CONNECTING CREATIVITY AND MOTIVATION RESEARCH WITH END USERS

It is often difficult to translate the findings of creativity and motivation researchers into language or activities that benefit end users. This is the problem driving the need for translational research, and this book fills the gap. It translates creativity and motivation research into language that teachers and their students, corporate trainers and their employees, and students' families or caregivers can immediately understand. Instructional modules and lesson plans provide readers with opportunities to network, give feedback, suggest new research needs, and access free assessments. Additional resources and opportunities for readers are available through the Freddie Reisman Center for Translational Research in Creativity and Motivation.

FREDRICKA REISMAN is Emerita Professor at Drexel University. She is also Founder of Drexel University's School of Education, Director of the Freddie Reisman Center for Translational Research in Creativity and Motivation, and Co-Director of the Drexel/Torrance Center for Creativity and Innovation. She has published numerous books, including *Creativity as a Bridge between Education and Industry* (2014) and *Using Creativity to Address Dyslexia, Dysgraphia, and Dyscalculia: Assessment and Techniques* (2021).

LARRY KEISER is Assistant Clinical Professor at Drexel University. He is also Program Director of Drexel University's Creativity and Innovation programs, Associate Director of the Freddie Reisman Center for Translational Research in Creativity and Motivation, and Co-Director of the Drexel/Torrance Center for Creativity and Innovation. He coauthored the Reisman Diagnostic Creativity Assessment and the Reisman Diagnostic Motivation Assessment, which evaluate creativity mindsets and motivation. Keiser has secured over $21 million in funding toward alternative teacher certification; science, technology, engineering, and math (STEM) education; and technology integration in preschool through college teaching.

JEFF WESTPHAL served as CEO and Chair of the Board of Vertex, Inc., the global leader in corporate tax technology, from 1996 to 2016.

He is Founder of both Mosaic™ and MeaningSphere®, platforms to enable intrinsically meaningful learning and work. For more information, visit his website: https://jeffwestphal.org/.

PENNY HAMMRICH was Dean of the School of Education and Distinguished Professor at Drexel University. Previously, she was Dean of Queens College of the City University of New York. She brought in over $50 million in grant funding, published over 150 articles and 18 books, and gave numerous conference presentations.

CONNECTING CREATIVITY AND MOTIVATION RESEARCH WITH END USERS

Lab to Learner

FREDRICKA REISMAN
Drexel University

LARRY KEISER
Drexel University

JEFF WESTPHAL
MeaningSphere, Inc.

PENNY HAMMRICH
Drexel University

Shaftesbury Road, Cambridge CB2 8EA, United Kingdom

One Liberty Plaza, 20th Floor, New York, NY 10006, USA

477 Williamstown Road, Port Melbourne, VIC 3207, Australia

314–321, 3rd Floor, Plot 3, Splendor Forum, Jasola District Centre, New Delhi – 110025, India

103 Penang Road, #05–06/07, Visioncrest Commercial, Singapore 238467

Cambridge University Press is part of Cambridge University Press & Assessment, a department of the University of Cambridge.

We share the University's mission to contribute to society through the pursuit of education, learning and research at the highest international levels of excellence.

www.cambridge.org
Information on this title: www.cambridge.org/9781009199186

DOI: 10.1017/9781009199193

© Fredricka Reisman, Larry Keiser, Jeff Westphal and Penny Hammrich 2024

This publication is in copyright. Subject to statutory exception and to the provisions of relevant collective licensing agreements, no reproduction of any part may take place without the written permission of Cambridge University Press & Assessment.

First published 2024

A catalogue record for this publication is available from the British Library

A Cataloging-in-Publication data record for this book is available from the Library of Congress

ISBN 978-1-009-19918-6 Hardback
ISBN 978-1-009-19921-6 Paperback

Cambridge University Press & Assessment has no responsibility for the persistence or accuracy of URLs for external or third-party internet websites referred to in this publication and does not guarantee that any content on such websites is, or will remain, accurate or appropriate.

We dedicate our book to Dean Penny Hammrich, one of this book's author team who sadly was taken from us unexpectedly. In addition to being a brilliant science educator and creative administrator, Penny was a leader in the burgeoning enterprise of micro-credentialling, which she describes in Chapter 11. She was excited about translating creativity and motivation research from journal articles and funded grant reports into an accessible format for practitioners, who will use this information to benefit their students, whether they are corporate employees or preschool through college learners – this is the intention of our book.

Fredricka Reisman
Larry Keiser
Jeff Westphal

Penny Hammrich

Contents

List of Figures and Tables		*page* ix
List of Modules		xi
List of Boxes		xii
Preface		xv
Acknowledgments		xvii

1 Translational Education Research — 1

2 Creativity — 15
  Appendix 2A Creativity Journals — 51
  Appendix 2B Glossary — 52

3 Motivation — 60
  Appendix 3 Glossary — 77

4 Assessment Attributes and Related Guidelines — 80
  Appendix 4 Glossary of Assessment Terms — 103

5 Assessment of Creativity — 109
  Appendix 5A Generic Influences on Learning and Definitions — 123
  Appendix 5B Additional Generic Influences on Learning — 127
  Appendix 5C Observation of Generic Influences on Learning: Tips for Teachers — 130
  Appendix 5D Reisman Diagnostic Creativity Assessment: Scoring Interpretation — 139
  Appendix 5E Glossary — 144

6 Assessment of Motivation — 160
  Appendix 6A Reisman Diagnostic Motivation Assessment – Teacher: Item Source Grid — 187
  Appendix 6B Reisman Diagnostic Motivation Assessment – Student: Item Source Grid — 190

	Appendix 6C	Reisman Diagnostic Motivation Assessment – Corporate: Item Source Grid	193
	Appendix 6D	Alternative Reisman Diagnostic Motivation Assessment Interpretation	195
7	Additional Theorists on Creativity and Motivation		201
8	Neuroscience of Creativity, Mindfulness, and Mind/Brain/Education Science		209
9	Creativity Modules		227
10	Motivation Modules		307
11	Dissemination and Communication Techniques for Translational Research		370
12	From Individual Compliance to Creative Collaboration: A Business Perspective		375
Index			381

Figures and Tables

Figures

1.1	Translational education research cycle	*page* 3
2.1	Creativity definitions	24
2.2	Creative-thinking process	27
3.1	Maslow's hierarchy of needs	64
3.2	Mnemonic for McGregor's X and Y theories	69
4.1	Diagnostic teaching process	84
7.1	Piaget's cognitive theory applied to motivation	202
9.1	Levels and descriptions of Bloom's taxonomy revised	251
9.2	Fluency self-assessment	262
9.3	Board showing zero	290
9.4	Board showing value of one	290
9.5	Counting board showing impending count of "ten"	291
9.6	Counting board showing count of "ten"	292
9.7	Units and tens counting boards showing that the horizontal move from units to tens remains "ten"	292
9.8	Tens and units boards representing "eleven"	293
9.9	Addition without renaming: 25+13	296
9.10	Addition with renaming: 35+9	297
9.11	Subtracting without renaming on the computation boards	298
9.12	Adding signed numbers on the computation boards to show the additive identity	299

Tables

4.1	Math content categorized by the developmental mathematics curriculum levels, RDCA factors, and cognitive generic influences on learning	93
9.1	RDCA score interpretation table	238
9.2	Creative problem-solving grid: find the real problem	243

9.3	Creative problem-solving grid: strategies	245
9.4	RDCA and RDMA K–8 assessment	256
9.5	Creative problem-solving grid: identifying the real problem	285
9.6	Creative problem-solving grid for a possible innovative pedagogy	286
10.1	Role play activities	316
10.2	RDMA-S item source interpretation grid	318
10.3	RDMA-T item source interpretation grid	329
10.4	Self-directed learning assessment grid	344

Modules

Creativity Module 9.1	What is creativity?	*page* 228
Creativity Module 9.2	Instructors and creativity	242
Creativity Module 9.3	Characteristics of creative teaching	246
Creativity Module 9.4	Critical thinking	248
Creativity Module 9.5	Originality	254
Creativity Module 9.6	Fluency	258
Creativity Module 9.7	Elaboration	263
Creativity Module 9.8	Tolerance of ambiguity	265
Creativity Module 9.9	Risk-taking	269
Creativity Module 9.10	Resistance to premature closure	272
Creativity Module 9.11	Flexibility	275
Creativity Module 9.12	Divergent thinking	278
Creativity Module 9.13	Convergent thinking	282
Creativity Module 9.14	Intrinsic and extrinsic motivation	287
Creativity Module 9.15	Creative place value pedagogy	288
Creativity Module 9.16	Counting boards computation	295
Creativity Module 9.17	Neuroscience of creativity	300
Creativity Module 9.18	Mindfulness and creativity	303
Motivation Module 10.1	What is motivation?	310
Motivation Module 10.2	Why should teachers know about motivation?	315
Motivation Module 10.3	Instructor motivation characteristics	325
Motivation Module 10.4	Self-determination theory	333
Motivation Module 10.5	Self-directed learning	335
Motivation Module 10.6	Intrinsic motivation	346
Motivation Module 10.7	Extrinsic motivation	350
Motivation Module 10.8	Gamification	354
Motivation Module 10.9	Mindfulness and motivation	356
Motivation Module 10.10	Neuroscience of motivation	362
Motivation Module 10.11	Diagnostic teaching	366

Boxes

1.1	Likert-type scales	page 6
1.2	Inverted-U theory	8
1.3	Example of a student talking through a math computation	9
2.1	The fourteen components of creativity	16
2.2	Torrance and the military	20
2.3	Four-C model of creativity	22
2.4	Domain-general versus domain-specific creativity	26
2.5	Creativity myths	28
2.6	Creativity facts	29
2.7	Creativity killers and response strategies	30
2.8	World Economic Forum 2016 report	49
2.9	World Economic Forum 2018 report	50
3.1	Types of motivation	62
3.2	Types of intrinsic and extrinsic motivation	63
3.3	Self-actualization	65
3.4	Self-actualizing characteristics	66
3.5	Theory Z features	70
3.6	Theory Z principles	71
3.7	Lock and Latham's ideas for effective goal setting	73
3.8	Three main components of Porter and Lawler's model	74
4.1	Pre- and post-testing	84
4.2	Difference between diagnostic and formative assessments	85
4.3	Diagnostic teaching and creative problem-solving compared	85
4.4	Creative problem-solving grid example	86
4.5	More complex creative problem-solving grid	87
4.6	Definitions and verbs for Bloom's taxonomy levels	88
4.7	Different meanings for the same symbol	100
5.1	Likert-type scale	110
5.2	Likert-type formats	111

List of Boxes

5.3	Types of aptitude tests	113
5.4	Aptitudes Research Project measures	115
5.5	Examples of remote associates test items	116
5.6	Advantages and disadvantages of self-reports	117
5.7	Examples of Gough personality scale items	118
5.8	Additional creative student characteristics	119
5.9	Examples of the creative product semantic scale	122
6.1	Teacher shortage data	163
6.2	Great resignation	164
6.3	Components of TARGET	166
6.4	The Self-Motivation Quiz	169
6.5	The Self-Motivation Quiz question categories	169
6.6	The Situational Motivation Scale sample items	170
6.7	Characteristics of a good questionnaire	171
6.8	Self-motivation questionnaire	172
6.9	Likert-type scales	173
6.10	The Rosenberg Self-Esteem Scale	174
6.11	Student Opinion items	175
6.12	Basic Psychological Need Satisfaction in General Checklist items	176
6.13	The Employee Motivation Survey	177
6.14	The Student Motivation Survey	177
6.15	Closed and open-ended questions	178
6.16	RDMA-T	179
6.17	RDMA-S	181
6.18	RDMA-C	183
6.19	RKW Student – Enhancing self-motivation diagnostic	185
6.20	Autonomy-supportive teachers	187
7.1	Maslow's and Rogers's ideas regarding self-actualization	203
7.2	Pygmalion effect	205
7.3	Golem effect	205
7.4	Types of metacognitive knowledge	206
8.1	Companies that have embraced mindfulness	220
9.1	*The Teaching Self-Reflection Tool and Skills Checklist*: permission statement	233
9.2	*The Teaching Self-Reflection Tool and Skills Checklist*: checklist	233
9.3	Voice from the field: elementary school teacher	244
9.4	Voice from the field: elementary grades teacher	251
9.5	Levels of Bloom's taxonomy	252

9.6	Voice from the field: fluency activity	259
9.7	Tolerance of ambiguity	267
9.8	Benefits of risk-taking	270
9.9	Example of premature closure	272
9.10	Six thinking hats definitions	273
9.11	Voice from the field: six thinking hats as an assessment strategy	274
9.12	Jerome Bruner	276
9.13	Absence thinking	277
9.14	Four rules of brainstorming	279
9.15	Voice from the field: divergent thinking	281
9.16	Bluma Wulfovna Zeigarnik	283
9.17	Counting board activities maximum sum of nine	298
9.18	Three distinct brain networks in creative thinking	300
10.1	Extrinsic and intrinsic motivation	308
10.2	Motivation-related characteristics	309
10.3	Sources of motivation	311
10.4	Duckworth grit scale scoring	312
10.5	Motivational quotes	313
10.6	Possible score interpretation for the RDMA-S	317
10.7	Instructor motivation characteristics self-assessment	327
10.8	Possible score interpretation for the RDMA-T	332
10.9	Difference between self-directed learning and self-determined learning	337
10.10	Double-loop learning	338
10.11	Difference between single-loop learning and double-loop learning	338
10.12	Story of a high schooler who opted into a self-directed learning school	339
10.13	Knowles's statement	345
10.14	Gamification related to learning	355
10.15	Mindfulness: psychological, physiological, and spiritual benefits	357
10.16	Mindfulness actions	360

Preface

This book is for those interested in applying creativity- and motivation-related research. Such research is typically found in journals or funded grant reports that are inaccessible to end users, including preschool through college classroom teachers and administrators, corporate trainers and talent managers, researchers in fields related to creativity and motivation, instructors and students of creativity and motivation courses, and parents. The book contains foundational knowledge regarding creativity and motivation, including contributions of trailblazing theorists and researchers, assessment strategies, and discussions on newer trends such as mindfulness, gamification, and the neuroscience of creativity. The book also sets out education and corporate applications – namely lesson plans in the form of modules that address creativity and motivation – which contain topic-related background information, activities, assessments, and related references.

Also described is the Freddie Reisman Center for Translational Research in Creativity and Motivation (FRC), including its goals, objectives, activities, and services. The main purpose of the FRC is to translate relevant creativity and motivation research for end-user applications. The FRC provides instructional modules, including those in this book, for helping end users to enhance creativity and motivation; simultaneously, these modules allow the FRC to receive feedback both on how the modules can be modified and giving suggestions for research that is needed. This two-pronged approach is synergistic, unlike the one-way, medical, bench-to-bedside model. Our feedback model – lab to learner and vice versa – exemplifies the interaction and cooperation of two or more entities to produce a combined effect that is greater than their separate contributions. Thus, the interaction between the FRC and end users regarding the translation of creativity and motivation research will lead to continuous improvements to the instructional modules and to proposals for new, related research. The FRC leadership and its stellar Advisory Board will seek creativity and motivation research that is worthy of translation but currently embedded in traditional research publications, from both national and international colleagues. The instructional modules (lesson plans) contained in Chapters 9 and 10 will serve as the channel for transmitting the research to education and corporate end users. In addition, the FRC will offer technical assistance in the form of credit- and noncredit-bearing workshops for translating educational research into practice. The Drexel FRC will collaborate across the university to provide nondegree options, such as certificates, badges, and micro-credentials, all of which are described in Chapter 11.

Acknowledgments

The authors would like to express our sincere gratitude to all the individuals who contributed to the creation of this book. Their support, expertise, and encouragement were invaluable throughout the entire process. First and foremost, we would like to thank our dedicated team of researchers, editors, and contributors for all their efforts in assisting the authors in gathering and organizing the vast amount of information presented in this book. Their commitment to excellence and their understanding of and passion for creativity helped bring this project to life.

Specifically, we would like to thank the following:

David Mattson, Post Doctoral Associate and Research Associate for the Freddie Reisman Center for Translational Research in Creativity and Motivation, who ensured that the manuscript was correct and complete, and we give him our profound thanks.

Stephanie Holmberg and Ericka Pitman, two Drexel University doctoral students in Drexel University's Educational Leadership and Management's Ed.D. program, and Dr. Melissa Schmitz, who received her doctorate from the program, for their contributions to several of the Lessons from the Field component of several of the creativity and motivation modules.

Ngaire Duncan, Chief Operations Officer of Westphal Philanthropy, who was instrumental in keeping Jeff connected to the process of developing the manuscript and provided immediate guidance to our frequent questions.

We are grateful to David Repetto, our Editor, for his unwavering patience as we endured the unexpected passing of our co-author, Penny Hammrich. David's understanding, caring, guidance and support have our deep appreciation.

Rowan Grout, Senior Editorial Assistant with Cambridge University Press, who was an unexpected and welcomed addition to our team. Rowan's guidance was clear, organized and on point from clarifying the book's title through all the steps to completed manuscript. We thank you, thank you, thank you, Rowan.

Finally, we thank the production arm of Cambridge University Press, Ruth Boyes, Senior Content Manager | Academic Books; Reshma Venkatachalapathy, Project Management Executive, Integra Software Services; and Melanie Woodward, Copy editor, TIDE Services.

This book would not have been possible without the collective efforts of all these individuals, and we are truly grateful for their contributions.

Fredricka Reisman

Larry Keiser

Jeff Westphal

CHAPTER I

Translational Education Research

Advance Organizer. Chapter 1 defines the concept of translational research and compares basic and applied research paradigms. The chapter includes Brabeck's (2008) quote that sets out the rationale for applying the translational medical research model known as bench to bedside to the authors' translational education research model: lab to learner. The chapter also sets out the dilemma of translational research for end users and describes the purpose and activities of the related Freddie Reisman Center for Translational Research in Creativity and Motivation (FRC) at Drexel University.

1.1 Introduction

Researchers publish their work for other academics in journals and funded grant reports and materials; however, these sources are not readily or easily accessible to teachers and their students, students' parents/guardians, or corporate trainers. As these individuals are not the target audience of researchers, it is difficult – if not impossible – for these non-researchers to translate the research findings into language or activities that would benefit their learners. Simply put, researchers' findings are not readily accessible or understandable to those who are in a position to implement the research. Generally, the research languishes in journals and reports for a subsequent researcher to read and utilize for the next research study. This problem is at the heart of the need for translational education research.

Evidence-based practice uses the best available research findings and is considered the gold standard in patient care. In medical research, it has typically taken hospitals and clinics about seventeen years to adopt a practice or treatment after the first systematic evidence showed it helped patients (AACN, 2016; NCATS, 2016; NIH, 2021; Niven, 2017). Although there has recently been movement in the medical model in decreasing the lag time as a result of the creation of Pfizer, Moderna, and Novavax vaccines in response to the COVID-19 epidemic, it is not yet known if the lag time decrease was the beginning of a trend or a temporary exception. Translational education research, however, aims to significantly decrease the lag time between the discovery of excellent research findings and those findings' potential impact on learning and instruction.

1.2 Translational Education Research Defined

"Translational research involves moving knowledge gained from the basic sciences to its application in clinical and community settings" (Davidson, 2011). Bench-to-bedside research is a summary phrase often used to describe this concept. This phrase describes the process of how laboratory research results are directly used to develop new ways to treat patients. That is, translational medical research derives from scientific discoveries made in the laboratory, clinic, or field. Those discoveries are then transformed into new approaches to medical care and into treatments that improve people's health. The bench-to-bedside translational medical research model served as the authors' prototype for their translational education research model, namely lab to learner. The lab to learner model underlies both this book and the FRC at Drexel University, with the FRC described later in this chapter (see Figure 1.1).

The term "translational research" first appeared around 1993 in medical journals and referred to transforming scientific discoveries in the laboratory into treatments for patients – mainly for individuals experiencing cancer. In that model, basic lab investigations were translated to benefit patients. Translational research in the medical field is one-directional, whereby research results go from the researcher's bench to the patient's bedside. However, the translational education model proposed by the authors of this book is a two-way, reiterative model. That is, research is translated into instructional-based modules (lesson plans) to benefit end users (e.g., teachers and their students, corporate trainers, and company employees), while feedback from end users can modify these lesson plans and possibly lead to the identification of new research goals, as shown in Figure 1.1. This is the translational education research cycle. Thus, the authors' model of translational education research is synergistic, as opposed to the one-way, linear, medical version.

Mary Brabeck, Dean Emerita of the Steinhardt School of Culture, Education, and Human Development at New York University, whose

1 Translational Education Research

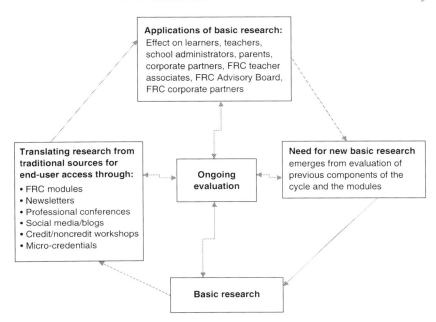

Figure 1.1 Translational education research cycle.

definition of translational research the authors apply to education, stated that:

> In medicine, translational research is often identified as *bench to bedside*. It recognizes the gap between basic research in the lab and the practice of medicine that can make a difference in health outcomes. The role or goal of translational research in medicine is to quickly provide practitioners with the latest information from basic research labs in usable form. The idea is to produce better medications, improve diagnostic and treatment strategies, and enhance health through the application of information from basic science research. (Brabeck, 2008, emphasis added)

The translational education research cycle (Figure 1.1) depicts the FRC's version of lab to learner translational education research. The process begins with FRC team members continually vetting the best of past and current research in creativity and motivation to extract the most important studies that affect learning. Instructional modules (lesson plans) for use in the education arena were created by the FRC as the initial vehicle for providing end users with access to the research in understandable terms and formats. The FRC will eventually branch out into translating research for corporate trainers and other relevant fields.

1.3 Value–Practice Gap

The authors' premise is that teachers and other end users must not only value basic educational research, but also use it. A UK study found a value–practice gap between teachers' value of research and their actual use of the research in their teaching (Jones, Proctor & Younie, 2015). Our two-pronged goal is for instructors to (1) *have access* to basic educational research and (2) understand and *apply* it for the benefit of their learners. The following section discusses and compares basic and applied research.

1.4 Basic and Applied Research

Research is most often categorized as either basic research or applied research. Bush (2020) distinguished between basic research and applied research as follows:

> Basic research is performed without thought of practical ends. It results in general knowledge and an understanding of nature and its laws. This general knowledge provides the means of answering a large number of important practical problems, though it may not give a complete specific answer to any one of them. The function of applied research is to provide such complete answers.

Definition of Basic Research

Basic research focuses on adding new scientific knowledge to an existing body of knowledge. Basic researchers create and test new theories with goals that do not address applications for end users.

Basic Research Tools

Basic research tools range from brain imaging to full-body exploration through various methods with varying degrees of specificity and invasiveness. Methods include:

- **functional magnetic resonance imaging**, a technique that measures brain activity through the detection of changes associated with blood flow

- **electroencephalogram**, a test that measures the electrical activity of the brain
- **positron emission tomography**, a functional imaging technique that uses radiotracers (a radioactive substance) to measure changes in metabolic processes and other physiological activities (e.g., blood flow, regional chemical composition, and absorption)
- **computerized tomography**, a computer imaging process that combines multiple X-ray images collected from different angles of the inside of a body; the results are cross-sectional images (slices) of the bones, blood vessels, and soft tissues
- **ultrasound imaging**, a technique that produces functional screen images created by sound waves (also known as a sonogram) of organs, tissues, and other structures inside the body.

Definition of Applied Research

Whereas basic research focuses on advancing knowledge rather than solving a problem, applied research seeks to identify solutions to specific problems.

Examples of Applied Education Research

Applied education research focuses on learners' generic influences on learning, which are used to design instructional modules. Generic influences on learning fall into several categories: cognitive, psychomotor, physical, and sensory influences, as well as social and emotional needs (Appendix 5A provides the definitions of these generic influences and Appendix 5C lists tips for teachers for implementing the generic influences). Generic influences include areas such as engaging in creativity and motivation activities, retaining information, applying visual discrimination, demonstrating low vitality and fatigue, and being aware of cues in the environment, as well as becoming overly upset, moody, sad, or happy, or other reactions that represent extremes of emotion that one typically learns to control under normative development.

Applied Education Research Methods

In education, applied research is used to understand teaching and learning behaviors in the classroom. The following are examples of common applied education research methods:

- **Experimentation.** Experiments in education research include observations, interviews, and administering surveys and questionnaires that tap attitudes and self-perception.
- **Observation.** This research method involves the researcher paying close attention to the subject's verbal and nonverbal behavior and actions.
- **Interview.** In this research method, the researcher asks participants questions in a one-to-one (interviewer/interviewee) manner or within a small, focused group of interviewees being questioned on a subject to gather in-depth information about an experience. Interviews may be structured or unstructured, depending on the research goals. In a structured interview, the researcher asks predetermined questions. In contrast, in an unstructured interview, the researcher starts with a question and then guides the subject to elaborate with relevant follow-up questions.
- **Questionnaire.** A questionnaire is a survey (generally a paper-and-pencil or online method of data collection) consisting of a series of questions. Participants' responses are often collected using a Likert-type scale (Box 1.1). Questionnaires may also be self-report assessments.

Box 1.1 Likert-type scales

Likert-type scales were introduced into research by the US social psychologist Rensis Likert (1932). They measure people's thoughts and feelings, including through opinion surveys, personality tests, and attitude responses. The scales comprise a series of statements to which the research participants provide response ratings. The statements express a positive or negative opinion. Such statements may be taken from a teacher self-assessment checklist such as the Reisman Diagnostic Creativity Assessment (RDCA), for example "I keep an open mind," "I will use more effort on an activity or task if there is some kind of incentive," and "I regularly come up with novel uses for things" (Reisman, Keiser & Otti, 2016). The scale used to rate each statement may be a 5-point, 6-point, or 7-point scale or some other appropriate point response ranging from "strongly disagree" to "strongly agree," "strongly disapprove" to "strongly approve," or "least like me" to "most like me." The RDCA assessment uses a 6-point Likert-type scale that ranges from "strongly disagree" to "strongly agree." Dr. Likert shared with Dr. E. Paul Torrance – a creativity researcher who is considered by many to be the "Father of Creativity" – his frustration with people modifying his scale without acknowledgment and suggested that it henceforth be cited as a Likert-type scale (and Dr. Torrance disclosed this to Dr. Reisman, the lead author of this book).

1   Translational Education Research   7

1.5   Example of Lab to Learner

This section sets out a real-life example of the authors' lab to learner model. In 1979, while on faculty at the University of Georgia in Athens, Georgia, Dr. Reisman was engaged in basic research with a colleague, John Braggio. Having refined his skills as a basic researcher at the Yerkes National Primate Research Center in Atlanta, Georgia, Dr. Braggio migrated to a faculty position at the University of North Carolina in Asheville, North Carolina. Braggio contributed his skills as a basic researcher to his collaboration with Reisman, the educator.

Reisman and Braggio recruited a group of Asheville 4th graders who were in their school's learning disabilities program. Physiological measures – namely a laryngograph and measures of respiration (including amplitude and frequency) – were taken while the students were engaged in a math computation test. The number of student participants is not recalled, but the subjects comprised an equal number of boys and girls. Each student was asked to complete a computation test created by Reisman in which 4th-grade-level items progressed from simple to difficult, while Braggio monitored students' physiological measures.

The laryngograph method consisted of placing a small disc on a student's larynx, while each student was simultaneously hooked up to a respiration machine. Acquiring physiological measures was made into a fun experience for each child so that each was comfortable with the procedure before starting the computation test. In testing of this sort, there is a phenomenon referred to as the U graph (Box 1.2). As shown by the graph, at first, participants typically experience a high level of activity (perhaps due to anxiety) as measured by the assessment tool. That period is followed by a period of calming down. In this specific instance, laryngograph activity increased as the computation problems got more difficult.

The U effect was apparent for those children who got the most items correct. These students were anxious at the start of the test (the upper left part of the U). They quickly calmed down as they completed the easy items (the low portion of the U). However, as the difficulty of the test items began to increase, the physiological measures increased (the upper right portion of the U). This reaction was expected and reflects the effort and anxiety expected in a normal U graph. The upper portions of the U graph were indicative of rapid laryngography muscular movement and rapid and deep breathing, while the bottom of the U indicated normal breathing and less muscular activity of the larynx. The physiological measures of the children who did poorly on the computation items varied. In other words,

8   Connecting Creativity and Motivation Research with End Users

---

Box 1.2   Inverted-U theory

Psychologists Robert Yerkes and John Dodson (1908) created the inverted-U theory. This theory uses the "U" shape to represent the relationship between pressure and performance in identifying the optimum level of positive pressure at which people perform at their best. Either too much or too little pressure can lead to decreased performance. The upper left of the U indicates too little pressure. Following the left side of the U down to the bottom represents the gradual rate of performance improvement in relation to the gradual increase in positive pressure, but only to a point. The mid-point of the bottom of the U represents the optimal intersection of positive pressure and performance. Past the mid-point of the U's bottom, the rise of the right-hand side of the U represents a decrease in performance related to increased pressure. It culminates at the upper right of the U, indicating the ultimate amount of pressure being applied coinciding with the lowest level of performance. The U shape illustration also provides a visual highlighting that the level of nonperformance is equal for both too little and too much pressure.

---

there was no pattern of physiological response related to item difficulty – no U curve was noted. Chapter 3 provides a more in-depth explanation of the U curve theory related to motivation.

The Ashville students' results are an example of translational education research. The lab findings were shared with the children's teachers, along with suggested pedagogy that translated the experimental results into classroom activities and environments, enhancing learning. Specifically, in this case, the following strategies were suggested, and the teachers stated that they would implement them:

- provide practice activities that involve different role-playing scenarios related to effort and anxiety that are appropriate to various tasks
- encourage and observe the development of the student's self-concept, self-efficacy (know you can do it), and perseverance to successfully complete a task
- use techniques such as relaxation imagery, centering, deep breathing, and affirmations (harnessing positive thinking)
- have students use concrete examples of arithmetic computations (see the discussion of Reisman counting boards in Chapter 9)
- encourage students to practice saying the steps aloud when solving computations
- allow students to create and solve their own math computation problems

- use formative evaluation to monitor changes in students' self-efficacy, self-concept, and task perseverance as they are involved in learning math and other subjects
- keep notes that document the move from a teacher-directed environment to a more creative student self-directed classroom

Although Ashville students' results suggested a possible relationship between the laryngograph results and subvocalization, a question still remains about this relationship. At the time of the research, Reisman and Braggio could say only that laryngograph activity demonstrated muscular activity in the larynx; they could not confirm their hypothesis of a connection between laryngograph activity, subvocalization, and metacognition.

Another question that arose was: Why might subvocalization be important to learning? Subvocalization while performing a task relates to Flavell's (1979) discussion of metacognition, also known as cognitive monitoring, and is a helpful strategy for problem-solving. Reisman and Braggio hypothesized that laryngograph activity, if it did indeed represent subvocalization, implied that the students talked themselves through the computation items while incorporating cognitive monitoring. Box 1.3 is an example of one of the children who did well on the computation test and shared their metacognitive activity aloud with us while attempting one of the assessment items in the Reisman and Braggio experiment (Braggio et al., 1979).

The following section describes the FRC, a university-wide research center that has been created to address the new model of translational research described in this book. The FRC provides specific lesson plans for end users in Chapters 9 and 10 in the form of instructional modules with an initial emphasis on creativity and motivation.

Box 1.3   Example of a student talking through a math computation

$$\begin{array}{r} 15 \\ + \ 23 \\ \hline \end{array}$$

The student said aloud, "I need to add the 5 and the 3," while looking at the "ones" column. They then said, "Ok . . . 5, 6, 7, 8," as they proceeded to total the column.

The student then moved to consider the "tens" column and said aloud, "Then I need to add the 2 and 1 to get 3."

1.6 FRC at Drexel University

Purpose

The FRC addresses the disconnect between research and its application. For example, one of the topics considered by the FRC is the research-derived characteristics of creative students in comparison with teachers' lack of knowledge of creative and motivated students and the resulting unfounded beliefs that affect how teachers stifle rather than nourish creative students.

The medical translational research model – referred to as bench to bedside – served as the prototype for the FRC's model, lab to learner. Through the lab to learner model, relevant research that is currently "hidden" in journals that are not accessible to educational end users will become available to teachers. The FRC will also address translational research for corporate trainers and talent managers. The FRC has expanded on the medical model of translational research and applied it to education, aiming to significantly decrease the lag between excellent research findings and teachers' and corporate trainers' access to these findings. In this way, education-related research can begin to be used for the benefit of end users.

How We Implement the FRC Purpose

A stellar group of researchers from the creativity and motivation fields make up the FRC's Advisory Board. The Advisory Board members assist in gathering basic creativity research for translation from the USA and around the world that relates to improving pedagogy in terms of understanding and valuing the roles of the learners and their cognitive, social, and emotional characteristics and needs. The results from translating the creativity research are disseminated to end users (e.g., teachers, school principals, college faculty, doctoral students, instructional designers, parents, corporate trainers, and business leaders) for use with their learners (e.g., preschool through college [K–16] students and corporate employees). Continuous updates on and biographies of the current FRC Administration and Advisory Board members can be found on the FRC website at www.frcenter.net/.

Why the Focus on Creativity and Motivation?

The spotlight on creativity and motivation purposely delimits the initial work of the FRC to these two areas that affect learning. Years of research have not changed the fact that teachers do not recognize their students' creative strengths. Teachers believe that their creative students agree with them, do not question teachers' statements, do not display behavior problems, and smile at the teacher (Aljughaiman & Mowrer-Reynolds, 2005; Getzels & Jackson, 1962; Torrance, 1975). Teachers described students whose creativity they do not acknowledge as nonconformist, disruptive, and troublemakers (Westby & Dawson, 1995). Research has suggested that teachers who recognize their own creative strengths may be able to better recognize and appreciate the creative strengths of their students, resulting in higher quality learning (Whitelaw, 2006). This dilemma is discussed more in Chapter 2 in the section "Education Definitions of Creativity."

Motivation is an essential part of almost every aspect of human behavior. When one makes a decision, the choices are often influenced by the decision-maker's motivational state. When studying mathematics, the motivation to study mathematics affects how one learns it. Despite its obvious importance, empirical research on motivation has been segregated in different areas for years, making it difficult to establish an integrative view on motivation. Researchers have begun to recognize the importance of a more unified and cross-disciplinary approach to studying motivation (Westby & Dawson, 1995). A multidisciplinary, multi-method pursuit called motivation science is emerging (Murayama, 2018), in which motivation researchers are now taking an integrative approach. They draw from multiple disciplines (e.g., cognitive, social, and educational psychology, as well as cognitive/social neuroscience) and multiple approaches (e.g., behavioral experiments, longitudinal data analysis, neuroimaging, meta-analysis, statistical simulation/computational modeling, and network analysis).

Services Provided

Key creativity and motivation research is obtained from creativity and motivation trailblazers from the USA and internationally. The research collected is translated into language that K–16 teachers and higher education faculty (and corporate trainers), their students (and corporate employees), and their students' families and caregivers can immediately understand, with strategies provided for implementing creativity and motivation research across these audiences.

Specifically, a team of Drexel University faculty, research students from across multiple disciplines within the university, and select, like-minded organizations are in contact with researchers from around the world, collecting the best creativity and motivation research that has been undertaken. The research is assessed and its content is evaluated for inclusion, that is, whether it is deemed essential for FRC-trained staff to translate the research for end user implementation. The FRC's funding also supports the recruitment of practicing teachers from across the nation (as well as globally, as appropriate) who collaborate with the FRC's leadership on designing authentic lessons based on relevant translated research. This includes the experiences and feedback of practicing teachers who have implemented these lessons and their interactions with their students. Teacher feedback is used to modify the lesson plans and identify areas for future research.

The FRC will also offer an evaluation plan for teachers to assess the results of the translational research. The FRC's leadership will instruct teachers and higher education faculty on how to use the evaluation plan that is provided as a template for them to create their own assessments. Thus, the FRC will offer suggestions on instructional and assessment activities derived from relevant research for teachers to implement with their students. It is noted that corporate trainers can apply the FRC's services to their own learners.

The recent disruption to established educational models in the context of the COVID-19 pandemic has created a ripe environment for research to be applied to new educational environments, such as virtual instruction and self-directed learning (sometimes referred to as unschooling). Due to this disruption of historic educational models, traditional instructor–learner interactions will need to be modified and documented through the translational efforts of the FRC. This includes providing tested, teacher-developed lesson plans and related strategies that educators can immediately implement in the classroom.

1.7 Summary

Chapter 1 provides a new definition of and rationale for the transformation and revision of the application of the medical translational research model, which is currently used in most translational research. The chapter includes examples of the revision of the model from the one-way information flow of the medical bench-to-beside model (Brabeck, 2008) to a two-way, interactive lab to learner model.

The chapter further provides insights into the dilemma of translational research from the perspective of the end users and discusses a new research center dedicated to breaking down the current silos that house research and findings in the areas of creativity and motivation, namely the FRC. The development of the FRC and its practice is discussed, including how the FRC identifies cutting-edge research in creativity and motivation journals across multiple disciplines and translates this into language and instructional modules to better and more quickly communicate the research to end users. With the support of the FRC's stellar Advisory Board, which is made up of worldwide trailblazing creativity and motivation researchers, the FRC is initially working to benefit teachers and their students, followed by corporate trainers and their students, in their quest for learning.

References

AACN (American Association of Critical-Care Nurses) (2016). AACN clinical scene investigator (CSI) academy. https://tinyurl.com/5n7b2k2p.

Aljughaiman, A. & Mowrer-Reynolds, E. (2005). Teachers' conceptions of creativity and creative students. *The Journal of Creative Behavior*, 39, 17–34. http://doi.org/10.1002/j.2162–6057.2005.tb01247.x.

Brabeck, M. (2008). Editorial: We need "translational" research: Putting clinical findings to work in the classroom. *Education Week*, 27(38), 28, 36.

Braggio, J. T., Braggio, S. M., Lanier, J. H., Simpson, L. & Reisman, F. K. (1979). Optimal response modes influence the performance of learning disabled children on academic tasks. *Journal of Learning Disabilities*, 12(6), 374–378.

Bush, V. (2020). Science: The endless frontier: 75th anniversary edition. National Science Foundation. www.nsf.gov/about/history/EndlessFrontier_w.pdf.

Davidson, A. (2011). Translational research: What does it mean? *Anesthesiology*, 115, 909–911. https://doi.org/10.1097/ALN.0b013e3182337a5e.

Flavell, J. H. (1979). Metacognition and cognitive monitoring: A new area of cognitive-developmental inquiry. *American Psychologist*, 34, 906–911.

Getzels, J. W. & Jackson, P. W. (1962). *Creativity and Intelligence: Explorations with Gifted Students*. Hoboken, NJ: Wiley.

Jones, S., Procter, R. & Younie, S. (2015). Participatory knowledge mobilization: An emerging model for translational research in education. *Journal of Education for Teaching*, 41(5), 555–574.

Likert, R. (1932). A technique for the measurement of attitudes. *Archives of Psychology*, (22)140, 55.

Murayama, K. (2018). The science of motivation: Multidisciplinary approaches advance research on the nature and effects of motivation. American Psychological Association.

NCATS (National Center for Advancing Translational Sciences) (2016). Website. https://ncats.nih.gov.

NIH (National Institutes of Health) (2021). NIH-wide strategic plan – fiscal years 2016–2020. www.nih.gov/about-nih/nih-wide-strategic-plan-fy-2016-2020.

Niven, D. (2017). Closing the 17-year gap between scientific evidence and patient care. https://tinyurl.com/ynuapwp7.

Reisman, F., Keiser, L. & Otti, O. (2016). Development, use and implications of diagnostic creativity assessment app, RDCA – Reisman diagnostic creativity assessment. *Creativity Research Journal*, 28(2), 177–187. https://doi.org/10.1080/10400419.2016.1162643.

Torrance, E. P. (1975). Sociodrama as a creative problem-solving approach to studying the future. *The Journal of Creative Behavior*, 9(3), 182–195.

Westby, E. & Dawson, V. (1995). Creativity: Asset or burden in the classroom? *Creativity Research Journal*, 8(1), 1–10.

Whitelaw, L. (2006). An evaluative study of teacher creativity, use of the heuristic diagnostic teaching process and student mathematics performance. Unpublished doctoral dissertation, Drexel University.

Yerkes, R. M. & Dodson, J. D. (1908). The relation of strength of stimulus to rapidity of habit-formation. *Journal of Comparative Neurology and Psychology*, 18(5), 459–482. https://doi.org/10.1002/cne.920180503.

CHAPTER 2

Creativity

Advance Organizer. Chapter 2 contains foundational knowledge regarding creativity, including definitions of creativity by discipline: engineering, architecture, corporate/business/industry, the military, education, scientists, psychologists, and creativity researchers/theorists. Further topics include creativity versus innovation, domain-general versus domain-specific creativity, the relationship between creativity and intelligence, the creative-thinking process, common creativity myths, and creativity killers and quick fixes. Biographies of trailblazing creativity theorists and researchers and their contributions are also presented. Appendix 2A lists popular creativity journals and Appendix 2B is a glossary of relevant terms.

2.1 Introduction

Guilford's (1950) incoming presidential speech to the American Psychological Association annual convention called for psychologists to investigate the neglected study of creativity; he was *appalled* at the neglect of the subject. The following excerpt from Guilford's landmark speech triggered a renaissance in creativity research:

> The neglect of this subject by psychologists is appalling. The evidences of the neglect are so obvious that I need not give proof. But the extent of the neglect I had not realized until recently. Of the approximately 121,000 titles listed in 11 Psychological Abstracts in the past 23 years, only 186 were indexed as definitely bearing on the subject of creativity. In other words, less than two-tenths of one percent of the books and articles indexed in the abstracts for approximately the past quarter century bear directly on the subject. (Guilford, 1950)

2.2 Creativity Defined

It was Moe Stein who published the first clear definition of creativity. Stein (1953) defined creativity as follows:

16   Connecting Creativity and Motivation Research with End Users

> The creative work is a novel work that is accepted as tenable or useful or satisfying by a group in some point in time. By "novel" I mean that the creative product did not exist previously in precisely the same form. The extent to which a work is novel depends on the extent to which it deviates from the traditional or the status quo. This may well depend on the nature of the problem that is attacked, the fund of knowledge or experience that exists in the field at the time, and the characteristics of the creative individual and those of the individuals with whom he (or she) is communicating.

Anna Jordanous (2012) stated:

> The components collectively provide a clearer "working" understanding of creativity in the form of components that collectively contribute to our understanding of what creativity is. Together these components act as building blocks for creativity, each contributing to the overall presence of creativity; individually, they make creativity more tractable and easier to understand by breaking down this seemingly impenetrable concept into constituent parts.

Jordanous's fourteen key themes and factors of creativity are defined in Box 2.1.

There are two main components of creativity that are pretty well accepted, namely originality and relevance. An original idea is one that is statistically rare or infrequent and deviates from the traditional or the status quo. The

---

Box 2.1   The fourteen components of creativity

The following descriptions of the meaning of each component are adapted from Jordanous (2012, 2014):

1. Active involvement and persistence – being actively involved, reacting, and having a deliberate effect; the tenacity to persist with a process throughout, even at problematic points.
2. Dealing with uncertainty – coping with incomplete, missing, inconsistent, uncertain, and/or ambiguous information. There is an element of risk and chance, with no guarantee that problems can or will be resolved. It includes not requiring every step of the process to be determined, and perhaps even avoiding routine or preexisting methods and solutions.
3. Domain competence – possessing domain-specific intelligence, knowledge, talent, skills, experience, and expertise. It involves having a thorough understanding of a particular domain, which enables one to identify gaps, needs, or problems that require solutions, as well as to create, validate, develop, and promote new ideas within that domain. It also involves flexible and adaptable mental capacity.
4. General Intellect – general intellectual ability and adaptable mental capacity.

2   *Creativity*   17

Box 2.1   (cont.)

5. Generation of results – working toward some end target or goal and producing something (tangible or intangible) that did not exist.
6. Independence and freedom – working independently with autonomy over actions and decisions, and the freedom to work outside preexisting solutions, processes, or biases.
7. Intention and emotional involvement – personal and emotional investment, immersion, self-expression, and involvement in a process, and an intention and desire to perform a task, a positive process giving fulfillment and enjoyment.
8. Novelty and originality – a new product, doing something in a new way, or seeing new connections between previously unassociated concepts; results that are unexpected, surprising, or out of the ordinary.
9. Progression and development – movement, advancement, evolution, and development during a process. While progress may not be linear, and the end goal may not be specified, the process should represent a developmental progression in a particular domain or task.
10. Social interaction and communication – communicating and promoting work to others persuasively and positively; mutual influence, sharing, and collaboration between society and the individual.
11. Spontaneity/subconscious processing – no need to control the whole process. Thoughts and activities may subconsciously inform a process without being fully accessible for conscious analysis; being able to react quickly and spontaneously during a process when appropriate, without spending too much time thinking about options.
12. Thinking and evaluation – consciously evaluating several options to recognize potential value in each and identify the best option, using reasoning and good judgment; proactively selecting from possible options without allowing the process to stagnate under indecision.
13. Value – making a valuable contribution valued by others and recognized as an influential achievement. The end product is relevant and appropriate.
14. Variety, divergence, and experimentation – generating a variety of different ideas to experiment with different options without bias; multitasking during a process.

idea should be something new that is not simply an extension of something else that already exists. Synonyms for *originality* include new, novel, unique, infrequent, unusual, and statistically rare. *Relevance* refers to an idea being useful, suitable, valuable, adaptive, appropriate, fitting, or functional.

It is interesting to note that there are differences in definitions of creativity, even within different domains of a discipline. For example,

Glück, Ernst & Unger (2002) found that artists with no constraints (sculptors or painters) and those with constraints (architects or designers) had different definitions, such as time pressure, a freely chosen or restricted topic, material, reward, or expectation of evaluation. The only agreed upon definition across the artist domain was that creatives must have many ideas (fluency). Next, we visit the definitions of creativity categorized by a variety of disciplines, commencing with artists.

Artists' Definitions of Creativity

Creativity is the mental capacity to generate novel and useful ideas. It isn't merely about art or design, writing or music. Creativity is, at its core, about ideas and how we develop, understand, and communicate them, not just in terms of the arts, but in every realm of thinking and work (Caslib, Garing & Casual, 2018). Artists' synonyms for creativity include cleverness, genius, imagination, imaginativeness, ingenuity, inspiration, inventiveness, and originality.

Engineering Definitions of Creativity

Creativity is a fundamental competence for engineers concerned with generating effective and novel solutions to problems. Identifying multiple solutions needed for a project is an important part of an engineer's work. Creativity enables them to improvise and successfully confront new situations. Creative engineers find more solutions to problems and are more independent, curious, and tolerant of ambiguous definitions. They are more willing to take risks and show persistence in solving problems. Today's engineers must be creative and innovative, as the problems engineers face today demand original thinking (Charyton, 2015).

Architects' Definitions of Creativity

Architects' definition of creativity mirrors that of engineers; however, in light of the importance of creativity in the design process, it is surprising that creativity theories and foundational knowledge are minimally included in the education architecture curricula.

Emerging innovative work environments coupled with the National Architectural Accreditation Board (NAAB, 2022) accreditation requirements call for a redesign of accredited architectural education, from a focus on solitary projects toward collaborative design dialogues and group creative production. Because creative collaboration depends upon social agreements of participants pooling their talents for common goals, collaborative design depends on perceptions as much as abilities. Although creativity research within the field of education is relatively new (Glăveanu & Kaufman, 2020), introducing design students to strategies that enhance creativity could surely help architectural education adapt to the emerging innovation economy (Sledge, 2021).

Corporate/Business/Industry Definitions of Creativity

Corporate/business/industry folk define creativity much like the current components described throughout this chapter, namely involving original ideas that are useful and relevant.

Scientists' Definitions of Creativity

Scientists define creativity as a process to determine which smaller questions are likely to yield results, imagine possible answers to their questions, and devise ways to test those answers.

Creativity Researchers'/Theorists' Definitions of Creativity

The various definitions of creativity provided by creativity theorists are listed later in this chapter with their biographies in Section 2.9, "Trailblazing Creativity Theorists and Researchers."

Military Definitions of Creativity

General Mark A. Milley, USA – the Chairman of the Joint Chiefs of Staff, that is, the presiding officer of the United States Joint Chiefs of Staff, since October 1, 2019 – believes that creative thinking is a critical element of strategic thought and is necessary for successful leadership of our military. The creativity of military commanders refers to their ability to find workable, novel solutions to problems – to be innovative and adaptable in fast-moving, potentially confusing situations. A creative intellect allows commanders to surprise enemy counterparts and render them impotent. Success in combat at all levels requires imagination on the part of commanders, who should possess a high degree of creativity in thinking and a readiness to take risks (Zais, 1985). Box 2.2 sets out E. Paul Torrance's application of creative problem-solving to military survival techniques.

> Box 2.2 Torrance and the military
>
> I have held that whenever one is faced with a problem for which he has no practiced or learned solution, some degree of creativity is required.
>
> E. Paul Torrance (1975)
>
> The following information about E. Paul Torrance is from Cramond (2021):
>
> In regard to teaching people to survive, Torrance worked with the U. S. Air Force Advanced Survival School (1951–1957). This school was established to prepare fighter pilots who are shot down to survive on the ground. Intrigued by the idea of developing a psychology of survival, Torrance took the job as Director of the Research Unit just as the Korean War began. Among the things they taught in the survival school were how to evade capture, what brainwashing techniques are used, how to live off of the land, how to be self-reliant and to cooperate with the group, how to use what they might have in different ways, and how to slow their pace to conserve their strength. It was tough training, but the men who finished it were well-prepared. Additionally, Torrance's published articles on survival – including adapting to torture, pain, and failure, climatic extremes, deprivation and isolation as well as group dynamics – provided new insights into survival psychology, group dynamics, and sociology (Millar, 2007, p. 32). Torrance gained an international reputation through the 135 research papers on survival in extreme conditions that he and his research team published (Neumeister & Cramond, 2004). Most important to his continuing research, Torrance saw that unpredictable circumstances required teaching them to be resourceful and think creatively.
>
> It was during his time working with U.S. Air Force Advanced Survival School that he conducted studies of jet aces. The basic question was, "What differentiates the approximately 5% of the pilots who are considered aces from other less successful pilots?" In observing and testing these aces, Torrance saw in them . . . that the aces had learned to focus their creativity productively (Hébert et al., 2002). It was also during this time that his basic survival definition of creativity was formulated. He concluded that the most successful pilots and the most likely survivors were those who could focus and use their creativity. His research demonstrated that creativity skills such as risk taking, courage, and independence (Neumeister & Cramond, 2004), as well as inventiveness, imagination, originality, flexibility, and decision-making (Millar, 2007, p. 32) were necessary for survival.
>
> Creativity is a distinctive trait of human excellence in all domains of behavior.
>
> E. Paul Torrance

2 Creativity

Education Definitions of Creativity

According to the National Advisory Committee on Creative and Cultural Education (NACCCE, 1999), creativity can be defined as "imaginative activity, fashioned so as to produce outcomes which are original and of value" (p. 29). The NACCCE report further argued for the integration of creativity in teaching and learning, curriculum, management, and leadership. It also argued for deepening young people's cultural knowledge and understanding, helping them to engage positively with cultural change and diversity (Csikszentmihalyi, 1996; Feldman, 1999; Sternberg & Lubart, 1999; Wallace & Gruber, 1989).

Reisman and Severino (2021) point out the result of teachers' lack of exposure to definitions of creativity, especially regarding students. Definitions of creativity affect teachers' ability to identify the hidden creativity of their students. In fact, students that are complacent, agreeable, subordinate, task-oriented, and smile are identified as creative by their teachers (Torrance, 1975; Whitelaw, 2006). Most teachers have a prejudicial perception of what a creative student looks like. In fact, one of the most consistent findings in educational studies of creativity has been that teachers dislike personality traits associated with creativity (Bachtold, 1974; Whitelaw, 2006). Research has indicated that teachers prefer traits that seem to run counter to creativity, such as conformity and unquestioning acceptance of authority. The reason for teachers' preferences is quite clear; creative people tend to have traits that some have referred to as obnoxious (Torrance, 1963). In fact, Torrance (1963) described creative people as not having the time to be courteous, as refusing to take *no* for an answer, and as being negativistic and critical of others.

Research has suggested that traits associated with creativity may not only be neglected, but actively punished (Myers & Torrance, 1961; Stone, 1980; Westby & Dawson, 1995). Stone (1980) found that second graders who scored highest on tests of creativity were also those identified by their peers as engaging in the most misbehavior (e.g., "getting in trouble the most"). Harrington, Block & Block (1987) suggest that a supportive environment is important to the fostering of creativity; it is quite possible that teachers are (perhaps unwittingly) extinguishing creative behaviors. The point is that current classrooms are not designed for impulsive expression – that is, talking out of turn, walking around without permission, responding with out-of-the-box answers to routine questions, daydreaming when bored, or demanding evidence for teacher or peer statements. Instead, in current classrooms, it's all about obeying rules and doing well on standardized tests. Such skills have little to do with fostering and dealing with creative thinkers.

Research has suggested that teachers who recognize their own creative strengths may be able to better recognize and appreciate the creative strengths of their students, resulting in higher quality learning (Robinson, 2018; Whitelaw, 2006). Previous research at high school level, which unveiled students' hidden talents, demonstrated that "when instructors become aware of their students' creative strengths, positive changes occur in their pedagogy and teacher–student interactions, as well as positively affecting student self-efficacy and academic performance" (Reisman & Torrance, 2002). Colleges and universities preparing teachers and school administrators for their careers in education are experiencing criticism from many arenas. Arthur Levine, former President of Teachers' College at Columbia University and former President of the Woodrow Wilson Foundation, was criticized for negatively assessing the state of teacher preparation. He commented that teacher preparation is archaic and stuck in an ivory tower. Not only do teachers squash kids' creativity, but, tragically, they do not recognize their students' or their own creative strengths (Levine, 2016).

Psychologists' Definitions of Creativity

Psychologists usually define creativity as the capacity to produce original and adaptive ideas. In other words, creative ideas must be new and workable or functional; thus, creativity enables a person to adjust (Simonton, 2001). Kaufman and Beghetto (Beghetto & Kaufman, 2011; Kaufman & Beghetto, 2009) proposed a "Four-C" model of creativity (mini-c, little-c, pro-c, and big-C), as shown in Box 2.3.

Box 2.3   Four-C model of creativity

Big-C	People achieve eminence and their work will be remembered throughout history.
Pro-C	Creativity takes place among professionals who are skilled and creative in their respective fields.
Little-C	Involves solving everyday problems that one may face and adapting to changing environments, thinking, and problem-solving.
Mini-C	Involves gaining new insights into learning and refers to the creative processes involved in constructing personal knowledge and understanding that are known only to the self.

2   *Creativity*   23

Another psychological framework for defining creativity is the 4P framework (process, person, product, and press) proposed by Rhodes (1961). Process refers to mental or physical processes involved in creative thought or work. Person involves personality traits or personality types associated with creative thought or work. Products are judged to be creative by a relevant social group. Press refers to external forces that affect creativity (e.g., the sociocultural context and trauma).

2.3   A Variety of Creativity Definitions

Figure 2.1 shows a free two-page poster produced by Demian Farnworth (2021) that addresses the following question: What is creativity? Farnworth asked: What exactly do we refer to when we talk about creativity? His poster answers this question and contains 21 definitions from a wide range of creative folk.

The definition of creativity is elusive, as de Sousa (2008) establishes in a scholarly review of the literature entitled "Still the elusive definition of creativity."

2.4   Creativity versus Innovation

Peek (2021) distinguished between creativity and innovation as follows:

> Although creativity and innovation are often used as interchangeable terms or meshed together as one concept, the difference between the two is an important one that actually helps us to understand each more fully. One way to differentiate between the two is to understand creativity as the mental precursor to innovation; creativity is about imagination and ideas where innovation is about action and process, evolutionary, or radical in its impact on the status quo.

Innovation requires creativity, but creativity does not always lead to innovation. Organizations seeking innovative thinking need workplaces and talent development systems that foster creativity and process systems that can translate creativity into innovation (Reisman & Hartz, 2011). Understanding these distinctions between creativity and innovation allows us to understand, learn, and maximize each more comprehensively. Since creativity is separate from, albeit necessary to, innovation, individuals can develop and utilize their personal creativity capabilities regardless of whether their jobs and workplaces explicitly require or seek innovation. To summarize, *creativity is the ability to produce new and unique ideas; innovation is the implementation of those ideas.*

Figure 2.1 Creativity definitions (free poster from Demian Farnworth, 2021).

2 *Creativity* 25

Figure 2.1 (cont.)

2.5 Domain-General versus Domain-Specific Creativity

Meihua, Plucker and Yang (2019) state that, "Creativity, as one of the key 21st century skills, has become increasingly important." However, despite the huge volume of research on creativity in the past sixty

> **Box 2.4 Domain-general versus domain-specific creativity**
>
> 1. There are many skills and dispositions that influence how creative someone is.
> 2. Those skills, traits, and dispositions might be domain-general or domain-specific.
> 3. If any skills, traits, or dispositions are in line with a domain-general theory of creativity, they are expected to show notable positive correlations between creative achievements across various domains. A greater correlation indicates a more potent domain-general effect.
> 4. While some skills, traits, and dispositions have a general impact on different domains, certain ones may have a domain-specific effect on creativity. For instance, conscientiousness may have a positive influence on creativity in certain domains, while, in other domains, it may have a negative impact.
> 5. Domain specificity predicts low (or zero) correlations between assessments of creative performances across domains.
> 6. Many domain specificity theorists acknowledge that intelligence is a domain-general factor that impacts creativity across different domains. As a result, they predict that low correlations exist among creative achievements across domains due to differences in intelligence, as measured by g-tests.
>
> Adapted from Baer (2016)

years, a fundamental debate about the nature of creativity still remains unsolved. Baumrind and Milgram (2010) concluded that different life experiences (schooling and culture) may have stronger impacts on domain-specific creative thinking than domain-general creative thinking. Some researchers support the hypothesis that creativity is relatively domain-general, rather than domain-specific (An & Runco, 2016; Diakidoy & Spanoudis, 2002). Others still ask: Is creativity domain-specific or domain-general?

Much of our creativity, such as musical improvisation, painting, and creative writing, is domain-specific. Each of these activities draws on a specific skill set that is different from others and is not fully dependent on domain-general creativity (Plucker, Beghetto & Dow, 2004). Baer (2016) provides a summary of the issue (Box 2.4).

2.6 Relationship between Creativity and Intelligence

Different conceptions about the relationship between intelligence and creativity exist (Jauk et al., 2013). Some researchers assert that, to be creative, a person needs to be intelligent. Still, not all intelligent people have high creative potential. MacKinnon (1965) argued that a basic level of IQ of about 120 is necessary for creative productivity. This is referred to as the threshold theory. The basic idea behind the threshold hypothesis is that high creativity requires high or above-average intelligence. Above-average intelligence is thought to be a necessary but not a sufficient condition for high creativity (Guilford, 1967). Torrance (1962) proposed that, in a general sample, there will be a positive correlation between low creativity and intelligence scores, but a correlation will not be found with higher scores. While earlier research mostly supported the threshold hypothesis, it has come under fire in recent investigations (Jauk et al., 2013). There is an inverse relation between scoring high on an IQ test and scoring high on a creativity assessment. To score high on an IQ test, the test taker must answer in line with the normative population. The opposite occurs regarding a creativity measure where the highly creative test taker's answers are unique, novel, and different from the normative population.

2.7 Creative-Thinking Process

Creative thinking comprises a sequence of divergent–convergent thinking as shown in Figure 2.2. Divergent thinking involves generating many ideas or solutions and is related to fluency. Convergent thinking involves coming to closure.

2.8 Common Creativity Myths

The following are myths about creativity: the inspiration just hasn't hit yet, you are born with it, you have to be right-brained, it falls into your lap, and you've got to be a little mad. Benedek et al. (2021)

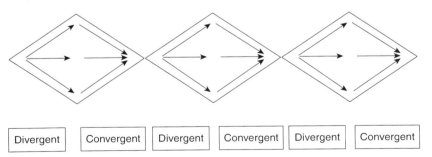

Figure 2.2 Creative-thinking process (from Tanner & Reisman, 2014, p. 98, with permission).

conducted a global study involving 1,417 recruits; the study "examined the prevalence of known creativity myths across six countries from diverse cultural backgrounds and explored why some people believe in them more than others." Fifteen myths and fifteen facts were identified concerning the definition of creativity, the creative process, the creative person, and ways to stimulate creativity. The creativity myths are presented in Box 2.5 and the creativity facts are presented in Box 2.6.

Regarding teachers' misconceptions of creative students, for decades studies have indicated that teachers prefer traits that seem to run

---

Box 2.5   Creativity myths

Creativity cannot be measured

Creativity is essentially the same as art

Creative ideas are naturally a good thing

Most people would not be able to distinguish abstract art from abstract children's drawings

Creative accomplishments are usually the result of sudden inspiration

Creative thinking mostly happens in the right hemisphere of the brain

Creativity tends to be a solitary activity

Creativity is a rare gift

People have a certain amount of creativity and cannot do much to change it

Children are more creative than adults

Exceptional creativity is usually accompanied by mental health disorders

People get more creative ideas under the influence of alcohol or marijuana

Long-term schooling has a negative impact on the creativity of children

Brainstorming in a group generates more ideas than if people were thinking by themselves

Individuals learn better when they receive information in their preferred learning style (e.g., auditory, visual, or kinesthetic)

Short bouts of coordination exercises can improve integration of left and right hemispheric brain function

Children are less attentive after sugary drinks and snacks

Differences in hemispheric dominance (left brain or right brain) can help to explain individual differences among learners

We mostly use only 10 percent of our brain

2 Creativity

> **Box 2.6 Creativity facts**
>
> To be considered creative, something has to be both novel and useful or appropriate
>
> Teachers appreciate the idea of creativity but not necessarily creative pupils
>
> Whether or not something is viewed as creative depends on zeitgeist and social norms
>
> Creativity is an important part of mathematical thinking
>
> Creative ideas are typically based on remembered information that is combined in new ways
>
> The first idea someone has is often not the best one
>
> Alpha activity (10 Hz, a measurement of frequency per second) in the brain plays an important role in creative thought
>
> Creative people are usually more open to new experiences
>
> Creative people are usually more intelligent
>
> Achieving a creative breakthrough in a domain (i.e., publishing a successful novel) typically requires at least ten years of deliberate practice and work
>
> Men and women generally do not differ in their creativity
>
> A man's creativity increases his attractiveness to potential partners
>
> When stuck on a problem, it is helpful to continue working on it after taking a break
>
> Positive moods help people get creative ideas
>
> Getting rewarded for creative performance at work increases one's creativity
>
> One is most creative when there is total freedom in one's actions
>
> We use our brains twenty-four hours a day
>
> Extended cognitive training can change the shape and structure of some parts of the brain
>
> The brains of boys are generally larger than those of girls
>
> Learning occurs through the modification of the brain's neural connections
>
> Normal development of the human brain involves the birth and death of brain cells

counter to creativity, such as conformity and unquestioning acceptance of authority (Bachtold, 1974; Cropley, 1992; Dettmer, 1981; Getzels & Jackson, 1962; Torrance, 1963). Getzels and Jackson's (1962) study, which triggered an explosion of research into the area of creativity, found that creative strengths were better predictors of academic achievement than IQ scores. Several research studies have replicated Getzels and Jackson's study and supported the finding that creativity is related to academic achievement. From the elementary level to the graduate level, creativity scores have been found to be either more effective or equivalent in predicting academic achievement (Esquivel & Lopez, 1988). Teachers' myths regarding the identification of their creative students are often a function of teacher preparation programs that do not address creativity.

Creativity Killers and Quick Fixes

Box 2.7 sets out characteristics referred to as *creativity killers* and strategies for addressing them. Readers may google "creativity killers" to access several related websites for additional creativity killers.

Box 2.7   Creativity killers and response strategies

Creativity killers	Response strategies
Pessimism is an overall negative mindset in which you're reluctant to build upon your creative ideas.	Reframe negative experiences by focusing on what went right, using positive language such as "and" instead of "but."
Fear is built on anxieties and an unwillingness to take any form of risk. It focuses on the uncertainties of an idea, rather than the potential benefits and positive outcomes.	Embrace fear as part of the creative process, as one learns from failure.
Pressure can cause one to shut down or freeze up due to stress, by putting a stranglehold on your ability to be creative.	Create a detailed schedule of your tasks and daily/weekly goals with space for free time to relax and unwind.
Isolation leads to always taking the "safe" route and avoiding risk taking, which is a creative characteristic.	Be receptive to the ideas of others, even if you don't agree with their ideas.
Narrow-mindedness means always circling back to the same ideas and same processes.	Resist premature closure.

Source: www.freshgigs.ca/blog/5-culprits-that-are-killing-your-creativity/

2.9 Trailblazing Creativity Theorists and Researchers

The following is a summary of the leading creativity researchers and theorists and their contributions to creativity. Our apologies for any inadvertent omittance.

Teresa Amabile

Amabile serves as the Edsel Bryant Ford Professor of Business Administration in the Entrepreneurial Management Unit at Harvard Business School. She was initially educated as a chemist but received her doctorate in psychology from Stanford. Her research focuses on creativity, productivity, innovation, and the junction of people's emotions, perceptions, and motivation. Amabile has published over 100 scholarly articles and chapters. She is also the author of *The Progress Principle: Using Small Wins to Ignite Joy, Engagement, and Creativity at Work*, which she coauthored with her husband and collaborator, Steven Kramer, Ph.D. (Amabile & Kramer, 2011). She also created the componential theory of creativity, which is a comprehensive model of the components necessary for creative work.

Ronald Beghetto

Beghetto is the Pinnacle West Presidential Chair and Professor in the Mary Lou Fulton Teachers College at Arizona State University, editor for the *Journal of Creative Behavior* and series editor for *Creative Theory and Action in Education* (Springer Books). His research explores the role uncertainty plays in creativity, learning, and instruction. Beghetto defines creative experience as engagement with the unfamiliar and a willingness to approach the familiar in unfamiliar ways (Glăveanu & Beghetto, 2021). Beghetto, with his colleagues Kaufman and Plucker, identified skills key for the twenty-first century, known as the "Four Cs": creativity, critical thinking, collaboration, and communication. These four Cs represent key skills identified by educational, business, and government leaders as essential to successfully deal with our complex future. Beghetto has published seven books and more than 100 articles and scholarly book chapters on creative and innovative approaches to teaching, learning, and leadership in schools and classrooms.

Kristen Betts

Dr. Kristen Betts, Clinical Professor in the School of Education at Drexel University, is affiliated with the Drexel Creativity and Innovation

Program and is Founder of the Drexel Education, Learning, and Brain Sciences (E-LaBS), a research collaborative. Dr. Betts has over twenty years of experience in higher education and online learning as a senior administrator (Chief Academic Officer, Senior Director for e-Learning with 90+ programs, and Director for Online and Blended Learning) and program director (EdD in Educational Leadership and Management and MS in Higher Education). Dr. Betts' expertise is in higher education, online and blended learning, course/program development, curriculum and instructional design, accreditation, and strategic planning. Her research intersects creativity and motivation with a focus on mind, brain, and education science, assessment, technology-enhanced learning, and professional development. A peer evaluator with the Middle States Commission on Higher Education and a Fulbright Specialist, she also is an instructor for the Online Learning Consortium certificate programs and a grant reviewer with the Hong Kong Research Grants Council. At Drexel University, Dr. Betts served as the National Faculty Academy Coordinator for the Urban Special Education Leaders for Tomorrow (USELT) grant project ($1.25 million). Dr. Betts has received distinguished national awards for her work in higher education and online learning and has been a keynote speaker at conferences and government-supported events in Sweden, South Korea, Canada, and across the United States. Dr. Betts is also engaged in innovative research initiatives with INTERACT123.com related to pedagogical practices and pivoting courses and programs seamlessly from on-campus to online learning for higher education and kindergarten to twelfth grade (K–12) education.

Jerome Bruner

Bruner defined the creative act as effective surprise – the production of novelty. He (Bruner, 1973) suggested that play and creativity are linchpins in constructivism epistemology and are clearly needed to the notion of "surprised amusement," which was central to Bruner's conception of creativity, as he writes that an act that produces *effective surprise* is the hallmark of the creative enterprise. Bruner distinguished between creativity and originality, as he proposed six essential conditions of creativity: (1) detachment and commitment, (2) passion and decorum, (3) freedom to be dominated by the object, (4) deferral and immediacy (there is an immediacy to creating anything), (5) the internal drama, and (6) the dilemma of abilities.

Bonnie Cramond

Professor Emerita in the Educational Psychology Department of the University of Georgia at Athens, Cramond has been director of the Torrance Center for Creativity and Talent Development, a member of the board of directors of the National Association for Gifted Children, editor of the *Journal of Secondary Gifted Education*, and a teacher. Currently on the advisory board for the Future Problem Solving Program International, the Global Center for Gifted and Talented Children, and a member of the Japan International Creativity Society, she is on the review board for several journals and a survivor of parenting two gifted and creative people.

Arthur Cropley

Arthur Cropley obtained his Ph.D. from the University of Alberta (Canada) and taught at the Universities of Regina (Canada) and Hamburg (Germany), with brief stints in Australia. He was founding editor of *High Ability Studies* and is on the board of the *Creativity Research Journal*. He has received awards and fellowships, as well as an honorary doctorate from the University of Latvia. In 2004, he received the Order of the Three Stars from the President of Latvia. He has published extensively on creativity and is the author of 25 books, with translations into a dozen languages including Hungarian, Latvian, Chinese, and Korean. He has become increasingly interested in recent years in using creativity concepts to examine areas not usually associated with creativity (such as engineering) and has looked closely at the dark side of creativity, and particularly crime.

David H. Cropley

David H. Cropley of the Centre for Change and Complexity in Learning of the University of South Australia is Professor of Engineering Innovation at the University of South Australia. He joined the School of Engineering at the South Australian Institute of Technology (SAIT) in 1990, after serving for four years in the United Kingdom's Royal Navy, including a deployment to the Arabian Gulf in 1988. His research interests lie in the measurement of product creativity, namely measuring innovation capacity in organizations, creativity in schools and education, creativity and innovation in terrorism and crime, and the nexus of creative problem-solving and engineering. Dr. Cropley is author of four books including *Creativity in Engineering: Novel Solutions to*

Complex Problems (Academic Press, 2015), *The Psychology of Innovation in Organizations* (Cambridge University Press, 2015), and *Creativity and Crime: A Psychological Analysis* (Cambridge University Press, 2013).

Mihalyi Cskiszentmihalyi

(pronounced me-HIGH chick-sent-me-HIGH-ee)

Mihalyi Cskiszentmihalyi is a founder of the positive psychology movement who created the Systems Model of Creativity (Csikszentmihalyi, 2014) that includes the individual, the domain (the gatekeepers of a discipline), and the field (society or humanity as a whole). He also proposed the concept of flow in his book *Flow: The Psychology of Optimal Experience* (Csikszentmihalyi, 1990). According to Csikszentmihalyi, people feel happy when in a state of flow. Flow is a type of intrinsic motivation where an individual is fully focused on a situation or task. He describes flow as "being completely involved in an activity for its own sake. The ego falls away, time flies" (Csikszentmihalyi, 1990). He defines creativity as "any act, idea, or product that changes an existing domain, or that transforms an existing domain into a new one ... What counts is whether the novelty he or she produces is accepted for inclusion in the domain" (Csikszentmihalyi, 1990, p. 28).

Edward de Bono

Edward de Bono died in June 2021 at 88 years of age. He was a Maltese physician, psychologist, author, inventor, philosopher, and consultant. He originated the term lateral thinking, wrote the book *Six Thinking Hats* (de Bono, 1985), and is a proponent of teaching thinking as a subject in schools. Lateral thinking "is a manner of solving problems using an indirect and creative approach via reasoning that is not immediately obvious. It involves ideas that may not be obtainable using only traditional step-by-step logic" (Syahrin et al., 2019).

The six hats are a process that involves taking different perspectives of a situation. The white hat is the objective hat, which focuses on facts and logic. The red hat is the intuitive hat, which focuses on emotion and instinct. The black hat is the cautious hat, which is used to predict negative outcomes. The yellow hat is the optimistic hat, which is used to look for positive outcomes. The green hat is the creative hat, where ideas are abundant and criticism spare. The blue hat is the hat of control and is used for management and organization.

His theory of lateral thinking is not recognized as a coherent and empirically validated theory within psychology (Moseley et al., 2005; Sternberg & Lubart 1999). However, his critics do recognize the potential usefulness of his tools and make a point not to reject them simply because they have not been studied and validated empirically (Sternberg, Kaufman & Pretz, 2002, p. 99; Sternberg & Lubart, 1999).

Howard Gardner

Gardner's theory of human intelligence contradicts the view that there is one type of intelligence. He described seven intelligence types: linguistic, logical/mathematical, spatial, bodily kinesthetic, musical, interpersonal, and intrapersonal, and later he added naturalist. He warned that teachers develop certain intelligence types in their students while placing less emphasis on other types – a practice that is detrimental, as it fails to recognize student cognitive strengths and creativity.

Vlad Glăveanu

Vlad Glăveanu is Professor of Psychology at Dublin City University. His work focuses on creativity, imagination, culture, collaboration, and societal challenges. There are multiple historical ways of defining and measuring creativity. He suggests that "Art based definitions are grounded in novelty, spontaneity and self-expression. Invention based definitions are grounded in utility, insight, and problem solving. Craft based definitions are grounded in collaboration, materiality, and culture. Understanding this multiplicity and fostering it is essential in education" (Glăveanu & Zittoun, 2018).

John Curtis Gowan

Gowan was a psychologist who studied the development of creative capabilities in children and gifted populations. He also had an interest in psychic (or psychedelic) phenomena in relation to human creativity. He described the entire spectrum of available states in his classic book *Trance, Art and Creativity* (Gowan, 1975), with its different modalities of spiritual and esthetic expression.

Joy Paul Guilford

Guilford is known for his study of human intelligence, including the distinction between convergent and divergent production. He identified three components of divergent thinking: fluency (the ability to quickly find multiple solutions to a problem), flexibility (being able to simultaneously consider a variety of alternatives), and originality (referring to ideas that differ from those of other people). His structure of the intellect theory comprises up to 180 different intellectual abilities organized along three dimensions: operations, content, and products. Guilford's structure of the intellect model of human abilities has few supporters today. Carroll (1993) summarized the view of later researchers:

> Guilford's SOI [structure of the intellect] model must, therefore, be marked down as a somewhat eccentric aberration in the history of intelligence models. The fact that so much attention has been paid to it is disturbing to the extent that textbooks and other treatments of it have given the impression that the model is valid and widely accepted, when clearly it is not.

Guilford's challenge at the 1950 American Psychological Association (APA) Conference triggered a renaissance in creativity research:

> Of approximately 121,000 titles listed in the past 23 years, only 186 were indexed as definitely bearing on the subject of creativity. The topics under which such references are listed include creativity, imagination, originality, thinking, and tests in these areas. In other words, less than two-tenths of one per cent of the books and articles indexed in the Abstracts for approximately the past quarter century bear directly on this subject. Few of these advance our understanding or control of creative activity very much. Of the large number of textbooks on general psychology, only two have devoted separate chapters to the subject during the same period. (Guilford, 1950, p. 445)

Scott G. Isaksen

Scott G. Isaksen is an academic scholar, practitioner, leader, and mentor. His contributions to the research and practice of creativity include the Cognitive Styles Project, which identifies links between person and process, and the integration of convergent thinking within creative problem-solving, as well as the development and validation of the VIEW tool (an assessment of problem-solving style) and the Situational Outlook Questionnaire.

Alan and Nadeen Kaufman

Alan and Nadeen Kaufman created the Kaufman Assessment Battery for Children (KABC and KABC-II) (Kaufman & Kaufman, 1983, 2004; Drozdick et al., 2018), an important contribution to the field of intelligence testing for assessing cognitive development. This assessment is based upon the planning, attention, simultaneous, and successive cognitive processing (PASS) intelligence theory and the Cattell–Horn–Carroll (CHC) theory of cognitive abilities (Benyamin et al., 2014). The updated version (KABC-II) helps to identify an individual's strengths and weaknesses in cognitive ability and mental processing. The information provided by the KABC-II can facilitate clinical and educational planning, treatment, and placement decisions. Alan and Nadeen Kaufman are the parents of James C. Kaufman.

James C. Kaufman

James C. Kaufman is Professor of Educational Psychology at the University of Connecticut. He is the author/editor of more than fifty books, including *Creativity 101* (2nd edition; Kaufman, 2016) and the *Cambridge Handbook of Creativity* (2nd edition; Kaufman & Sternberg, 2019). He has published more than 300 papers, including the study that spawned the "Sylvia Plath effect," and three well-known theories of creativity, including (with Ron Beghetto) the Four-C model of creativity (Beghetto & Kaufman, 2010; Kaufman & Beghetto, 2009). He is a past president of Division 10 of the APA. Dr. Kaufman has won many awards, including Mensa's research award, the Torrance Award from the National Association for Gifted Children, and the APA's Berlyne and Farnsworth awards. He cofounded two major journals (*Psychology of Aesthetics, Creativity, and the Arts* and *Psychology of Popular Media Culture*) and wrote the book and lyrics to *Discovering Magenta*, which had its Manhattan premiere in 2015.

Kyung-Hee Kim (Kay)

Dr. Kim is originally from Korea and came to the USA in 2000. Through the support of one of her teachers at a young age, she became the first female from her village to progress to high school. Thanks to that teacher, Kim avoided a future as a worker in a sock shop. She already had a master's degree and a Ph.D. from Korea, but when she came to the USA, she did a second Ph.D. under the supervision of Dr. Torrance and found an additional mentor, Dr. Bonnie Cramond, during graduate study at the Torrance Center.

Kim's paper "The creativity crisis: The decrease in creative thinking scores on the Torrance Tests of Creative Thinking" was published in the *Creativity Research Journal* in 2011 (Kim, 2011) and publicized in *Newsweek* magazine (Bronson & Merryman, 2010); in this paper, she reported a significant decrease in creativity scores, which had been on the rise prior to 1990. Kim discovered that there is a negligible relationship between IQ and creativity: "You can have a low IQ and be creative." Kim also noted that "The Torrance Tests of Creative Thinking predicts creative achievement three times better than IQ tests." She is professor at William and Mary College.

Nathan Kogan

Dr. Nathan Kogan was Professor Emeritus of Psychology at the New School for Social Research, New York City, and Visiting Scholar at the Center for New Constructs, Educational Testing Service, Princeton, New Jersey. Dr. Kogan served two terms as President of APA Division 10 (Society for the Psychology of Aesthetics, Creativity, and the Arts). He received the Sir Francis Galton award from the International Association for Empirical Aesthetics, the SAGES award from the Society for the Psychological Study of Social Issues, and the Farnsworth Award from Division 10 of the APA. Over the course of his career, Dr. Kogan's research has been supported in part or in whole by the Office of Naval Research, the National Science Foundation, the National Institute of Mental Health, the Advanced Research Projects Agency, the Cooperative Research Program of the US Office of Education, and the National Institute of Child Health and Human Development. Kogan indicated that creativity measures are influenced when creativity tests are administered as serious tests rather than as fun activities, especially for children in kindergarten or in the early grades (Wallach & Kogan, 1965).

Stanley Krippner

Krippner investigated altered states of consciousness, dream telepathy, hypnosis, shamanism, dissociation, and parapsychological subjects. Krippner served as a leader in Division 32 of the APA, the division concerned with humanistic psychology, serving as president of the division from 1980 to 1981. He also served as president of Division 30, the Society for Psychological

Hypnosis, and is a fellow of four APA divisions. In 2002, Krippner won the APA Award for Distinguished Contributions to the International Advancement of Psychology.

Todd Lubart

Todd Lubart is Professor of Psychology at the University Paris Descartes and is a former member of the Institute Universiatire de France. He received his Ph.D. from Yale and collaborated with Robert Sternberg on the investment theory of creativity (Sternberg & Lubart, 1991). He is author or coauthor of approximately 100 scientific reports (journal papers and book chapters) on creativity, as well as the book *Defying the Crowd: Cultivating Creativity in a Culture of Conformity* (Sternberg & Lubart, 1995).

Colin Martindale

Colin Martindale was Professor of Psychology at the University of Maine for 35 years. He studied creativity and the artistic process. In his book *The Clockwork Muse* (Martindale, 1990), he argued that artistic development was the result of a search for novelty and could be studied quantitatively. Martindale earned the American Association for the Advancement of Science Prize for Behavioral Science Research in 1984.

Michael Mumford

Dr. Mumford has held faculty positions at the Georgia Institute of Technology and George Mason University. He has also been a Senior Research Fellow and Managing Partner of the American Institutes for Research. Dr. Mumford has published more than 150 articles on creativity, leadership, integrity, and planning. He serves on the editorial boards of *Leadership Quarterly*, the *Creativity Research Journal*, and the *Journal of Creative Behavior*. He is a fellow of the APA (Divisions 3, 5, and 14), the American Psychological Society, and the Society for Industrial and Organizational Psychology. In 2002, he received the Society for Industrial and Organizational Psychologies' Myers Applied Research Award. He received his master's (1981) and Ph.D. (1983) degrees from the University of Georgia and his B.A. from Bucknell University in 1979. He defined creativity as follows: "creativity is the process of producing something that is both original and worthwhile or which is characterized by originality and expressiveness and imaginative." He further adds that creativity involves the production of novel and useful products.

Kobus Neethling

Neethling is President of the South African Creativity Foundation and the creator of the Neethling Brain Instruments. Neethling's interactions with Torrance and Parnes opened the door to creativity in South Africa, supported by his relations with Nelson Mandela.

Ruth Noller

Dr. Ruth Noller was a noted mathematician, computer programmer, and professor of creativity studies. During World War II, she participated in the pioneering work of programming the Mark 1 computer at Harvard University – as the second known woman computer programmer in the country. Noller merged her loves of math and creativity, resulting in her formula for creativity, $C = fa(K,I,E)$, which claimed that creativity is a function of knowledge (semantics), imagination (divergence), and evaluation.

Alex Faickney Osborn

Osborn coined and popularized the creative-thinking tool known as "brainstorming" – using the brain to storm a creative problem. In his book *Your Creative Power* (Osborn, 1948), he laid out the basic tenets of brainstorming, the most important of which was that no idea should be discouraged or judged. The objective of brainstorming was to generate as many ideas or suggestions around one specific issue as possible. Brainstorming, by the 1950s, was employed in planning and research in eight out of ten of the largest companies in the USA. However, when brainstorming was subject to its first empirical study at Yale University in 1958, groups were found to work far less effectively than individuals on a series of creative puzzles. In the sixty or so independent studies that have since been conducted, the evidence has stacked up against the claims made by Osborn and others.

Sidney Parnes

Sidney Parnes, cofounder of what is today the Center for Applied Imagination at Buffalo State University, partnered with advertising executive Dr. Alex Osborn to develop the Osborn–Parnes creative problem-solving model, based on Osborn's brainstorming techniques. Parnes published more than a dozen books and hundreds of articles on creativity, perhaps most notably the *Creative Behavior Guidebook* (Parnes, 1967). He spoke at conferences, workshops, and seminars around the world and received numerous awards, including a Lifetime Achievement Award from the Innovation Network.

Jean Piaget

Piaget's theory is an interactive theory in which the basis of all actions, growth, and invention is the interaction of individuals with their environment. Within this theory of creative thinking developed from Piaget's dialectic notions of assimilation and accommodation, this interaction is vital. Ayman-Nolley (1999) challenged the widely accepted myth that Piaget did not address the concept of creativity in his theoretical interpretation of the development of the mind. Using Piaget's own explanations, Ayman-Nolley explored the possibility of a dialectic approach to creativity. The proposed explanation does not focus on Piaget's stage theory but utilizes his explanation of development (assimilation and accommodation). Thus, Piaget explores the integration of creative thought as integral to understanding thought processes in general.

Jonathan Plucker

Jonathan Plucker's work includes the following aspects: (1) defining creativity (and how researchers can push its boundaries), (2) the assessment and psychometrics of creativity, (3) assessing the evidence of creativity, (4) creativity across the globe, (5) creativity in the classroom, and (6) talent development through gifted education and reducing excellence gaps across students from different demographic backgrounds. He defined creativity as follows: "creativity is the interaction among aptitude, process, and environment by which an individual or group produces a perceptible product that is both novel and useful as defined within a social context" (Plucker, Beghetto & Dow, 2004).

Steven Pritzker

Steven Pritzker started in the arts and later recreated himself as a scholar of creativity. He began his career as a comedy writer on network television, rising from Executive Story Editor of the Emmy-winning Room 222 and the Mary Tyler Moore Show to eventually become an executive producer on subsequent sitcoms. In the 1990s, Pritzker left television to pursue a doctorate in educational psychology. With backgrounds in business and counseling, Pritzker pursued topics ranging from organizational culture and expressive arts to substance abuse and humanistic therapies. He applied his expertise to writing, teaching, and life coaching before founding the master's and doctoral specializations in creativity at Saybrook University, Pasadena, California. Pritzker conceived and became Co-Editor-in-Chief of the *Encyclopedia of Creativity*, which provides a wealth of information on creativity research. Pritzker defined creativity as influencing each of our lives and is essential for the advancement of society.

Gerard J. Puccio

Gerard is the department chair of the Center for Applied Imagination (formerly the International Center for Studies in Creativity) at Buffalo State University, where they have created the Doctor of Professional Studies (DPS) program as part of the Creativity and Change Leadership program. Puccio received the State University of New York Chancellor's Recognition Award for Research Excellence and the President's Medal for Scholarship and Creativity. He developed the FourSight model, which comprises the following four steps: (1) you clarify, (2) you ideate, (3) you develop, and (4) you implement. When you clarify, you define the problem. You are working to make sure that you are solving the right problems, creating the right work, using the right voice/medium, etc. When you ideate, you come up with lots of possible ideas to meet the challenges. When you develop, you are finding a solution. When you implement, you find and tap into acceptance of the idea and/or product.

Ruth Richards

Dr. Ruth Richards is an Educational Psychologist and Board Certified Psychiatrist and has been a Professor for almost 25 years at Saybrook University in Creativity Studies and in Consciousness, Spirituality, and Integrative Health. She is also a fellow with the APA in Divisions 10, 32, 34, and 48. She has published numerous articles, has edited/written four books on everyday creativity, and has received the Rudolf Arnheim Award from APA Division 10 for Outstanding Lifetime Accomplishment in Psychology and the Arts. Dr. Richards' 2018 book *Everyday Creativity and the Healthy Mind* (Richards, 2017) won a Silver Nautilus Award ("Better Books for a

Better World"). Dr. Richards' work spans education, clinical areas, social action, spirituality, esthetics and awareness, and the importance of chaos and complexity theories in areas including our dynamic identity, interconnection, mutual awareness, expanded empathy, and forward potentials for evolution in a challenged world and evolving cosmos. She also is a creative poet.

Ken Robinson

Sir Ken Robinson asked: Do schools continue to kill creativity? In 2006, Robinson declared that the school system alienated students and did not provide a place for creativity. According to him (Robinson, 2017), this is contradictory with the needs of contemporary organizations that look for creative thinkers. He pointed out the problem of the current design of the educational system, sharing a view of it as one of a non-synchronized system that was created for children from a different era. Moreover, he suggested that many people are unaware of the variety of their talents, indicating that many of our institutions are failing the people they're meant to serve and the energies of those who work in them. Sir Ken Robinson believed that creativity is essential for navigating a fundamentally unpredictable world. He defined creativity as the process of having original ideas that have value. Ken and his daughter Kate coauthored their 2022 book, *Imagine If . . . Creating a Future for Us All* (Robinson & Robinson, 2022).

Mark Runco

Mark Runco earned his Ph.D. in cognitive psychology from the Claremont Graduate School in California. He is currently Director of Creativity Research and Programming at Southern Oregon University. Nearly thirty years ago, Runco founded the *Creativity Research Journal*. In 2014, he founded two more journals: *Business Creativity and the Creative Economy* and the *Journal of Genius and Eminence*. Runco coedited the *Encyclopedia of Creativity* in 1999, 2011, and 2020. He has published approximately 200 articles, book chapters, and books on creativity and its measurement and enhancement. Runco posits that creativity requires originality or novelty because, if something is not unusual, novel, or unique, it is commonplace, mundane, or conventional. In addition, original things must be effective to be creative. Effectiveness is often labeled functional, fit, or appropriate (Runco & Jaeger, 2012).

Robert Keith Sawyer

Sawyer is the Morgan Distinguished Professor in Educational Innovations at University of North Carolina at Chapel Hill. Sawyer's research explores the subtle and often hidden roles of collaboration, conversation, interaction, and improvisation. He posits that creativity researchers can be grouped into two major traditions of research: an individualist approach and a sociocultural approach. Each type of researcher has its own analytic focus and each defines creativity slightly differently. The individualist definition posits that creativity is a new mental combination that is expressed in the world. The sociocultural definition states that creativity is the generation of a product that is judged to be novel and also to be appropriate, useful, or valuable by a suitably knowledgeable social group (Sawyer, 2007). Sawyer is noted for studying group creativity.

Dean Keith Simonton

Simonton investigated creative trailblazers to map patterns and predictors of creative productivity (Simonton, 1997). He supplied the field of creativity studies with a wealth of evidence-based insights and directions for future research (Simonton, 2014). He defines creativity as follows: "Creativity is simply used to create a new, appropriate, original and effective for a task whose outcome is unknown, to design a new product and to find new answers solution" (Simonton, 2018). He also argued that any attempt to define creative ideas cannot fully succeed without also defining uncreative ideas (Simonton, 2016).

Dorothy Sisk

Sisk and Torrance developed the following definition related to their beliefs about spirituality: "spiritual intelligence (SQ) is defined as the capacity to use a multisensory approach – including intuition, meditation, and visualization – to access one's inner knowledge in order to solve problems of a global nature" (Sisk & Torrance, 2001). Sisk explores definitions of creativity, theories and models of creativity, and the classic stages of creativity. She concludes that creativity is best defined in terms of an interactive process. The creative process in adults often results in creative and useful products, and such creativity is judged in terms of the quantity and quality of patents, theories, books, and more. In children, however, the product may be original with the child, but not original with the culture.

Morris "Moe" Stein

Morris "Moe" Stein was on the faculty of New York University from 1960 and headed the Doctoral Program in Social Psychology. Well known for his work on personality and the nature and encouragement of creativity, he authored over ten books and accrued many honors. He was born in the Bronx, educated at De Witt Clinton High School, the City College of New York, and Harvard, and taught at Wheaton College and Chicago University before returning to New York City. In Stein's *Stimulating Creativity* Volumes 1 and 2 (Stein, 1974, 1975), he developed a framework for stimulating creativity.

Robert Sternberg

Robert Sternberg defined creativity as "the production of something original and worthwhile" (Sternberg, 2011). Sternberg's triarchic theory of human intelligence distinguished between three types of intellectual abilities: analytic, creative, and practical. According to Sternberg, these abilities are interdependent constructs, and every student demonstrates a distinct blend of strengths in one, two, or all three triarchic ability categories. Analytic abilities are those needed to analyze, evaluate, explain, and compare or contrast. The stereotype for students high in analytic abilities is that of the "good student" – that is, such students have been found to excel at the kinds of tasks fostered and reinforced within the United States school system (Sternberg, 1997). Creative abilities are those involved in creating, designing, discovering, or inventing. Creative thinking entails applying problem-solving processes to relatively novel and unfamiliar problems. Students with dominant creative abilities are valued for being able to generate new ideas. Practical abilities are those needed to utilize, implement, and apply problem-solving processes to concrete and relatively familiar everyday problems. Practical students are motivated by and appreciative of knowledge that they can take with them when they leave the classroom. Students with strong practical abilities are considered "street smart" – that is, able to quickly adapt to and shape their environment to achieve a concrete goal. Sternberg also is noted for his investment theory of creativity, in which original ideas are at first not valued by the field (buy low) but then are enthusiastically accepted (sell high) (Sternberg & Davidson, 2005).

Ellis Paul Torrance

Paul Torrance, who is regarded worldwide as the father of creativity, developed benchmarks for quantifying creativity, which proved that IQ is not the only measure of intelligence. Torrance was born in Milledgeville, Georgia, and earned his bachelor's degree from Mercer University and then a doctorate from the University of Michigan. He was very prolific, publishing 1,871 publications, namely 88 books; 256 parts of books or cooperative volumes; 408 journal articles; 538 reports, manuals, tests, etc.; 162 articles in popular journals or magazines; 355 conference papers; and 64 forewords or prefaces. He also created the Future Problem-Solving Program International, the Incubation Curriculum Model, and the Torrance Tests of Creative Thinking. Because of this one man's work, children and adults worldwide have the opportunity and wherewithal to develop their creative talent.

Torrance defined creativity as a process of becoming sensitive to problems, deficiencies, gaps in knowledge, missing elements, disharmonies, and so on; of identifying difficulties; of searching for solutions, making guesses, or formulating hypotheses about the deficiencies; of testing and retesting these hypotheses and possibly modifying and retesting them; and finally of communicating the results (Torrance, 1984).

Kim (2006) wrote: "Torrance's research into creativity as a measure of intelligence shattered the theory that IQ tests alone can measure real intelligence." The Torrance Tests of Creative Thinking provided a physical measure and groundwork for the idea that creative levels can be scaled and then increased through practice. Torrance and Reisman, as math teachers, coauthored a trilogy on teaching math creatively (Reisman & Torrance, 2002; Torrance & Reisman, 2000a, b).

Paul Torrance will best be remembered by those closest to him for his huge heart as much as for his colossal intellect.

Donald John Treffinger

Treffinger's primary interest was in creative problem-solving. He is the author or coauthor of more than 350 publications (Treffinger, 1986; Treffinger & Isaksen, 2005). Treffinger's professional career has extended over fifty years, including appointments at Purdue and the University of Kansas, the Directorship of the Creative Studies Program at Buffalo State, and founding the Center for Creative Learning in Sarasota, Florida.

Lev Semyonovich Vygotsky

Vygotsky believed that creativity arises from any human activity that produces something new. Creative acts could produce anything from physical objects to a music score to a new mental construct. Creativity is therefore present when major artistic, scientific, and technical discoveries are made. "Psychology has for a long time ascribed too great a significance to just such established stereotypic forms of development that were themselves the result of already developed and fixed processes of development, that is, processes that are concluded and are only repeated and reproduced" (Vygotsky, 1967). Vygotsky considered "creative intelligence" as fundamental to the effective, dialectical interaction of an individual with his or her environment and the intersubjective understandings among members of a community (Vygotsky, 2004, 2010).

Michael A. Wallach

Wallach's early work included contributions on modes of thinking in young children, the distinction between intelligence and creativity, and risk-taking behavior. Wallach and Kogan (1965a, 1965b) proposed that creativity measures were weakly related to one another and were not related to IQ, but they seemed also to draw upon non-creative skills. McNemar (1964) noted that there were major measurement issues, namely that the IQ scores were a mixture from three different IQ tests. Wallach and Kogan administered five measures of creativity, each of which resulted in a score for originality and fluency, and ten measures of general intelligence. These tests were untimed and given in a game-like manner aiming to facilitate creativity. See Crockenberg (1972) for an excellent discussion of the Wallach–Kogan assessment.

Graham Wallas

Wallas dissected the act of creativity into four stages in *The Art of Thought* (Wallas, 1926): preparation, incubation, illumination, and verification. During the preparation stage, the problem is investigated from all angles and includes the accumulation of information from which emerge new ideas. The incubation stage involves unconscious processing, whereby one is unaware that cognitive activity is going on. Wallas found Poincaire's ideas on illumination critical, as Poincaire talks about the value of "procrastination," which is in fact a valuable part of illumination. The verification stage involves a conscious and deliberate effort to test the validity of an idea. Wallas's (1926) classic was published almost nine decades ago and is still widely referenced today. His work still serves as a "conceptual anchor" for many creativity researchers (e.g., Orlet, 2008; Pagel & Kwiatkowski, 2003; Reisman & Severino, 2021; to name only a few). Although some creativity researchers have proposed a five-stage model (e.g., Cropley & Cropley, 2012), most have held to Wallas's four-stage model.

2.10 What Is the Future of Creativity?

Developing and using personal creativity in the workplace is no longer relegated to the "creative arts" or deemed as "nice to have." Regardless of the setting, creativity is quickly becoming a competitive differentiator and a core competency for leadership. An IBM survey of more than 1,500 chief executives from over sixty countries and thirty industries found that "chief executives believe that – more than rigor, management discipline, integrity, or even vision – successfully navigating an increasingly complex world will require creativity" (IBM, 2010).

According to the World Economic Forum's *Future of Jobs Report* (World Economic Forum, 2018), the top ten skills that employers see as rising in importance leading up to 2025 are:

1. analytical thinking and innovation
2. active learning and learning strategies
3. complex problem-solving
4. critical thinking and analysis
5. resilience, stress tolerance, and flexibility
6. creativity, originality, and initiative
7. leadership and social influence
8. reasoning, problem-solving, and ideation
9. emotional intelligence
10. technology design and programming

Source: https://lepaya.com/en/top-10-skills-of-the-future/#10-skills-of-2025

In addition, LinkedIn's *Global Talent Trends* report, published in 2019 (LinkedIn, 2019), emphasized that the soft skills identified as most important by industry talent managers, in order of importance, were:

1. creativity
2. persuasion
3. collaboration
4. adaptability
5. time management

Source: www.upsidelms.com/blog/linkedin-global-talent-trends-2019-report/

> Box 2.8   World Economic Forum 2016 report
>
> | Skills for future jobs 2020 | Skills for future jobs 2015 |
> |---|---|
> | 1. Complex problem-solving | 1. Complex problem-solving |
> | 2. Critical thinking | 2. Coordinating with others |
> | 3. Creativity | 3. People management |
> | 4. People management | 4. Critical thinking |
> | 5. Coordinating with others | 5. Negotiation |
> | 6. Emotional intelligence | 6. Quality control |
> | 7. Judgment and decision-making | 7. Service orientation |
> | 8. Service orientation | 8. Judgment and decision-making |
> | 9. Negotiation | 9. Active listening |
> | 10. Cognitive flexibility | 10. Creativity |
>
> *Sources:* Idea to Value (2020), World Economic Forum (2016)

The following historical data (see Box 2.8 and Box 2.9) indicate that the future of creativity is an extension of the past. According to the World Economic Forum, creativity will be the third-most-important skill for employees by 2020. A report by the World Economic Forum (2019) stated that, "With the avalanche of new products, new technologies, and new ways of working, workers are going to have to become more creative in order to benefit from these changes." The World Economic Forum's *Future of Jobs* report (Box 2.9) predicted creativity, innovation, and ideation as key skills for the workforce of the future. These so-called soft skills, which sit alongside analytic thinking and problem-solving, will replace manual tasks that become automated.

Companies that want to realize their full potential must prioritize creativity as an essential component of success. Creative problem-solving will unlock innovation in the workplace in many ways – for example by finding new approaches to problems inherent to the business, developing new products, or improving existing processes. Creativity will allow companies to address their customers' biggest challenges.

Regarding how creativity is defined in the future, computational creativity (also known as artificial creativity, mechanical creativity, creative computing, or creative computation) combines the fields of artificial intelligence, cognitive psychology, philosophy, and the arts. Computational creativity (Jordanous, 2014) allows companies to model, simulate, or replicate creativity using artificial intelligence or software. Some goals of computational

Box 2.9 World Economic Forum 2018 report

2018	Trending 2022	Declining 2022
Analytical thinking and innovation	Analytical thinking and innovation	Manual dexterity, endurance, and precision
Complex problem-solving	Active learning and learning strategies	Memory, verbal, auditory, and spatial abilities
Critical thinking and analysis	Creativity, originality, and initiative	Management of financial and material resources
Active learning and learning strategies	Technology design and programming	Technology installation and maintenance
Creativity, originality, and initiative	Critical thinking and analysis	Reading, writing, math, and active listening
Attention to detail, trustworthiness	Complex problem-solving	Management of personnel
Emotional intelligence	Leadership and social influence	Quality control and safety awareness
Reasoning, problem-solving, and ideation	Emotional intelligence	Coordination and time management
Leadership and social influence	Reasoning, problem-solving, and ideation	Visual, auditory, and speech abilities
Coordination and time management	Systems analysis and evaluation	Technology use, monitoring, and control

Source: World Economic Forum (2018)

creativity include to (1) construct a program or computer capable of human-level creativity, (2) better understand human creativity and formulate an algorithmic perspective on creative behavior in humans, and (3) design programs that can enhance human creativity without necessarily being creative themselves.

The field of computational creativity addresses theoretical and practical issues related to creativity. Theoretical investigation into the nature and proper definition of creativity is performed simultaneously with explorations of practical work on developing systems that exhibit creativity. Each strand of research informs the other. This applied form of computational creativity is known as media synthesis.

2.11 Summary

The chapter acknowledges Joy Paul Guilford's APA Presidential Address entitled "Creativity milestone" that precipitated a renewal of creativity research and an explosion of creativity definitions, many of which are presented in this chapter. The definition that underlies this chapter emphasizes two components: uniqueness and relevance. Creativity is ubiquitous and complex; thus, the assessment of creative thinking and creative action is a challenge.

In this chapter, distinctions are made between creativity and innovation and domain-general and domain-specific creativity, and the relationship between creativity and intelligence is valued. The creative-thinking process and creativity myths also are discussed. This chapter also provides various tools and techniques for teachers, corporate trainers, and talent managers, including by highlighting some creativity killers and suggesting quick fixes to address these killers. Creativity trailblazers and their contributions are also listed.

Appendix 2A Creativity Journals

The *Journal of Creative Behavior* is a quarterly peer-reviewed academic journal published by Wiley-Blackwell on behalf of the Creative Education Foundation and established in 1967. The journal focuses on creativity and problem-solving, including ways to foster creative productivity, giftedness, the management of creative personnel, testing, creativity in business and industry, the development of creative curricula, and creativity in the arts and the sciences. This journal appears to focus on advancing the understanding of creativity as a field of study on a broad spectrum of ideas. A quick look at the articles in the journal reveals a wide variety of topics, ranging from group creativity in children to culinary creativity and associative algorithms for computational creativity.

Creativity and Innovation Management appears to delve into the system implementation of the creativity and innovation. The articles focus on the motivational aspects of creative work such as employee points of view, creative performance, communication, entrepreneurship, and teamwork in relation to creative products, and teamwork in relation to creative products.

The *International Journal of Innovation, Creativity and Change* publishes papers (scholarly works) to "promote and foster" innovation creativity. This journal seeks to influence the field to create a broader understanding.

The *International Journal of Design Creativity and Innovation* provides a forum for discussing the "nature and potential" of creativity and innovation. Its description suggests that it covers theories on design creativity, inventive and innovative processes, methods and tools for design creativity, and education for design creativity.

Thinking Skills and Creativity is a quarterly peer-reviewed academic journal that covers research into the teaching of thinking skills and creativity. The journal was established in 2006 and is published by Elsevier. It provides a forum for researchers to discuss and debate the ideas behind teaching for thinking and creativity. According to the description, the journal welcomes studies of teaching, reports of research, and relevant theoretical and methodological studies.

The *Creativity Research Journal* is a quarterly peer-reviewed academic journal that covers research into all aspects of creativity. The journal was established in 1988 and is published by Routledge. This journal looks at creativity through behavioral, clinical, cognitive, cross-cultural, educational, genetic, organizational, social, and psychoanalytical lenses. The journal also looks at issues such as genius, imagery, intuition, metaphor., and problem-solving/problem-finding.

Psychology of Aesthetics, Creativity, and the Arts is a quarterly peer-reviewed academic journal published by the American Psychological Association. The journal covers research on the psychology of the production and appreciation of the arts and all aspects of creative endeavor.

The *International Journal of Creative Computing* is a quarterly peer-reviewed scientific journal published by Inderscience Publishers covering creativity in computing.

Appendix 2B   Glossary

Cognitive psychology	The study of mental processes such as attention, language use, memory, perception, problem-solving, creativity, and thinking.
Convergent thinking	The ability to find a single correct solution for a given problem.
Creativity	The ability to make new things or think of new ideas. Such ideas should be original and useful.

Crystallized intelligence	The part of intelligence resulting from acquired information; it is most often obtained through education.
Divergent thinking	The ability to think of as many solutions as possible for a certain problem.
Domain	A field or an academic area.

References

Amabile, T. & Kramer, S. (2011), *The Progress Principle – Using Small Wins to Ignite Joy, Engagement and Creativity at Work*. Boston: Harvard Business Review Press.

An, D. & Runco, M. A. (2016). General and domain-specific contributions to creative ideation and creative performance. *Europe's Journal of Psychology*, 12(4), 523–532.

Ayman-Nolley, S. (1999). A Piagetian perspective on the dialectic process of creativity, *Creativity Research Journal*, 12(4), 267–275. https://doi.org/10.1207/s15326934crj1204_4.

Bachtold, L. (1974). The creative personality and the ideal pupil revisited. *Journal of Creative Behavior*, 8, 47–54.

Baer, J. (2016). Creativity doesn't develop in a vacuum. *Special Issue: Perspectives on Creativity Development*, 2019(151), 9–20.

Baumrind, D. & Milgram, S. (2010). Classic dialogue: Was Stanley Milgram's study of obedience unethical? In B. Slife (ed.), *Clashing Views on Psychological Issues* (pp. 26–42). New York: McGraw-Hill.

Beghetto, R. A. & Kaufman, J. C. (2010). *Nurturing Creativity in the Classroom*. New York: Cambridge University Press.

Beghetto, R. A. & Kaufman, J. C. (2011). Teaching for creativity with disciplined improvisation. In R. K. Sawyer (ed.), *Structure and Improvisation in Creative Teaching* (pp. 94–109). Cambridge, UK: Cambridge University Press.

Benedek, M., Karstendiek, M., Ceh, S., et al. (2021). Creativity myths: Prevalence and correlates of misconceptions on creativity. *Personality and Individual Differences*, 182, 111068.

Benyamin, B., Pourcain, B., Davis, O. S., et al. (2014). Childhood intelligence is heritable, highly polygenic and associated with FNBP1L. *Molecular Psychiatry*, 19(2), 253–258. https://doi.org/10.1038/mp.2012.184.

Bronson, P. & Merryman, A. (2010). The creativity crisis. *Newsweek*. www.newsweek.com/creativity-crisis-74665.

Bruner, J. S. (1973). Organization of early skilled action. *Child Development*, 44(1), 1–11. https://doi.org/10.2307/1127671.

Carroll, J. B. (1993). *Human Cognitive Abilities: A Survey of Factor-Analytic Studies*. Cambridge, UK: Cambridge University Press. https://doi.org/10.1017/CBO9780511571312.

Caslib Jr., B. C., Garing, D. & Casual, J. A. (2018). *Art Appreciation*. Quezon City, PH: Rex Book Store.

Charyton, C. (2015). Creative engineering design: The meaning of creativity and innovation in engineering. In C. Charyton (ed.), *Creativity and Innovation among Science and Art: A Discussion of the Two Cultures* (pp. 135–152). Hamburg, Germany: Springer-Verlag Publishing. https://doi.org/10.1007/978-1-4471-6624-5_7.

Cramond, B. (2021). E. Paul Torrance, father of creativity, minority of one (October 8, 1915–July 12, 2003). In F. Reisman, (ed.), *Celebrating Giants and Trailblazers: A–Z of Who's Who in Creativity Research and Related Fields* (pp. 732–752). London: KIE Publications.

Crockenberg, S. B. (1972). *Creativity Tests: A Boon or Boondoggle for Education?* Thousand Oaks, CA: Sage Journals.

Cropley, A. J. (1992). *More Ways than One: Fostering Creativity*. Norwood, NJ: Ablex Publishing Corporation.

Cropley, D. & Cropley, A. (2012). A psychological taxonomy of organizational innovation: Resolving the paradoxes. *Creativity Research Journal*, 24(1), 29–40.

Csikszentmihalyi, M. (1990). *Flow: The Psychology of Optimal Experience*. New York: Harper & Row.

Csikszentmihalyi, M. (1996). *Creativity*. New York: Harper Collins.

Csikszentmihalyi, M. (2014). The concept of flow. In *Flow and the Foundations of Positive Psychology* (pp. 239–263). Heidelberg: Springer Netherlands.

de Bono, E. (1985). *Six Thinking Hats*. New York: Little Brown and Co.

de Sousa, F. (2008). Still the elusive definition of creativity. *International Journal of Psychology: A Biopsychosocial Approach*, 2, 55–82.

Dettmer, P. (1981). Improving teacher attitudes toward characteristics of the creatively gifted. *Gifted Child Quarterly*, 25, 11–16.

Diakidoy, I.-A. N. & Spanoudis, G. (2002). Domain specificity in creativity testing: A comparison of performance on a general divergent-thinking test and a parallel, content-specific test. *The Journal of Creative Behavior*, 36(1), 41–61. https://doi.org/10.1002/j.2162-6057.2002.tb01055.x.

Drozdick, L. W., Singer, J. K., Lichtenberger, E. O., et al. (2018). The Kaufman Assessment Battery for Children – second edition and KABC-II normative update. In D. P. Flanagan & E. M. McDonough (eds.), *Contemporary Intellectual Assessment: Theories, Tests, and Issues* (pp. 333–359). New York: The Guilford Press.

Esquivel, G. B. & Lopez, E. (1988). Correlations among measures of cognitive ability, creativity, and academic achievement for gifted minority children. *Perceptual and Motor Skills*, 67(2), 395–398. https://doi.org/10.2466/pms.1988.67.2.395.

Farnworth, D. (2021). What is creativity? 21 authentic definitions you'll love. https://copyblogger.com/define-creativity/.

Feldman, D. H. (1999). The development of creativity. In R. J. Sternberg (ed.), *Handbook of Creativity* (pp. 169–186). Cambridge, UK: Cambridge University Press.

Getzels, J. W. & Jackson, P. W. (1962). *Creativity and Intelligence*. New York: Wiley.
Glăveanu, V. P. & Zittoun, T. (2018). The future of imagination in sociocultural research. In T. Zittoun & V. Glăveanu (eds.), *Handbook of Imagination and Culture* (pp. 347–367). Oxford, UK: Oxford University Press.
Glăveanu, V. P. & Kaufman, J. C. (2020). The creativity matrix: Spotlights and blind spots in our understanding of the phenomenon. *Journal of Creative Behavior*, 54, 884–896. https://doi.org/10.1002/jocb.417.
Glăveanu, V. P. & Beghetto, R. A. (2021). Creative experience: A non-standard definition of creativity. *Creativity Research Journal*, 33(2), 75–80.
Glück, J., Ernst, R. & Unger, F. (2002). How creatives define creativity: Definitions reflect different types of creativity. *Creativity Research Journal*, 14(1), 55–67, https://doi.org/10.1207/S15326934CRJ1401_5.
Gowan, J. (1975). Trance, art and creativity. *Journal of Creative Behavior*, 9(1), 1–11. https://doi.org/10.1002/j.2162-6057.1975.tb00551.x.
Guilford, J. P. (1950) Creativity. *American Psychologist*, 5, 444–454. http://dx.doi.org/10.1037/h0063487.
Guilford, J. P. (1967). Creativity: Yesterday, today and tomorrow. *Journal of Creative Behavior*, 1, 3–14.
Harrington, D. M., Block, J. H. & Block, J. (1987). Testing aspects of Carl Rogers's theory of creative environments: Child-rearing antecedents of creative potential in young adolescents. *Journal of Personality and Social Psychology*, 52, 851–856.
Hébert, T. P., Cramond, B., Neumeister, K. L., Millar, G. & Silvian, A. F. (2002). *E. Paul Torrance: His Life, Accomplishments, and Legacy*. Storrs, CT: University of Connecticut, The National Research Center on the Gifted and Talented.
IBM (2010). Global CEO study: Creativity selected as most crucial factor for future success. News provided by IBM. May 18, 2010.
Idea to Value (2020). Leaders agree: Creativity will be 3rd most important work skill by 2020. www.ideatovalue.com/inno/nickskillicorn/2016/09/leaders-agree-creativity-will-3rd-important-work-skill-2020/.
Jauk, E., Benedek, M., Dunst, B. & Neubauer, A. C. (2013). The relationship between intelligence and creativity: New support for the threshold hypothesis by means of empirical breakpoint detection. *Intelligence*, 41(4), 212–221. https://doi.org/10.1016/j.intell.2013.03.003.
Jordanous, A. (2012). A standardized procedure for evaluating creative systems: Computational creativity evaluation based on what it is to be creative. *Cognitive Computation*, 4, 246–279. https://doi.org/10.1007/s12559-012-9156-1.
Jordanous, A. (2014). Four PPPPerspectives on computational creativity in theory and in practice. *Connection Science*, 28, 194–216.
Kaufman, A. S. & Kaufman, N. L. (1983). *Kaufman Assessment Battery for Children*. Circle Pines, MN: American Guidance Service.
Kaufman, A. S. & Kaufman, N. L. (2004). *Kaufman Assessment Battery for Children Second Edition*. Circle Pines, MN: American Guidance Service.
Kaufman, J. & Beghetto, R. (2009). Beyond big and little: The four C model of creativity. *Review of General Psychology*, 13, 1–12.

Kaufman, J. C. (2016). *Creativity 101* (2nd ed.). New York: Springer.
Kaufman, J. & Sternberg, R. (eds.) (2019). *The Cambridge Handbook of Creativity* (2nd ed.). Cambridge, UK: Cambridge University Press. https://doi.org/10.1017/9781316979839.
Kim K. H. (2006). Can we trust creativity tests? A review of the Torrance Tests of Creative Thinking (TTCT). *Creativity Research Journal*, 18(1), 3–14.
Kim K. H. (2011). The creativity crisis: The decrease in creative thinking scores on the Torrance Tests of Creative Thinking. *Creativity Research Journal*, 23(4), 285–295.
Levine, A. (2016). The changing face of teacher preparation 7 Arthur Levine. YouTube. www.youtube.com/watch?v=4ev_5XQBQRA.
LinkedIn (2019). LinkedIn releases 2019 Global Talent Trends report. https://news.linkedin.com/2019/January/linkedin-releases-2019-global-talent-trends-report.
MacKinnon, D. W. (1965). Personality and the realization of creative potential. *American Psychologist*, 20, 273–281.
Martindale, C. (1990). *The Clockwork Muse: The Predictability of Artistic Change*. New York: Basic Books.
McNemar, Q. (1964). Lost: Our intelligence? Why? *American Psychologist*, 19(12), 871–882. https://doi.org/10.1037/h0042008.
Meihua, Q., Plucker, J. & Yang, X. (2019). Is creativity domain specific or domain general? Evidence from multilevel explanatory item response theory models. *Thinking Skills and Creativity*, 33, 100571.
Millar, G. W. (2007). *E. Paul Torrance: The Creativity Man*. Bensenville, IL: Scholastic Testing Service.
Moseley, D., Baumfield, V., Elliott, J., et al. (2005). *Frameworks for Thinking: A Handbook for Teaching and Learning*. Cambridge, UK: Cambridge University Press.
Myers, R. E. & Torrance, E. P. (1961). Can teachers encourage creative thinking? *Educational Leadership*, 19, 156–159.
NAAB (National Architectural Accreditation Board) (2022). www.naab.org/2022/.
NACCCE (National Advisory Committee on Creative and Cultural Education) (1999). *All Our Futures: Creativity, Culture and Education*.
Neumeister, K. L. S. & Cramond, B. (2004). E. Paul Torrance (1915–2003). *American Psychologist*, 59(3), 179. https://doi.org/10.1037/0003-066X.59.3.179.
Orlet, S. (2008). An expanding view on incubation. *Creativity Research Journal*, 20(3), 297–308.
Osborn, A. (1948). *Your Creative Power: How to Use Imagination*. New York: Charles Scribner's Sons.
Pagel, J. F. & Kwiatkowski, C. F. (2003). Creativity and dreaming: Correlation of reported dream incorporation into waking behavior with level and type of creative interest. *Creativity Research Journal*, 15(2–3), 199–205.
Parnes, S. (1967). *Creative Behavior Guidebook*. New York: Scribner.

Peek, S. (2021). Creativity is not innovation (but you need both). Business News Daily. www.businessnewsdaily.com/6848-creativity-vs-innovation.html.

Plucker, J. A., Beghetto, R. A. & Dow, G. T. (2004). Why isn't creativity more important to educational psychologists? Potentials, pitfalls, and future directions in creativity research. *Educational Psychologist*, 39, 83–96.

Reisman, F. K. & Torrance, E. P. (2002). *Learning and Using Primes, Fractions and Decimals Creatively*. Bensenville, IL: Scholastic Testing Service.

Reisman, F. K. & Hartz, T. A. (2011). Generating a culture for creativity and innovation. In L. A. Berger & D. R. Berger (eds.), *Talent Management Handbook* (2nd ed.). New York: McGraw Hill.

Reisman, F. & Severino, L. (2021). *Using Creativity to Address Dyslexia, Dysgraphia, and Dyscalculia: Assessment and Techniques*. London: Routledge, Taylor & Francis Group.

Richards, R. (2017). *Everyday Creativity: Coping and Thriving in the 21st Century*. Research Triangle, NC: Lulu Company.

Rhodes, M. (1961). An analysis of creativity. *The Phi Delta Kappan*, 42(7), 305–310.

Robinson, K. (2017). *Out of Our Minds: The Power of Being Creative*. New York: John Wiley & Sons.

Robinson, K. (2018). *You, Your Child, and School: Navigating Your Way to the Best Education*. New York: Viking Press.

Robinson, K. & Robinson, K. (2022). *Imagine If... Creating a Future for Us All*. New York: Penguin Books.

Runco. M. & Jaeger, G. (2012). The standard definition of creativity. *Creativity Research Journal*, 24(1), 92–96.

Sawyer, K. (2007). *Group Genius: The Creative Power of Collaboration*. New York: Basic Books.

Simonton, D. K. (1997). Creative productivity: A predictive and explanatory model of career trajectories and landmarks. *Psychological Review*, 104(1), 66–89. https://doi.org/10.1037/0033-295X.104.1.66.

Simonton, D. K. (2001). Talent development as a multidimensional, multiplicative, and dynamic process. *Current Directions in Psychological Science*, 10(2), 39–43. https://doi.org/10.1111/1467-8721.00110.

Simonton, D. K. (2014). The mad-genius paradox: Can creative people be more mentally healthy but highly creative people more mentally ill? *Perspectives on Psychological Science*, 9(5), 470–480.

Simonton, D. K. (2016). Defining creativity: Don't we also need to define what is not creative? *Journal of Creative Behavior*, 52(1), 80–90.

Simonton, D. (2018). Defining creativity: Don't we also need to define what is not creative? *Journal of Creative Behavior*, 52(1), 80–90.

Sisk, D. A. & Torrance, E. P. (2001). *Spiritual Intelligence: Developing Higher Consciousness*. Buffalo, NY: Creative Education Foundation Press.

Sledge, D. C. (2021). Collaboration, dialogue, and creativity as instructional strategies for accredited architectural education programs: A mixed methods exploratory investigation. Dissertation, Drexel University.

Stein, M. (1953). Creativity and culture. *The Journal of Psychology*, 36(2), 311–322, https://doi.org/10.1080/00223980.1953.9712897.
Stein, M. (1974). *Stimulating Creativity* (vol. 1). Cambridge, MA: Academic Press.
Stein, M. (1975). *Stimulating Creativity* (vol. 2). New York: Academic Press.
Sternberg, R. J. & Lubart, T. I. (1991). An investment theory of creativity and its development. *Human Development*, 34(1), 1–31.
Sternberg, R. J. & Lubart, T. I. (1995). *Defying the Crowd: Cultivating Creativity in a Culture of Conformity*. New York: Free Press.
Sternberg, R. J. (1997). The concept of intelligence and its role in lifelong learning and success. *American Psychologist*, 52(10), 1030–1037. https://doi.org/10.1037/0003-066X.52.10.1030.
Sternberg, R. J. & Lubart, T. I. (1999). The concept of creativity: Prospects and paradigms. In R. J. Sternberg (ed.), *Handbook of Creativity*. Cambridge, UK: Cambridge University Press.
Sternberg, R., Kaufman, J. C. & Pretz, J. E. (2002). *The Creativity Conundrum: A Propulsion Model of Kinds of Creative Contribution*. New York: Psychology Press.
Sternberg, R. J. & Davidson, J. E. (eds.) (2005). *Conceptions of Giftedness* (vol. 2). New York: Cambridge University Press.
Sternberg, R. J. (2011). The theory of successful intelligence. In R. J. Sternberg & S. B. Kaufman (eds.), *Cambridge Handbook of Intelligence* (pp. 504–527). New York: Cambridge University Press.
Stone, B. G. (1980). Relationship between creativity and classroom behavior. *Psychology in the Schools*, 17, 106–108.
Syahrin, A., Dawud, D., Suwignyo, H. & Priyatni, E. T. (2019). Creative thinking patterns in student's scientific works. *Eurasian Journal of Educational Research* 81, 21–36.
Tanner, D. & Reisman, F. (2014). *Creativity as a Bridge between Education and Industry: Fostering New Innovations*. North Charleston, NC: CreateSpace.
Torrance, E. P. (1962). *Guiding Creative Talent*. Englewood Cliffs, NJ: Prentice-Hall.
Torrance, E. P. (1963). The creative personality and the ideal pupil. *Teachers College Record*, 65, 220–226.
Torrance, E. P. (1975). Sociodrama as a creative problem-solving approach to studying the future. *Journal of Creative Behavior*, 9(3), 182–195.
Torrance, E. P. (1984). *Torrance Tests of Creative Thinking: Norms Technical Manual*. Bensenville, IL: Scholastic Testing Service Inc.
Torrance, E. P. & Reisman, F. K. (2000a). *Learning to Use Place Value Creatively*. Bensenville, IL: Scholastic Testing Service.
Torrance, E. P. & Reisman, F. K. (2000b). *Learning to Solve Mathematics Word Problems Creatively*. Bensenville, IL: Scholastic Testing Service.
Treffinger, D. J. (1986). Research on creativity. *Gifted Child Quarterly*, 30(1), 15–19. https://doi.org/10.1177/001698628603000103.

Treffinger, D. J. & Isaksen, S. G. (2005). Creative problem solving: The history, development, and implications for gifted education and talent development. *Gifted Child Quarterly*, 49(4), 342–353. https://doi.org/10.1177/001698620504900407.
Vygotsky, L. S. (1967). Play and its role in the mental development of the child. *Soviet Psychology*, 5(3), 6–18.
Vygotsky, L. S. (2004). Imagination and creativity in childhood. *Journal of Russian and East European Psychology*, 42, 7–97.
Vygotsky, L. S. (2010). The Vygotsky family archive (1912–1934): New findings. *Journal of Russian and East European Psychology*, 48(1), 14–33.
Wallace, D. B. & Gruber, H. E. (eds.) (1989). *Creative People at Work: Twelve Cognitive Case Studies*. Oxford, UK: Oxford University Press.
Wallach, M. A. & Kogan, N. (1965a). A new look at the creativity-intelligence distinction. *Journal of Personality*, 33(3), 348–369. https://doi.org/10.1111/j.1467-6494.1965.tb01391.x.
Wallach, M. A. & Kogan, N. (1965b). *Modes of Thinking in Young Children: A Study of the Creativity-Intelligence Distinction*. New York: Holt, Rinehart, and Winston.
Wallas, G. (1926). *The Art of Thought*. London: J. Cape.
Westby, E. L. & Dawson, V. L. (1995). Creativity: Asset or burden in the classroom? *Creativity Research Journal*, 8, 1–10.
Whitelaw, L. (2006). An evaluative study of teacher creativity, use of the heuristic diagnostic teaching process and student mathematics performance. Dissertation, Drexel University.
World Economic Forum (2016). *The Future of Jobs Employment, Skills and Workforce Strategy for the Fourth Industrial Revolution*. www3.weforum.org/docs/WEF_Future_of_Jobs.pdf.
World Economic Forum (2018). 5 things you need to know about creativity. Your Article Library. www.yourarticlelibrary.com/human-resources/motivation-introduction-definition-and-characteristics-of-motivation.
World Economic Forum (2018). *The Future of Jobs Report 2018 Insight Report Centre for the New Economy and Society*. https://www3.weforum.org/docs/WEF_Future_of_Jobs_2018.pdf.
World Economic Forum (2019). *World Economic Forum Annual Meeting 2019. Shaping a Global Architecture in the Age of the Fourth Industrial Revolution*.
Zais, M. (1985). Strategic vision and strength of will: Imperatives for theater command. *Parameters*, 15(1), 33. https://doi.org/10.55540/0031-1723.1404.

CHAPTER 3

Motivation

Advance Organizer. This chapter addresses motivation by sharing the ideas of leading motivation researchers. These include Maslow's hierarchy of needs, Herzberg's two-factor motivation–hygiene theory, Alderfer's existence, relatedness, and growth (ERG) theory, and a more recent theory of needs proposed by Richard Ryan and Edward Deci, namely their self-determination theory (SDT) of motivation. Other theories presented include Vroom's expectancy theory, McClelland's achievement theory, Merton's self-fulfilling prophecy, and Locke and Latham's and Porter and Lawler's goal-setting theories. Also included are elements of motivation, processes of motivation, types of motivation, and the neuroscience of motivation. Appendix 3 is a glossary.

3.1 Introduction

The term "motivation" is a derivative of the word "motive." Motive drives needs, wants, and impulses within an individual. In the context of creativity, it can be defined as a person's processes that account for their intensity, direction, and persistence toward attaining a goal. Motivation initiates, guides, and maintains goal-oriented behaviors. It is what causes one to act. One can increase motivation, as well as motivate others, by understanding the science and theories behind motivation, the various types of motivation that are used, and its component parts. Motivation levels vary between and within individuals at different times.

In corporate settings, goal-oriented behavior is vital as a motivation variable to predict sales performance, corporate goal setting, training needs, and leadership development. Goal-directed activities involve active, voluntary participation toward a goal that the individual considers meaningful. In education, involving students in setting learning or behavior goals is represented by the self-directed learning initiative that has emerged within the "unschooling" movement. Motivation involves the biological, emotional, social, and cognitive forces referred to here as generic factors that influence learning and behavior and discussed in Chapter 5 (Reisman, 2020). Generic factors are an integral component in the assessment of motivation. They are listed in Appendix 5A, which addresses this topic.

3.2 Elements of Motivation

Three key elements in motivation are intensity, direction, and persistence.

1. **Intensity** describes how hard a person tries and is the element most focused upon when considering motivation.
2. **Direction** refers to the intensity of effort being consistent with the direction that benefits the organization goals.
3. **Persistence** involves staying with a task long enough to achieve the goal.

Adapted from Paper Tyari (2019)

3.3 Process of Motivation

Motivation concerns those processes that produce goal-directed behavior. The three basic components of the process of motivation are as follows:

1. **Motives** prompt people to action and energize behavior.
2. **Behavior** is a series of activities generally motivated by a desire to achieve a goal.
3. **Goals** are what motives are directed toward. Motives create a state of disequilibrium – a physiological or psychological imbalance – within individuals. Attaining a goal will restore balance.

Adapted from Paper Tyari (2019)

3.4 Types of Motivation

Motivation may be classified as positive or negative, extrinsic or intrinsic, and financial or nonfinancial, as shown in Box 3.1.

Subsets of Intrinsic and Extrinsic Motivation

Intrinsic and extrinsic motivation can be used together to achieve an optimal balance of motivating factors. Intrinsic motivation describes all motivational types driven by internal incentives. Extrinsic motivation describes all

	Box 3.1 Types of motivation
Positive motivation	The process of influencing one's behavior through efforts and contributions toward the achievement of specified goals.
Negative motivation	Influences on behavior that are based upon fear (e.g., the fear of not graduating, demotion, or being laid off).
Extrinsic motivation	Arises from a need for external rewards to complete a task, such as grades, salary, promotion, or praise.
Intrinsic motivation	Provides a sense of satisfaction or fulfillment while doing a certain task.
Financial motivation	Associated with money and includes wages and salaries, fringe benefits, bonuses, retirement benefits, etc.
Nonfinancial motivation	Not associated with monetary rewards; instead, it includes intangible incentives such as ego satisfaction, self-actualization, and responsibility.

motivational types driven by external rewards. However, within these two broad categories are subsets of motivation that highlight specific motivating factors, as shown in Box 3.2.

3.5 Motivation Theories and Their Researchers

There are several categories of motivation theories. Needs-based theories deal with internal feelings and are deficiencies that energize or trigger behaviors to satisfy these deficiencies. Self-determination theory (SDT) addresses intrinsic and extrinsic motivation further. SDT explains motivation in terms of self-regulation "where extrinsic motivation reflects external control of behavior, and inherent motivation relates to true self-regulation" (Ryan & Deci, 2000). "Expectancy theory, originally developed to explain how the work environment can motivate employees, strives to show the relationship between the expectations of success and anticipation of rewards and the amount of effort expended on a task and how it relates to the overall performance" (Gopalan, Aida Abu Bakar & Zulkifli, 2017). A focus on satisfaction and dissatisfaction is another direction for explaining motivation, as is David McClelland's (1978) acquired-needs theory. The following are leading motivation theorists and researchers.

> **Box 3.2 Types of intrinsic and extrinsic motivation**
>
> Types of intrinsic motivation include the following:
>
> - Learning – people are motivated by the process of learning itself rather than by a subsequent reward.
> - Attitude – this involves one's way of thinking and behaving, point of view, mindset, opinion, and outlook. People engage in interactions that make them and those around them feel better in a positive and uplifting way.
> - Achievement – people who are driven by this type of motivation value the process of improving more than the end result.
> - Creative – people are compelled to create and express themselves through original and unique endeavors (e.g., writing a book, acting in a movie, playing an instrument, designing something, or starting a business).
> - Physiological – one is driven by some internal force beyond explanation.
>
> Types of extrinsic motivation include the following:
>
> - Incentive – one is motivated by an expected reward.
> - Fear – one is driven into action to avoid pain or consequences.
> - Power – people are motivated by control over their own lives and the lives of others. Power motivation in its extreme can be seen in real-world horrors such as the Russian invasion of Ukraine or Nazi Germany, where the hunger to control others outweighed any moral obligation.
> - Affiliation/social – people are motivated by social factors such as belonging and acceptance. Humans have an innate desire to connect with others, and social motivation causes us to seek connections by contributing to a social group.
>
> Source: Tarver (2020)

Abraham Maslow

Maslow was concerned with creativity, freedom of expression, personal growth, and fulfillment. He believed that people simultaneously have partially satisfied and partially unsatisfied needs and that a lower level need may be only partially met before a higher level need emerges. The order in which needs emerge is not fixed. A ladder may be a better visual representation of Maslow's hierarchy of needs. The pyramid has horizontal lines between levels of need, making it difficult to imagine a person simultaneously affected by different needs. However, using the ladder to represent needs, multiple rungs are occupied by the feet and hands at the same time. Other rungs may also be leaned on. Therefore, a ladder better

64 Connecting Creativity and Motivation Research with End Users

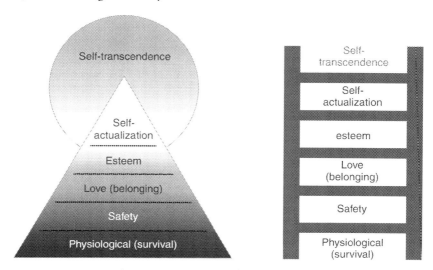

Figure 3.1 Maslow's hierarchy of needs. Visual conceptual adaptation of Maslow (1969).

represents Maslow's idea that people can simultaneously move up and down the hierarchy (Taormina & Gao, 2013). Figure 3.1 shows a ladder representation of Maslow's hierarchy of needs.

Most theorists interpret Maslow's hierarchy of needs as beginning with the basic necessities, namely physiological needs. Physiological needs are the most basic human survival needs, including food and water, rest, clothing, and shelter. Maslow stated that these basic physiological needs must be satisfied before humans move on to the following levels of needs. Once the physiological needs are satisfied, the next level is safety, comprising physical and psychological safety. An example of physical safety might be feeling assured that, at a traffic light, you are physically safe to move forward when you have the green light. An example of psychological safety might be that you feel safe emotionally and mentally while driving down a dark narrow road that at one time was scary but now is familiar, and you are comfortable. The next level is the belongingness and love level, which involves the need to love and be loved. This need requires emotional and social acceptance, affiliations, a sense of belonging, and being welcome. Next are needs referred to as self-esteem, self-respect, self-concept, and self-efficacy. Fulfilling these needs indicates that an individual has self-confidence, competence, knowledge, and independence. The inability to fulfill these needs results in feelings of inferiority, weakness, and helplessness. Once

> **Box 3.3 Self-actualization**
>
> The term "self-actualization" was originally introduced by Kurt Goldstein, a physician specializing in neuroanatomy and psychiatry in the early half of the twentieth century (Modell, 1993). As conceived by Goldstein, self-actualization is the ultimate goal of all organisms. He saw all behaviors and drives as manifestations of this overarching motivation.

these needs are met, individuals are primed to achieve self-actualization (Gleitman & Gross, 2010). In his later work, Maslow suggested that there are two additional phases that an individual must fulfill before attaining self-actualization. These are cognitive needs, whereby a person will desire knowledge and an understanding of the world around them, and aesthetic needs, which include a need for "symmetry, order, and beauty" (Reason and Meaning, 2017). Messerly added a further step beyond self-actualization: self-transcendence. Self-transcendence occurs at the "very highest and most inclusive or holistic levels of human consciousness" (Reason and Meaning, 2017). See Box 3.3 for the origin of the term "self-actualization."

Maslow considered self-actualizing people to possess "an unusual ability to detect the spurious, the fake, and the dishonest in personality, and in general to judge people correctly and efficiently" (Maslow, 1954). Maslow examined the lives of select people to assess the common qualities that led each to become self-actualized. Maslow found that self-actualizers had similarities (Reber, 1995). Whether famous or unknown, educated or not, rich or poor, self-actualizers tend to fit the profile in Box 3.4 (Feist & Feist, 2009).

It is interesting that other motivation theories rest upon the shoulders of Maslow's hierarchy of needs (e.g., those of Herzberg, Alderfer, and McClelland).

Frederick Herzberg

Herzberg extended the work of Maslow and proposed a two-factor theory – also known as the motivation–hygiene factor theory – that addressed employee motivation and recognized two sources of job satisfaction (Herzberg, 1987). **Motivating factors** influence job satisfaction because they are based on an individual's need for personal growth. They include achievement, recognition, the job itself, responsibility, and advancement. **Hygiene factors** represent deficiency needs in the job. They include institutional politics, the management approach, supervision, salary, workplace

> **Box 3.4 Self-actualizing characteristics**
>
> Maslow's self-actualizing characteristics, which refer to "social interest, community feeling, or a sense of oneness with all humanity," are as follows:
>
> - **Efficient perceptions of reality.** Self-actualizers are able to judge situations correctly and honestly. They are very sensitive to the superficial and dishonest.
> - **Comfortable acceptance of self, others, and nature.** Self-actualizers accept their own human nature with all its flaws. The shortcomings of others and the contradictions of the human condition are accepted with humor and tolerance.
> - **Reliant on own experiences and judgment.** Self-actualizers are independent and are not reliant on culture or the environment to form opinions and views.
> - **Spontaneous and natural.** Self-actualizers are true to themselves, rather than being how others want.
> - **Task centering.** Most of Maslow's subjects had a mission to fulfill in life or some task or problem "beyond" themselves (instead of outside themselves) to pursue. Humanitarians such as Albert Schweitzer are considered to have possessed this quality.
> - **Autonomy.** Self-actualizers are free from a reliance on external authorities or other people. They tend to be resourceful and independent.
> - **Continued freshness of appreciation.** Self-actualizers seem to constantly renew their appreciation of life's basic goods. A sunset or a flower will be experienced as intensely, time after time, as it was the first time. There is an "innocence of vision," like that of a child.
> - **Profound interpersonal relationships.** The interpersonal relationships of self-actualizers are marked by deep, loving bonds.
> - **Comfort with solitude.** Despite their satisfying relationships with others, self-actualizers value solitude and are comfortable being alone.
> - **Nonhostile sense of humor.** This refers to the ability to laugh at oneself.
> - **Peak experiences.** All of Maslow's subjects reported the frequent occurrence of peak experiences (temporary moments of self-actualization). These occasions were marked by feelings of ecstasy, harmony, and deep meaning. Self-actualizers reported feeling at one with the universe, stronger and calmer than ever before, filled with light, beauty, goodness, and so forth.
> - **Socially compassionate.** Self-actualizers possess humanity.
> - **Few friends.** Self-actualizers have a few, close, intimate friends rather than many perfunctory relationships.
> - *Gemeinschaftsgefühl.* According to Maslow, self-actualizers possess "*Gemeinschaftsgefühl*" (i.e., community spirit).
>
> Source: Feist & Feist (2009)

relationships, and working conditions. Satisfaction and dissatisfaction in relation to these factors are independent phenomena, such that one may increase as the other diminishes or vice versa. According to Herzberg, the opposite of satisfaction is not dissatisfaction, as the removal of dissatisfying characteristics from a job does not necessarily make the job satisfying (Herzberg, 1987).

Clayton P. Alderfer

Alderfer's existence, relatedness, and growth (ERG) theory of motivation expands on the work of Maslow and observes that, when lower needs are satisfied, they occupy less of our attention, as the higher needs become more important. He described a situation that he called the frustration-regression process, whereby, when higher needs are constrained, folk may regress to lower needs (Alderfer, 1969). The ERG motivation theory condenses Maslow's five human needs into three needs: existence, relatedness, and growth. **Existence** needs include physiological needs (e.g., food, water, air, clothing, and safety). **Relatedness** needs correspond to Maslow's third and fourth levels (belonging and esteem) and involve relationships with family, friends, coworkers, and employers. **Growth** needs overlap with Maslow's fourth need (esteem) and also include the fifth level (self-actualization), which includes creativity and productivity. The ERG theory resembles Maslow's theory in that it is hierarchical. Alderfer emphasizes that a lower level need does not necessarily have to be met for a higher level to become relevant (i.e., a person may satisfy a particular need, whether or not a different need has been satisfied).

Henry Murray

Murray believed that specific needs may be more important to some than to others and, to measure this idea, he developed the thematic apperception test. Murray's needs are not based on a hierarchy; individuals may be high in one and low in another, and multiple needs may be affected by a single action (Murray, 1973). His suggestion was that, by having individuals narrate a story about an image, they would unknowingly lower their guard and reveal sensitive, personal information to the examiner without realizing it (Murray, 1973).

David McClelland

McClelland's achievement motivation theory (McClelland, 1978), based on Henry Murray's list of motives and manifest needs, believed that needs are developed and learned, and he focused his research away from satisfaction. McClelland categorized motives or needs into the following three categories: achievement, affiliation, and power. He held the belief that only a single dominant motive could manifest in our behavior at any given time, with its expression being shaped by internal or extrinsic factors. **Achievement** needs include (1) liking to receive regular feedback on progress and achievements, (2) tending to set moderately difficult goals and take calculated risks, (3) having a strong desire to perform well, (4) often liking to work alone, (5) setting moderately difficult goals, and (6) taking calculated risks. **Affiliation** needs comprise (1) having a strong desire for acceptance and approval from others, (2) tending to conform to the wishes of those people whose friendship and companionship are valued, and (3) valuing the feelings of others. **Power** needs encompass (1) wanting to control and influence others, (2) liking to win arguments, (3) enjoying competition and winning, (4) enjoying status and recognition, (5) having the desire to influence others, (6) having the desire to influence and direct somebody else, and (7) having the desire to exercise control over others.

Chris Argyris

Argyris's theory (Argyris, 1997) argues that motivation increases as individuals move from immaturity to maturity. The following are seven areas in which an employee can grow and become more motivated: (1) passivity to activity, (2) dependence to independence, (3) responsibility for a few behaviors to responsibility for many behaviors, (4) little interest to deep interest, (5) a short-term perspective to a long-term perspective, (6) subordination to superiority, and (7) a lack of self-awareness to self-awareness. In Argyris's view, these seven changes in one's personality facilitate maturity. Argyris believed immaturity exists in individuals mainly because of organizational settings and management practices such as task specialization, chain of command, and commonality of direction. He proposed gradual shifts from the existing hierarchal organization structure to a humanistic system, that is, from existing management systems to more flexible and participative management to make individuals more mature. These ideas may be adapted to educational settings.

3 Motivation

Figure 3.2 Mnemonic for McGregor's X and Y theories.

Douglas McGregor

McGregor proposed theory X and theory Y, addressing employee motivation and its implications for management (McGregor, 1970). He divided employees into theory X employees, namely those who avoid work and dislike responsibility, and theory Y employees, namely those who enjoy work and exert effort. He suggested that organizations use different approaches to motivate these two types of employees. To motivate theory X employees, the organization should enforce rules. For theory Y employees, management must develop opportunities for employees to take on responsibility and show their creativity. Figure 3.2 shows a mnemonic for the two theories: a person refusing to work (X) and a person "cheering" the opportunity to work (Y).

William Ouchi

In response to McGregor's theory, a third theory – theory Z – was developed by Ouchi. Ouchi's theory proposes that providing employees with lifelong jobs and focusing on their well-being would increase their loyalty to the company. This increased loyalty and well-being would facilitate group work and positive social interaction, leading to higher employee motivation. According to Ouchi (1981), theory Z is a hybrid system that incorporates the strengths of US management (individual freedom, risk-taking, quick decision-making, etc.) and Japanese management (job security, group decision-making, social cohesion, holistic concern for employees, etc.). The distinguishing features of theory Z are presented in Box 3.5.

> **Box 3.5 Theory Z features**
>
> 1. **Mutual trust.** When trust and openness exist between employees, work groups, unions, and management, conflict is reduced to the minimum and employees cooperate fully to achieve the organization's objectives.
> 2. Strong bond between the organization and employees. Employees may be granted lifetime employment, which leads to loyalty toward the organization. During adverse business conditions, shareholders may forgo dividends to avoid retrenchment of workers.
> 3. Employee involvement. The involvement of employees in decisions improves their commitment and performance. Involvement implies meaningful participation of employees in the decision-making process, particularly in matters directly affecting them.
> 4. Integrated organization. The focus is on the sharing of information and resources. An integrated organization improves understanding about the interdependence of tasks.
> 5. Coordination. In order to develop a common culture in the organization, the leader must use the processes of communication, debate, and analysis.
> 6. Informal control system. The emphasis is on mutual trust and cooperation rather than on superior–subordinate relationships.
> 7. Human resource development. Managers should develop new skills among employees so that the potential of every person is recognized and attempts are made to develop and utilize this potential.
>
> Adapted from Chand (2014) and Ouchi (1981)

Theory Z management tends to promote stable employment, high productivity, and high employee morale and satisfaction.

Victor Vroom

Vroom's theory (Vroom, 1968) states that people will be motivated to exert more effort when they perceive a connection between their action, their performance, and the outcomes or rewards for their effort. Vroom's expectancy theory assumes that behavior results from individuals' choices, which are aimed at maximizing pleasure and minimizing pain. He recognized that many factors influence employee behavior, including personality, skills, knowledge, experience, and ability. Vroom's theory integrates needs, equity, and reinforcement theories to explain how we choose from alternative behaviors. Expectancy theory posits that individuals are motivated to pursue an activity by appraising three factors: (1) expectancy or the belief that more effort will result in better performance, (2) instrumentality means performance is related to rewards, and (3) valence is the value or strength that one places on a particular outcome or reward.

Lyndall F. Urwick

Urwick applied theory Z, which states that an optimal managerial style would help cultivate worker creativity, insight, meaning, and moral excellence (Urwick, 1944). Theory Z includes goals of long-term job security, consensual decision-making, employee–management collaborative evaluation, promotion procedures, and individual responsibility within a group context. With this foundation, Urwick created the principles of administration shown in Box 3.6.

Theresa Amabile and Steven Kramer

Amabile is noted for the componential theory of creativity (Amabile & Kramer, 2011). Her definition of creativity is "the production of ideas or

---

Box 3.6 Theory Z principles

1. The principle of the objective – the overall purpose of an organization is its reason for existence.
2. The principle of specialization – one group, one function.
3. The principle of coordination – the purpose of organizing is to facilitate coordination or unity of effort.
4. The principle of authority – in every organized group, supreme authority must be located somewhere, and there should be a clear line of authority to every member of the group.
5. The principle of responsibility – a superior may be held accountable for the actions of subordinates.
6. The principle of definition – jobs, duties, and relationships should be clearly defined.
7. The principle of correspondence – in every position, responsibility and authority should correspond with one another.
8. The principle of span of control – no person should supervise more than five or six line reports whose work is interlocked.
9. The principle of balance – it is essential that the various units of an organization are kept in balance.
10. The principle of continuity – reorganization is a continuous process and provision should be made for it.

Adapted from Urwick (1944)

outcomes that are both novel and appropriate to some goal" and includes four components: (1) domain-relevant skills, (2) creativity-relevant processes, (3) intrinsic task motivation, and (4) social environment. Amabile and her husband, Steven Kramer, wrote *The Progress Principle* (Amabile & Kramer, 2011), which states that "progress contributes to positive inner work life, which contributes to progress, creating an upward spiral of creativity, engagement, and performance." They ask: How can you make work more meaningful? Whether a task is meaningful depends a lot on the perception of the person doing the job. A manager can influence meaningfulness by adhering to this advice taken from *The Progress Principle* (Amabile & Kramer, 2011):

1. Implement the ideas of your team. By listening to your team and acting on their input, you show that you value their knowledge, which in turn leads to them valuing their own input.
2. Leave ownership with the team as much as possible. When people are responsible for actions, the perception of importance of that action grows.
3. Prevent meaningless work. Linked to clear goals, it is important as a manager to share the work that has been done by your team and is used in the future.
4. Make the job challenging.

George Elton Mayo

George Elton Mayo is noted for the Hawthorne effect, which states that an employee's productivity increases when someone is watching them. Mayo popularized the results of several experiments at the Hawthorne plant of Western Electric in Chicago. The plant had over 29,000 employees, who mainly manufactured telephone equipment for AT&T. Mayo's management theory states that employees are motivated more by attention and camaraderie than by financial bonuses or environmental factors such as lighting or humidity (Mayo, 2007).

Robert K. Merton

In 1948, Robert K. Merton coined the term "self-fulfilling prophecy," defining it as "a false definition of the situation evoking a behavior which makes the originally false conception come true" (Merton, 1948). A false reality can become true because of how humans respond to predictions and fears about the future. Self-fulfilling prophecies can take two forms: self-imposed and other-imposed. In a self-imposed self-fulfilling prophecy, an individual's expectations become the cause of actions that align with their expected result. Other-imposed self-fulfilling prophecies arise when other people's expectations shape the actions of an individual. Both kinds of self-fulfilling prophecies show how a false notion causes behavior that, in turn, makes a person act as if an idea is accurate until, eventually, these behaviors cause the prophecy to come true.

Edwin Locke and Gary Latham

Locke and Latham's (1990) goal-setting theory is an integrative model of motivation that views goals as key determinants of behavior. Goals that are too difficult or too easy do not increase motivation. In fact, Locke and Latham's research showed that goals that individuals perceive as difficult and specific result in greater effort exerted toward achieving those goals. Box 3.7 introduces Lock and Latham's ideas for effective goal setting.

Lyman Porter and Edward E. Lawler

Porter and Lawler's theory further develops Vroom's expectancy theory by clarifying that motivation does not equal satisfaction or performance, namely that effort or motivation does not lead directly to performance (Porter & Lawler, 1968). The three main components in their model shown in Box 3.8 are effort, performance, and satisfaction.

Porter and Lawler suggest that an individual's view regarding the attractiveness and fairness of the rewards will affect motivation. They provide advice for managers on motivating their employees, as follows: (1) match employees' abilities and traits to the right job, (2) communicate

---

Box 3.7 Lock and Latham's ideas for effective goal setting

- Ensure goals are specific, measurable, and quantifiable.
- Obtain goal commitment to ensure adequate effort toward reaching the goals.
- Encourage broad participation in the goal-setting process.
- Provide encouragement, the resources required, and moral support.
- Ensure knowledge of results is widespread.
- Encourage feedback.

> **Box 3.8 Three main components of Porter and Lawler's model**
> 1. **Effort.** The two factors that affect effort are the value of the reward and the perception of the effort–reward relation.
> 2. **Performance.** Effort leads to performance, and the amount of performance is determined by the ability of the individual.
> 3. **Satisfaction.** Performance leads to satisfaction, and the level of satisfaction depends upon whether or not the expected rewards meet or exceed perceived expectations.

what is expected of employees, as they must satisfy expectations to be rewarded, (3) provide appropriate rewards for successful performance, and (4) ensure that the rewards dispensed are valued by employees. These suggestions for managers can also be applied to education, that is, from teachers to students, from principals to teachers, and from superintendents to principals and district-wide supervisors.

Edward L. Deci and Richard Ryan

Edward Deci and Richard Ryan developed the self-determination theory (SDT) of motivation, which called into question the predominant reinforcement theory and stated that "the best way to get human beings to perform tasks is to reinforce their behavior with rewards" (Deci & Ryan, 2012; Ntoumanis et al., 2020). They identified three basic needs that comprise SDT and fuel intrinsic motivation: (1) competence, that is, we need to perceive that we are good at something, (2) autonomy, that is, we have choices and control over our decisions, and (3) relatedness, that is, we are connected to others through positive relationships. They also suggested that there are two main types of motivation – intrinsic and extrinsic – and that both are powerful forces in shaping who we are and how we behave (Deci & Ryan, 2008). The following are the effects of external motivators on intrinsic motivation (Talbot, 2017; Vansteenkiste et al., 2004). The first group of external motivators tend to **decrease** intrinsic motivation and include monetary rewards, other tangible rewards, deadlines, threats of punishment, competition against others, directives and evaluations, negative feedback, and controlling interpersonal climates. The external motivators that tend to **increase** intrinsic motivation include choice, acknowledgment, encouragement for self-initiation, positive feedback, and autonomy-supportive interpersonal climates.

Deci et al. (1991) proposed that "when significant adults – most notably, teachers and parents – are involved with students in an autonomy-supportive way, the students will be more likely to retain their natural curiosity (their intrinsic motivation for learning) and to develop autonomous forms of self-regulation through the process of internalization and integration." They further state:

> The specific supports for self-determination we suggest include offering choice, minimizing controls, acknowledging feelings, and making available information that is needed for decision making and for performing the target task. With a general attitude of valuing children's autonomy and by providing the type of autonomy support just mentioned, we stand the greatest chance of bringing about the types of educational contexts that facilitate conceptual understanding, flexible problem solving, personal adjustment, and social responsibility. This is so whether one's analysis focuses on the classroom, the school system, or society. (Deci et al., 1991)

3.6 Self-Determined Motivation and Education

In several studies, self-determined motivation has been linked to conceptual understanding and personal adjustment from early elementary school to college students. Some of these studies (e.g., Vallerand & Reid, 1990) have shown that students who had more self-determined motivation for doing schoolwork were more likely to stay in and enjoy school. Self-determination refers to people's ability to make choices and manage their own lives and empowers individuals to feel they control their choices and life outcomes.

Regarding teachers, the degree to which they support autonomy has an important effect on students' motivation and self-determination. Evidence has indicated that, when teachers become more controlling, students perform less well in problem-solving activities. Deci et al. (1982) found that, when teachers are pressured or controlled by their superiors, they are likely to respond by being more controlling with their students.

Another influence on teachers' behavior is the students themselves or the teachers' beliefs about the students. Students who are highly motivated and autonomous in school elicit more autonomy support from their teachers. In contrast, students who are more distracted and less motivated elicit more controlling behaviors from their teachers. Motivation also affects post-secondary levels that involve other situations such as interviewing for a job, satisfying promotion and tenure requirements, promotion to a leadership position, submitting to journals for publication, and being selected as a reviewer or editor.

Self-determination is important for students with disabilities. People with disabilities have emphasized that having control over their lives, rather than having others make decisions for them, is crucial for their self-esteem and self-worth. Enhanced self-determination skills such as goal setting, problem-solving, and decision-making empower students to take on more responsibility and control. Additionally, when students with disabilities demonstrate their ability to take charge of planning and decision-making, others' perceptions and expectations of them are altered (Ward & Kohler, 1996).

3.7 Neuroscience of Motivation

Recent studies have increased our understanding of how the brain deals with motivation. The motivational drive involves both internal states and external environmental conditions, as well as the organism's past history and experiences through the coordinated action of molecules (peptides, hormones, neurotransmitters, etc.) acting within specific circuits that integrate multiple signals for complex decisions to be made (Simpson & Balsam, 2016). Research approaches for studying motivation include clinical and experimental approaches and several neuroscience models, including cognitive, molecular, cellular, behavioral, and systems neuroscience and functional magnetic resonance imaging studies. Motivation research (Redish et al., 2007) also involves computational models of decision-making and tests these models by measuring neural activity during deliberative behavior.

3.8 Summary

Motivational theory is the study of understanding what drives a person to work toward a particular goal or outcome. The belief is that motivation is rooted in a basic impulse to optimize well-being, minimize physical pain, and maximize pleasure. Intrinsic motivation is represented by personal enjoyment, interest, or pleasure. Extrinsic motivation is governed by reinforcement contingencies. This chapter has presented the contributions of leading researchers and theorists in motivational theory. Chapter 8 provides more on neuroscience and Chapter 10 contains modules that serve as lesson plans related to motivation.

Appendix 3 Glossary

Drive theory	Deviations from homeostasis create physiological needs that result in psychological drive states that direct behavior to meet the need and ultimately bring the system back to homeostasis.
Goal-directed behavior	Behavior that is oriented toward attaining a particular goal.
Hierarchy of needs	A spectrum of needs ranging from basic biological needs to social needs to self-actualization.
Motivation	Wants or needs that direct behavior toward some goal.
Persistence	Prolonged efforts made while trying to find a creative solution to an impasse.
Self-efficacy	An individual's belief in their own capabilities or capacities to complete a task.

References

Alderfer, C. P. (1969). An empirical test of a new theory of human needs. *Organizational Behavior and Human Performance*, 4(2), 142–175.

Amabile, T. & Kramer, S. (2011). *The Progress Principle – Using Small Wins to Ignite Joy, Engagement and Creativity at Work*, Boston: Harvard Business Review Press.

Argyris, C. (1997). Learning and teaching: A theory of action perspective. *Journal of Management Education*, 21(1), 9–26. https://doi.org/10.1177/105256299702100102.

Chand, S. (2014). William Ouchi's theory Z of motivation: Features and limitations. Your Article Library. www.yourarticlelibrary.com/motivation/william-ouchis-theory-z-of-motivation-features-and-limitations/28024.

Deci, E. L., Spiegel, N. H., Ryan, R. M., Koestner, R. & Kauffman, M. (1982). Effects of performance standards on teaching styles: Behavior of controlling teachers. *Journal of Educational Psychology*, 74(6), 852–859. https://doi.org/10.1037/0022-0663.74.6.852.

Deci, E., Vallerand, R., Pelletier, L. & Ryan, R. (1991). Motivation and education: The self-determination perspective. *Educational Psychologist*, 26(3–4), 325–346.

Deci, E. L. & Ryan, R. M. (2008). Self-determination theory: A macrotheory of human motivation, development, and health. *Canadian Psychology/Psychologie canadienne*, 49(3), 182–185. https://doi.org/10.1037/a0012801.

Deci, E. L. & Ryan, R. M. (2012). Self-determination theory. In P. A. M. Van Lange, A. W. Kruglanski & E. T. Higgins (eds.), *Handbook of Theories of Social*

Psychology (pp. 416–436). Newbury Park, CA: Sage Publications Ltd. https://doi.org/10.4135/9781446249215.n21.

Feist, J. & Feist, G. (2009). *Theories of Personality*. Boston: McGraw-Hill.

Gleitman, H. & Gross, J. (2010). *Psychology: Eighth International Student Edition*. New York: WW Norton & Company.

Gopalan, V., Aida Abu Bakar, J. & Zulkifli, A. (2017). A review of the motivation theories in learning. *AIP Conference Proceedings*, 1891, 020043. https://doi.org/10.1063/1.5005376.

Herzberg, F. (1987). One more time: How do you motivate employees? *Harvard Business Review*, 65, 5.

Locke, E. A. & Latham, G. P. (1990). *A Theory of Goal Setting & Task Performance*. Upper Saddle River, NJ: Prentice-Hall, Inc.

Maslow, A. H. (1954). *Motivation and Personality*. New York: Harper & Row Publishers.

Maslow, A. H. (1969). Theory Z. *The Journal of Transpersonal Psychology*, 1(2), 31–47.

Mayo, G. (2007). *The Social Problems of an Industrial Civilization*. New York: Routledge.

McClelland, D. C. (1978). Managing motivation to expand human freedom. *American Psychologist*, 33(3), 201–210. https://doi.org/10.1037/0003-066x.33.3.201.

McGregor, D. (1970). Beyond theory Y. *Harvard Business Review*. www.langston.edu/sites/default/files/basic-content-files/TransformationalLeadership.pdf.

Merton, R. (1948). The self fulfilling prophecy. *Antioch Review*, 8(2), 193–210.

Modell, A. (1993). *The Private Self*. Cambridge, MA: Harvard University Press.

Murray, H. (1973). *The Analysis of Fantasy*. Huntington, NY: Robert E. Krieger Publishing Company.

Ntoumanis, N., Ng, J., Prestwich, A., et al. (2020). A meta-analysis of self-determination theory-informed intervention studies in the health domain: Effects on motivation, health behavior, physical, and psychological health. *Health Psychology Review*, 15(2), 214–244.

Ouchi, W. G. (1981). *Theory Z: How American Business Can Meet the Japanese Challenge*. Boston: Addison-Wesley.

Paper Tyari (2019). Motivation: Process, elements, types of motivation. www.papertyari.com/general-awareness/management/motivation.

Porter, L. & Lawler, E. (1968). *Managerial Attitudes and Performance*. Homewood, IL: R. D. Irwin.

Reason and Meaning (2017). Summary of Maslow on self-transcendence. https://reasonandmeaning.com/2017/01/18/summary-of-maslow-on-self-transcendence/.

Reber, A. (1995). *Dictionary of Psychology*. London: Penguin Group.

Redish, A. D., Jensen, S., Johnson, A. & Kurth-Nelson, Z. (2007). Reconciling reinforcement learning models with behavioral extinction and renewal: implications for addiction, relapse, and problem gambling. *Psychological Review*, 114, 784–805.

Reisman, F. (2020). 70 years of research into creativity: JP Guilford's role and today's focus. KIE Conference, virtual.
Ryan, R. M. & Deci, E. L. (2000). Intrinsic and extrinsic motivations: Classic definitions and new directions. *Contemporary Educational Psychology*, 25(1), 54–67.
Simpson, E. H. & Balsam, P. D. (2016). The behavioral neuroscience of motivation: An overview of concepts, measures, and translational applications. *Current Topics in Behavioral Neuroscience*, 27, 1–12. https://doi.org/10.1007/7854_2015_402.
Taormina, R. J. & Gao, J. H. (2013). Maslow and the motivation hierarchy: Measuring satisfaction of the needs. *The American Journal of Psychology*, 126(2), 155–177.
Talbot, D. M. (2017). Effect of external motivators on intrinsic motivation. Master's dissertation, Lakehead University.
Tarver, E. (2020). 11 types of motivation: What they are & how to use them. https://evantarver.com/types-of-motivation/.
Urwick, L. (1944). *The Elements of Administration*. New York: Harper & Brothers.
Vallerand, R. J. & Reid, G. (1990). Motivation and special populations: Theory, research, and implications regarding motor behaviour. *Advances in Psychology*, 74, 159–197.
Vansteenkiste, M., Simons, J., Lens, W., Sheldon, K. M. & Deci, E. L. (2004). Motivating learning, performance, and persistence: The synergistic effects of intrinsic goal contents and autonomy-supportive contexts. *Journal of Personality and Social Psychology*, 87(2), 246–260. https://doi.org/10.1037/0022-3514.87.2.246.
Vroom, V. H. (1968). Towards a stochastic model of managerial careers. *Administrative Science Quarterly*, 13(1), 26–46. https://doi.org/10.2307/2391260.
Ward, M. & Kohler, P. D. (1996). Teaching self-determination: Content and process. In L. E. Powers, G. H. S. Singer & J. Sowers (eds.), *Promoting Self-Competence in Children and Youth with Disabilities: On the Road to Autonomy* (pp. 275–322). Baltimore: Brookes.

CHAPTER 4

Assessment Attributes and Related Guidelines

Advance Organizer. This chapter includes a description of essential creativity and motivation assessment attributes and types of assessments, reviews Bloom's taxonomy of behavioral objectives, and introduces the developmental math and literacy curricula. In addition, the chapter provides background information for Chapters 5 and 6, which address the assessment of creativity and motivation. Appendix 4 is a glossary.

4.1 Introduction

The strength of creativity and motivation assessments lies in the quality of the questions. For example, do the items that make up these assessments relate to research and underlying theories? See Appendices 6A, 6B, and 6C, which contain Reisman Diagnostic Motivation Assessment (RDMA) item source grids, for examples of building a motivation assessment directly from research and/or theories that underlie motivation. Motivational and creativity assessments help teachers to determine how to teach effectively. In the corporate world, these assessments assist managers in selecting the best-fit employees for specific tasks. Assessments should incorporate relevant attributes such as those summarized in Section 4.2.

4.2 Attributes of Measurement

Being familiar with different attributes of measurement aids the selection of the best fit for the purpose of the assessment. The two major features are *validity*, which refers to whether a test measures what it aims to measure, and *reliability*, which refers to an assessment producing the same results over time. A measurement can be reliable without being valid. However, if a measurement is valid, it is usually also reliable.

Validity

There are four main types of validity: construct, content, face, and criterion validity. **Construct** validity asks: Does the test measure the concept that it is intended to measure? Some common constructs include self-esteem, logical reasoning, academic motivation, social anxiety, intelligence, happiness, and job satisfaction. **Content** validity judges if the test fully represents what it aims to measure, that is: Is it representative of the related instruction and material presented? **Face** validity requires that the measure be clearly relevant for what it is measuring, appropriate for the participants, and adequate for its purpose. **Criterion** validity involves comparing test results to another assessment that is often referred to as a "gold standard" measurement and that is widely accepted as a valid measure of a similar construct. A gold standard criterion variable must measure the same construct that is conceptually relevant regarding behavior or performance. Criterion validity is comprised of three subtypes: retrospective, concurrent, and predictive validity. **Retrospective** validity represents the extent to which an instrument that purports to measure a particular behavior can be shown to correlate with past occurrences of this behavior. For example, to evaluate a new measure of accident proneness, a group of employees is sampled and then their company medical records are checked to determine if higher test scores on a measure correlate with the number of past injuries. **Concurrent** validity represents the extent of the agreement between two measures or assessments taken at the same time. **Predictive** validity refers to the ability of a measurement to predict a future outcome. For example, a preemployment test has predictive validity when it can accurately identify the applicants who will perform well after a given amount of time on the job and is further used in education and psychology when a test can predict a future outcome. For example, SAT scores are considered predictive of student retention: Students with higher SAT scores are more likely to return for their sophomore year; thus, the outcome is assessed at a point in the future.

Reliability

Reliability is comprised of four types: **test–retest**, whereby the same test is administered over time; **interrater**, whereby the same test is conducted by different people; **parallel**, whereby different versions of a test are intended to be equivalent; and **split-half**, which focuses on evaluation of internal consistency and involves randomly splitting a set of measures into two sets and finding the correlation (r) between them.

4.3 Types of Assessment

In this section, the types of assessment categories and processes are discussed. Categories include formative, summative, standard, and nonstandard testing. Processes comprise interviews, observations, impartial assessments, direct and indirect assessments, and diagnostic assessments.

Assessment Categories

Formative assessments include tests, quizzes, games, and group work designed to evaluate how well a student is learning the material. Such assessments involve continuously assessing a learner's progress and indicating what has to be reviewed or taught in a different way, rather than waiting to the end of a curricular unit – it informs instruction. For further information on formative assessment, see www.edglossary.org/formative-assessment/.

Summative assessments evaluate what and how much a student has learned at the end of a unit or topic and may include final exams, in-depth reports, papers, end-of-class projects, etc.

Standard assessments apply consistency to the testing methods; for example, they have the same set of questions for all participants and all the answers are graded using the same criteria.

Nonstandard testing methods include case studies, interviews, rating scales, questionnaires, observations, biographies, and anecdotal records that measure one's skills or progress, but do not compare one to a group of age or experience peers. Nonstandard assessments are sometimes used to describe accommodations of standard testing conditions for students with disabilities; these nonstandard assessment accommodations are intended to "level the playing field" for the student without altering the concepts to be learned.

Assessment Processes

Interviews

An interview is a structured conversation in which one participant asks questions and the other provides answers. Types of interviews include:

- **Formal and informal interviews.** The questions are prepared in advance, and the time, date, venue, dress code, etc., is decided prior to the interview. In informal interviews, the questions are random and emerge from the interchange.

4   *Assessment Attributes and Related Guidelines*   83

- **Sequential and panel interviews.** Sequential interviews consist of several interviews in which the same set of questions is asked repeatedly by several interviewers to check if the interviewee answers in the same manner or not. Panel interviews involve a group of interviewers simultaneously asking the interviewee questions.
- **Situational interviews.** A situation or a problem is presented and the interviewee is asked how they will solve it.
- **Phone or video call interviews.**

Observations
Observation assessments involve obtaining evaluative information through direct observation that provides documented evidence of what is seen and heard.

Impartial Assessments
Impartial assessment doesn't favor or disfavor any test taker. Impartial or equitable assessments involve testing students using the methods and procedures that are most appropriate to them.

Direct and Indirect Assessments
Direct evidence of student learning is tangible, visible, and measurable, and is evidence of what students have and have not learned. Examples of direct assessment include observations, tests or writing summaries, presentations, interviews, portfolios projects, papers, and performances. **Indirect** evidence relies upon proxy signs, such as self-reports, that ask students to specify what they have learned. A disadvantage of self-repots is that it is not uncommon for students to either inflate or undervalue what they have actually learned. Indirect evidence is further exemplified by surveys, exit interviews, and curriculum and syllabus analysis.

Diagnostic Assessments
Diagnostic assessments comprise pretests that help the teacher (and the student) to understand how much they know and don't know about an upcoming topic. This helps to inform the teacher's lesson planning and learning objectives and to identify areas that may require more or less instructional time or different pedagogy. Components of a diagnostic assessment are illustrated in Figure 4.1.

As Figure 4.1 shows, first, the *real* problem must be diagnosed, then possible reasons for the problem must be hypothesized and learning

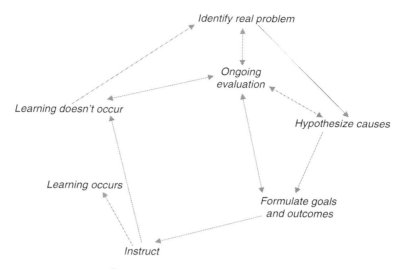

Figure 4.1 Diagnostic teaching process.

Box 4.1 Pre- and post-testing

When combined with a post-test, change scores emanating from a pre-test show students how much knowledge they have gained. Using the same items for pre- and post-testing highlights a student's growth.

---

outcomes that will drive instruction must be formulated, which will result in the problem being solved – or, if the problem is not solved, the cycle will be repeated again. If the problem was not solved, it may have been that the *real* problem was not diagnosed, the hypotheses were faulty, etc.

Box 4.1 discusses pre- and post-testing and Box 4.2 discusses the difference between diagnostic and formative assessments.

4.4 Diagnostic Teaching and Creative Problem-Solving

Diagnostic teaching is a creative problem-solving instructional/learning model framed around generic or core influences on learning, in-depth content knowledge, and pedagogy knowledge (see Appendix 5A). Creativity theories and their applications to diagnostic teaching suggest ways that individuals may integrate intervention strategies in identifying "real"

> **Box 4.2 Difference between diagnostic and formative assessments**
>
> Although both diagnostic and formative assessments aim to inform teachers about instruction, they emphasize different aspects. Formative assessments are taken during a unit to assess how students are learning the material. Diagnostic assessments comprise pre-tests that reveal what students have learned in the past on this topic. Both results identify gaps in students' knowledge of specific materials and where more instruction is needed (Reisman & Severino, 2021).

> **Box 4.3 Diagnostic teaching and creative problem-solving compared**
>
> The diagnostic teaching approach involves (1) identifying strengths and weaknesses that the learner displays, (2) theorizing possible causes for the results of the previous step, (3) formulating expected learning outcomes based upon the previous steps, (4) designing and implementing instructions that address the previous steps, and (5) evaluating the results: Does the learner now demonstrate success related to the listed outcomes (goals)?
>
> Creative problem-solving, similar to diagnostic teaching, involves (1) identifying the *real* problem through brainstorming activities, (2) generating possible solutions and creating assessment criteria through which the possible solutions can be ranked, (3) selecting the top-ranked possible solution, (4) implementing that option, and (5) solving the *real* problem; if the problem is not solved, the process is repeated with the second highest ranked solution, and so on.

problems and pathways to their solutions. Box 4.3 compares diagnostic teaching and creative problem-solving, Box 4.4 provides an example of using the creative problem-solving grid to identify one's preferred behaviors, and Box 4.5 presents a more complex grid.

4.5 Bloom's Taxonomy

Benjamin Bloom (1956) was motivated to create a system for matching learning levels to behavioral objectives. Bloom's book *Taxonomy of Educational Objectives: The Classification of Educational Goals* (Bloom, 1969) categorized observable verbs as a function of the type of cognition involved and served as the structure for writing behavioral objectives (now referred to as learner outcomes).

> **Box 4.4 Creative problem-solving grid example**
>
> The following grid is a simplification of the problem-solving grids in Tables 9.2 and 9.6. This creative problem-solving assesses the presence or non-presence of ideal behaviors. The directions are as follows:
>
> 1. Place an X in the cell that indicates whether a behavior is apparent or not apparent.
> 2. Count the number of Xs in each column and record this in the totals columns.
> 3. Analyze which behaviors are strengths (apparent) and which are weaknesses (not apparent).
> 4. Use these data to structure instructional goals and related activities and assessments.
>
> | Goal: identify the presence of ideal behaviors | Behavior is apparent | Behavior is not apparent | Behavior is apparent – total | Behavior is not apparent – total |
> |---|---|---|---|---|
> | Shows persistence (grit) | X | | 3 | 6 |
> | Triggers original/novel ideas | | X | | |
> | Generates many ideas | | X | | |
> | Resists premature closure | | X | | |
> | Tolerates ambiguity | X | | | |
> | Displays divergent thinking | X | | | |
> | Displays convergent thinking | | X | | |
> | Displays intrinsic motivation | | X | | |
> | Displays extrinsic motivation | | X | | |

Bloom's taxonomy presents six levels of thinking skills ranked from the most basic to the most abstract. Each level of these cognitive skills is associated with a verb that allows for observing student cognitive performance. Using Bloom's taxonomy can help teachers to ensure that assessments and assignments reflect many levels of thinking. Assessments such as multiple-choice, matching, and fill-in-the-blank questions usually

Box 4.5 More complex creative problem-solving grid

The following grid is based on an identified problem in a senior design project. The directions are as follows:

1. Rank each possible solution for each evaluation criteria (i.e., 6 represents the most important/desirable/effective and 1 represents the least).
2. Add up the scores of the evaluation criteria for each row and enter the sum in totals column.
3. Consider the possible solution with the highest score as your first activity to engage in.
4. If you are not comfortable with the possible solution with the highest score, then consider the next highest. Remember, this grid is merely a heuristic (tool) for making a decision.

			Evaluation criteria			
Possible solutions	Feasible	Creative	Little cost in effort	Little cost in time	Attainable	Based in research	Projected profitability	Totals
1. Collaborate with industry partner								
2. Research problem								
3. Develop projected budget								
4. Build a prototype								
5. Ask coop site for a project								

concentrate on the two lower levels of Bloom's taxonomy (i.e., remembering and understanding). Conversely, essay responses, experiments, portfolios, and performances are types of assessments that assess the higher levels of Bloom's original taxonomy.

In 2001, the taxonomy was revised by a team of researchers led by David Krathwohl, a colleague of Bloom, and Lorin Anderson, one of Bloom's students, with the aim of offering learners more precise instructional objectives (Anderson & Krathwohl, 2001). Armstrong (2010) suggested that incorporating Bloom's taxonomy into lessons ensures that the full range of thinking is utilized, from the most basic (remembering) at the beginning of a unit to the highest levels of Bloom's taxonomy in the final lessons of a unit. Box 4.6 presents the definitions and verbs for each level of Bloom's updated taxonomy.

Box 4.6   Definitions and verbs for Bloom's taxonomy levels

Create. Putting elements together to form a new coherent or functional whole, or reorganizing elements into a new pattern or structure. Examples include arranging, assembling, building, collecting, combining, compiling, composing, constituting, constructing, creating, designing, developing, devising, formulating, generating, hypothesizing, integrating, inventing, making, managing, modifying, organizing, performing, planning, preparing, producing, proposing, rearranging, reconstructing, reorganizing, revising, rewriting, specifying, synthesizing, and writing.

Evaluate. Making judgments based on criteria and standards. Examples include appraising, apprizing, arguing, assessing, comparing, concluding, considering, contrasting, convincing, criticizing, critiquing, deciding, determining, discriminating, evaluating, grading, judging, justifying, measuring, ranking, rating, recommending, reviewing, scoring, selecting, standardizing, supporting, testing, and validating.

Analyze. Breaking material into its constituent parts and determining how they relate to one another and/or to an overall structure or purpose. Examples include analyzing, arranging, breaking down, categorizing, classifying, comparing, connecting, contrasting, deconstructing, detecting, diagramming, differentiating, discriminating, distinguishing, dividing, explaining, identifying, integrating, inventorying, ordering, organizing, relating, separating, and structuring.

Apply. Using information or a skill in a new situation. Examples include applying, calculating, carrying out, classifying, completing, computing, demonstrating, dramatizing, employing, examining, executing, experimenting, generalizing, illustrating, implementing, inferring, interpreting, manipulating, modifying, operating, organizing, outlining, predicting, solving, transferring, translating, and using.

4 Assessment Attributes and Related Guidelines 89

> Box 4.6 (cont.)
>
> **Understand.** Demonstrating comprehension through explanation. Examples include abstracting, arranging, articulating, associating, categorizing, clarifying, classifying, comparing, computing, concluding, contrasting, defending, diagramming, differentiating, discussing, distinguishing, estimating, exemplifying, explaining, extrapolating, generalizing, giving examples of, illustrating, inferring, interpreting, matching, outlining, paraphrasing, predicting, rearranging, reordering, rephrasing, representing, restating, summarizing, transforming, and translating.
>
> **Remember.** Recalling or recognizing relevant knowledge from long-term memory. Examples include citing, defining, describing, identifying, listing, outlining, quoting, recalling, reproducing, retrieving, showing, stating, tabulating, and telling.
>
> Source: Anderson & Krathwohl (2001)

4.6 Developmental Math and Literacy Curricula

Reisman and Severino (2021), based on Reisman and Kauffman (1980), created a complementary way for structuring learning activities that supplements Bloom (1969), namely focusing on the curriculum as it directly affects pedagogy. Whereas Bloom emphasizes levels of thinking, Reisman and Severino focus on the curriculum regarding what teaching methods relate to different content, and they ask: (1) What pedagogies are involved in acquiring math and literacy content? and (2) Why is knowing this important? Of course, thinking levels are also involved, but the focus is different.

Regarding the nature of curricula, it is the ascension from arbitrary associations to lower level relationships to lower level generalizations to concepts and then from concepts to higher level relationships to higher level generalizations that underlies the selection of appropriate instruction. This process makes apparent what on the surface appears simple but is often complex; thus, it has a bearing on the design of instruction. For example, in math, the idea of "basic facts" (e.g., 3+3=6) is considered an easy topic for students to learn. Basic facts are often taught as though they reside at the lowest levels of Bloom's taxonomy and the developmental math curriculum. However, upon analyzing the curriculum, we see that basic facts sit at the top of the developmental math curriculum, as they depend on learning at many prerequisite levels. Section 4.7 defines the levels of the developmental curriculum.

4.7 Developmental Curriculum Levels

Arbitrary Associations

Math and literacy ideas and skills are communicated by means of various symbol systems. "In order to communicate thoughts ... there must be a conventional system of signs or symbols which when used by some persons, are understood by other persons receiving them" (Gelb, 1963). These symbols are arbitrarily associated with the ideas that they represent. Math incorporates logographs (digits, the addition sign, the square root sign, etc.) in which the symbol represents one or more words, which in turn represent a complete thought.

In literacy, sound–symbol relationships require the ability to connect visual stimuli and auditory stimuli. The abstract logographs of a mathematical language know few language boundaries: 1+1=2 can be read by speakers of many languages. A concrete pictograph of a cow represents that animal in any language, while the word "cow" alphabetically written is decipherable only to readers of English.

Lower Level Relationships

An example of a lower level relationship in math is sequencing and matching elements of a set to elements of another set that is equal in number on a one-for-one match. The ability to sequence involves attending in succession and then arranging objects or events into a progression. Out of the ability to sequence emerges the notion of one-to-one correspondence. One-to-one correspondence is one of the most basic relationships in math. Unless a child understands the one-to-one relationship, they do not comprehend identity or the relation of equality. One-to-one correspondence underlies the following mathematical ideas: many-to-one, equality, and greater than/less than.

An example of a lower level relationship in literacy is one of the early developing skills in phonological awareness: the ability to hear that words are made up of sentences. Once children understand that sentences are made up of words, they can then begin to hear that words are made up of syllables. These skills are necessary, as they lead to higher relationships and generalizations that lead to reading and spelling.

4 Assessment Attributes and Related Guidelines

Lower Level Generalizations

An example of a lower level generalization in math is when the one-to-one relationship is applied to more than two sets and the generalization of equivalent sets is developed. For example, when the child recognizes that several sets have the same number of elements, they are generalizing from the specific number concept (e.g., three) to equivalent sets of objects – all have the same number. Extending set situations involving many-to-one correspondence or greater/less than as well as sorting and seriation are further examples of lower level generalizations in math.

Some examples of lower level generalizations in literacy include when children recognize whether or not two words rhyme, as well as onset and rime. The onset of a word is the initial consonant or consonant blend in a word followed by the rime, which is the vowel and any consonants that follow. In the word "flock," "fl" is the onset and "ock" is the rime. The ability to recognize onset/rime will later help a child to decode.

Concepts

A concept is an abstraction or idea that may or may not have physical manifestations. For example, the concept of trees may represent evergreen trees, tall or short trees, or deciduous trees (which shed their leaves annually), all of which are physical/concrete examples of the concept of trees. Some concepts do not have a physical representation, such as respect, culture, and freedom; they can't be directly perceived or measured.

The child who can identify the cardinal number property of equivalent sets is displaying the specific concept of the number (e.g., three). Similarly, sorting involves classifying according to some criterion such as color, size, texture, function, thickness, or shape. Thus, concepts involve developing an idea formed by consideration of selected characteristics.

In literacy, a few important concepts are understanding that words are made of syllables, knowing what those syllables are, understanding how the syllable type influences how we pronounce the vowel, and knowing how to spell words. A syllable is a word or word part that has a vowel sound and is pronounced as a unit. Words can have one syllable or multiple syllables. Alphabetic systems use symbols, in combinations, to form thousands of different words. In some languages, there is a highly phonemic orthography that translates into highly predictable spelling, making the language easier to learn to read and write. In written English, however, there are forty-four phonemes yet only twenty-six graphemes, which makes reading and writing the language complicated.

92 Connecting Creativity and Motivation Research with End Users

Higher Level Relationships

Examples of higher order relationships in math are binary operations (including addition, multiplication, subtraction, and division) and unary operations (e.g., squaring or cubing a number and finding the root of a number). Higher level relationships connect concepts and lower level generalizations.

In literacy, vocabulary (word choice) and background knowledge are higher level relationships that allow for greater comprehension of texts (McNamara & Kintsch, 1996; Rawson & Van Overschelde, 2008).

Higher Level Generalizations

When a child applies an arithmetic operation to numbers, they are generalizing at the rule or principal level. For example, putting two concepts together into some sort of relationship, such as "two plus three equals five" (2+3=5), is an example of a higher level generalization. Additional examples of the math developmental curriculum categorized by both the Reisman Diagnostic Creativity Assessment (RDCA) factors and the cognitive generic influences on learning are shown in Table 4.1.

In regard to literacy, verbal reasoning is also a higher level generalization. The reader or writer needs to extract the meaning and implications in what is read or needs to be able to deliver their thoughts in speaking or writing. Reading comprehension is the ultimate goal. Examples of higher order generalizations in literacy involve language structures. Semantics builds from the concept of vocabulary and the meaning of words and relates those meanings to how they can be used in reading and writing. Understanding whether an author meant to use a sentence or phrase literally or figuratively requires the student to use higher order thinking and make generalizations.

4.8 Basic Fact Task Analysis

This section sets out a 22-step basic fact (3+3=6) task analysis, with steps categorized by their level on the developmental math curriculum. These steps form the structure for designing instruction-related learning activities.

Arbitrary Associations

Arbitrary associations are man-made agreements about the meaning of symbols. For example, the + sign means "to add" and the = sign means "equals" in any language. However, there is an exception: In the USA, the

Table 4.1 Math content categorized by the developmental mathematics curriculum levels, RDCA factors, and cognitive generic influences on learning

Math content	Developmental curricula level	RDCA factors	Cognitive generic influences on learning
Learning to write digits, symbols (e.g., +, −, ×, ÷, >, <, =)	Arbitrary associations: symbols (e.g, digits, words)	Tolerate ambiguity Resist premature closure	Ability to learn symbol systems/arbitrary associations Ability to attend to salient aspects of a situation Ability to recognize a visual stimulus when it appears in different spatial positions Visual discrimination
Succession	Lower level relationships	Tolerate ambiguity Resist premature closure	Ability to form rules Visual perception Visual discrimination Sensory limitation
Sequencing	Lower level relationships	Flexibility Elaboration Risk-taking	Ability to separate figure from the background Ability to process or recall a series of visual stimuli in sequential memory Ability to form rules Visual perception Visual discrimination
One-to-one correspondence	Lower level relationships	Fluency Flexibility Elaboration Divergent thinking	Ability to form relationships, concepts, and generalizations Ability to attend to salient aspects of a situation Physical impairments Sensory limitation Ability to separate figure from the background Visual perception Visual discrimination

Table 4.1 (cont.)

Math content	Developmental curricula level	RDCA factors	Cognitive generic influences on learning
Topological relationships (e.g., proximity, enclosure, order, separateness)	Lower level relationships	Fluency Flexibility Elaboration Divergent thinking	Rate and amount of learning Ability to retain information Ability to form relationships, concepts, and generalizations Ability to attend to salient aspects of a situation Ability to make decisions and judgments Visual discrimination
Sorting	Lower level generalization	Flexibility Convergent thinking Intrinsic motivation Resist premature closure	Ability to form relationships, concepts, and generalizations Ability to attend to salient aspects of a situation Ability to make decisions and judgments Visual discrimination
Many-to-one correspondence	Lower level generalization	Flexibility Fluency Elaboration Divergent thinking	Ability to form relationships, concepts, and generalizations Ability to make decisions and judgments Ability to form rules
Equivalent sets	Lower level generalization	Originality Flexibility Fluency Elaboration Convergent thinking	Ability to form relationships, concepts, and generalizations Ability to make decisions and judgments Ability to form rules

Seriation	Lower level generalization	Flexibility Originality Fluency Elaboration Convergent thinking	Ability to form relationships, concepts, and generalizations Ability to make decisions and judgments Ability to attend to salient aspects of a situation Ability to make decisions and judgments Ability to draw inferences and conclusions and to hypothesize Ability in general to abstract and to cope with complexity Ability to form rules
Greater/less than	Lower level generalization	Flexibility Fluency Elaboration Convergent thinking	Ability to form relationships, concepts, and generalizations Ability to make decisions and judgments
Number	Concept	Flexibility Originality Fluency Elaboration Convergent thinking	Ability to form relationships, concepts, and generalizations Ability to attend to salient aspects of a situation Ability to make decisions and judgments Visual discrimination
Shape	Concept	Flexibility Originality Fluency Elaboration Convergent thinking	Ability to form relationships, concepts, and generalizations Ability to attend to salient aspects of a situation Ability to make decisions and judgments Visual discrimination
Color	Concept	Flexibility Originality Fluency Elaboration Convergent thinking	Ability to form relationships, concepts, and generalizations Ability to attend to salient aspects of a situation Ability to make decisions and judgments Visual discrimination
Weight	Concept	Flexibility Originality Fluency Elaboration Convergent thinking	Ability to form relationships, concepts, and generalizations Ability to attend to salient aspects of a situation Ability to make decisions and judgments Visual discrimination

Table 4.1 (*cont.*)

Math content	Developmental curricula level	RDCA factors	Cognitive generic influences on learning
Time	Concept	Flexibility Originality Fluency Elaboration Convergent thinking Risk-taking Avoid premature closure Tolerate ambiguity	Ability to form relationships, concepts, and generalizations Ability to attend to salient aspects of a situation Ability to make decisions and judgments Visual discrimination
Mathematical language	Higher level relationships	Fluency Flexibility Elaboration Divergent thinking Risk-taking Avoid premature closure Tolerate ambiguity	Ability to learn symbol systems/arbitrary associations Size of vocabulary Ability to form relationships, concepts, and generalizations Understanding another's point of view Auditory perception Auditory discrimination
Number operations (+, −, ×, ÷) Symbols (>, <, =, √)	Higher level relationships	Fluency Flexibility Elaboration Divergent thinking	Ability to form relationships, concepts, and generalizations Ability to make decisions and judgments Ability to form rules
Set operations and relationships	Higher level relationships	Fluency Flexibility Elaboration Divergent thinking	Ability to form relationships, concepts, and generalizations Ability to make decisions and judgments Ability to form rules

Rigid transformations (reflections, rotations, translations)	Higher level relationships	Fluency Flexibility Elaboration Divergent thinking
Cause–effect Example: we received seven inches of rain in four hours (cause), how many inches of rain is expected in eight hours (effect)	Higher level relationships	Elaboration Flexibility
Conservation (e.g., number, volume, time, length) This is the principle, which Piaget called the theory of conservation, in which the child realizes that properties of objects (such as mass, volume, and number) remain the same, despite changes in the form of the objects	Higher level relationships	Fluency Flexibility Elaboration Convergent thinking
Word problems	Higher level generalizations	Originality Fluency Flexibility Elaboration Divergent thinking Convergent thinking Risk-taking Intrinsic motivation

Ability to form relationships, concepts, and generalizations
Ability to make decisions and judgments
Ability to form rules

Ability to form relationships, concepts, and generalizations
Ability to make decisions and judgments
Ability to form rules

Ability to form relationships, concepts, and generalizations
Ability to make decisions and judgments
Ability to form rules

Ability to form relationships, concepts, and generalizations
Ability to make decisions and judgments

Table 4.1 (*cont.*)

Math content	Developmental curricula level	RDCA factors	Cognitive generic influences on learning
Place value	Higher level generalizations	Originality Fluency Flexibility Elaboration Divergent thinking Convergent thinking Risk-taking Intrinsic motivation	Ability to form relationships, concepts, and generalizations Ability to make decisions and judgments Ability to form rules
Axioms	Higher level generalizations	Originality Fluency Flexibility Elaboration Divergent thinking Convergent thinking Risk-taking Intrinsic motivation	Ability to form relationships, concepts, and generalizations Ability to make decisions and judgments Ability to form rules
Basic facts This refers to all the addition and multiplication problems formed by combinations of one-digit numbers. There are 100 basic addition facts and 100 basic multiplication facts	Higher level generalizations	Originality Fluency Flexibility Elaboration Divergent thinking Convergent thinking Risk-taking Intrinsic motivation	Ability to form relationships, concepts, and generalizations Ability to make decisions and judgments Ability to form rules

Primes, fractions, and decimals	Higher level generalizations	Originality Fluency Flexibility Elaboration Divergent thinking Convergent thinking Risk-taking Intrinsic motivation	Ability to form relationships, concepts, and generalizations Ability to make decisions and judgments Ability to form rules
Applied mathematics This is the application of mathematics to real-world problems	Higher level generalizations	Originality Fluency Flexibility Elaboration Divergent thinking Convergent thinking Risk-taking Intrinsic motivation	Ability to form relationships, concepts, and generalizations Ability to make decisions and judgments Ability to form rules
Probability, statistics, graphs	Higher level generalizations	Fluency Flexibility Elaboration Divergent thinking	Ability to form relationships, concepts, and generalizations Ability to make decisions and judgments Ability to form rules

Adapted with permission from Reisman & Kauffman (1980)

symbol × may be substituted by a dot (•) to mean multiply (3×2=6 or 3•2=6); however, in the UK, the dot in 3•2 could be confused with a decimal (meaning three and two-tenths), as a dot for multiplication is less common. Box 4.7 reiterates this difference in meaning for the same symbol (i.e., the placement of the dot in math). This is unusual, since arbitrary associations are usually consistent in their meaning.

1. Recognize the digits 3 and 6, as well as the symbols + and =.
2. Write the digits 3 and 6, as well as the symbols + and =.
3. Read aloud the digits 3 and 6, as well as the symbols + and =.
4. Count aloud the number of objects in a set of three red wooden blocks (***).
5. Select the digit 3 from a group of cut-out cardboard digits comprising 1, 1, 2, 2, 3, 3, 4, 4, 5, 5, 6, 6, 7, 7, 8, 8, 9, 9 and have the child match it with the set of three red blocks.
6. Introduce a second set of three red blocks and repeat step 5 with this set of three red blocks and another cardboard digit (3).
7. Count aloud the number of objects in the two sets of red blocks – (***) and (***) – and get six.

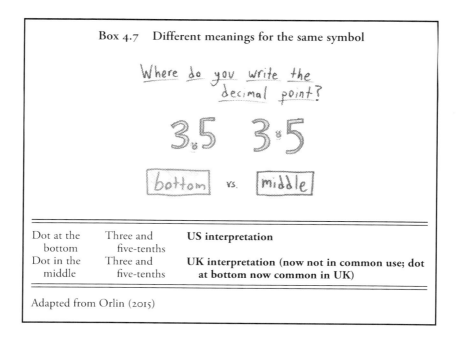

Box 4.7 Different meanings for the same symbol

Dot at the bottom	Three and five-tenths	US interpretation
Dot in the middle	Three and five-tenths	UK interpretation (now not in common use; dot at bottom now common in UK)

Adapted from Orlin (2015)

4 Assessment Attributes and Related Guidelines

8. Select the digit 6 from a group of cut-out cardboard digits comprised of 1, 1, 2, 2, 3, 3, 4, 4, 5, 5, 6, 6, 7, 7, 8, 8, 9, 9, and have the child match it with the combined sets of red blocks.
9. Recognize that there was a combining operation represented by the + sign.
10. Have the child place the sets of red blocks on a surface as follows: (***) (***).
11. Have the child place the relevant cardboard digits under its set: $\frac{(***)}{3} \frac{(***)}{3}$.
12. Have the child place cardboard signs that show adding the number of objects, the equals sign and the digit that shows the total number of objects in both sets: $\frac{(***)}{3} + \frac{(***)}{3} = 6$.
13. State that the combined sets of red blocks now equal six and the = sign shows the sum resulting from the addition operation (+).

Lower Level Relationships

Lower level relationships link connections such as one-to-one correspondence between objects.

14. Provide an additional group of ten red blocks and ask the child to make another set that has the same number as the original set, utilizing one-to-one correspondence.

Lower Level Generalizations

Lower level generalizations are general statements obtained by inference from specific cases.

15. Provide several different objects (a key, a rubber ball, a yellow block, etc.) and ask the child to make another set with these objects that has the same number as the original set, utilizing one-to-one correspondence.

Concept

Concept is an abstraction from examples – an idea.

16. Provide two sets of three yellow blocks and ask what is the same about these two sets: color, shape, size, number, wooden blocks.

17. Add another set of three blocks made up of one blue block, one yellow block, and one green block and ask what is the same about these sets: shape, size, number, wooden blocks (color is eliminated).
18. Add another set of three objects made up of a wooden block, a wooden doll, and a wooden ruler and ask what is the same about these sets (shape and size are eliminated).
19. Add another set of three objects made up of a pen, a pencil, and a hankie and ask what is the same about these sets (wooden is eliminated and only number remains).
20. Ask: How many items are in each of these sets? If the child answers "three," they show they know the concept of *threeness*.

In this way, the complex abstraction of the concept of numbers is given meaning for the learner. Now let us continue to the basic fact (3+3=6). The following steps of the task analysis build upon the previous steps in learning a number concept.

Higher Level Relationships

Higher level relationships incorporate concepts and extend the one-to-one correspondence that underlies equivalence to many sets. A further activity can include many-to-one and less/more than relationships.

21. Provide seven sets of different objects with some sets comprising three objects and some comprising five objects. Ask for all the sets with the same number of objects to be put close together. This expands the basic one-to-one relation between two sets to several with the same number (equivalent sets).

Higher Level Generalization

Higher level generalization puts together the concept of number, addition and equivalence relations, and higher level relationships.

22. Solve a basic fact computation using concrete objects if necessary: 3+3=6, 3+5=8, etc.

Gaps in learning at lower levels of the curriculum cause difficulty learning higher levels. Many adults do not understand place value because the traditional teaching of bundling 10 ones to make a ten is a wrong pedagogy, as our notation system changes place value after nine, not ten. In addition, adults can have trouble with algebra because they never mastered computation with integers (includes negative numbers).

As discussed earlier in this chapter, diagnostic teaching identifies such gaps in the curriculum hierarchy and then suggests appropriate instruction for relevant outcomes.

4.9 Characteristics of a "Good" Assessment

A "good" assessment consistently measures what it claims to measure. This means that there is a connection between assessment items and the real-world situation to be assessed (validity) and a similar result would occur on a reassessment (reliability). These characteristics – validity and reliability – were discussed previously in Section 4.2.

However, reliability is affected by the stability of the characteristic or construct being measured. Some constructs are more stable than others. For example, one would expect an individual's assessment of color recognition in a design course to be more stable than a panic attack score over time in a psychology program. Therefore, you would expect a higher level of reliability on a color recognition test than on a test that measures anxiety.

4.10 Summary

Being cognizant of assessment attributes and types of assessments helps inform the correct selection and use of assessments. Appropriate assessment selection, in turn, helps to ensure fair and proper evaluation in education or corporate settings.

Appendix 4 Glossary of Assessment Terms

Source: US Department of Labor (1999)

Ability test	A test that measures the current performance or estimates the future performance of a person in some defined area of cognitive, psychomotor, or physical functioning.
Achievement test	A test that measures acquired knowledge or skills, usually as the result of previous instruction.

Adverse impact	A situation in which members of a particular race, sex, or ethnic group have a substantially lower rate of selection in hiring, promotion, or other employment decisions.
Alternate forms	Two or more forms of a test that are similar in nature and intended to be used for the same purpose.
Assessment	Any test or procedure used to measure an individual's employment or career-related qualifications or characteristics.
Basic skills test	Assessments of competence in reading, simple math, and other skills that are widely required in training and employment settings.
Coaching	Instructional activities designed to improve the test performance of prospective test takers.
Compensatory approach	See *Counterbalanced approach*.
Concurrent validity	See *Criterion-related validity*.
Construct	A theoretical characteristic or concept (e.g., numerical ability, conscientiousness) that has been constructed to explain observable patterns of behavior.
Construct-related validity	The extent to which a test measures a specific theoretical construct, characteristic, or trait. In employment testing, this characteristic should be important for job success. Examples of constructs are mechanical ability and physical endurance.
Content-related validity	The extent to which the content of a test samples or represents the subject area or behavior it is intended to measure.
Converted score	A raw score that has been converted by numerical transformation (e.g., to percentile ranks or standard scores) to facilitate comparison of individual scores with group norms.
Correlation	A statistic that indicates the degree to which two variables relate to each other, such as a test score and job performance or one test with another test.

4 Assessment Attributes and Related Guidelines

Counterbalanced approach	An approach to personnel assessment that allows high scores in one area or more to be counterbalanced with low scores in another area.
Criterion	A measure of performance, such as productivity rate, accident rate, or supervisory ratings. Test scores are used to predict criteria.
Criterion-related validity	The degree to which scores on an assessment instrument correlate with some external criterion, such as job performance. When the assessment instrument and the criterion are measured at about the same time, it is called *concurrent validity*; when the criterion is measured at some future time, it is called *predictive validity*.
Derived score	See *Converted score*.
Equivalent forms	See *Alternate forms*.
Expectancy table	A table that shows the probability of different criterion outcomes for each test score.
Hurdles approach	See *Multiple hurdles approach*.
Inventory	A questionnaire or checklist that elicits information about an individual in areas such as work values, interests, attitudes, and motivation.
Job analysis	A systematic process used to identify the tasks, duties, responsibilities, and working conditions associated with a job and the knowledge, skills, abilities, and other characteristics required to perform that job.
Mean	The average score in a group of scores, computed by adding all the scores and dividing the sum by the number of cases.
Median	The middle score in a group of ranked scores. It is the point or score that divides the group into two equal parts. The median is also known as the fiftieth percentile.
Multiple hurdles approach	An approach to personnel assessment that requires a candidate to pass all tests in sequence in order to qualify.

Normal curve	A mathematical curve that is the basis of many statistical analyses. The curve is bilaterally symmetrical, with a single bell-shaped peak in the center. Most distributions of human traits – such as height, mathematical ability, and manual dexterity – approximate the normal curve.
Norms	Descriptive statistics that are used to summarize the test performance of a specified group, such as a sample of workers in a specific occupation. Norms are often assumed to represent a larger population, such as all workers in an occupation.
Parallel forms	See *Alternate forms*.
Percentile score	The score on a test below which a given percentage of scores fall. For example, a score at the sixty-fifth percentile is equal to or higher than the scores obtained by 65 percent of the people who took the test.
Predictive validity	See *Criterion-related validity*.
Rank ordering	The process of ranking individuals based on their relative test scores, from the highest to the lowest score.
Raw score	The score obtained on a test, usually determined by counting the number of correct answers.
Reference group	The group of individuals used to develop a test.
Reliability	The degree to which test scores are consistent, dependable, or repeatable.
Reliability coefficient	A coefficient of correlation that indicates the degree to which test scores are dependable or repeatable.
Standard deviation	A statistic used to describe the variability within a set of scores. It indicates the extent to which scores vary around the mean or average score.

Standard score	A score that describes the location of a person's score within a set of scores in terms of its distance from the mean in standard deviation units.
Standardized test	A test developed using professionally prescribed methods that provides specific administration requirements, instructions for scoring, and instructions for interpreting scores.
Target group	The population or group of individuals whom the employer wishes to assess.
Test	Any instrument or procedure that samples behavior or performance. A personnel or employment test is the general term for any assessment tool used to measure an individual's employment qualifications, capabilities, or characteristics.
Validity	The degree to which actions or inferences based on test results are meaningful or supported by theory and empirical evidence.
Validity coefficient	A numerical index that shows the strength of the relationship between a test score and a criterion, such as job performance.

References

Anderson, L. & Krathwohl, D. (eds.) (2001). *A Taxonomy for Learning, Teaching, and Assessing: A Revision of Bloom's Taxonomy of Educational Objectives*. New York: Addison Wesley.

Armstrong, P. (2010). *Bloom's Taxonomy*. Nashville: Vanderbilt University Center for Teaching. https://cft.vanderbilt.edu/guides-sub-pages/blooms-taxonomy/.

Bloom, B. S. (1956) *Taxonomy of Educational Objectives, Handbook: The Cognitive Domain*. David McKay, New York.

Bloom, B. S. (1969). *Taxonomy of Educational Objectives: The Classification of Educational Goals: Handbook I, Cognitive Domain*. New York: McKay.

Gelb, I. (1963). *Study of Writing*. Chicago: University of Chicago Press.

McNamara, D. S. & Kintsch, W. (1996). Learning from texts: Effects of prior knowledge and text coherence. *Discourse Processes*, 22(3), 247–288. https://doi.org/10.1080/01638539609544975.

Orlin, B. (2015). US vs. UK: Mathematical terminology. Math with Bad Drawings. https://mathwithbaddrawings.com/2015/05/20/us-vs-uk-mathematical-terminology/comment-page-1.

Rawson, K. A. & Van Overschelde, J. P. (2008). How does knowledge promote memory? The distinctiveness theory of skilled memory. *Journal of Memory and Language*, 58(3), 646–668. https://doi.org/10.1016/j.jml.2007.08.004.

Reisman, F. & Severino, L. (2021). *Using Creativity to Address Dyslexia, Dysgraphia, and Dyscalculia: Assessment and Techniques*. Oxford, UK: Routledge.

Reisman, F. K. & Kauffman, S. H. (1980). *Mathematics Instruction for Children with Special Needs*. Columbus, OH: Charles E. Merrill.

Tanner, D. & Reisman, F. (2014). *Creativity as a Bridge between Education and Industry: Fostering New Innovations*. North Charleston, NC: CreateSpace, an Amazon subsidiary.

US Department of Labor (1999). *Testing and Assessment: An Employer's Guide to Good Practices*.

CHAPTER 5

Assessment of Creativity

Advance Organizer. Chapter 5 includes assessments of creative processes, including the Torrance Tests of Creative Thinking, the Reisman Diagnostic Creativity Assessment (RDCA), Amabile's componential model and many others, reflecting standardized tests, self-reports, rating scales, and assessments of products. Also included in this chapter are the advantages and disadvantages of self-reports, generic influences on learning, and five appendices. Appendix 5A defines the generic influences on learning, Appendix 5B sets out additional generic influences on learning, Appendix 5C describes observations of generic influences on learning and gives tips for teachers, Appendix 5D sets out the RDCA scoring interpretation, and Appendix 5E is a glossary.

5.1 Introduction

Most creativity tests in use today are based at least partially on the theory of creativity developed by J. P. Guilford (1950), who posited that the ability to envision multiple solutions to a problem lay at the core of creativity. He called this process *divergent thinking* and its opposite – the tendency to narrow down all options to a single solution – *convergent thinking*. Guilford identified three components of divergent thinking: (1) fluency (the ability to quickly find multiple solutions to a problem), (2) flexibility (being able to simultaneously consider a variety of alternatives), and (3) originality (referring to ideas that differ from those of other people).

5.2 Assessment of Creative Processes

Creativity assessment attempts to measure an individual's potential for creativity, which is defined as one's ability to generate novel and useful ideas. A variety of assessments have been used for studying creativity and creative processes, including standardized tests, self-assessments or

> **Box 5.1 Likert-type scale**
>
> The Likert-type scale was developed by Rensis Likert (1932). The Likert scale is frequently employed for measuring attitudes, knowledge, perceptions, values, and behavioral changes. This type of scale presents respondents with a range of statements to choose from in order to rate their responses to evaluative questions. When it comes to scoring and analysis, each item can be assessed individually or, in certain cases, item responses can be added together to generate a score for a group of items.

self-reports, rating scales including checklists, and products produced. Several assessments incorporate a Likert-type scale, as described in Boxes 5.1 and 5.2, as well as in Box 1.1 in Chapter 1. Creativity assessments are measures of creative *potential*, as creative achievement depends on factors beyond a test, such as practical problem-solving, knowledge of a discipline, or self-efficacy (i.e., an individual's confidence in their ability to complete a task or achieve a goal). Thus, "assessments should be based on several tests, rather than relying on a single score" (Cropley, 2000). Runco and Pritzker (2011) presented an exhaustive summary of tests of creativity, and Bonnie Cramond (2020), former Director of the University of Georgia Torrance Center for Creativity and Talent Development, provided an excellent summary of creativity assessments.

Box 5.2 presents a summary of useful Likert-type formats for creating an assessment (Vagias, 2006).

5.3 Standardized Assessments

A standardized assessment requires all test takers to answer the same or related questions or activities, is scored in a "standard" or consistent manner (which makes it possible to compare the relative performance of individuals), and usually is timed. Included in these types of assessments are the three types of standardized tests: achievement, aptitude, and diagnostic (Woolfolk, 2004). Achievement tests measure how much of the material has been mastered. Tests such as the American College Testing, the Iowa Test of Basic Skills, and the Iowa Tests of Educational Development are all norm-referenced achievement tests (Woolfolk & Shaughnessy, 2004). An aptitude test is an exam used to determine an individual's skill or propensity to succeed in a given activity. Aptitude tests assume that individuals have inherent strengths and weaknesses and have a natural inclination toward success or failure in specific areas based on

5   Assessment of Creativity

Box 5.2   Likert-type formats

Level of acceptability	1, totally unacceptable; 2, unacceptable; 3, slightly unacceptable; 4, neutral; 5, slightly acceptable; 6, acceptable; 7, perfectly acceptable
Knowledge of action	1, never true; 2, rarely true; 3, sometimes but infrequently true; 4, neutral; 5, sometimes true; 6, usually true; 7, always true
Level of appropriateness	1, absolutely inappropriate; 2, inappropriate; 3, slightly inappropriate; 4, neutral; 5, slightly appropriate; 6, appropriate; 7, absolutely appropriate
Does is reflect me?	1, very untrue of me; 2, untrue of me; 3, somewhat untrue of me; 4, neutral; 5, somewhat true of me; 6, true of me; 7, very true of me
Level of importance	1, not at all important; 2, low importance; 3, slightly important; 4, neutral; 5, moderately important; 6, very important; 7, extremely important
My beliefs	1, very untrue of what I believe; 2, untrue of what I believe; 3, somewhat untrue of what I believe; 4, neutral; 5, somewhat true of what I believe; 6, true of what I believe; 7, very true of what I believe
Level of agreement	1, strongly disagree; 2, disagree; 3, somewhat disagree; 4, neither agree nor disagree; 5, somewhat agree; 6, agree; 7, strongly agree
Priority (seven-point scale)	1, not a priority; 2, low priority; 3, somewhat priority; 4, neutral; 5, moderate priority; 6, high priority; 7, essential priority
Priority (five-point scale)	1, not a priority; 2, low priority; 3, medium priority; 4, high priority; 5, essential
Level of desirability	1, very undesirable; 2, undesirable; 3, neutral; 4, desirable; 5, very desirable
Level of concern	1, not at all concerned; 2, slightly concerned; 3, somewhat concerned; 4, moderately concerned; 5, extremely concerned

> Box 5.2 (cont.)
>
> | | |
> |---|---|
> | Level of participation | 1, no, and not considered; 2, no, but considered; 3, yes |
> | Level of problem | 1, not at all a problem; 2, minor problem; 3, moderate problem; 4, serious problem |
> | Affect on X | 1, no affect; 2, minor affect; 3, neutral; 4, moderate affect; 5, major affect |
> | Level of consideration | 1, would not consider; 2, might or might not consider; 3, definitely consider |
> | Level of support/opposition | 1, strongly oppose; 2, somewhat oppose; 3, neutral; 4, somewhat favor; 5, strongly favor |
> | Level of probability | 1, not probable; 2, somewhat improbable; 3, neutral; 4, somewhat probable; 5, very probable |
> | Level of agreement | 1, strongly disagree; 2, disagree; 3, neither agree or disagree; 4, agree; 5, strongly agree |
> | Frequency (five-point scale) | 1, never; 2, rarely; 3, sometimes; 4, often; 5, always |
> | Level of familiarity | 1, not at all familiar; 2, slightly familiar; 3, somewhat familiar; 4, moderately familiar; 5, extremely familiar |
> | Level of awareness | 1, not at all aware; 2, slightly aware; 3, somewhat aware; 4, moderately aware; 5, extremely aware |
> | Level of difficulty | 1, very difficult; 2, difficult; 3, neutral; 4, easy; 5, very easy |
> | Level of satisfaction (five-point scale) | 1, not at all satisfied; 2, slightly satisfied; 3, moderately satisfied; 4, very satisfied; 5, extremely satisfied |

their innate characteristics. Diagnostic assessment is mainly known for its use in medicine; however, in education, mathematics in particular has been an application. Academic diagnosis can help identify one's current knowledge of a discipline, skill sets, and capabilities, and can clarify misconceptions before instruction takes place. Knowing learners' strengths and weaknesses can help instructors plan what to teach and how to teach it. However, in the case of the Reisman Diagnostic Creativity Assessment (RDCA; as discussed later in Section 5.5), the goal is to help one become aware of one's own strengths and weaknesses as regards eleven creativity factors, including originality, risk-taking, and elaboration. Creativity assessments can be categorized as both aptitude and diagnostic tests. Box 5.3 sets out the different types of aptitude tests.

The following are examples of standardized assessments.

Torrance Tests of Creative Thinking (TTCT). The TTCT, which are mainly based on Guilford's structure-of-intelligence battery, are the most widely used and studied creativity tests (Swartz, 1988). The TTCT consist of

---

Box 5.3 Types of aptitude tests

Abstract Reasoning Test. This test is designed to evaluate an individual's mental capacity to comprehend alterations in shapes, generate novel ideas on the spot, and create fresh drawings based on prior illustrations. Additionally, it measures an individual's ability to derive logical connections among various sets of information. Typically, this assessment is employed to assess a person's creativity and their proficiency in rapidly solving new problems.

Numerical Reasoning Test. This test analyses a person's aptitude for numbers. It assesses their ability to make correct decisions based on numerical or statistical data, such as graphs, equations, and fractions. Such tests are popular among firms that recruit accountants and bankers and among students who want to hone their mathematical skills.

Verbal Reasoning Test. This test assesses comprehension, communication, and capability to understand, analyze, and draw accurate conclusions related to a standard text.

Spatial Reasoning Test. Spatial reasoning pertains to an individual's ability to contemplate objects in three dimensions and deduce implications about them from incomplete information. A person with strong spatial skills may also excel in visualizing the appearance of an object after undergoing rotation.

Psychometric Test. There are essentially three categories of psychometric measures: aptitude tests, skills tests, and personality tests. Aptitude tests are designed to evaluate a particular set of skills or overall abilities, such as creative thinking. Skills tests meausre a person's skills in a specific area, i.e., sofware development, typing or math. Personality tests measure characteristic patterns of traits that people exhibit across various situations.

Logical Reasoning Test. This test measures a person's ability or aptitude to extract rules, analogies, and structures, which are used to find a correct answer among a set of options. Logical thinking is the process of applying a chain of reasoning to overcome a problem and reach a conclusion. A good example is playing chess, which involves working through a sequence of individual steps to attain victory. Logical thinking is important because it can facilitate applying reason to important decisions, solving problems, generating creative ideas, and setting goals.

Adapted from *India Today* (2021)

verbal and figural assessments. The TTCT-verbal is entitled "Thinking creatively with words" and the TTCT-figural is entitled "Thinking creatively with pictures." The TTCT-verbal is scored on fluency, originality, and elaboration. The TTCT-figural battery is scored on resistance to premature closure and abstractness of titles, in addition to originality, fluency and elaboration. Flexibility was removed as a scoring factor because of the close correlation between fluency and flexibility scores (Hebert et al., 2003). The TTCT use a normalized standard score with a mean of 100 and a standard deviation of 20. The TTCT-verbal consists of seven activities entitled asking, guessing causes, guessing consequences, product improvement, unusual uses, unusual questions, and just suppose. The TTCT-figural consists of three subtests, namely picture construction, picture completion, and parallel lines. The TTCT incorporate time limitations and recommend the administration of a game-like environment. The TTCT may be obtained from the ScholasticTesting Service (www.ststesting.com/).

Aptitudes Research Project. The most extensive work on divergent thinking was done under Guilford's direction at the University of Southern California by the Aptitudes Research Project. The Aptitudes Research Project tests were divided into verbal and figural categories, as shown in Box 5.4.

Alternative Uses Test. (This test is also known as Guilford's test of divergent thinking.) Developed by Guilford in 1967, the alternative uses test stretches one's creativity by providing the test taker with two minutes to think of as many uses as possible for an everyday object such as a chair, coffee mug, shoe, paper clip, or brick. Scoring involves divergent thinking: (1) fluency, that is, the number of given uses; (2) uniqueness, namely how rare a given use is, and (3) multiple experts rate creativity on a Likert-type scale. Using the percentage of occurrence as a measure of novelty, it was found that participants that produced more responses had more novel responses and a higher average novelty score (Kudrowitz & Dippo, 2013). Research suggests that the first handful of ideas that one thinks of are likely to have been suggested already by others and thus to be not original. To get more novel solutions, one must build upon the ideas generated first to arrive at the less obvious ideas and associations. In this specific test, nine ideas appear to be the limit before ideas begin to be highly novel. The alternative uses test only measures divergent thinking ability and so it may not fully represent general creativity (Kudrowitz & Dippo, 2013). Further information is available at https://davebirss.com/altuses/.

Remote Associates Test. This 30-item test was developed by Sarnoff and Martha Mednick (Mednick & Mednick, 1962). The Mednicks, instead of solely focusing on divergent thinking, argued that convergent

> **Box 5.4   Aptitudes Research Project measures**
>
> The verbal measures include the following:
>
> - Word fluency – writing words containing a given letter
> - Ideational fluency – naming things that belong to a given class (i.e., fluids that will burn)
> - Associational fluency – writing synonyms for a specified word
> - Expressional fluency – writing four-word sentences in which each word begins with a specified letter
> - Alternative uses – listing as many uses as possible for a given object
> - Plot titles – writing titles for short-story plots
> - Consequences – listing consequences for a hypothetical event (e.g., "What if no one needed to sleep?")
> - Possible jobs – listing all jobs that might be symbolized by a given emblem
>
> The figural measures of spatial aptitude include the following:
>
> - Making objects – drawing specified objects using only a given set of shapes, such as a circle, square, etc.
> - Sketches – elaborating on a given figure to produce sketches of recognizable items
> - Match problems – removing a specified number of matchsticks from a diagram to produce a specified number of geometric shapes
> - Decorations – using as many different designs as possible to outline drawings of common objects
>
> Adapted from Psychology Encyclopedia (n.d.)

thinking also should be considered. Each remote associates test task presents three cue words that are linked by a fourth word, which is an abstraction of the other three words' meanings. A typical person can solve most of the items marked as easy, about half of those marked medium, and few of the hard ones. Box 5.5 presents examples of remote associates test items.

5.4   Self-Assessments/Self-Reports

Self-assessments involve obtaining information about people's creativity from the responses they provide to questions about themselves and their behavior (e.g., their own skills, abilities, and activities). Self-assessments include the act or process of analyzing and evaluating oneself or one's actions and often employ a Likert-type scale (as described previously in

> **Box 5.5 Examples of remote associates test items**
>
> Easy items:
> - square/cardboard/open – BOX
> - broken/clear/eye – GLASS
> - coin/quick/spoon – SILVER
> - time/hair/stretch – LONG
>
> Medium-level items:
> - sense/courtesy/place – COMMON
> - flower/friend/scout – GIRL
> - opera/hand/dish – SOAP
> - wheel/hand/shopping – CART
> - fox/man/peep – HOLE
>
> Hard items:
> - home/sea/bed – SICK
> - fence/card/master – POST
> - illness/bus/computer – TERMINAL
> - wise/work/tower – CLOCK
>
> Additional remote associates test items may be accessed at: www.remote-associates-test.com/.

Box 5.1). Self-report data enable researchers to examine an individual's self-image in relation to their creativity, and such factors are important for theoretical and pedagogical reasons. In regard to creativity, self-assessments show the amount of creativity a person feels that they exhibit. Instruments to measure an individual's perception of themselves include self-reports, checklists, questionnaires, and attitude and biographical inventories. Box 5.6 presents the advantages and disadvantages of self-reports.

Thus, data obtained from self-assessments are affected by truthfulness, mood, intention, environment, and internal biases (Reisman, Keiser & Otti, 2016). There are also other challenges in using self-report instruments, such as them not being easily verifiable and open to halo-effect bias on the participant's part (Lubart & Guignard, 2004; Paulhus & Vazire, 2007). Although alternative methods have an equally long history, self-reports remain the most popular choice. The following sets out some self-assessment tests.

Gough Personality Scale. The Gough (1979) scale is a self-assessment whereby the test taker checks off characteristics that apply to themselves. A scoring key is provided to determine which characteristics are indicative

> **Box 5.6 Advantages and disadvantages of self-reports**
>
> **Advantages.** Self-report assessments allow researchers to study large groups and are easily interpretable. Self-report assessments frequently use Likert-type scales to allow respondents to show how strongly they agree or disagree with the scale statements rather than providing a simple yes-or-no answer.
>
> **Disadvantages.** Self-report assessments are affected by circumstances. When taking the assessment, do the test takers respond to the items truthfully or do they want to please the assessor? Are they in a good mood or depressed when responding? Do they overreport socially acceptable behavior or underreport undesirable behavior? Do they shy away from stating that they work for rewards rather than for the love of the task? Do they respond mainly to what they perceive as positive traits, such as elaboration when explaining something or making a point, avoiding risks, or exaggerating their tolerance of the unknown? (These disadvantages are adapted from Reisman & Severino, 2021.) Disadvantages of self-reports also include credibility and self-deception, as they often rely on memory.

of creativity. In terms of scoring, specific items reflect higher creativity. Higher total points indicate higher creativity. Box 5.7 provides sample items on the Gough personality scale (Gough, 1979; Gough & Heilbrun, 1965).

Reisman Diagnostic Creativity Assessment. The RDCA (Reisman, Keiser & Otti, 2011) is a free, online, forty-item self-report creativity assessment (available at https://drexel.qualtrics.com/jfe/form/SV_exPnH xf9uPfptrv; Reisman, Keiser & Otti, 2016). The results of the RDCA are intended "to diagnostically identify one's creative strengths, rather than to predict creativity" (Tanner & Reisman, 2014, p. 25). The RDCA assesses an individual's self-perception on eleven major creativity factors that have emerged from the creativity research: originality, fluency, flexibility, elaboration, resistance to premature closure, tolerance of ambiguity, convergent thinking, divergent thinking, risk-taking, intrinsic motivation, and extrinsic motivation. Some of the RDCA factors are similar to those tapped by the TTCT (Torrance, 1974), which in turn stem from Guilford's (1967) creativity research. The RDCA requires approximately ten minutes. The test is automatically scored and provides immediate results that users can email to themselves or others. Researchers have established the reliability and validity of the RDCA (Reisman, Keiser & Otti, 2016).

> **Box 5.7   Examples of Gough personality scale items**
>
> Please indicate which of the following adjectives best describe yourself. Check all that apply.
>
> *Items with example scores (+, apply; –, do not apply)*
>
> | | |
> |---|---|
> | + Capable | – Honest |
> | – Artificial | + Intelligent |
> | + Clever | – Well mannered |
> | – Cautious | + Wide interests |
> | + Confident | + Inventive |
> | + Egotistical | + Original |
> | – Commonplace | – Narrow interests |
> | + Humorous | + Reflective |

The RDCA score interpretation (Appendix 5D) is a diagnostic tool that provides a profile of one's RDCA assessment. Each interpretation includes the RDCA factor maximum points possible, the total score and equivalent percent score for each creativity factor, the classification of score meanings (very high, moderately high, average, low, or very low), factor definitions, RDCA items categorized by factor, and two scoring examples. Test takers rate themselves on a six-point Likert-type scale from strongly disagree to strongly agree. The test taker immediately gets a profile of relative strengths and weaknesses, ranked from very high to very low on each of the eleven factors. In addition to the eleven creativity factors tapped by the RDCA, Box 5.8 lists additional creative student characteristics.

In addition to the RDCA creativity and RDMA motivation factors, awareness of the social and emotional generic influences (Appendix 5A) that have an impact on learning helps educators understand students' learning needs and provides data for effective instruction. Additional resources include Appendix 5B, which provides further generic influences on learning; Appendix 5C, which sets out observations of generic influences on learning and tips for teachers; and Appendix 5D, which provides the RDCA scoring interpretation and the glossary in Appendix 5E.

5 Assessment of Creativity 119

> **Box 5.8 Additional creative student characteristics**
>
> A creative student also might:
>
> - have a high level of curiosity
> - engage in disruptive behaviors
> - disengage
> - daydream due to boredom
> - show high levels of energy
> - need positive ways to show their creativity
> - question, question, question!
> - have a subtle sense of humor

5.5 Rating Scales, Checklists, and Questionnaires

Rating scales provide specific descriptions of qualities or behaviors associated with creativity characteristics and ask teachers, parents, mentors, peers, or others to rate a person in relation to those qualities. Examples of rating scales are given in the following.

Counting the Muses: Development of the Kaufman Domains of Creativity Scale. This scale is included as an appendix to Kaufman (2012). The fifty items are assessed with the following Likert-type scale:

1. much less creative
2. less creative
3. neither more or less creative
4. more creative
5. much more creative

Scales Used for Rating Behavioral Characteristics. This scale (Renzulli, 1976) assesses the following: (1) learning characteristics, (2) creativity characteristics, (3) motivation characteristics, (4) leadership characteristics, (5) artistic characteristics, (6) musical characteristics, (7) dramatics characteristics, (8) communication characteristics, (9) planning characteristics, (10) mathematics characteristics, (11) reading characteristics, (12) technology characteristics, and (13) science characteristics. Each of the Renzulli scales contains multiple items using a Likert-type scale. The first four scales focus on learning, creativity, motivation, and leadership; the remaining ten focus on specific areas. According to research, gifted children commonly display identifiable behaviors, such as utilizing sophisticated terminology, comprehending fundamental concepts, and generalizing from complex data. The Renzulli scales request that educators evaluate children against their peers in several of these behaviors, assuming that students who score well on the scales are more likely to qualify for a gifted program. Reproduction of the Renzulli scales in any form is prohibited without express permission of the publisher Prufrock Press Inc. (www.routledge.com/contacts/rights-and-permissions).

5.6   Products

Creativity is often defined in terms of products. MacKinnon (1978) argued that "the bedrock of all studies of creativity ... is an analysis of creative products, a determination of what it is that makes them different from more mundane products" (p. 187). Judgments about products can be quite reliable (Runco, 1989) compared with the study of creative processes or related personality characteristics. Products such as paintings, publications, and compositions are indicators of creative achievement, while ideas can be treated as the products of original, divergent, and even creative thinking. The following are assessments that utilize products as a measure of creativity.

Runco Ideational Behavior Scale. The Runco ideational behavior scale is a creativity self-report based upon the notion that ideas can be treated as products of original, divergent, and creative thinking, as proposed by Guilford (1967). The Runco ideational behavior scale contains twenty-three statements evaluated by a five-point Likert-type scale indicating to what degree each statement describes one's usual behavior. Runco (2013) argued that ideas are common to all domains and are evident in eminent and everyday creativity. Thus, this scale measures the creativity of ideas, which do not always result in tangible products. Three factors were identified in the scale: quantity of ideas, absorption, and originality. Items in the Runco ideational behavior scale include (Runco, Plucker & Lim, 2001):

- I am able to think about things intensely for many hours.
- I often find that one of my ideas has led me to other ideas that have led me to other ideas.
- I end up with an idea and do not know where it came from.

Thus, the purpose of the Runco ideational behavior scale is to measure idea generation, defined as the process of creating, developing, and communicating abstract, concrete, or visual ideas. Further information is available at www.coursehero.com/file/16610110/Runco-Ideational-Behaviour-Scale/.

Amabile's Consensual Assessment Technique. (This test is also called the componential model of creativity.) The consensual assessment technique has been described as the gold standard of creativity assessment. It has been used extensively by creativity researchers for the past thirty years. The consensual assessment technique defines creativity as the production of ideas or outcomes that are both novel and appropriate to some goal (Amabile, 1983). Amabile's (1983) componential model of creativity predicts that three significant components contribute to creativity: (1) skills specific to the task domain, (2) general (cross-domain) creativity-relevant skills, and (3) task motivation. Amabile (2012) proposed that, for any idea, product, performance, or accomplishment to be considered creative, it must be recognized as valuable by experts in a relevant field. Therefore, Amabile suggested that the consensual assessment technique modifies the use of subjective judgment of creativity. Ultimately, a response or product is creative to the extent that it is seen as creative by people familiar with the domain in which it was produced (Amabile et al., 1994). Several articles regarding this methodology may be accessed by searching for Amabile's consensual assessment technique.

Creative Product Semantic Scale. This scale (O'Quin & Besemer, 1989, 2006) is an online assessment tool for evaluating creative products and uses the following three product features: (1) novelty (the product is original or surprising), (2) resolution (the product is valuable, logical, useful, or understandable), and (3) elaboration/synthesis (the product is complex and well crafted). The creative product semantic scale, contains fifty-five bipolar adjective pairs scored on a seven-point Likert-type scale and can be used by untrained judges to evaluate a product's creativity. Box 5.9 provides examples of the creative product semantic scale.

5.7 Summary

Over the past half-century, numerous creativity assessments have provided evidence of the reliable and valid measurement of creativity. Researchers developed these tests because of growing interest in creativity and because of the limitations inherent in non-testing methods for judging creativity. Creativity assessment provides opportunities to use content in new ways through examining multiple perspectives, solving problems, and applying ideas in original situations. This chapter provides

> **Box 5.9 Examples of the creative product semantic scale**
>
> The following are examples of bipolar adjective pairs in the creative product semantic scale:
>
> **Novelty**
> - overused–fresh
> - predictable–novel
> - usual–unusual
> - unique–ordinary
> - original–conventional
>
> **Resolution**
> - illogical–logical
> - makes sense–senseless
> - irrelevant–relevant
> - appropriate–inappropriate
> - adequate–inadequate
>
> **Elaboration and Synthesis**
> - skillful–bungling
> - well made–botched
> - crude–well crafted
> - careless–careful
> - meticulous–sloppy
>
> Source: Product Enthusiast (n.d.)

a variety of research-based tools for assessing creative thinking activities that include standardized tests, self-reports, rating scales, and products as evidence of creativity. The generic influences on learning that emerged from the special education research both expand how to observe learners and provide a basis for individualizing instruction (as presented in Chapters 9 and 10). This chapter's appendices are a source of tools that support the assessment activities.

Appendices

Being aware of cognitive, psychomotor, physical, sensory, social, and emotional impacts on learning helps in understanding students' learning needs and provides data for effective instruction. The appendices include definitions of the generic influences on learning and serve as foundation material for Chapters 9 and 10, which comprise instructional modules. The material in Appendices 5A, 5B, and 5C focuses on the generic influences. Appendix 5D contains the scoring interpretation for the RDCA and Appendix 5E is the glossary.

The instructional modules presented in Chapters 9 and 10 can be enhanced by applying the generic influences on learning. This approach helps teachers to design learning activities that unlock students' creative strengths and that consider the psychological nature of curricula from basic acquisition of labels to high-level abstractions.

Appendix 5A   Generic Influences on Learning and Definitions

This appendix lists the generic influences on learning and defines each.

Cognitive

Rate and Amount of Learning Compared with Age Peers. This refers to the length of time taken to learn a given amount of material in comparison with other members of a similar age group.

Speed of Learning Related to Specific Content. This involves the consideration of a student's strengths and weaknesses, in particular learning tasks such as verbal comprehension (e.g., reading and listening), perceptual organization (e.g., puzzles, geometry, and spelling), and numerical reasoning (e.g., mathematics).

Ability to Retain Information. This refers to tasks that utilize memory, such as repeating digits, obeying simple commands, role counting, and naming the days of the week.

Need for Repetition. This refers to the amount of practice necessary for mastery.

Verbal Skills. These involve tasks such as comprehending and producing written and spoken words and sentences.

Ability to Learn Symbol Systems and Arbitrary Associations. This refers to the communication of thoughts through a conventional system of signs or symbols that are understood simultaneously by the sender and by the receiver.

Size of Vocabulary Compared to Peers. This refers to the number of words a student understands and uses, as well as the number of different meanings and nuances for a given word.

Ability to Form Relationships, Concepts, and Generalizations. This refers to the psychological nature of the content that is being learned, for example constructing one-to-one correspondence and thus forming a relationship, abstracting the number property (e.g., the concept of three from a set of three objects), and putting two or more concepts together into some kind of relationship and thus forming a generalization (e.g., combining the concepts two and three into an addition relationship).

Ability to Attend to Salient Aspects of a Situation. This refers to the ability to notice the important and most relevant aspect(s) or attribute(s) of a situation and simultaneously disregard extraneous cues, as well as the ability to attend to detail and to differentiate the essential from the nonessential (e.g., to select the thinner blocks when given blocks of various color, shape, size, and thickness).

Use of Problem-Solving Strategies. This refers to a systematic organized approach to tasks, compared with those who flounder randomly, never moving beyond a trial-and-error approach.

Ability to Make Decisions and Judgments. This involves recognizing salient aspects of a situation, using any important information given, being aware of missing information, abstracting essential from nonessential details, evaluating relationships embedded in a situation, and making choices between alternatives, It also involves generating a set of possible alternatives, dealing with future ideas, and making judgments according to a set of criteria.

Ability in General to Abstract and to Cope with Complexity. This includes classifying objects or ideas, finding logical relationships or analogies, performing simple operations of logical deductions, and using similes and metaphors.

Demonstrates Creativity Factors. These creativity factors include originality (generating unique and novel ideas), fluency (generating many ideas), flexibility (generating many categories of ideas), elaboration (adding detail), tolerance of ambiguity (being comfortable with the unknown), resistance to premature closure (keeping an open mind), divergent thinking (generating many solutions [related to fluency]), convergent thinking (coming to a closure), risk-taking (adventuresome), intrinsic motivation (inner drive), and extrinsic motivation (needing reward or reinforcement).

Psychomotor

Visual Perception. This involves the child understanding the world through visual experience – through what they see.

Visual Discrimination. This refers to the ability to perceive the difference between two similar visual symbols (e.g., + and ×, 6 and 9, 3 and E).

Visual Field Dependence/Field Independence. This refers to the ability to separate figures from the background (i.e., to screen out irrelevant visual stimuli).

Visual Form Constancy. This involves the ability to recognize a visual stimulus when it appears in different spatial positions or in slightly different forms (e.g., the digit 5 placed around the classroom in different sizes or colors).

Visual-Sequential Memory. This involves the ability to process or recall a series of visual stimuli in sequential memory (e.g., saying the digits 0–9 in a counting order).

Auditory Perception. This involves the child understanding the world through auditory experience – through what they hear.

Auditory Discrimination. This refers to the ability to perceive the difference between two similar auditory symbols (e.g., a child with a problem in this area might draw hair instead of a chair or get in instead of on a box).

Auditory Field Dependence/Field Independence. This refers to the ability to screen out irrelevant auditory stimuli and focus on the primary auditory message (e.g., a child with a problem in this area may not be able to concentrate on what the teacher is saying in the classroom because of noises outside).

Auditory Form Constancy. This is the ability to recognize sounds spoken by different people or presented in different environments (e.g., recognizing the sound of a train on a recording or understanding language when spoken with a dialect different from what the student is accustomed to).

Auditory-Sequential Memory. This involves the ability to process or recall a series of auditory events in order (e.g., repeat a telephone number, retell a story, or name the days of the week in order).

Ability to Form Rules (Phonological, Morphological, Syntactical, Semantic). This involves interpretation and the expression of combinations of sounds, inflectional endings, word order, and word meaning.

Physical and Sensory

Physical Impairments. These include cardiac conditions, diabetes, epilepsy, rheumatic fever, cerebral palsy, muscular dystrophy, etc.
Low Vitality and Fatigue. This may result from chronic medical problems and from effects of medication.
Sensory Processing. This includes tolerance or intolerance to light, sounds, or touch, being able to feel, and being distracted due to noise or light.
Physical Attributes. This includes athletics, good motor hand–eye coordination, good balance, and awareness of their body in space.
Levels of Energy. This includes high energy and stamina.

Emotional

Feeling Afraid, Anxious, Frustrated, Joyous, Angry, Surprised. This involves conscious experience that can be communicated to another person.
Becoming Overly Upset, Moody, Sad, Happy. This represents the extremes of emotion that one learns to control under normative development.

Social

Rules of Conduct, Moral Codes, Values, Customs. These involve being able to relate well to peers and adults.
Modeling Other's Behavior. This can be positive if acceptable behavior is modeled.
Being Aware of Cues in the Environment. This involves knowing when to quiet down, when to speak up, and responding appropriately to others behavior.
Relating to and Interacting with Other People. This includes cooperation and consideration.
Using Diplomacy. This includes tactfulness.
Understanding Another's Point of View and Empathizing. This includes having an emotional and a cognitive view of another's needs.

Appendix 5B   Additional Generic Influences on Learning

This appendix provides an expanded list of traits that represent how one either excels or struggles intellectually, physically, emotionally, and/or socially and regarding psychomotor influences on learning.

Intellectual

- Highly curious, divergent thinker
- Intellectually advanced
- Creative problem-solver
- Insatiable need for information/learning
- Learns "systems" to a high degree of competency
- Can see obscure connections not easily seen by others
- Advanced creativity
- Strong metacognitive (thinking about their thinking) skills
- Unique insight into complex issues
- Has different, often surprising, perspectives
- Likes to explore wide-ranging, often esoteric, subjects
- Can rapidly accelerate learning to high levels of expertise
- Advanced, wicked, and often bizarre sense of humor
- Extraordinary perceptions and/or abilities in one area or more
- Autodidactic (ability to successfully teach one's self)
- Responds well to academic flexibility and self-directed learning
- May seem introverted; spends a lot of time daydreaming/thinking
- Long attention span when working in areas of high interest
- Passionate about areas of interest; fully focused and invested
- Persistent
- Demonstrates superior spatial skills
- Enjoys codes, puzzles, and games of strategy
- Good at developing compensatory strategies
- May have difficulty with auditory instructions/learning
- Advanced reader; can read and understand highly complex material
- Superior vocabulary
- Unusual imagination
- Very motivated to achieve mastery; may abandon subject due to perfectionism/unrealistic expectations
- Hyper-focus, often to the exclusion of all else
- Likes to see the big picture first and then fill in details; is dismissive of details in the quest for the big picture
- Asynchronous intellectual development

- Often has learning (dis)abilities
- Dislikes linear learning or rote practice
- Overreaction to timed tests
- Slower processing speed than displayed by typical children
- Tendency to overthink questions; may take a long time to answer a question

Physical

- Issues with food, multiple food aversions, needs eating rituals
- Problems with digestion, gut health, and/or food allergies
- Sensory processing issues
- Likes to handle items; may have oral fixation
- Can be hypersensitive to touch and often does not like to be touched; conversely, may be hyposensitive to touch and seek rough physical interaction
- Extremely sensitive to stimuli
- Unusual sleep cycles, difficulty sleeping, and less need for sleep
- Trouble controlling body movements, awkward, and clumsy
- Poor fine motor skills
- Trouble with modulating voice levels
- Difficulty sitting still, standing in line, or walking with a group
- Difficulty with personal hygiene and managing personal care
- May not be aware of physical sensations or needs (forgets to eat, drink, sleep, or go to the bathroom)
- Even if appearing chaotic or messy, needs underlying system of order and routine
- May have weak muscle tone, poor gross motor skills, or asynchronous physical development

Emotional

- Empathetic
- Deeply connected to loved ones
- Often mature beyond their years
- Intense feelings; may be confused by their emotions
- Asynchronous emotional development
- Overwhelmed by other's emotions and emotional intensity
- Very sensitive; easily wounded emotionally
- May have existential sorrow/depression

- Perfectionist
- Compulsive and obsessive
- Impulsive
- Has issues with anxiety and phobias
- Has unrealistic expectations of themselves
- Low self-esteem; feels like an imposter
- Emotional response out of sync with what is typical
- Rigid about rules and fairness; struggles with gray areas and inflexibility
- May need time to prepare for changes to routine; surprises may be difficult for them to manage
- Arrogant or may appear arrogant
- Bored, frustrated, feels held back by traditional pacing and learning practices
- Less interested in typical external motivators and reward systems
- Falls apart under pressure
- Has trouble understanding facial expressions and body language

Social

- Often feels lonely or out of sync with others
- Asynchronous social development
- Is concerned about social justice
- Has a mature understanding of world problems and social injustice
- Cares deeply about the future of the world
- Questions the status quo; comes up with creative alternatives
- Often outwits adults
- Sensitive to patronizing or hypocritical behavior; may confront adults in authority on their own behavior
- May not follow rules for rules' sake; may challenge underlying logic/illogic of rules, even if punished for doing so
- May have trouble with authority; can be oppositional and argumentative
- May want to be the center of attention in some instances; conversely, may have high social anxiety in other instances
- Comments and actions are out of sync with what others are doing
- May have extremes with imaginative play: difficulty understanding imaginative play or obsessively engages in imaginative play throughout childhood
- May struggle to express themselves verbally
- Gullible, socially awkward, and often bullied
- Gets along with adults, as well as much younger/much older children

- Behavioral issues often resolve when intellectually or creatively satisfied
- Loves to challenge themselves and/or others
- Often misunderstood or ostracized
- Confused by social protocol

Psychomotor

- Overexcitability, which may manifest as hyperactivity, sleeplessness, rapid speech, intense athletic activities, restlessness, and acting out on impulse
- Sensual overexcitability, which may manifest as an increased need for touching and handling things, the need for physical contact with others, oral fixation, or the need to be the center of attention
- Imaginational overexcitability, which may manifest through a vivid imagination, detailed descriptions of images and impressions, high anxiety, phobias, inventiveness, animated visualization, intense dreams and nightmares, mixing of truth and fiction, and fears of the unknown
- Intellectual overexcitability, which may manifest in an insatiable need for information; delights in the analysis of difficult problems, is persistent in asking probing questions, has an inordinate desire for increasing levels of knowledge, has a reverence for logic, and has a preoccupation with theoretical problems
- Emotional overexcitability, which may manifest in phobias, fears, obsessions, inhibition (timidity or shyness), concerns with death, anxieties, depression, feelings of loneliness, and concern for others.

Adapted from Dabrowski & Piechowski (1977)

Appendix 5C Observation of Generic Influences on Learning: Tips for Teachers

The following material expands on the generic influences and serves as a guide for teachers' observations of students.

Cognitive Generic Influences on Learning

Quite simply, cognition refers to thinking. The term "cognition" has its origin in the Latin word *cognosco* and means "to conceptualize" or "to recognize." It refers to the mental processes (thinking, learning, remembering, abstraction, judgment, problem-solving, language, imagination, perception, planning, and execution) involved in acquiring knowledge and awareness about one's self and environment.

5 Assessment of Creativity

The evolution of the science of cognition has its beginning in philosophy. Aristotle (384–322 BC) portrayed cognitive domains pertaining to memory, perception, and mental imagery. Cognition found a dominant place in psychology in the early nineteenth century. In psychology, conventionally, the study of behavior has been divided into two broad categories: cognitive (pertaining to processes such as memory, association, concept formation, pattern recognition, language, attention, perception, motor programming, problem-solving, and mental imagery) and affective (pertaining to emotions that were not earlier considered as a cognitive process). This division is now considered largely artificial, and much research is currently being undertaken to examine the cognitive psychology of emotion, metacognition, and metamemory.

The cognitive generic influences listed in Appendix 5A form the structure for adaptations and modifications in instruction that will accommodate learners' needs. Notice that creative thinking is a crucial cognitive influence.

Psychomotor Generic Influences on Learning

Generic factors that affect learning involve inefficiency in the use of psychomotor abilities, including those abilities needed in searching and in producing spoken or written responses.

Children with visuomotor deficits have difficulty recognizing shapes, matching, discriminating forms, and attending to salient attributes of a situation. These skills of spatial ability underlie the development of number concepts in young children. To a young child, the concept of four takes up more space than the concept of two. Number is a spatial idea; number is also a temporal idea. When one enumerates objects in a set by matching, in order, a number name to each element of a set, the elements are attended to in sequenced time. We cannot count simultaneously. The ability to search – that is, to scan in a controlled manner – is therefore essential to developing concepts of number, geometric shapes, and spatial relationships underlying topological ideas (order, proximity, separateness, and enclosure).

Psychomotor learning appears to develop in three stages: the reception of experience (stage 1), the central organization of received experience (stage 2), and the expression of what has been learned (stage 3). Interference in the development of any of these stages will affect the acquisition of learning.

Disorders of Visual Perception

Visual perception involves the child understanding their world through visual experience – that is, through what they see. Visuoperceptual disorders underlie difficulties in spatial orientation, recognizing position, discriminating figure from ground, and distinguishing near–far relationships.

Clumsiness often accompanies visuoperceptual difficulties. The severity of clumsiness varies with respect to the child's chronological age and general level of intelligence. This causes difficulty in arithmetic computation involving writing. A child with poor fine motor coordination skills in addition to perceptual problems has trouble aligning digits according to place value and processing the various algorithms. The child may also have difficulty with handwriting and this may cause difficulty in writing letters and digits.

Behaviors that children display consistently that interfere with efficient visual processing include:

- poor visual discrimination – the inability to perceive the difference between two similar visual symbols
- visual figure–ground distractibility – the inability to screen out irrelevant visual stimuli
- form-constancy problems – the inability to perceive similarity in meaning in visual stimuli with slightly different forms; a generalization process
- deficit in visual-sequential memory – the inability to process or recall a series of visual stimuli in sequential order
- difficulties in spatial relationships and directionality – the inability to organize visual stimuli in space and difficulties with left-to-right or top-to-bottom orientation

The following subsections set out examples of how these behaviors represent psychomotor factors that affect mathematics learning.

Poor Visual Discrimination

- Confuses operational signs: + and × or − and +
- Confuses set notation: ∩ ∪ C
- Confuses digits (e.g., 6 and 9) and confuses letters with digits (e.g., 3 and E)
- Confuses geometric shapes

5 *Assessment of Creativity* 133

Visual Figure-Ground Distractibility

- Unable to disregard irrelevant attributes, such as in the Piagetian task dealing with conservation of mass. Here, the child is shown two equivalent balls of clay. When one is rolled into a longer, thinner shape, the nonconserving child believes that a change in mass has also occurred
- Unable to attend to the number property of equivalent sets and simultaneously disregard the color, size, shape, texture, or function of objects in the sets
- Unable to notice topological equivalents such as simple closed curves; for example, o and D are topologically equivalent, whereas and 8 and G are not
- Difficulty in solving mazes

Form-Constancy Problems

- Does not recognize the digits 0, 1, 2, 3, 4, 5, 6, 7, 8, 9 if they are presented with variation in size, color, or position in a room
- Does not recognize that there are an infinite number of names for a number; for example, 4 can be represented as 2+2, 8÷2, 100−96, 1×4, 32/8, etc.

Difficulties in Spatial Relationships

- Confuses decimal notation: 7.34 and .734
- Confuses multiplication and division notation: 3×5 and 3÷5
- Writes "e" for 6 and "B" for 3
- Difficulty comprehending topological notions: enclosure (the dot is inside the circle), order (the triangle is third in line to the right), proximity (draw a ball next to the tree), and separateness (an open curve, e.g., Z)
- Difficulty seeing rotations and projections

Disorders of Auditory Perception

Auditory perception is described as the organization and interpretation of auditory stimuli – both speech sounds and environmental sounds. It is the internal process of organizing things that we hear and interpreting them on the basis of previous experience. It is discriminating, categorizing, and giving meaning to sounds. The process takes place in the brain and not in the ears.

As speech has a temporal underpinning involving rhythm, as does number, disability in auditory perception is a basic factor that affects mathematics and reading (phonemic awareness issues).

Poor Auditory Discrimination. The inability to perceive the difference between two similar sounds; that is, the misperception of one word for another (e.g., cat/hat/bat, etc.).

Auditory Figure–Ground Distractibility. The inability to screen out irrelevant auditory stimuli and focus on the primary auditory message.

Poor Auditory Analysis. The inability to break down a spoken word into individual sounds and analyze their number and order.

Sound Blending Difficulty. The inability to perceive a sequence of individual sounds and then blend them into a word; also called auditory synthesis.

Problems in Auditory Sequential Memory. The inability to recall a series of auditory events in order; a child cannot repeat a telephone number or a sentence, retell a story, or name the days of the week in order.

Examples of how these factors affect learning are as follows:

- poor auditory discrimination – a child draws hair instead of a square or gets in instead of on a box
- poor auditory analysis – a child has difficulty in expressing plurals, for example "I have three sister" for "I have three sisters"
- sound blending difficulty – a child cannot write numerals to represent dictated numbers, for example writes 345 for "three tens, four hundreds, five units"

A major characteristic of psychomotor factors that affect learning is difficulty in integrating information derived from one sense modality with that gained from others. This is called sensory integration. Prominent among this type of difficulty are perceptual and visuomotor disturbances. Birch and Belmont (1964) stated that "many children with specific learning disabilities show themselves to be significantly defective in their ability to integrate information derived from the auditory, visual, tactile, and kinesthetic sense modalities with one another" (p. 295). As so many mathematical and language ideas are abstracted from the child's perceived actions upon objects in the real world, the ability for sensory integration is essential to learning.

Physical and Sensory Generic Influences on Learning

Factors that influence learning include those that prevent or inhibit the development of spatial and temporal relationships. Younger children build up knowledge of objects in space through information from bodily movements transmitted along various sensory channels. If they are restricted in their activities, particularly early in life, they can become deprived of a wide range of sensorimotor experiences.

Low-Vitality and Fatigue Conditions

Children with low-vitality conditions can be presented with instructional material at a slower than usual rate of instruction. This adjustment depends on how much instruction the child can tolerate. The result is introducing the child to only a portion of the total curriculum. Thus, the selection of appropriate and relevant topics and skills is essential.

Severe weakness may place limitations on the amount and degree of movement in space. Thus, the effect of a low-vitality condition will be determined by concomitant cognitive, sensory, social, and emotional factors. The age of onset and the severity of the condition will also be involved in the effect on learning.

Children with dyslexia, dysgraphia, and/or dyscalculia may experience fatigue when learning and mastering skills. The teacher wants to create enough tension that the child continues to learn, but not so much that the child becomes completely frustrated and gives up. Incorporating creative activities when working on the difficult skills may help to increase vitality and energy.

Sensory Limitation

Sensory awareness involves a nonverbal stimulus (light or sound) activating a sense organ (eye or ear) and being detected by the receiver.

Sensory impairment of a visual nature affects skills in object identification, discrimination, sorting, classification, quantitative comparisons (size of objects, weight, length, and surface measure), orientation and mobility, handwriting, reading temperature, identifying time on a clock face, and using a calendar. Reduced vision limits the child's experiences with their environment, development of spatial orientation, and learning facilitated by imitating others.

Social and Emotional Generic Influences on Learning

Problems of learning usually relate to either a general learning problem or an emotional difficulty. In our culture, mathematics is considered to involve superior reasoning ability and is thought to be a powerful tool. Successful performance in mathematics carries with it positive connotations. Being "good in math" is "being bright," and being bright in mathematics is associated with control, mastery, quick understanding, and leadership. Unsuccessful mathematics achievement implies the opposite of these positive connotations. This value system is a cultural problem that has a subtle harmful effect on a number of children and adults. Parents sometimes give their child the impression that learning mathematics is difficult and that they would like the child to do it. Some may wish that the success in mathematics that eluded them be realized in their child. Parental pressure may bear upon general learning, but it is particularly evident for mathematics learning.

A teacher can help a child who displays anxiety as a result of learning problems. The level of anxiety may be exemplified as follows: A child has a perceptual, spatial, temporal, or motor problem, or a combination of these. They want to learn but cannot produce. The child tries, but the results are inadequate. The child becomes anxious. In this case, the teacher should try to determine what is going wrong at the learning level. Is the work too difficult? Are there missing portions of a curriculum not learned? Does the child need more work at the concrete level? Once an instructional problem is diagnosed and corrected, the teacher may be instrumental in decreasing the child's anxiety by providing success situations.

A distinction is made here between social and emotional factors that influence learning. Social factors include the following:

- rules of conduct, moral codes, values, and customs
- modeling others' behavior, being aware of cues in the environment, and relating to and interacting with other people
- using diplomacy, understanding another's point of view, empathizing, enjoying the company of others, and including in one's decisions the desires and intentions of others
- accepting needed help and forming a balance between autonomy and dependency

5 Assessment of Creativity

Emotional factors include feeling:

- afraid
- anxious
- frustrated
- joyous
- angry
- surprised
- overly upset, moody, sad, or happy

Social Factors

Cooperation. Group participation requires the ability to follow directions without unduly disrupting the activities of others. The child may be unable to inhibit their reactions; may speak out randomly, not wait their turn, or engage in other inappropriate acts; and disruptiveness may be episodic. They may be aware that their behavior is unsuitable, but are incapable of altering it.

Attention. Inattention has two major types: distraction from within and distraction from without. The child who cannot control inner distractions is described as disinhibited, whereas the child who overreacts to the surrounding environment is considered distractible. Examples of inattention include never being attentive, being very distractible, rarely listening, and attention frequently wandering.

Organization. The child lacks facility in planning, cannot organize tasks sequentially, always needs suggestions as to the next step, is careless, and is inexact.

New Situations. The child shows low tolerance for any change. Some overreact only to particularly stressful situations involving surprise, complex social demands, fatigue, excitability, or a lack of self-control.

Social Acceptance. The child lacks the ability to relate well, especially to other children. They are often viewed as unfriendly, disobedient, naughty, or to be avoided.

Responsibility. The child is deficient in the ability to assume responsibility and lacks general initiative and self-sufficiency.

Completion of Assignments. The child often cannot finish assigned work, even with supervision.

Tactfulness. The child is often rude, disregarding the feelings of others. This relates to a lack of perception in discerning the wishes of others. This deficiency in social perception precludes learning the significance of cues, especially of certain nonverbal aspects of life. Thus, the child is not aware of the meaning of the actions of others or of themselves.

Emotional Factors. Adults can help alleviate fears and anxieties that have an effect on learning by providing information, reassurance, and comfort. Krutetskii (1976, p. 347) commented on the role of emotion in learning mathematics:

> The emotions a person feels are an important factor in the development of abilities in any activity, including mathematics. A joy in creation, a feeling of satisfaction from intense mental work, and an emotional enjoyment of this process heighten a person's mental tone, mobilize their powers, and force them to overcome difficulties. An indifferent person cannot be a creator.

Emotional problems may cause and also result from mathematics difficulty.

Failure in arithmetic can be caused by emotional problems but it also can cause emotional problems. Some children have already developed a fear of arithmetic before they come to school. They may have heard a parent talk about their difficulty or failure in arithmetic and subconsciously may identify with this parent. Sometimes, a parent's occupation is mathematically oriented. Such children may have difficulty in arithmetic either because they would rather fail than compete with their parents or because they try so hard to succeed that they block their learning.

Anxiety has generally been regarded as a response that may be expressed at various levels of intensity and may involve physiological and motor behaviors such as excessive fidgeting, squirming, blushing, and sweaty palms. Investigators have done extensive research regarding the nature of anxiety and its relationship to need achievement, school achievement, test situations, fear, intelligence, and other variables.

Hyperactivity, Distractibility, Impulsivity

These three factors, although involving different behaviors, are interrelated and occur frequently in those students with emotional disturbance, learning disabilities, and mental retardation. They have been delineated by Hallahan and Kauffman (1977, p. 146) as follows:

> Hyperactivity or hyperkinesis involves excessive motor activity of an inappropriate nature. Distractibility is the inability to selectively attend to the appropriate or relevant stimuli in a given situation, or

over-selectivity of attention to irrelevant stimuli. Impulsivity is disinhibition or a tendency to respond to stimuli quickly and without considering alternatives.

Aggressiveness

Group interaction in a classroom requires cooperation among members of the social environment. Rules of conduct that facilitate learning involve following directions, taking turns, and, in general, not being a disruptive force. The child who is unable to inhibit verbal or motor activity will have difficulty in engaging in suitable behavior. Bandura (1973) listed considerations for identifying aggressive behavior, including evaluating (1) the behavior itself, (2) the apparent intentions of the aggressor, and (3) the type of reactions on the part of the target of the behavior.

Appendix 5D Reisman Diagnostic Creativity Assessment: Scoring Interpretation

The individual RDCA score interpretation is a diagnostic tool that provides a profile of one's RDCA, the meaning of the results reported as a percentage on the related creativity factors scale, and an indication of strong creativity characteristics and those that one might wish to enhance.

Example 1: A total score of 240 means that you selected the highest scoring option for each item for 100 percent of the items.

Example 2: A score of 22 for the originality factor reflects that you obtained 61 percent of the possible thirty-six originality factor points comprised of the six originality RDCA items.

Note, RDCA items 10, 15, 22, and 33 were reversed score (i.e., "Strongly disagree" was the highest scoring option instead of "Strongly agree").

RDCA score interpretation

RDCA maximum possible score	Score and equivalent percentage	Classification	Factor definition	RDCA items related to factors
Total score (240: highest possible score)	199–240 (83–100 percent) 146–198 (61–82 percent) 120–145 (50–60 percent) 94–119 (39–49 percent) 41–93 (17–38 percent)	Very high Moderately high Average Low Very low		
Originality (36: highest possible score)	30–36 (83–100 percent) 22–29 (61–82 percent) 18–21 (50–60 percent) 14–17 (39–49 percent) 6–13 (17–38 percent)	Very high Moderately high Average Low Very low	Unique and novel	3. I regularly come up with novel uses for things. 4. I come up with new and unusual ideas. 8. I come up with unique suggestions, thought up wholly or partly independently of other people. 13. I think in unconventional ways. 20. I usually think out of the box. 29. I am very innovative.
Fluency (24: highest possible score)	20–24 (83–100 percent) 15–19 (62–82 percent) 12–14 (50–61 percent) 9–11 (34–49 percent) 4–8 (17–33 percent)	Very high Moderately high Average Low Very low	Generates many ideas	7. I can generate many relevant solutions. 28. I can rapidly produce a lot of ideas relevant to a task. 36. I generate many ideas when I draw. 40. I generate many ideas.

Flexibility (18: highest possible score)	15–18 (83–100 percent) 11–14 (61–82 percent) 9–10 (50–60 percent) 7–8 (39–49 percent) 3–6 (17–38 percent)	Very high Moderately high Average Low Very low	Generates many categories of ideas	14. I come up with different categories of approaches to solving problems. 21. I come up with different types of responses to a situation. 31. I can generate different categories of uses for a specific item.
Elaboration (24: highest possible score)	20–24 (83–100 percent) 15–19 (63–82 percent) 12–14 (50–62 percent) 9–11 (38–49 percent) 4–8 (17–37 percent)	Very high Moderately high Average Low Very Low	Adds detail	9. I fill in details when drawing. 19. I tend to elaborate on my ideas when speaking. 27. I tend to keep adding to my drawings. 39. I tend to elaborate on my ideas when writing.
Tolerance of ambiguity (12: highest possible score)	11–12 (91–100 percent) 9–10 (75–90 percent) 7–8 (58–74 percent) 4–6 (33–57 percent) 2–3 (17–32 percent)	Very high Moderately high Average Low Very low	Comfortable with the unknown	24. I can tolerate the unknown. 35. I can cope with uncertainty.
Resistance to premature closure (24: highest possible score)	20–24 (83–100 percent) 15–19 (62–82 percent) 12–14 (50–61 percent) 9–11 (38–49 percent) 4–8 (17–37 percent)	Very high Moderately high Average Low Very low	Keeps an open mind	1. I keep an open mind. 11. When faced with a problem, I evaluate possible solutions and select the best one. 23. I gather as much information as possible before making a decision. 32. I keep listening even when I think I know what someone is saying.

(cont.)

RDCA maximum possible score	Score and equivalent percentage	Classification	Factor definition	RDCA items related to factors
Divergent thinking (18: highest possible score)	15–18 (83–100 percent) 11–14 (52–61 percent) 9–10 (50–60 percent) 7–8 (39–49 percent)	High Moderately high Average Low	Generates many solutions (related to fluency)	6. I follow many paths to come up with possible solutions. 18. I come up with multiple possibilities when analyzing a problem by looking at every angle of the situation. 37. I prefer problems where there are many or several possible right answers.
Convergent thinking (18: highest possible score)	15–18 (83–100 percent) 11–14 (52–61 percent) 9–10 (50–60 percent) 7–8 (39–49 percent) 3–6 (17–38 percent)	Very high Moderately high Average Low Very low	Comes to closure	5. I can make a decision when there are multiple possibilities or choices. 26. I can select one solution from many possibilities. 30. I do well on standardized tests that require a single correct response.
Risk-taking (24: highest possible score)	20–24 (83–100 percent) 15–19 (62–82 percent) 12–14 (50–61 percent) 9–11 (38–49 percent) 4–8 (17–37 percent)	Very high Moderately high Average Low Very low	Adventuresome	2. I am willing to tackle challenging tasks even when success is uncertain. 10. I am afraid of the unknown. 16. I share and advocate ideas I believe in, even when those ideas are unconventional. 34. I am willing to take calculated risks

Intrinsic motivation (24: highest possible score)	20–24 (83–100 percent) 15–19 (62–82 percent) 12–14 (50–61 percent) 9–11 (38–49 percent) 4–8 (17–37 percent)	Very high Moderately high Average Low Very Low	Inner drive	12. I do well on activities or tasks that I find personally challenging. 17. I engage in activities that are personally satisfying. 25. Curiosity, enjoyment, and interest energize me to complete a task. 38. My motivation to perform well does not depend on external recognition.
Extrinsic motivation (18: highest possible score) Note: These items are reversed scored	15–18 (83–100 percent) 11–14 (61–82 percent) 9–10 (50–60 percent) 7–8 (39–49 percent) 3–6 (17–38 percent)	Very high Moderately high Average Low Very low	Needs reward or reinforcement	15. I will use more effort on an activity or task if there is some kind of incentive. 22. I perform tasks better knowing there will be a reward or recognition. 33. Knowing that I am going to be rewarded enhances my creativity.

Appendix 5E Glossary

Elaboration	The level of detail in responses; for instance, "keeping headphones from getting tangled up" would be worth more than "bookmark" in the paper clip test.
Flexibility	The ability to switch between thinking about two different concepts or tasks, and to think about multiple concepts simultaneously.
Fluency	The rate of responses per minute in a test of creativity, such as discrete solutions generated for various objects.
Functional fixedness	A cognitive bias that limits a person to using an object only in the way it is traditionally used. The bias can prevent us from seeing the full range of ways in which an object can be used.
Lateral inhibition	A person's ability to filter out irrelevant stimuli.
Lateral thinking	Solving problems through an indirect and creative approach, using reasoning that is not immediately obvious and involving ideas that may not be obtainable by using only traditional step-by-step logic. The term was coined in 1967 by Edward de Bono.
Overcoming knowledge constraints	The ability to override "functional fixedness," the constraining influence imposed by salient or pertinent knowledge.
Originality	The rarity of responses in a creativity test.
Perseverance	The ability to use many or broad cognitive categories but also to generate many ideas within a few categories.

The following terms are from: www.mvcc.edu/institutional-effectiveness/assessment/assess-terms-glossary.php

Accountability	The demand by a community (public officials, employers, and taxpayers) for school officials to prove that money invested in education has led to measurable learning.

Achievement test	Standardized test designed to measure the amount of knowledge and/or skill a person has acquired. Such testing evaluates the test taker's learning in comparison with a standard or norm.
Alternative assessment	Used to describe alternatives to traditional, standardized, norm- or criterion-referenced traditional paper and pencil testing. Portfolios and instructor observation of students are also alternative forms of assessment.
Analytic scoring	Evaluating student work across multiple areas of performance rather than from an overall impression (*see* "Holistic scoring"). In analytic scoring, individual scores for each area are scored and reported.
Anchor	A sample of student work that exemplifies a specific level of performance. An anchor would be used to score student work, usually comparing the student performance to the anchor.
Assessment	The process of observing learning; describing, collecting, recording, scoring, and interpreting information about courses/programs/services undertaken for the purpose of improving the institution, services, programs, and student learning and development. Note, assessment is not and should not be associated with evaluation. The object of analysis is the program, activity, or service, not the individual. Assessment is about improving, not judging, the performance of a faculty or staff member.

Assessment activities (methods)	Mechanisms by which achievement of an outcome is determined. Examples include surveys, interviews, standardized tests, portfolios, juried performances, research data from outside sources, peer review, etc.
Assessment for accountability	This involves the summative assessment of units or individuals to satisfy external stakeholders.
Assessment for improvement	This type of assessment feeds directly, and often immediately, back into revision of the course, program, service, or institution to improve student learning, programs, or services. Assessment for improvement can be formative and/or summative.
Authentic assessment	Involves asking students to demonstrate the behavior that the learning is intended to produce. Rather than choosing from a set of responses, students are asked to accomplish a task or to solve problems.
Benchmark	A description of a specific level of expected performance. Benchmarks for student learning are often represented by samples of student work.
Capstone experience	Holistic activities designed to assess students' knowledge, skills, and problem-solving abilities using concepts learned at the end of the program.
Classroom-embedded assessment	Activities used by an individual instructor to determine if students are meeting the outcomes in a single class meeting or a small number of consecutive class meetings. The instructor evaluates the results to decide if changes are needed to help improve student learning.

Cohort	A group of individuals whose progress is tracked by examining identified measurements at specified points in time.
Competencies	Knowledge, skills, or behavior that a student can perform or demonstrate.
Competency test	A test used to determine if a student has met established minimum standards of skills and knowledge.
Course-embedded assessment	Activities selected by faculty members, who teach a course, to determine if students are meeting the learning outcomes for that given course. The results of the assessments should be used to decide if changes in the course are needed to help improve student learning.
Criteria	Measures or characteristics that are used to determine or verify student knowledge, attitudes, and performance.
Criterion-referenced assessment	An assessment comparing an individual's performance to a specific learning outcome or performance standard and not to the performance of other students.
Curriculum mapping	The process for documenting the link between course learning outcomes and program goals and outcomes.
Curriculum-embedded assessment	Assessment that occurs simultaneously with learning and as a natural part of the teaching-learning process. These would include activities such as projects, portfolios, and assignments. The assessments occur in the classroom setting, where tasks or tests are developed from the curriculum or instructional materials.

Cutoff score	Minimum score used to determine the performance level needed to pass a competency test.
Dimensions	Desired knowledge, attitudes, or skills to be measured in an assessment as represented in a scoring rubric.
Direct assessment of learning	Assessment activities that gather evidence of student knowledge and skills based upon student performance, rather than perception.
Educational objectives	Objectives that describe the knowledge, skills, abilities, or attitudes that students are expected to acquire as a result of completing the academic program. Objectives are sometimes treated as synonymous with outcomes.
Evaluation	The use of qualitative and quantitative descriptions to judge individual, course, program, and institutional effectiveness. Depending on the level, evaluation information is used for making decisions about individual performance review, student grades, and course, program, and institutional changes for improvement.
Evaluation of faculty and staff	A process where employee performance is measured at an institution.
External assessment	This uses criteria (i.e., a rubric) or an instrument developed by an external source and is usually summative, quantitative, and standardized.
Formative assessment	Specific assessments identifying what individuals know or are able to do

5 Assessment of Creativity

	and not do for a given learning task. This is a specific focus of student learning assessment within a course.
Norm-referenced assessment	An assessment where student performance or performances are compared with a norm group.
Objective test	A test for which the scoring procedure is completely specified and not subjective, enabling agreement of the correct answer among different scorers.
Outcome	An observable act that can be measured, usually a culminating activity or product.
Outcome (student)	A measurable activity, product, or performance that involves students.
Outcome (student learning)	Descriptions of what a student should be able to know, think, or do when they have completed a course or program.
Performance-based assessment	Direct observation and rating of an individual's performance of an educational objective. The assessment may be conducted over a period of time and usually includes the use of a rubric or scoring guide to provide for objectivity. A test of the ability to apply knowledge in a real-life setting is an example of performance-based assessment.
Performance criteria or standards	Specific descriptions of what individuals must do to demonstrate proficiency at a defined level.
Portfolio	A collection of work, usually drawn from students' classroom work. Portfolios can be designed to assess student progress, effort, and/or

	achievement, and encourage students to reflect on their learning.
Portfolio assessment	Reviewers assess student work on meeting outcomes by use of a portfolio and established criteria of performance. Each item in the portfolio may be individually scored, or a holistic scoring process may be used to present an overall impression of the student's collected work.
Primary trait rubric	A scoring rubric constructed to assess a specific trait, skill, behavior, or format.
Program assessment	Processes identified by faculty and staff members of an academic or nonacademic program to measure identified outcomes as a result of participation in the program or service. The results of the assessments should be used to decide if changes are needed to improve the program or service.
Qualitative assessment	Provides data that are analyzed by interpretive criteria and do not lend themselves to be analyzed by quantitative methods.
Quantitative assessment	Provides data that can be analyzed using quantitative methods.
Rating scale	Qualities of a performance on an assessment that is based on descriptive words or phrases that indicate levels of achievement.
Reliability	The measure of consistency for an assessment indicating that the assessment yields similar results over time when applied to similar populations in similar circumstances. Reliability provides

	an indication of the consistency of scores over time and across raters and different items that measure the same thing.
Rubric	A scoring guide that defines the criteria of how an assignment or task will be assessed. A rubric typically provides an explicit description of performance characteristics corresponding to a point on a rating scale.
Sampling	Method to obtain information about characteristics of a population by examining a smaller, randomly chosen selection (the sample) of the group members. If conducted correctly, sampling results will be representative of the population as a whole.
Standardization	Procedures for designing, administering, and scoring an assessment in an effort to ensure that all students are assessed under the same conditions and scores are not influenced by extraneous conditions.
Standardized test	An objective test that is given and scored in a uniform manner, often with scores being norm-referenced. Standardized tests are often accompanied by guidelines for administration and scoring in an effort to reduce influence on the results.
Standards	Statements of expectations for outcomes, which may include content standards, performance standards, and benchmarks.

Student learning outcomes assessment	The systematic collection, examination, and interpretation of qualitative and quantitative data about student learning and the use of that information to document and improve student learning. Note, assessment is not synonymous with evaluation. The object of analysis of assessment results is about improving learning, and the results should never be used for judging the performance of a faculty or staff member.
Subjective assessment	An assessment whereby the impression or opinion of the assessor contributes to the determination of the score or evaluation of performance.
Summative assessment	Provides a summary at the culmination of a course, unit, or program.
Unit	The designation used for the instructional and noninstructional departments, programs, and college services under the Mohawk Valley Community College Institutional Effectiveness process.
Validity	The extent to which an assessment measures what it is designed to measure and that the results are used to make appropriate and accurate inferences. An assessment cannot be valid if it is not reliable.
Value added	The increase in learning that occurs during a course, program, or activity. This can focus either on the individual student (how much better a student does something at the end than at the beginning) or on

5 Assessment of Creativity

a cohort of students (whether senior projects demonstrate greater critical thinking skills [in the aggregate] than freshmen projects). Value added requires pre- and post-assessment for comparison.

The following assessment terms are from www.potsdam.edu/sites/default/files/documents/offices/ie/assessment/Assessment_Glossary_of_Terms-2.pdf

Assessment	The systematic collection, review, and use of information about educational programs undertaken for the purpose of improving student learning and development.
Benchmark	A description or example of candidate or institutional performance that serves as a standard of comparison for evaluation or judging quality.
Bloom's taxonomy of cognitive objectives	Six levels arranged in order of increasing complexity (1=low, 6=high). (1) Knowledge – recalling or remembering information without necessarily understanding it; includes behaviors such as describing, listing, identifying, and labeling. (2) Comprehension – understanding learned material; includes behaviors such as explaining, discussing, and interpreting. (3) Application – the ability to put ideas and concepts to work in solving problems; includes behaviors such as demonstrating, showing, and making use of information. (4) Analysis – breaking down information into its component parts to see interrelationships and ideas; related

	behaviors include differentiating, comparing, and categorizing. (5) Synthesis – the ability to put parts together to form something original; involves using creativity to compose or design something new. (6) Evaluation – judging the value of evidence based on definite criteria; includes behaviors such as concluding, criticizing, prioritizing, and recommending.
Course-embedded assessment	Reviewing materials generated in the classroom. In addition to providing a basis for grading students, such materials allow faculty to evaluate approaches to instruction and course design.
Direct measures of learning	Students (learners) display knowledge and skills as they respond directly to the instrument itself. Examples include objective tests, essays, presentations, and classroom assignments.
Formative evaluation	Improvement-oriented assessment. The use of a broad range of instruments and procedures during a course of instruction or during a period of organizational operations in order to facilitate mid-course adjustments.
Goals for learning	Goals are used to express intended results in general terms. The term "goals" is used to describe broad learning concepts, for example clear communication, problem-solving, and ethical awareness.
Indirect measures of learning	Students (learners) are asked to reflect on their learning rather than to demonstrate it. Examples include exit surveys, student interviews (e.g., graduating seniors), and alumni surveys.

5 Assessment of Creativity

Institutional effectiveness	The measure of what an institution actually achieves.
Learning outcomes (outcome behaviors)	Observable behaviors or actions on the part of students that demonstrate that the intended learning objective has occurred.
Measurements	Design of strategies, techniques, and instruments for collecting feedback data that provide evidence of the extent to which students demonstrate the desired behaviors.
Methods of assessment	Techniques or instruments used in assessment.
Modifications	Recommended actions or changes for improving student learning, service delivery, etc., that respond to the respective measurement evaluation.
Objectives for learning	Objectives are used to express intended results in precise terms. Furthermore, objectives are more specific as to what needs to be assessed and thus are a more accurate guide in selecting appropriate assessment tools. Example: Graduates in speech communication will be able to interpret nonverbal behavior and to support arguments with credible evidence.
Performance assessment	The process of using student activities or products, as opposed to tests or surveys, to evaluate students' knowledge, skills, and development. Methods include essays, oral presentations, exhibitions, performances, and demonstrations. Examples include reflective journals (daily/weekly), capstone experiences, demonstrations of student work (e.g., acting in a theatrical production, playing an instrument, observing

	a student teaching a lesson), products of student work (e.g., art students produce paintings/drawings, journalism students write newspaper articles, geography students create maps, computer science students generate computer programs, etc.).
Portfolio	An accumulation of evidence about individual proficiencies, especially in relation to learning standards. Examples include, but are not limited to, samples of student work including projects, journals, exams, papers, presentations, videos of speeches, and performances.
Quantitative methods of assessment	Methods that rely on numerical scores or ratings. Examples include surveys, inventories, institutional/departmental data, and departmental/course-level exams (locally constructed, standardized, etc.).
Reliability	Reliable measures are measures that produce consistent responses over time.
Rubrics	(Scoring guidelines) Written and shared for judging performance that indicate the qualities by which levels of performance can be differentiated, and that anchor judgments about the degree of achievement.
Student outcomes assessment	The act of assembling, analyzing, and using both quantitative and qualitative evidence of teaching and learning outcomes, in order to examine their congruence with stated purposes and educational objectives and to provide meaningful feedback that will stimulate self-renewal.

Summative evaluation	Accountability-oriented assessment. The use of data assembled at the end of a particular sequence of activities, to provide a macro view of teaching, learning, and institutional effectiveness.
Teaching-improvement loop	Teaching, learning, outcomes assessment, and improvement may be defined as elements of a feedback loop in which teaching influences learning, and the assessment of learning outcomes is used to improve teaching and learning.
Validity	As applied to a test refers to a judgment concerning how well a test does in fact measure what it purports to measure.

References

Amabile, T. M. (1983). The social psychology of creativity: A componential conceptualization. *Journal of Personality and Social Psychology*, 45(2), 357–376. https://doi.org/10.1037/0022-3514.45.2.357.

Amabile, T. M., Hill, K. G., Hennessey, B. A. & Tighe, E. M. (1994). The Work Preference Inventory: Assessing intrinsic and extrinsic motivational orientations. *Journal of Personality and Social Psychology*, 66(5), 950–967. https://doi.org/10.1037/0022-3514.66.5.950.

Amabile, T. M. (2012). Componential theory of creativity. *Harvard Business School Working Paper*, No. 12–096.

Bandura, A. (1973). *Aggression: A Social Learning Analysis*. Upper Saddle River, NJ: Prentice-Hall.

Birch, H. G. & Belmont, L. (1964). Auditory-visual integration in normal and retarded readers. *American Journal of Orthopsychiatry*, 34(5), 852–861. https://doi.org/10.1111/j.1939-0025.1964.tb02240.x.

Cramond, B. (2020). *Assessing Creativity: A Palette of Possibilities*. Billund, Denmark: Lego Foundation. https://cms.learningthroughplay.com/media/ynrbfpi4/appendix_assessingcreativity_pdf.pdf.

Cropley, A. J. (2000). Defining and measuring creativity: Are creativity tests worth using? *Roeper Review*, 23, 2, 72–79. https://doi.org/10.1080/02783190009554069.

Dabrowski, K., & Piechowski, M. M. (1977). *Theory of Levels of Emotional Development: Vol. 1B. Multilevelness and Positive Disintegration*. Oceanside, NY: Dabor Science.

Gough, H. G. & Heilbrun, A. B., Jr. (1965). *The Adjective Check List Manual*. Palo Alto, CA: Consulting Psychologists Press.

Gough, H. G. (1979). A creative personality scale for the Adjective Check List. *Journal of Personality and Social Psychology*, 37(8), 1398–1405. https://doi.org/10.1037/0022-3514.37.8.1398.

Guilford, J. P. (1950). Creativity. *American Psychologist*, 5, 444–454. http://dx.doi.org/10.1037/h0063487.

Guilford, J. P. (1967). *The Nature of Human Intelligence*. New York: McGraw-Hill.

Hallahan, D. P. & Kauffman, J. M. (1977). Labels, categories, behaviors: ED, LD, and EMR reconsidered. *The Journal of Special Education*, 11(2), 139–149. https://doi.org/10.1177/002246697701100202.

Hebert, P. D., Cywinska, A., Ball, S. L. & deWaard, J. R. (2003). Biological identifications through DNA barcodes. *Proceedings of the Royal Society B: Biological Sciences*, 270(1512), 313–321. https://doi.org/10.1098/rspb.2002.2218.

India Today (2021). 7 different types of aptitude test candidates must know about. www.indiatoday.in/education-today/featurephilia/story/7-different-types-of-aptitude-test-candidates-must-know-about-1876904-2021-11-15.

Kaufman, J. (2012). Counting the muses: Development of the Kaufman Domains of Creativity Scale (K-DOCS). *Psychology of Aesthetics, Creativity, and the Arts*, 6(4), 298–308. https://doi.org/10.1037/a0029751.

Krutetskii, V. A. (1976). *The Psychology of Mathematical Abilities in Schoolchildren*. Chicago: The University of Chicago Press.

Kudrowitz, B. & Dippo, C. (2013). When does a paper clip become a sundial? Exploring the progression of originality in the alternative uses test. *Journal of Integrated Design and Process Science*, 17(4), 3–18. https://doi.org/10.3233/jid-2013-0018.

Likert, R. (1932). A technique for the measurement of attitudes. *Archives of Psychology*, 140, 5–55.

Lubart, T. & Guignard, J.-H. (2004). The generality-specificity of creativity: A multivariate approach. In R. J. Sternberg, E. L. Grigorenko & J. L. Singer (eds.), *Creativity: From Potential to Realization* (pp. 43–56). Washington, DC: American Psychological Association. https://doi.org/10.1037/10692-004.

MacKinnon, D. (1978). *In Search of Human Effectiveness: Identifying and Developing Creativity*. Scituate, MA: Creative Education Foundation.

Mednick, S. A. & Mednick, M. T. (1962). A theory and test of creative thought. In G. Nielson (ed.), *Proceedings of the XIV International Congress of Applied Psychology. Vol. 5. Industrial and Business Psychology* (pp. 40–47). Copenhagen: Munksgaard.

O'Quin, K. & Besemer, S. P. (1989). The development, reliability, and validity of the revised Creative Product Semantic Scale. *Creativity Research Journal*, 2(4), 267–278.

O'Quin, K. & Besemer, S. P. (2006). Using the Creative Product Semantic Scale as a metric for results-oriented business. *Creativity and Innovation Management*, 15(1), pp. 34–44. http://doi.org/10.1111/j.1467-8691.2006.00367.x.

Paulhus, D. L. & Vazire, S. (2007). The self-report method. In R. W. Robins, R. C. Fraley & R. F. Krueger (eds.), *Handbook of Research Methods in Personality Psychology* (pp. 224–239). New York: The Guilford Press.
Product Enthusiast (n.d.). CPSS. https://alicarnold.wordpress.com/cpss/.
Psychology Encyclopedia (n.d.). Creativity tests. https://psychology.jrank.org/pages/155/Creativity-Tests.html.
Reisman, F., Keiser, L. & Otti, O. (2011). Development, use and implications of diagnostic creativity assessment phone app, RDCA – Reisman Diagnostic Creativity Assessment. (co-presented with L. Keiser, C. Schmitt & O. Otti, Drexel University), American Creativity Association (ACA) International Conference, Art Institute of Fort Lauderdale, FL.
Reisman, F., Keiser, L. & Otti, O. (2016). Development, use and implications of diagnostic creativity assessment app, RDCA – Reisman Diagnostic Creativity Assessment. *Creativity Research Journal*, 28(2), 177–187.
Reisman, F. & Severino, L. (2021). *Using Creativity to Address Dyslexia, Dysgraphia, and Dyscalculia: Assessment and Techniques*. Abingdon-on-Thames, UK: Routledge.
Renzulli, J. S. (1976). The enrichment triad model: A guide for developing defensible programs for the gifted and talented. *Gifted Child Quarterly*, 20, 303–326.
Runco, M. A. (1989). Parents' and teachers' ratings of the creativity of children. *Journal of Social Behavior & Personality*, 4(1), 73–83.
Runco, M. A., Plucker, J. A. & Lim, W. (2001). Development and psychometric integrity of a measure of ideational behavior. *Creativity Research Journal*, 13, 393–400. https://doi.org/10.1207/S15326934CRJ1334_16.
Runco, M. & Pritzker, S. (eds.) (2011). *Encyclopedia of Creativity* (2nd ed.). New York: Elsevier.
Runco, M. A. (2013). Divergent thinking. In E. G. Carayannis (ed.), *Encyclopedia of Creativity, Invention, Innovation and Entrepreneurship*. New York: Springer. https://doi.org/10.1007/978-1-4614-3858-8_430.
Swartz, J. D. (1988). Torrance Tests of Creative Thinking. In D. J. Keyser & R. C. Sweetland (eds.), *Test Critique* (vol. 7, pp. 619–622). Kansas, MS: Test Corporation of America.
Tanner, D. & Reisman, F. (2014). *Creativity as a Bridge between Education and Industry: Fostering New Innovations*. North Charleston, NC: CreateSpace.
Torrance, E. P. (1974). *The Torrance Tests of Creative Thinking: Norms-Technical Manual. Research Edition. Verbal Tests, Forms A and B. Figural Tests, Forms A and B*. Princeton, NJ: Personnel Press.
Vagias, W. M. (2006). *Likert-Type Scale Response Anchors. Clemson International Institute for Tourism & Research Development, Department of Parks, Recreation and Tourism Management*. Clemson, SC: Clemson University. www.clemson.edu/centers-institutes/tourism/documents/sample-scales.pdf.
Woolfolk, A. (2004). *Educational Psychology* (9th ed.). Boston: Allyn and Bacon.
Woolfolk, A. & Shaughnessy, M. F. (2004). An interview with Anita Woolfolk: The educational psychology of teacher efficacy. *Educational Psychology Review*, 16(2), 153–175.

CHAPTER 6

Assessment of Motivation

Advance Organizer. Chapter 6 presents an array of techniques for assessing motivation, including self-reports, questionnaires, rating scales, checklists, surveys, interviews, and a diagnostic protocol. In addition to these assessments, Appendices 6A, 6B, and 6C – designed for teachers, students, and corporate folk, respectively – contain the Reisman Diagnostic Motivation Assessment (RDMA) items that emerged from and are categorized by motivation theorists (see Chapter 3). Appendix 6D provides an alternative RDMA interpretation. This chapter also addresses why motivation in education is important, with sections on students and motivation, teachers and motivation, corporate employer and employee motivation, self-esteem and motivation, and motivation and creativity.

6.1 Introduction

Motivation is an internal process – a drive, a need, a desire to change either the self or the environment (Reeve, 2018) – and is related to Maslow's hierarchy of needs (described in Chapters 3 and 7). For example, physiological needs for food and water maintain life and provide satisfaction when achieved. Psychological needs for safety, autonomy, and belonging direct our behavior, as do the needs for love, meaning, and self-esteem (Reeve, 2015). Thus, motivation is one of the driving forces behind human behavior.

Motivation is described in Chapter 3 as a force that triggers the identification of goal-directed behaviors and subsequently provides the energy and will to achieve them. The forces that trigger motivations include personal needs and environmental variables. Generic influences on learning – including cognitive, social, emotional, physical, sensory, and psychomotor influences (as delineated in Chapter 5) – offer a framework for understanding a learner's motivation. This chapter addresses both education and corporate workplace motivation.

6 Assessment of Motivation   161

Why Is Motivation in Education Important?

Motivation sustains students' attention and provides the energy needed to complete tasks. In education, motivation has various effects on students' behavior, preferences, and outcomes as follows:

- helps direct attention toward tasks that need to be done
- allows tasks to be completed in shorter periods of time and attention to be maintained for a longer time
- minimizes and helps resist distractions
- affects how much information is retained
- influences the perception of how easy or difficult a task may appear

Most importantly, motivation drives one to perform an action; without it, completing the action can be hard or even impossible (adapted from Team, 2015).

6.2 Students and Motivation

The following are suggestions for enhancing student motivation.

- **Students should be aware of expectations, objectives, and rules.** This allows them to have a clear understanding of what they should do to succeed in studying.
- **Track the way studying improves.** This allows students to see their progress and achievements and allows the emphasis to be placed on improvement.
- **Give students control.** Allow special days of the week for activities when students elect what they would like to do.
- **Vary pedagogy.** Different students prefer different types of instruction, and if only one technique is used it is likely that students will be bored and unmotivated.
- **Make sure your material is clear and understandable.** Including many examples is a good way to clarify instruction.
- **Set a spirit of collaboration rather than competition.** Students should be encouraged to help one another and thus become a community of learners.
- **Provide the right motivation.** Students need recognition for their efforts and accomplishments rather than an emphasis on external rewards such as stars or trophies.
- **Classroom jobs are good ways to develop student motivation.** These can range from mundane tasks such as the weekly chalkboard manager

to somebody who moderates discussions in the class or edits the class newspaper.
- **Set high but achievable goals.** Easy-to-achieve goals may produce boredom while attaining high but realistic goals is motivating.
- **Give chances to improve.** Students need to embrace mistakes as a learning opportunity because they aren't afraid of failure in an environment that allows for chances to "redo."

There are ways that teachers can inspire and motivate students. For example, enthusiasm is contagious, and students relate to their teachers' excitement and love of the subject during instruction. Small gestures such as saying "great job!" make a difference in a student's attitude and approach to learning. The following are some additional ways in which teachers can motivate students. These examples are adapted from Education World (n.d.).

Have Empathy. Empathy involves connecting with students, sharing both their tears and their laughter, discerning their emotions, and understanding their sentiments. It entails acknowledging that students may be experiencing immense stress, which they may express through anger, aggression, negative demeanor, or impatience. During such moments, demonstrating compassion and comprehension can motivate and support them.

Appreciate. The National Education Association (NEA) surveyed almost 1,000 teachers in 2013 to discover what they truly desired for National Teacher Appreciation Day. The findings revealed that teachers wanted their administrators to place more confidence in their expertise, grant them increased control over their teaching, and provide equitable evaluations of their efficacy in meeting their students' requirements.

Address Needs. For teachers to reach different types of learners, they need relevant supplies, realistic student-to-teacher ratios, and time to evaluate and work with each child.

Pay Them What They Deserve. As per the NEA survey conducted in 2013, teachers desire fair compensation for their efforts, without any undue favor or deficit. Research by the Economic Policy Institute in 2011 showed that teachers earned lesser salaries than professionals with comparable educational qualifications in other industries. Although boosting basic wages is a daunting task that requires significant structural changes, one fact remains irrefutable: If you want to retain effective teachers, ensure that they can afford to provide their best effort.

6.3 Teachers and Motivation

Besides student motivation, attention should be directed toward teacher motivation, particularly as many are exiting the field. This is of utmost significance given that motivation is a vital factor in retaining teachers. Box 6.1 presents teacher shortage data.

School leadership is key to motivating teachers. Principals can work at making things less difficult and complicated by cutting down the amount of paperwork faculty must do, limit the number of staff meetings, and establish the following strategies that are applicable to enhancing teacher motivation:

- seek input regarding higher level decisions
- communicate appreciation for hard work
- allow and encourage teachers to address selected goals via their own methods
- assist individuals under work-related pressure
- implement team-building opportunities or exercises to improve morale, collaboration, and communication
- send thank-you notes to express gratitude
- set clear and reachable goals
- maintain regular communication
- encourage teachers to stay positive and remain calm – especially during unexpected circumstances
- encourage highly skilled teachers to mentor

Box 6.1   Teacher shortage data

Almost two in five or about 44 percent of teachers quit in their first five years of teaching, according to a June 2022 survey of members of the American Federation of Teachers union. The most common reasons cited for general lack of employee retention are person–job fit, lack of growth opportunities, lack of appreciation, lack of trust, low levels of support from supervisors, stress from overload, work–life imbalance, and low compensation (Sandhya & Kumar, 2011). The Bureau of Labor Statistics reports 567,000 fewer educators in US public schools today than there were before the pandemic and the NEA's analysis of the Bureau of Labor Statistics data indicates that 43 percent of jobs posted are going unfilled.

164 Connecting Creativity and Motivation Research with End Users

6.4 Corporate Employer and Employee Motivation

Retention of employees has been an issue in the USA in the past couple of years. Box 6.2 describes the situation that came to be referred to as the "great resignation."

Similar to teachers, approximately 70 percent of employees feel that their managers expressing gratitude more frequently would boost their motivation and morale. Maintaining employee motivation is the most significant challenge for companies, as a positive work environment encourages employees to be more productive and creative. Conversely, demotivated employees are unable to perform effectively and can slow down progress at the workplace.

Several factors contribute to employee motivation. First, monetary compensation and benefits such as gross salary, perks, and performance bonuses are essential motivators. Second, recognition of an individual's hard work can serve as a source of motivation, encouraging them to strive for better performance. Third, work ethics play a crucial role in keeping employees motivated. In an ethical working environment, honesty, integrity, and moral values are important factors for a company. Additionally, the culture at work is essential, and collaboration among individuals from diverse backgrounds, religions, sexual orientations, and countries in the workplace fosters a sense of social connection. Fourth, providing opportunities for career development has a positive impact on employee motivation. Furthermore, health benefits, insurance, and other incentives can serve as motivational factors for

---

Box 6.2   Great resignation

In 2022, an average of four million US citizens resigned from their jobs every month. Notably, 4.2 million quit their jobs in August 2022, and the highest number of resignations occurred in November 2021, with a staggering 4.5 million individuals leaving their jobs. Throughout 2021, approximately 3.98 million workers resigned from their jobs each month and, by the end of the year, over 47 million US citizens had left their jobs. In 2022, 40 percent of employees reported that they were considering quitting their jobs within the next three to six months.

Low pay was cited by at least 63 percent as a reason for leaving their jobs, while other common reasons included a lack of opportunities for advancement (63 percent), feeling disrespected at work (57 percent), childcare issues (48 percent), a lack of flexibility (45 percent), and a lack of benefits (43 percent).

Adapted from Flynn (2023)

employees. Finally, establishing positive and transparent communication between managers and subordinates creates a sense of belonging and motivates employees. Overall, these factors are important in keeping employees motivated, engaged, and committed to their work.

6.5 Self-Esteem and Motivation

Self-esteem is a person's overall subjective sense of self-worth or value, or how much one likes and appreciates themselves regardless of circumstances. Self-esteem has an impact on your decision-making process, your relationships, and your emotional health, and also influences motivation, as confidence in one's abilities generally enhances motivation. Those who strive to achieve goals are more likely to be successful. Upon completing their goals, they will feel encouraged and more motivated and use the feelings of success to boost their self-esteem. Thus, healthy self-esteem directly influences motivation, as people with a healthy self-esteem also display healthy motivation levels.

6.6 Motivation and Creativity

Students' ability to generate novel and useful ideas and solutions to everyday problems is a crucial competence and requires high levels of motivation. Amabile's (1996) research made the link between intrinsic motivation and creativity apparent. Csikszentmihalyi and Rathunde (1993) concluded that genuinely creative people work for work's own sake, and their motivation drives them more than extrinsic reward.

Box 6.3 describes a model for integrating ideas about motivation entitled TARGET (Ames, 1992), which is an acronym for six elements of effective motivation, namely (1) task, (2) authority, (3) recognition, (4) grouping, (5) evaluation, and (6) time. These elements contribute to students' motivation either directly or indirectly.

The foundational knowledge presented in Chapter 3 sets the stage for the remaining portion of this chapter, which focuses on the assessment of motivation.

6.7 What Is Motivation Assessment?

First, a distinction is made between assessment and evaluation. Assessment can be defined as a systematic process of collecting information about something or someone to gauge their skills or knowledge. Evaluation concerns

> **Box 6.3 Components of TARGET**
>
> **Task.** Tasks can be perceived by students based on their value, expectation of success, and authenticity. The value of a task can be evaluated by its significance, level of interest for the student, usefulness or practicality, and the effort and time required to complete it. The expectation of success depends on how difficult the task is perceived to be by the student. Authenticity refers to the extent to which a task mirrors real-life experiences, with greater authenticity leading to increased relevance to the student's interests and goals, ultimately making it more meaningful and motivating.
>
> **Authority.** If students feel responsible for their learning tasks, this can enhance their motivation. Autonomy plays a crucial role in this aspect, and it can be promoted by offering students the opportunity to choose their assignments and encouraging them to take the initiative in their own learning.
>
> **Recognition.** Teachers can support students' motivation by recognizing their achievements appropriately – that is, by not being too general or lacking in detailed reasons.
>
> **Grouping.** The way students are grouped for their work can have an impact on their motivation, and this grouping typically falls into three types: cooperative, competitive, and individualistic.
>
> **Evaluation.** Competitive structures can divert students' attention from the material to be learned, leading them to focus instead on how their performance will be evaluated by the teacher. This can negatively affect their motivation to learn. To create optimal motivation, it is important to strike a balance between cooperative and individualistic structures.
>
> **Time.** Students vary in the amount of time needed to learn, and accommodating these differences will involve flexible scheduling. For example, larger blocks of time may be needed for large group long-term activities, whereas short-term enrichment and extra-help activities can be arranged for some students while others receive attention from the teacher on core or basic tasks.
>
> Adapted from Seifert & Sutton (2018)

making a judgment about the quality or importance of something or someone. Assessment involves an individual's performance level; evaluation addresses how much of a goal is attained. Evaluation involves a value judgment and, indeed, the word "value" is embedded in the word evaluation.

The assessment of motivation is designed to discover what persuades one to take a particular action, make a decision, or choose one thing over another. It is about considering an individual's interests, desires, and preferences, and using these samples of information to understand what drives them to pursue specific opportunities.

In the corporate world, data from motivation assessments drive informed decision-making, especially when it is time to choose individuals for certain positions. In addition to other variables (e.g., experience, education, training, and personality idiosyncrasies), including an assessment of an individual's motivation to apply for a particular job enables management to identify best-fit applicants for a position.

In the education world, the assessment of motivation helps to identify a student's drive – or lack of drive – to do something (e.g., engage in lessons, behave, act up, daydream, cooperate, or collaborate). The assessment process itself helps students to develop critical-thinking and analysis skills. Students who assess themselves are learning and improving their cognitive skills and other generic influences while assessment is happening. The process of classroom assessment can serve an important role in enhancing student motivation and achievement. Teachers can help enrich student performance by sharing clearly defined learning goals and the nature of the assessment. Activities to assess motivation are rarely found in schools today and so this chapter presents an array of options to assess both student and teacher motivation.

6.8 Motivation Assessments

A search for motivation assessments uncovered several for use in business settings, but few for education and classroom use. The motivation assessments presented here are in the forms of self-reports, questionnaires, rating scales, checklists, surveys, interviews, and diagnostic assessment.

Self-Reports

A self-report refers to a methodology that involves requesting participants to provide information about their attitudes, beliefs, feelings, and other subjective experiences. Self-reports include surveys, interviews, questionnaires, rating scales, or diagnostic forms in which test takers read the question and select a response by themselves without any outside interference (Jupp, 2006). Self-report methods have strengths and weaknesses.

The strengths of self-reports include their ease of obtainment, low cost, and ability to reach a larger number of participants than could be observed through other methods. Additionally, self-reports can be conducted quickly and allow participants to express their feelings, attitudes, and opinions.

The weaknesses of self-reports include the fact that collecting information through self-reporting has limitations. People are often biased when they report on their own experiences (Devaux & Sassi, 2016). Self-reports can be biased due to various factors, including social desirability, which means that individuals tend to report socially acceptable or preferred experiences, either consciously or unconsciously. Another weakness of self-reports is that the usefulness of the information gathered about thoughts or feelings heavily depends on participants' willingness to disclose them truthfully. Participants may be inclined to give responses that they believe are expected by the assessor or deliberately provide opposite answers. In addition, they may try to present themselves in a socially desirable way, leading to inaccurate or untruthful responses.

The following are examples of self-assessment items that might be evaluated using a Likert-type scale within categories such as achievement, goals, professional advancement, communication skills, time management, and creativity.

Achievement items might include the following: (1) I have identified areas that I believe I can improve in, (2) I could have done better at work (or school) over the past year, and (3) I am aware of my strengths. **Goals** items might include the following: (1) I set achievable goals for myself this year and (2) I achieved most of my goals for the year. **Professional advancement** items might include the following: (1) I have taken part in professional development programs that the company (or school) offered, (2) I feel that there are particular skills that I am not using, and (3) I would like to have a leadership position in the future. **Communication skills** might focus on the following items: (1) I believe that I communicate effectively with my supervisor and colleagues and (2) I often ask for help to help clarify an assignment. **Creativity** items might comprise the following: (1) I think "outside the box" when it comes to finding solutions to problems, (2) I generate many ideas, (3) I elaborate to get an idea across, (4) I can tolerate ambiguous situations, (5) I resist coming to a premature closure, (6) I take smart risks, (7) I come up with novel ideas, and (8) I do things for the love of the task rather than for an award.

The following are two examples of a motivation self-report assessment, namely The Self-Motivation Quiz and The Situational Motivation Scale (SIMS).

The Self-Motivation Quiz

This is a free self-report quiz assessed on a Likert-type scale comprising five options: not at all, rarely, sometimes, often, and very often. Box 6.4 contains the items.

Box 6.5 sets out the categories of questions in The Self-Motivation Quiz, according to their related self-motivation factor.

> **Box 6.4 The Self-Motivation Quiz**
>
> The following twelve items of The Self-Motivation Quiz may be accessed for free at www.mindtools.com/adosk97/how-self-motivated-are-you:
>
> 1. I'm unsure of my ability to achieve the goals I set for myself.
> 2. When working on my goals, I put in maximum effort and work even harder if I've suffered a setback.
> 3. I regularly set goals and objectives to achieve my vision for my life.
> 4. I think positively about setting goals and making sure my needs are met.
> 5. I use rewards (and consequences) to keep myself focused. For example, if I finish my report on time, I allow myself to take a coffee break.
> 6. I believe that if I work hard and apply my abilities and talents, I will be successful.
> 7. I worry about deadlines and getting things done, which causes stress and anxiety.
> 8. When an unexpected event threatens or jeopardizes my goal, I tend to walk away, set a different goal, and move in a new direction.
> 9. When I come up with a really good idea, I am surprised by my creativity. I figure it is my lucky day, and caution myself not to get used to the feeling.
> 10. I tend to do the minimum amount of work necessary to keep my boss and my team satisfied.
> 11. I tend to worry about why I won't reach my goals, and I often focus on why something probably won't work.
> 12. I create a vivid and powerful vision of my future success before embarking on a new goal.

> **Box 6.5 The Self-Motivation Quiz question categories**
>
> Self-confidence and self-efficacy (questions 1, 2, 6, and 8).
> Positive thinking, and positive thinking about the future (questions 4, 9, 11, and 12).
> Focus and strong goals (questions 3 and 7).
> Motivating environment (questions 5 and 10).

The Situational Motivation Scale

The SIMS is designed to assess intrinsic motivation, identified regulation, external regulation, and amotivation (Deci & Ryan, 1985, 1991; Guay, Vallerand & Blanchard, 2000). Situational motivation refers to the motivation that individuals experience when they are currently engaging in an activity. It refers to the here-and-now of motivation (Pelletier et al., 1995; Vallerand, 1997). Intrinsically motivated behaviors are those that are engaged in for their own sake (Deci, 1971). Identified regulation is a motivational concept whereby an individual perceives a behavior as self-chosen, but the activity is still performed for an external purpose. On the other hand, external regulation occurs when an individual regulates their behavior based on rewards or avoiding negative consequences. Deci and Ryan (1985) introduced a third concept to better comprehend human behavior, known as amotivation. This concept describes the state in which individuals perceive a lack of connection between their actions and their consequences. Individuals who are amotivated experience a lack of connection between their behaviors and outcomes, which leads to a sense of purposelessness and no expectation of reward or possibility of changing the outcome. Behaviors that are amotivated are neither intrinsically nor extrinsically motivated and are considered to be the least self-determined. Amotivation can thus be seen as similar to learned helplessness (Abramson, Seligman & Teasdale, 1978) whereby the individual experiences feelings of incompetence and expectations of uncontrollability. Box 6.6 presents sample items from the SIMS assessment.

Box 6.6   The Situational Motivation Scale sample items

The following SIMS sample items may use Likert-type scale scoring:

- I find this activity interesting.
- I do it for my own sake.
- I am expected to do so.
- There may be many good reasons to do this activity, but personally I do not see any.
- I find this activity enjoyable.
- I think this activity is good for me.
- I am doing this activity, but I am not sure if it is worth it.
- This activity is fun.
- It feels good to do this activity.
- This activity is important to me.
- I feel like I have to do it.
- I am doing this activity now, but I am not sure if it is right to continue.

> **Box 6.7 Characteristics of a good questionnaire**
>
> **A Clear Objective.** Identify the purpose of the questionnaire: What goal do you want to achieve and how you will use the results? Then, align every question with the questionnaire objective.
> **Simple Questions.** Avoid complicated question phrases. Use clear and concise questions that the test takers can understand and respond to immediately.
> **A Reliable Design.** Collect only valid and quality data that measures the aspects that your survey is intended to measure.
> **Brief.** Each question's length should not exceed twenty words, there should not be more than three commas in the question text, the use of multi-syllable words should be restricted, and ambiguous words and phrases should be avoided that have the potential to be interpreted differently by different respondents.

Questionnaires

Questionnaires are a type of self-report consisting of open and closed questions. Questionnaires can be used to study large samples of people fairly easy and quickly and examine a large number of variables. However, individuals may not respond truthfully because they cannot remember or because of social pressure. Social desirability bias can have an impact, as test takers may respond in a way that portrays them in a good light. If questionnaires are emailed, the response rate can be very low. Box 6.7 sets out characteristics of a good questionnaire.

A self-motivation questionnaire covers four elements: personal drive (to improve and achieve and to meet standards), commitment (to both personal and organizational goals), initiative (a "readiness to act"), and optimism (being willing to persevere when facing hurdles). Box 6.8 includes items from the free questionnaire developed by Daniel Goleman, the authority on emotional intelligence, which can be accessed at http://questmeraki.com/self-motivation-questionnaire/. A Likert-type scale for this questionnaire is as follows: never, rarely, sometimes, often, and always.

Rating Scales

Rating scales allow one to indicate the degree or frequency of the behaviors, skills, and strategies displayed by the test taker. One way for teachers to document observations and for students to engage in self-assessment is by

Box 6.8 Self-motivation questionnaire

PERSONAL DRIVE
1. I enjoy taking responsibility for new projects out of interest and willingness.
2. I love to take on a leadership role for challenging tasks.
3. I take ownership of my problems and do not blame others.
4. I am willing to learn new skills that will help me in my work.
5. I readily accept tasks even if they are not within my job description.
6. I continue to identify areas of improvement in my work and try to develop in those areas.
7. I have a strong desire to achieve and excel.
8. I feel good when I get positive feedback from my team members.
9. I am open to criticism and willing to improve myself for my betterment.
10. I get very excited about working with new team members and enjoy my work time with them.

COMMITMENT
11. I am willing to work hard to meet my personal and organizational goals.
12. I do my job with commitment because I try to be perfect.
13. I do not mind working for longer hours in order to complete my work.
14. I will not compromise on quality of work, although it takes a lot of time and energy.
15. I go to work on time.
16. I believe in dedication and perseverance to achieve my goals and visions.
17. I set my personal goals in line with organizational goals.
18. I get a sense of satisfaction when I achieve goals that I have set for myself.
19. I like to set goals that are realistic and achievable.

INITIATIVE
20. I am constantly on the lookout for new and innovative tasks.
21. I will not hesitate to extend my support at work even though it is not within my job scope.
22. I try to see the future directions of my organization and equip myself to meet the needs.
23. I get enthusiastic when I am a part of a challenging task.
24. If a colleague asks me for help, I will go out of my way to help them.
25. I am very quick to identify and take advantage of opportunities.
26. I am ready to implement innovative ideas in my work.
27. I volunteer my services for organizational growth without any internal motive.
28. I am a person who helps others without expecting anything in return.

6 Assessment of Motivation

Box 6.8 (cont.)

OPTIMISM (POSITIVE ATTITUDE)

29. I take on feedback from my colleagues for self-development.
30. I do not give up on tasks started even if I meet setbacks and obstacles at work.
31. Even when I feel like giving up, I push myself to work and complete what I have started.
32. I do not expect my colleagues' help to complete my work.
33. I train myself to be focused at work and do not give in to criticisms or wasted talk.
34. I periodically self-evaluate my work against set standards.
35. I do not expect others to motivate me.
36. I do not take to heart any conflicts or arguments raised by my colleagues at work.
37. I like to progress with my work in spite of unsupportive or disobliging team members.
38. I do not get discouraged by failures and believe that there is always a next time.

Box 6.9 Likert-type scales

Likert-type scales are a common method of assessing opinions or attitudes. They present a list of statements for participants to rate their level of agreement or disagreement. A significant benefit of using Likert-type scales is that they provide more detailed information than a simple yes or no response. Additionally, the use of quantitative data enables easy statistical analysis. However, there is a common tendency for participants to select responses in the middle of the scale, potentially to avoid appearing too extreme. Similarly, as with any questionnaire, there may be social desirability biases influencing participants' responses. Another limitation of quantitative data is that such data do not provide in-depth information.

---

using rating scales. The Likert scale is a widely used example of such a scale (as described in Chapters 1, 3, and 5). Box 6.9 reviews Likert-type scales.

The Rosenberg Self-Esteem Scale (RSES) is a questionnaire designed by Dr. Morris Rosenberg to measure an individual's global self-esteem, that is, their overall sense of self-worth (Rosenberg, 1965). Participants rate their level of agreement with each statement using a 4-point Likert-type response format: strongly agree, agree, disagree, and strongly disagree. The RSES consists of ten items that, along with their scoring directions, are shown in Box 6.10.

> **Box 6.10 The Rosenberg Self-Esteem Scale**
>
> The scores for all ten of the following items are summed. Higher scores indicate higher self-esteem.
>
> 1. On the whole, I am satisfied with myself.
> 2. At times I think I am no good at all.*
> 3. I feel that I have a number of good qualities.
> 4. I am able to do things as well as most other people.
> 5. I feel I do not have much to be proud of.*
> 6. I certainly feel useless at times.*
> 7. I feel that I'm a person of worth, at least on an equal plane with others.
> 8. I wish I could have more respect for myself.*
> 9. All in all, I am inclined to feel that I am a failure.*
> 10. I take a positive attitude toward myself.
>
> *Denotes items that are reverse scored (i.e., strongly agree=0, agree=1, disagree=2, and strongly disagree=3).
> Adapted from Department of Sociology (2019)

The Student Opinion (SOS) consists of ten items that use a five-point Likert-type scale: 1=strongly disagree, 2=disagree, 3=neutral, 4=agree, and 5=strongly agree. The scores from these items are added to create three scores: total motivation, importance, and effort. To calculate the SOS total motivation score, the responses to all ten items are added together. The importance scale is obtained by adding responses to items 1, 3, 4, 5, and 8, which measures the significance of the test to the examinee. The effort scale consists of the remaining items (2, 6, 7, 9, and 10) and is intended to assess the amount of effort students put into the assessment task. Higher scores on the SOS total motivation score indicate higher self-reported motivation. Four of the items (3, 4, 7, and 9) need to be reverse scored. Box 6.11 sets out the SOS items.

The Motivation Assessment Scale (MAS) is a rating scale designed to identify those situations in which a student is likely to behave in certain ways. From this information, more informed decisions can be made concerning the selection of appropriate instruction (Durand & Crimmins, 1988, 1992; Haim, 2002). The MAS may be accessed at www.scribd.com/document/350812470/MOTIVATION-ASSESSMENT-SCALE1-pdf.

> **Box 6.11   Student Opinion items**
>
> 1. Doing well on this test was important to me.
> 2. I engaged in good effort throughout this test.
> 3. I am not curious about how I did on this test relative to others.*
> 4. I am not concerned about the score I receive on this test.*
> 5. This was an important test to me.
> 6. I gave my best effort on this test.
> 7. While taking this test, I could have worked harder on it.*
> 8. I would like to know how well I did on this test.
> 9. I did not give this test my full attention while completing it.*
> 10. While taking this test, I was able to persist to complete the task.
>
> *Denotes items that are reversed scored.
> Adapted from Sundre (n.d.).

Checklists

Checklists can be used for formative and summative assessments as well as for diagnostic evaluation. The Basic Psychological Need Satisfaction in General Checklist (Deci & Ryan, 2000; Gagné, 2003) is a twenty-one-item checklist that assesses self-reflection related to motivation. According to the Self-Determination Theory, needs for competence, autonomy, and relatedness must be continually satisfied for people to develop and function in healthy and optimal ways (Deci & Ryan, 2000). Items from this checklist are included in Box 6.12.

Surveys

A survey, which is a type of self-report, is defined as "the collection of information from a sample of individuals through their responses to questions" (Check & Schutt, 2012, p. 160). A survey is the process of collecting, analyzing, and interpreting data.

The Employee Motivation Survey is designed to evaluate the level of motivation and productivity in the workplace. The three goals for the employee motivation questionnaire are (1) measure employees' interest toward their work, (2) discover the factors that are affecting their work performance, and (3) use this feedback to accomplish a lively work environment with happier teams and improved morale. Employers can use items such as those in Box 6.13, scored on a Likert-type scale such as strongly agree, agree, neutral, disagree, and strongly disagree, as a diagnostic assessment to find out why employees are not motivated and offer solutions to promote motivation in the workplace.

> **Box 6.12 Basic Psychological Need Satisfaction in General Checklist items**
>
> 1. I feel like I am free to decide for myself how to live my life.
> 2. I really like the people I interact with.
> 3. Often, I do not feel very competent.
> 4. I feel pressured in my life.
> 5. People I know tell me I am good at what I do.
> 6. I get along with people I come into contact with.
> 7. I pretty much keep to myself and don't have a lot of social contacts.
> 8. I generally feel free to express my ideas and opinions.
> 9. I consider the people I regularly interact with to be my friends.
> 10. I have been able to learn interesting new skills recently.
> 11. In my daily life, I frequently have to do what I am told.
> 12. People in my life care about me.
> 13. Most days I feel a sense of accomplishment from what I do.
> 14. People I interact with on a daily basis tend to take my feelings into consideration.
> 15. In my life I do not get much of a chance to show how capable I am.
> 16. There are not many people that I am close to.
> 17. I feel like I can pretty much be myself in my daily situations.
> 18. The people I interact with regularly do not seem to like me much.
> 19. I often do not feel very capable.
> 20. There is not much opportunity for me to decide for myself how to do things in my daily life.
> 21. People are generally pretty friendly toward me.
>
> Scoring information: To form self-reflection subscale scores for each of the three needs, first, all items that are worded in a negative way are reverse scored (marked with (R) after the item numbers below). To reverse score an item, the item response is subtracted from the total Likert-type scale (e.g., if the scale has eight options, a two would be converted to a six). Once you have reverse scored the items, average the items on the relevant subscale as follows:
>
> - autonomy: items 1, 4(R), 8, 11(R), 14, 17, and 20(R)
> - competence: items 3(R), 5, 10, 13, 15(R), and 19(R)
> - relatedness: items 2, 6, 7(R), 9, 12, 16(R), 18(R), and 21

The Student Motivation Survey (Martin, 2001) has several functions, including providing a structure for self-reflection, for discussion with a peer or adult, and to be used diagnostically to access motivation strengths and limitations. Box 6.14 contains items that may be evaluated on the following Likert-type scale: strongly disagree, disagree, neutral, agree, and strongly agree.

> **Box 6.13   The Employee Motivation Survey**
>
> - My work is stimulating and engaging.
> - My job is challenging and exciting.
> - I am always excited to go to work every day.
> - I always look forward to going to work Monday.
> - My job allows me to grow and develop new skills.
> - I feel I am contributing to the overall goals of my organization.
> - I feel that my work is seen and appreciated within my organization.
> - A superior has shown sincere interest in my career goals.
> - The recognition I receive from my direct superior motivates me to do my best.
> - My direct superior entrusts me with a high level of responsibility.
>
> This survey can be accessed at https://surveysparrow.com/blog/employee-motivation-questionnaire.

> **Box 6.14   The Student Motivation Survey**
>
> - I work hard at school.
> - I concentrate on my schoolwork.
> - I am good at staying at focused in my goals.
> - It's important to me that I improve my skills this year.
> - There's at least one adult in this school I can talk to if I have a problem.
> - I can come up with new ideas.
> - Setbacks don't discourage me.
> - I can learn the things taught in school.
> - What we do in school will help me succeed in life.
>
> For more information, see Formplus (n.d.).

Interviews

An interview is a research technique that allows you to ask a series of questions to gather relevant information. Interviews can use open or closed questions or both, as described next.

Closed questions restrict the answer choices and often require choosing from a predetermined list, such as the participant's age or favorite food. While these questions provide quantitative data, which can be easily analyzed, they do not allow for in-depth responses or insights from participants.

Open questions allow the test taker to provide answers in their own words. Open-ended questions can be more challenging to analyze, but they can provide richer and more detailed insights into a participant's thoughts and feelings. Box 6.15 provides examples of closed and open-ended questions.

Box 6.15   Closed and open-ended questions

Closed questions	Open questions
Are you satisfied?	How satisfied or dissatisfied are you with this process?
Did it act as you expected?	What would (did) you expect to happen when you … ?
Did you find it?	• How did you find that … ? • Where did you find the answer? • Where was the item? • What did you find?
Do you think you would use this?	How would this fit into your work? How might this change the way you do that today?
Does that work for you?	What do you think about that?
Have you done this before?	What kinds of questions or difficulties have you had when doing this in the past? What happened when you did this before? Please describe your level of experience with …
Is this easy to use?	What's most confusing or annoying about … ? What worked well for you?
Did you know … ?	How do you know … ?
Do you normally … ?	How do you normally … ?
Did you see that?	What just happened? What was that?
Do you like this?	What would you most want to change about … ? Which things did you like the best about … ?
Did you expect this kind of information to be in there?	What kinds of information would likely be in there? What were you expecting?

For more information, see www.nngroup.com/articles/open-ended-questions/.

Diagnostic Assessment

A diagnostic assessment allows the instructor to ascertain what the learner already knows about a topic and to discover any hidden learning gaps they might have. The task analysis of basic facts in math that is presented in the developmental mathematics and literacy curricula in Chapter 4 exemplifies how diagnostic teaching that includes diagnostic assessment can reveal hidden aspects of curricula that cause gaps that block future learning. The following are examples of diagnostic assessment.

Box 6.16 RDMA-T

1. I do something for the pleasure of accomplishing a task with no expectation of outside reward such as promotion or increase in salary.
2. I adapt my thinking and needs to incoming information.
3. I adapt to my environment.
4. My self-confidence and feeling that I can do a specified task (self-efficacy) motivate me.
5. Challenging work, recognition, and responsibility give me positive satisfaction.
6. Status, job security, salary, fringe benefits, and work conditions do not give me positive satisfaction, but dissatisfaction results from their absence.
7. I value money, promotion, time-off, and benefits.
8. I am confident about what I am capable of doing.
9. My perception as to whether I will actually get what I desire as was promised by my superior(s) affects my motivation.
10. My superior(s) ensure that promises of rewards are fulfilled and that I am aware of that.
11. I act in ways that bring me pleasure and avoid pain.
12. I have a strong need to set and accomplish challenging goals.
13. I take calculated risks to accomplish my goals.
14. I like to receive regular feedback on my progress and achievements.
15. I often like to work alone.
16. I want to belong to the group.
17. I want to be liked.
18. I will often go along with whatever the rest of the group wants to do.
19. I favor collaboration over competition.
20. I don't like high risk or uncertainty.
21. I want to control and influence others.
22. I like to win arguments.
23. I enjoy competition and winning.
24. I enjoy status and recognition.
25. I need to enjoyably share with another.
26. I need to be free and independent of others.
27. I need to control or influence others.
28. I need to be seen and heard and to entertain.
29. I need to avoid injury and take precaution.
30. I need to help, console, and support my students.
31. I need organization and neatness.
32. I need enjoyment and fun.
33. I need to form stimulating relationships.
34. I need to be loved.
35. I need to analyze, speculate, and generalize.
36. My motivation influences my behavior.

Box 6.16 (cont.)

37. My need for achievement is positively related to my teaching success.
38. I repeat behavior that leads to positive consequences and avoid behavior that has had negative effects.
39. My perceived self-efficacy leads me to set higher goals.
40. My motivation becomes directed toward the satisfaction of others' expectations.
41. I will be motivated to exert a high level of effort when I believe there are relationships between the effort I put forth, the performance I achieve, and the outcomes/rewards I receive.
42. My effort will improve my performance.
43. My performance will lead to rewards.
44. Rewards will satisfy my individual goals.
45. In contrast with a person refusing to teach, I am a person who relishes the opportunity to teach.
46. A supportive supervisor style helps cultivate my creativity.
47. I believe supervision focused on increasing teacher loyalty to the school setting by providing tenure with a strong focus on the well-being of the teacher tends to promote high teacher morale and satisfaction.
48. I believe an individual's view regarding the attractiveness and fairness of rewards will affect motivation.
49. I believe a person may satisfy a particular need whether or not a previous need has been satisfied.
50. I have a need to perceive that I am good at something,
51. I have choices and control over my decisions.
52. I am connected to others through positive relationships.

Reisman Diagnostic Motivation Assessment – Teacher

(Note, the RDMA is currently undergoing initial administrations and analysis.)

The RDMA – Teacher (RDMA-T) (Box 6.16; Reisman et al., 2024) is designed to gauge the level of motivation of teachers (see Table 10.7 in Chapter 10 for the RDMA-T item source grid for teachers that categorizes each item). Each theory related to an item in the RDMA-T is described in Chapter 3. Appendices 6B and 6C offer the same information for the RDMA – Student (RDMA-S) and the RDMA – Corporate (RDMA-C), which can be tailored to the test taker as regards content and length.

6 Assessment of Motivation

The items may be inserted into a Likert-type format, as follows: 1=very untrue of me, 2=untrue of me, 3=somewhat untrue of me, 4=neutral, 5=somewhat true of me, 6=true of me, and 7=very true of me.

Reisman Diagnostic Motivation Assessment – Student

The RDMA-S (Box 6.17) is designed to gauge the level of motivation of post-secondary school students (see Table 10.5 in Chapter 10 for the RDMA-S item source grid for students, which provides data on each item). Each theory related to an item in the RDMA-S is described in Chapter 3. The RDMA-S contains a bank of items that can be selected as appropriate and thus the assessment can be tailored to the test taker in regard to content and length (see Box 6.17).

The items may be inserted into a Likert-type format, as follows: 1=very untrue of me, 2=untrue of me, 3=somewhat untrue of me, 4=neutral, 5=somewhat true of me, 6=true of me, and 7=very true of me.

Box 6.17   RDMA-S

1. I do something for the pleasure of accomplishing a task with no expectation of outside reward such as grade or money.
2. I adapt my thinking and needs to incoming information.
3. I adapt to my environment.
4. My self-confidence and feeling that I can do a specified task motivate me.
5. Challenging classes, recognition, and responsibility give me positive satisfaction.
6. Teachers liking me does not give me positive satisfaction, but dissatisfaction results from their not liking me.
7. I value learning what interests me.
8. I am confident about what I am capable of doing.
9. My perception as to whether I will actually get what I desire as was promised by my teacher(s) affects my motivation.
10. My teacher(s) ensure that promises of rewards are fulfilled and that I am aware of that.
11. I act in ways that bring me pleasure and avoid pain.
12. I have a strong need to set and accomplish challenging goals.
13. I take calculated risks to accomplish my goals.
14. I like to receive regular feedback on my progress and achievements.
15. I often like to work alone.
16. I want to belong to the group.
17. I want to be liked.
18. I will often go along with whatever the rest of the group wants to do.

Box 6.17 (cont.)

19. I favor collaboration over competition.
20. I don't like high risk or uncertainty.
21. I want to control and influence others.
22. I like to win arguments.
23. I enjoy competition and winning.
24. I enjoy status and recognition.
25. I need to enjoyably share with another.
26. I need to be free and independent of others.
27. I need to control or influence others.
28. I need to be seen and heard and to entertain.
29. I need to avoid injury and take precaution.
30. I need to help, console, and nurse the weak.
31. I have a need for organization and neatness.
32. I need enjoyment and fun.
33. I need to form stimulating relationships.
34. I need to be loved.
35. I need to analyze, speculate, and generalize.
36. My motivation influences my behavior.
37. My need for achievement is positively related to my self-concept.
38. I repeat behavior that leads to positive consequences and avoid behavior that has had negative effects.
39. My perceived self-efficacy (i.e., my belief that I can do something) leads me to set higher goals.
40. My motivation becomes directed toward the satisfaction of others' expectations.
41. I will be motivated to exert a high level of effort when I believe there are relationships between the effort I put forth, the performance I achieve, and the outcomes/rewards I receive.
42. My effort will improve my performance.
43. My performance will lead to rewards.
44. Rewards will satisfy my individual goals.
45. In contrast with a person refusing to learn, I am a person who relishes the opportunity to learn.
46. A supportive teaching style helps cultivate my creativity.
47. I believe a person may satisfy a particular need whether or not a previous need has been satisfied.
48. I have a need to perceive that I am good at something.
49. I have choices and control over my decisions.
50. I am connected to others through positive relationships.
51. I do not believe that the best way to get human beings to perform tasks is to reinforce their behavior with rewards.
52. I believe that a basic psychological need is autonomy.

Reisman Diagnostic Motivation Assessment – Corporate

The RDMA-C (Box 6.18) is designed to gauge the level of motivation of corporate employees (see Appendix 6C for the RDMA-C item source grid for employees, which provides data on each item). Each theory related to an item in the RDMA-C is described in Chapter 3. The RDMA-C contains a bank of items that can be selected as appropriate and thus the assessment can be tailored to the test taker as regards content and length.

Box 6.18   RDMA-C

1. I do something for the pleasure of accomplishing a task with no expectation of outside reward such as grade or money.
2. I adapt my thinking and needs to incoming information.
3. I adapt to my environment.
4. My self-confidence and feeling that I can do a specified task (self-efficacy) motivate me.
5. Challenging work, recognition, and responsibility give me positive satisfaction.
6. Status, job security, salary, fringe benefits, and work conditions do not give me positive satisfaction, but dissatisfaction results from their absence.
7. I value money, promotion, time-off, and benefits.
8. I am confident about what I am capable of doing.
9. My perception as to whether I will actually get what I desire as was promised by my boss affects my motivation.
10. My boss ensures that promises of rewards are fulfilled and that I am aware of that.
11. I act in ways that bring me pleasure and avoid pain.
12. I have a strong need to set and accomplish challenging goals.
13. I take calculated risks to accomplish my goals.
14. I like to receive regular feedback on my progress and achievements.
15. I often like to work alone.
16. I want to belong to the group.
17. I want to be liked.
18. I will often go along with whatever the rest of the group wants to do.
19. I favor collaboration over competition.
20. I don't like high risk or uncertainty.
21. I want to control and influence others.
22. I like to win arguments.
23. I enjoy competition and winning.
24. I enjoy status and recognition.
25. I need to enjoyably share with another.
26. I need to be free and independent of others.

Box 6.18 (cont.)

27. I need to control or influence others.
28. I need to be seen and heard and to entertain.
29. I need to avoid injury and take precaution.
30. I need to help, console, and nurse the weak.
31. I need organization and neatness.
32. I need enjoyment and fun.
33. I need to form stimulating relationships.
34. I need to be loved.
35. I need to analyze, speculate, and generalize.
36. My motivation influences my behavior.
37. My need for achievement is positively related to my occupational and financial success.
38. I repeat behavior that leads to positive consequences and avoid behavior that has had negative effects.
39. My perceived self-efficacy leads me to set higher goals.
40. My motivation becomes directed toward the satisfaction of others' expectations.
41. I will be motivated to exert a high level of effort when I believe there are relationships between the effort I put forth, the performance I achieve, and the outcomes/rewards I receive.
42. My effort will improve my performance.
43. My performance will lead to rewards.
44. Rewards will satisfy my individual goals.
45. In contrast with a person refusing to work, I am a person who relishes the opportunity to work.
46. An optimal managerial style helps cultivate my creativity.
47. I believe management focused on increasing employee loyalty to the company by providing a job for life with a strong focus on the well-being of the employee, both on and off the job, tends to promote stable employment, high productivity, and high employee morale and satisfaction.
48. I believe an individual's view regarding the attractiveness and fairness of rewards will affect motivation.
49. I believe a person may satisfy a particular need whether or not a previous need has been satisfied.
50. I have a need to perceive that I am good at something.
51. I have choices and control over my decisions.
52. I am connected to others through positive relationships.
53. I prefer a job that involves just one skill.
54. When I receive clear, actionable information about my work performance, I have a better understanding of what specific actions I need to take (if any) to improve.

The items may be inserted into a Likert-type format, as follows: 1=very untrue of me, 2=untrue of me, 3=somewhat untrue of me, 4=neutral, 5=somewhat true of me, 6=true of me, and 7=very true of me.

It is suggested that, for a fuller picture of the test taker, the relevant RDMA should be administered along with the Reisman Diagnostic Creativity Assessment (RDCA) (Reisman, Keiser & Otti, 2016), as described in Chapter 5.

RKW Student – Enhancing Self-Motivation Diagnostic

RKW Student (Reisman, Keiser & Westphal, 2023) is an assessment designed for teachers to reflect upon their classroom environment and to encourage student self-motivation. This assessment (Box 6.19) may be inserted into a Likert-type scale, a checklist format, or a questionnaire.

Box 6.19 RKW STUDENT – ENHANCING SELF-MOTIVATION DIAGNOSTIC

1. I provide students with freedom of choice in a range of options.
2. I provide useful feedback to encourage student competence.
3. I take a genuine interest in my students.
4. I encourage my students to be aware that what they are learning is relevant to their own lives.
5. I guide my students to apply time management skills to become more organized and productive.
6. I encourage collaboration rather than competition in my classroom.
7. I encourage my students' creative strengths.
8. I reteach where gaps emerge in a student's learning.
9. I welcome student feedback on my classroom behavior.
10. I address student motivational needs.
11. I encourage students to challenge assumptions.
12. I model finding the dominant idea in situations.
13. I encourage students to generate alternatives in a variety of situations.
14. I model using analogies.
15. I have students engage in brainstorming as a problem-solving strategy.
16. I model suspending judgment and resisting premature closure.
17. I appropriately challenge students, which involves my expectations as well as my support.
18. I point out the relevance of lesson goals by integrating real-world problems.
19. I make sure students have the skills and materials to reach their goals.
20. I monitor student progress and provide relevant feedback.
21. I develop good rapport with students.
22. I model enthusiasm for the material.

Box 6.19 (cont.)

23. I employ appropriate humor in my instruction.
24. I provide lessons that offer choice, are connected to students' goals, and provide both challenges and opportunities for success that are appropriate to students' level of skill.
25. I scaffold a lesson by breaking it down into manageable pieces to eliminate gaps in student learning.
26. I foster positive relationships by valuing student inputs.
27. I cultivate students' concentration by limiting distractions and interruptions.
28. I limit students' use of passive activities such as lectures or videos.
29. I avoid allowing student learned helplessness by encouraging their personal sense of control.
30. I have created a classroom that is most conducive to the way my students learn best.
31. I nurture my creative students by allowing them to daydream when bored, respect their insistence on evidence to back up statements from me and their classmates, and acknowledge their need to vent abundant energy.
32. I emphasize autonomy in students rather than control students.
33. I embrace student curiosity and motivation to learn, which encourages them to approach unfamiliar and often challenging circumstances with the expectation to succeed.
34. I pay attention to students' motivation and preferences as fundamental factors in fostering effective learning and achievement in addition to their cognitive development.
35. I arrange for students to participate in academic activities where they experience fun, challenge, and novelty without expectations of rewards.
36. I acknowledge that intrinsic motivation can lead to greater levels of self-motivation and that extrinsic motivation may offer that initial boost that engages students in the activity.

Autonomy-Supportive Intervention Program

The Autonomy-Supportive Intervention Program (ASIP) is a needs-based intervention program to help teachers develop a motivating style designed to support students' needs (Cheon, Reeve & Moon, 2012; Cheon & Reeve, 2014). The ASIP may be used diagnostically to create a student self-directed environment. Box 6.20 describes what autonomy-supportive teachers do during instruction.

Box 6.20 Autonomy-supportive teachers

During instruction, autonomy-supportive teachers:

- adopt the perspective of students
- actively listen to students' concerns with empathy
- utilize teaching techniques that foster intrinsic motivation
- accommodate diverse learning preferences
- provide clear explanations
- use inviting language
- exhibit patience
- acknowledge and validate students' expressions of negative emotions

6.9 Summary

All human actions are motivated, either positively or negatively. Although it may be challenging to identify the underlying reasons for people's choices, this chapter discussed various assessment tools intended to uncover them. Motivation assessments help to understand why individuals make particular decisions. Data from motivation assessments drive informed decision-making (e.g., planning instruction, understanding student behavior, meeting with parents of students, applying for a particular job, or hiring a best-fit employee).

Appendices

Appendices 6A, 6B, and 6C each contain a bank of items that can be selected as appropriate and thus the assessment can be tailored to the test taker as regards content and length. The following is the key for categorizing RDMA test items according to the motivation theorist from whom they emerged. In addition, Appendix 6D provides an alternative RDMA interpretation.

Appendix 6A Reisman Diagnostic Motivation Assessment – Teacher: Item Source Grid

Motivation theorist and theory	RDMA-T items related to motivation theory
Amabile: intrinsic motivation	1. I do something for the pleasure of accomplishing a task with no expectation of outside reward such as evaluation, tenure, or money.

(cont.)

Motivation theorist and theory	RDMA-T items related to motivation theory
Piaget: adaptation	2. I adapt my thinking and needs to incoming information.
	3. I adapt to my environment.
Maslow: needs hierarchy	4. I am motivated when my self-confidence and feeling that I can do a specified task are satisfied.
Herzberg: motivating and hygiene factors	5. Challenging classes, recognition, and responsibility give me positive satisfaction.
	6. Status, job security, salary, fringe benefits, and teaching conditions do not give me positive satisfaction, but dissatisfaction results from their absence.
Vroom: expectancy theory	7. I value money, promotion, time-off, and benefits.
	8. I am confident about what I am capable of doing.
	9. My perception as to whether I will actually get what I desire as was promised by my supervisor(s) affects my motivation.
	10. My supervisor(s) ensure that promises of rewards are fulfilled and that I am aware of that.
	11. I act in ways that bring me pleasure and avoid pain.
McClelland: needs theory	12. I have a strong need to set and accomplish challenging goals.
	13. I take calculated risks to accomplish my goals.
	14. I like to receive regular feedback on my progress and achievements.
	15. I often like to work alone.
	16. I want to belong to the group.
	17. I want to be liked.
	18. I will often go along with whatever the rest of the faculty want to do.
	19. I favor collaboration over competition.
	20. I don't like high risk or uncertainty.
	21. I want to control and influence others.
	22. I like to win arguments.
	23. I enjoy competition and winning.
	24. I enjoy status and recognition.
Murray: needs	25. I need to enjoyably share with another.
	26. I need to be free and independent of others.
	27. I need to control or influence others.

(cont.)

Motivation theorist and theory	RDMA-T items related to motivation theory
	28. I need to be seen and heard and to entertain.
	29. I need to avoid injury and take precaution.
	30. I need to help, console, and nurse the weak.
	31. I need organization and neatness.
	32. I need enjoyment and fun.
	33. I need to form stimulating relationships.
	34. I need to be loved.
	35. I need to analyze, speculate, and generalize.
	36. My motivation influences my behavior.
	37. My need for achievement is positively related to my occupational and financial success.
Skinner: reinforcement theory and operant conditioning	38. I repeat behavior that leads to positive consequences and avoid behavior that has had negative effects.
Bandura: self-efficacy	39. My perceived self-efficacy (belief that I can do something) leads me to set higher goals.
Rogers: humanistic theory	40. My motivation becomes directed toward the satisfaction of others' expectations.
Argyris: there are relationships between the effort put forth, performance, and rewards	41. I will be motivated to exert a high level of effort when I believe there are relationships between the effort I put forth, the performance I achieve, and the outcomes/rewards I receive.
	42. My effort will improve my teaching.
	43. My teaching will lead to rewards.
	44. Rewards will satisfy my individual goals.
McGregor: high supervision versus self-directed employees	45. In contrast with a person refusing to learn, I am a person who relishes the opportunity to learn.
Urwick: an optimal managerial style would help cultivate worker creativity, insight, meaning, and moral excellence	46. A supportive supervisor helps cultivate my creativity.
Ouchi: focus is on the well-being of the employee needs	47. I believe a person may satisfy a particular need whether or not a previous need has been satisfied.
Porter and Lawler: based their work on Victor Vroom's expectancy theory	48. I have a need to perceive that I am a good teacher.

(*cont.*)

Motivation theorist and theory	RDMA-T items related to motivation theory
Alderfer: expands on the work of Maslow – when lower needs are satisfied, they occupy less of our attention, and the higher needs tend to become more important and so the more we pursue them	49. I have choices and control over my decisions.
Deci and Ryan: self-determination theory	50. I am connected to others through positive relationships.
	51. I do not believe that the best way to get students to perform tasks is to reinforce their behavior with rewards.
	52. I believe that a basic psychological need is autonomy.
Hackman and Oldham: job characteristics theory – characteristics (i.e., skill variety, task identity, task significance, autonomy, and feedback) affect work	53. I prefer a job that involves just one skill.
	54. When I receive clear, actionable information about my teaching performance, I have a better understanding of what specific actions I need to take (if any) to improve.

Items 20 and 53 should be reverse scored.

Appendix 6B Reisman Diagnostic Motivation Assessment – Student: Item Source Grid

Motivation theory and theorist	RDMA-S items related to motivation theory
Amabile: intrinsic motivation	1. I engage in my classwork for the pleasure of learning with no expectation of outside reward such as grade or other approval.
Piaget: adaptation	2. I adapt my thinking and needs to incoming information
	3. I adapt to my environment.
Maslow: needs hierarchy	4. My self-confidence and feeling that I can do a specified task motivate me.

(cont.)

Motivation theory and theorist	RDMA-S items related to motivation theory
Herzberg: motivating and hygiene factors	5. Challenging lessons, recognition, and responsibility give me positive satisfaction.
	6. Teacher or other positive recognition does not give me satisfaction, but dissatisfaction results from their absence.
Vroom: expectancy theory	7. I mostly value grades.
	8. I am confident about what I am capable of doing.
	9. My perception as to whether I will actually get what I desire as was promised by my teacher affects my motivation.
	10. My teacher ensures that promises of rewards are fulfilled and that I am aware of that.
	11. I act in ways that bring me pleasure and avoid pain.
McClelland: needs theory	12. I have a strong need to set and accomplish challenging goals.
	13. I take calculated risks to accomplish my goals.
	14. I like to receive regular feedback on my progress and achievements.
	15. I often like to work alone.
	16. I want to belong to a group.
	17. I want to be liked.
	18. I will often go along with whatever the rest of my classmates want to do.
	19. I favor collaboration over competition.
	20. I don't like high risk or uncertainty.
	21. I want to control and influence others.
	22. I like to win arguments.
	23. I enjoy competition and winning.
	24. I enjoy status and recognition.
Murray: needs	25. I need to enjoyably share with another.
	26. I need to be free and independent of others.
	27. I need to control or influence others.
	28. I need to be seen and heard and to entertain.
	29. I need to avoid injury and take precaution.
	30. I need to help, console, and nurse the weak.
	31. I prefer neatness.

(*cont.*)

Motivation theory and theorist	RDMA-S items related to motivation theory
	32. I need enjoyment and fun.
	33. I need to form stimulating relationships.
	34. I need to be loved.
	35. I need to analyze, speculate, and generalize.
	36. My motivation influences my behavior.
	37. My need for achievement is positively related to my schoolwork and future career success.
Skinner: reinforcement theory and operant conditioning	38. I repeat behavior that leads to positive consequences and avoid behavior that has had negative effects.
Bandura: self-efficacy	39. My perceived self-efficacy (I can do it) leads me to set higher goals.
Rogers: humanistic theory	40. My motivation becomes directed toward the satisfaction of others' expectations.
Argyris: there are relationships between the effort put forth, performance, and rewards	41. I will be motivated to exert a high level of effort when I believe there are relationships between the effort I put forth, the performance I achieve, and the outcomes/rewards I receive.
	42. My effort will improve my performance.
	43. My performance will lead to rewards.
	44. Rewards will satisfy my individual goals.
McGregor: high supervision versus self-directed employees	45. In contrast with a student refusing to learn, I am a person who relishes the opportunity to learn.
Urwick: an optimal managerial style would help cultivate worker creativity, insight, meaning, and moral excellence	46. An exciting teaching style helps cultivate my creativity.
Ouchi: focus is on the well-being of the employee needs	47. I believe a school environment focused on increasing student autonomy tends to promote high productivity, morale, and satisfaction.
Porter and Lawler: based their work on Victor Vroom's expectancy theory	48. I believe an individual's view regarding the attractiveness and fairness of rewards will affect motivation.
Alderfer: expands on the work of Maslow – when lower needs are satisfied, they occupy less of our attention, and the higher needs tend to become more important and so the more we pursue them	49. I believe a person may satisfy a particular need whether or not a previous need has been satisfied.

(cont.)

Motivation theory and theorist	RDMA-S items related to motivation theory
Deci and Ryan: self-determination theory	50. I have a need to perceive that I am good at something.
	51. I have choices and control over my decisions.
	52. I am connected to others through positive relationships.
Hackman and Oldham: job characteristics theory – characteristics (i.e., skill variety, task identity, task significance, autonomy, and feedback) affect work	53. I prefer a lesson that involves just one concept.
	54. When I receive clear, actionable information about my performance, I have a better understanding of what specific actions I need to take (if any) to improve.

Items 20 and 53 should be reverse scored.

Appendix 6C   Reisman Diagnostic Motivation Assessment – Corporate: Item Source Grid

Motivation theory and theorist	RDMA-C items related to motivation theory
Amabile: intrinsic motivation	1. I do something for the pleasure of accomplishing a task with no expectation of outside reward such as promotion or money.
Piaget: adaptation	2. I adapt my thinking and needs to incoming information.
	3. I adapt to my environment.
Maslow: needs hierarchy	4. My self-confidence and feeling that I can do a specified task motivate me.
Herzberg: motivating and hygiene factors	5. Challenging work, recognition, and responsibility give me positive satisfaction.
	6. Status, job security, salary, fringe benefits, and work conditions do not give me positive satisfaction, but dissatisfaction results from their absence.
Vroom: expectancy theory	7. I value money, promotion, time-off, and benefits.
	8. I am confident about what I am capable of doing.
	9. My perception as to whether I will actually get what I desire as was promised by my boss affects my motivation.
	10. My boss ensures that promises of rewards are fulfilled and that I am aware of that.
	11. I act in ways that bring me pleasure and avoid pain.
McClelland: needs theory	12. I have a strong need to set and accomplish challenging goals.

(cont.)

Motivation theory and theorist	RDMA-C items related to motivation theory
Murray: needs	13. I take calculated risks to accomplish my goals. 14. I like to receive regular feedback on my progress and achievements. 15. I often like to work alone. 16. I want to belong to the group. 17. I want to be liked. 18. I will often go along with whatever the rest of the group wants to do. 19. I favor collaboration over competition. 20. I don't like high risk or uncertainty. 21. I want to control and influence others. 22. I like to win arguments. 23. I enjoy competition and winning. 24. I enjoy status and recognition. 25. I need to enjoyably share with another. 26. I need to be free and independent of others. 27. I need to control or influence others. 28. I need to be seen and heard and to entertain. 29. I need to avoid injury and take precaution. 30. I need to help, console, and nurse the weak. 31. I need organization and neatness. 32. I need enjoyment and fun. 33. I need to form stimulating relationships. 34. I need to be loved. 35. I need to analyze, speculate, and generalize. 36. My motivation influences my behavior. 37. My need for achievement is positively related to my occupational and financial success.
Skinner: reinforcement theory and operant conditioning	38. I repeat behavior that leads to positive consequences and avoid behavior that has had negative effects.
Bandura: self-efficacy	39. My perceived self-efficacy leads me to set higher goals.
Rogers: humanistic theory	40. My motivation becomes directed toward the satisfaction of others' expectations.
Argyris: theory of management – there are relationships between the effort put forth, performance, and rewards	41. I will be motivated to exert a high level of effort when I believe there are relationships between the effort I put forth, the performance I achieve, and the outcomes/rewards I receive. 42. My effort will improve my performance. 43. My performance will lead to rewards.

6 Assessment of Motivation

(*cont.*)

Motivation theory and theorist	RDMA-C items related to motivation theory
	44. Rewards will satisfy my individual goals.
McGregor: high supervision versus self-directed employees	45. In contrast with a person refusing to work, I am a person who relishes the opportunity to work.
Urwick: management theory of motivation – an optimal managerial style would help cultivate worker creativity, insight, meaning, and moral excellence	46. A supportive managerial style helps cultivate my creativity.
Ouchi: increasing employee loyalty – focus is on the well-being of the employee and needs	47. I believe management focused on increasing employee loyalty to the company by providing a job for life with a strong focus on the well-being of the employee, both on and off the job, tends to promote stable employment, high productivity, and high employee morale and satisfaction.
Porter and Lawler: expectancy theory	48. I believe an individual's view regarding the attractiveness and fairness of rewards will affect motivation.
Alderfer: needs	49. I believe a person may satisfy a particular need whether or not a previous need has been satisfied.
Deci and Ryan: self-determination theory of motivation	50. I have a need to perceive that I am good at something.
	51. I have choices and control over my decisions.
	52. I am connected to others through positive relationships.

Item 20 should be reverse scored.

Appendix 6D Alternative Reisman Diagnostic Motivation Assessment Interpretation

The following is an alternative RDMA interpretation based upon a similar underpinning of theory groupings. Notice that several theories, although named differently and with slightly different emphasis, are abstractions of a particular motivation theory. It appears that the two

196 Connecting Creativity and Motivation Research with End Users

main motivation theories are *expectancy* and *needs*. This RDMA interpretation focuses on the Likert-type scale score instead of percentile rankings; for example, find the mean for the six expectancy items by dividing the score sum by 6. The mean (average) score is then interpreted using the following Likert-type scale: 1=very untrue of me, 2=untrue of me, 3=somewhat untrue of me, 4=neutral, 5=somewhat true of me, 6=true of me, and 7=very true of me.

Motivation main theory	Related theorists	Related items
Expectancy Expectancy motivation theory centers on people thinking about the future and formulating expectations about what they think will happen	Vroom Porter and Lawler	7. I value money, promotion, time-off, and benefits. 8. I am confident about what I am capable of doing. 9. My perception of whether I will get what I desire, as promised by my teacher(s), affects my motivation. 10. My teacher(s) ensure that promises of rewards are fulfilled and that I am aware of that. 11. I act in ways that bring me pleasure and avoid pain. 47. I have a need to perceive that I am good at something.
Needs A person's motivation is a result of personal needs.	Piaget Maslow McClelland Murray Alderfer Deci and Ryan McGregor	2. I adapt my thinking and needs to incoming information. 3. I adapt to my environment. 4. My self-confidence and feeling that I can do a specified task motivate me. 25. I need to enjoyably share with another. 26. I need to be free and independent of others. 27. I need to control or influence others. 28. I need to be seen and heard and to entertain. 29. I need to avoid injury and take precautions. 30. I need to help, console, and nurse the weak.

(cont.)

Motivation main theory	Related theorists	Related items
		31. I have a need for organization and neatness.
		32. I need enjoyment and fun.
		33. I need to form stimulating relationships.
		34. I need to be loved
		35. I need to analyze, speculate, and generalize.
		36. My motivation influences my behavior.
		37. My need for achievement is positively related to my self-concept.
		45. In contrast with a person refusing to learn, I am a person who relishes the opportunity to learn.
		48. I have choices and control over my decisions.
		49. I am connected to others through positive relationships.
		50. I do not believe that the best way to get someone to perform tasks is to reinforce their behavior with rewards.
		51. I believe that a basic psychological need is autonomy.
Satisfaction	Herzberg	5. Challenging classes, recognition, and responsibility give me positive satisfaction.
		6. Status, job security, salary, fringe benefits, and work conditions do not give me positive satisfaction, but dissatisfaction results from their absence.

References

Abramson, L. Y., Seligman, M. E. & Teasdale, J. D. (1978). Learned helplessness in humans: Critique and reformulation. *Journal of Abnormal Psychology*, 87(1), 49–74.

Amabile, T. M. (1996). *Creativity in Context: Update to "The Social Psychology of Creativity."* Boulder, CO: Westview Press.

Ames, C. (1992). Achievement goals and the classroom motivational climate. *Student Perceptions in the Classroom*, 1, 327–348.

Check, J. & Schutt, R. (2012). *Research Methods in Education*. Thousand Oaks, CA: Sage Publishing.

Cheon, S. H., Reeve, J. & Moon, I. S. (2012). Experimentally based, longitudinally designed, teacher-focused intervention to help physical education teachers be more autonomy supportive toward their students. *Journal of Sport & Exercise Psychology*, 34, 365–396.

Cheon, S. H. & Reeve, J. (2014). A classroom-based intervention to help teachers decrease student amotivation. *Contemporary Educational Psychology*, 40, 99–111.

Csikszentmihalyi, M. & Rathunde, K. (1993). The measurement of flow in everyday life: Toward a theory of emergent motivation. In J. E. Jacobs (ed.), *Nebraska Symposium on Motivation, 1992: Developmental Perspectives on Motivation* (pp. 57–97). Lincoln, NE: University of Nebraska Press.

Deci, E. L. (1971). Effects of externally mediated rewards on intrinsic motivation. *Journal of Personality and Social Psychology*, 18(1), 105–115. https://doi.org/10.1037/h0030644.

Deci, E. L. & Ryan, R. M. (1985). *Intrinsic Motivation and Self-Determination in Human Behavior*. Berlin: Springer Science & Business Media. https://doi.org/10.1007/978-1-4899-2271-7.

Deci, E. L. & Ryan, R. M. (1991). A motivational approach to self: Integration in personality. In R. A. Dienstbier (ed.), *Nebraska Symposium on Motivation, 1990: Perspectives on Motivation* (pp. 237–288). Lincoln, NE: University of Nebraska Press.

Deci, E. L. & Ryan, R. M. (2000). The "what" and "why" of goal pursuits: Human needs and the self-determination of behavior. *Psychological Inquiry*, 11, 227–268.

Department of Sociology (2019). Using the Rosenberg Self-Esteem Scale. University of Maryland. https://socy.umd.edu/about-us/using-rosenberg-self-esteem-scale.

Devaux M. & Sassi F. (2016). Social disparities in hazardous alcohol use: Self-report bias may lead to incorrect estimates. *European Journal of Public Health*, 26(1), 129-134. https://doi.org/10.1093/eurpub/ckv190.

Durand, V. M. & Crimmins, D. B. (1988). Identifying the variables maintaining self-injurious behavior. *Journal of Autism and Developmental Disorders*, 18(1), 99–117.

Durand, V. M. & Crimmins, D. B. (1992). *The Motivation Assessment Scale (MAS) Administration Guide*. Topeka, KS: Monaco and Associates.

Education World (n.d.). Six ways to really motivate teachers. www.education world.com/a_admin/six-ways-motivate-teachers.shtml.

Formplus (n.d.). Free student motivation survey template. www.formpl.us/tem plates/student-motivation-surve.

Flynn, J. (2023). 20 stunning great resignation statistics [2023]: How many people quit their jobs in 2022. Zippia. www.zippia.com/advice/great-resignation-statistics/.

Gagné, M. (2003). The role of autonomy support and autonomy orientation in prosocial behavior engagement. *Motivation and Emotion*, 27, 199–223.

Guay, F., Vallerand, R. J. & Blanchard, C. (2000). On the assessment of situational intrinsic and extrinsic motivation: The Situational Motivation Scale (SIMS). *Motivation and Emotion*, 24(3), 175–213. https://doi.org/10.1023/A:1005614228250.

Haim, A. (2002). The analysis and validation of the Motivation Assessment Scale-II test version: A structural equation model. ProQuest Dissertations Publishing, State University of New York at Albany.

Jupp, V. (ed.) (2006). Self-report study. *The SAGE Dictionary of Social Research Methods*. Washington, DC: Sage Publications.

Martin, A. J. (2001). The Student Motivation Scale: A tool for measuring and enhancing motivation. *Australian Journal of Guidance and Counselling*, 11, 1–20.

MindTools (n.d.). How self-motivated are you? www.mindtools.com/adosk97/h ow-self-motivated-are-you.

Pelletier, L. G., Fortier, M. S., Vallerand, R. J., Tuson, K. M., Brière, N. M. & Blais, M. R. (1995). Toward a new measure of intrinsic motivation, extrinsic motivation, and amotivation in sports: The Sport Motivation Scale (SMS). *Journal of Sport & Exercise Psychology*, 17, 35–53.

Reeve, J. (2015). *Understanding Motivation and Emotion* (6th ed.). Hoboken, NJ: John Wiley & Sons, Inc.

Reeve, J. (2018). *Understanding Motivation and Emotion* (7th ed.). Hoboken, NJ: Wiley.

Reisman, F., Keiser, L. & Otti, O. (2016). Development, use and implications of diagnostic creativity assessment app, RDCA – Reisman Diagnostic Creativity Assessment. *Creativity Research Journal*, 28(2), 177–187.

Reisman, F., Keiser, L. & Westphal, J. (2023). RKW Student – Enhancing Self-Motivation Diagnostic in Reisman. In F., Keiser, J., Westphal & P. Hammrich (eds.), *Creativity and Motivation Research Translated to Benefit Teachers and Students: Lab to Learner*. Cambridge, UK: Cambridge University Press.

Reisman, F., Keiser, L., Bach, C. & Fourie, M. (2024). Reisman Diagnostic Motivation Assessments (RDMA-T, RDMA-S, RDMA-C). In F., Keiser, J., Westphal & P. Hammrich (eds.), *Creativity and Motivation Research Translated to Benefit Teachers and Students: Lab to Learner*. Cambridge, UK: Cambridge University Press.

Rosenberg, M. (1965). Rosenberg Self-Esteem Scale (RSE). Acceptance and commitment therapy. *Measures Package*, 61, 52.

Sandhya, K. & Kumar, D.P. (2011). Employee retention by motivation. *Indian Journal of Science and Technology*, 4, 1778–1782. https://doi.org/10.17485/ijst/2011/v4i12.34.

Seifert, K. & Sutton, R. (2018). Motivation theories on learning. In R. E. West (ed.), *Foundations of Learning and Instructional Design Technology*. Provo, UT: EdTech Books.

Sundre, D. (n.d.). *Motivation Scale Background and Scoring Guide*. Harrisonburg, VA: Center for Assessment and Research Studies James Madison University.

Team, U. (2015). 14 best techniques to increase students' motivation. Unicheck Blog for Education Junkies. https://unicheck.com/blog/motivating-students.

Vallerand, R. J. (1997). Toward a hierarchical model of intrinsic and extrinsic motivation. *Advances in Experimental Social Psychology*, 29, 271–360. https://doi.org/10.1016/S0065-2601(08)60019-2.

CHAPTER 7

Additional Theorists on Creativity and Motivation

Advance Organizer. The additional theorists presented in this chapter provide a basis for understanding creativity and motivation. The theorists discussed include Piaget, Carl Rogers compared with Maslow, Skinner (reinforcement theory), Bandura (the self-efficacy concept), Festinger (a focus on cognitive dissonance), Flavell (the concept of metacognition), Adams (equity theory), and Rosenthal and Jacobson (the Pygmalion effect).

7.1 Introduction

The theorists presented in this chapter embody the foundation of knowledge that underlies this book's first chapters. Although they don't fit the typical creativity and motivation categories, these researchers/theorists provide historical value to complement the book's content.

7.2 Theorists

Jean Piaget

In addition to the material presented in Chapters 2 and 3, this chapter further explores Piaget's work. Piaget noted parallels between the processes of creativity and development: "The real problem is how to explain novelties. I think that novelties, i.e., creations, constantly intervene in development" (Piaget, 1971, p. 192). Piaget proposed that intrinsic motivation was the best way to motivate a child. Intrinsic motivation drives an individual to do something for the pleasure of satisfying a task with no expectation of outside reward such as grades or money. Although Piaget is noted for his emphasis on cognitive development, in terms of Piagetian theory, motivation is related to his concept of equilibration (Figure 7.1). Equilibration encompasses assimilation (i.e., people transform incoming information so that it fits within their existing thinking or needs) and accommodation

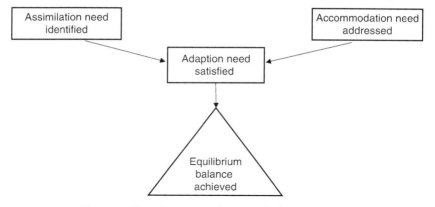

Figure 7.1 Piaget's cognitive theory applied to motivation.

(i.e., people adapt their thinking and needs to incoming information), which are components of adaptation (i.e., the individual's ability to adapt to their environment). Just as new learning stops when balance is reached and it is time for practice to consolidate the new learning, a similar application occurs in needs-based motivation. For example, a carrot can be mashed and is chewable for one with no teeth who is hungry and motivated to eat (assimilation); the eater either grows teeth as a baby or obtains false teeth as an adult so they can eat (accommodation) so the hunger need becomes satisfied (equilibrium). In relation to Piaget's theory, the individual is now ready to advance to the next developmental level.

Albert Einstein once described Piaget's observations on children's intellectual growth and thought processes as a discovery "so simple only a genius could have thought of it."

Carl Rogers

Carl Rogers maintained that there exists a social need for the creative behavior of creative individuals and believed the following:

> In education we turn out conformists and stereotypic rather than freely creative and original thinkers. In our leisure time activities, passive entertainment and regimented group action are predominant while creative activities are much less in evidence. In the sciences, there is an ample supply of technicians but the number who can creatively formulate fruitful hypothesis and theories is small. In industry creation is reserved for the few – the manager, the designer, the head of the research department; for many life is devoid of original or creative

endeavor. In individual and family life the same picture holds true in the clothes we wear, the food we eat, the books we read and the ideas we hold. There is a strong tendency toward conformity. Unfortunately, to be original or different is felt to be dangerous. (These remarks were in a paper delivered by Rogers at the creativity conference in Granville, OH, 1952.)

Central to Rogers's theory of motivation is that the self-concept is shaped by praise and acceptance often obtained from others, without conditions (Arts et al., 2009). To Rogers, self-concept is an individual's knowledge of who they are and has three components: (1) self-image, (2) self-esteem, and (3) the ideal self. Self-concept is active, dynamic, and malleable; it can be influenced by social situations and even one's motivation to seek self-knowledge. However, Rogers acknowledged that discrepancies for this occurring lead to inconsistencies between self-actualizing behavior and societal expectations (Rogers, 1989). Thus, human motivation becomes directed toward the satisfaction of others' expectations and may result in self-defeating behaviors.

According to Carl Rogers's theory of person-centered therapy (Rogers, 1959), humans have a fundamental motive – the tendency to self-actualize. This involves fulfilling one's potential and attaining the highest level of "human-beingness." In order to achieve self-actualization, Rogers believed that individuals must continually reflect upon and reinterpret their experiences, allowing for recovery, development, change, and growth. Rogers also posited that, by providing empathy, congruence, and unconditional positive regard, therapists could create a safe environment for clients to access their potential and progress toward self-actualization. Box 7.1 compares Maslow's and Rogers's ideas regarding self-actualization.

> **Box 7.1 Maslow's and Rogers's ideas regarding self-actualization**
>
> Maslow (see Chapter 3) believed that people would motivate themselves to achieve self-actualization only after their basic needs were met. For Maslow, self-actualization refers to one's desire for self-fulfillment; to become what they are potentially. Carl Rogers described self-actualization as the continuous lifelong process whereby an individual's self-concept is maintained and enhanced via reflection and the reinterpretation of various experiences, which enable the individual to recover, change, and develop (Rogers, 1951). Maslow found self-actualized people to be spontaneous, purposeful, and creative (Shultz & Schultz, 2019). Rogers's approach to self-actualization was similar to Maslow's, although Rogers's approach replaces a needs hierarchy with levels of congruence.

Burrhus Frederic Skinner

Skinner is noted for his reinforcement theory of motivation, which is referred to as operant conditioning theory. Behavior changes occur in response to stimuli or events that take place in the environment. An individual will repeat behavior that previously led to positive consequences and will avoid behavior that had negative effects. Skinner identified positive reinforcements as praise, appreciation, a good grade, trophy, money, promotion, or any other reward (Gordon, 1987). Negative reinforcement intends to stop the undesired behavior by inflicting unwanted consequences.

Albert Bandura

In 2002, Bandura was ranked as the fourth most frequently cited psychologist of all time in a survey. The psychologists who were ranked higher than him were B. F. Skinner, Sigmund Freud, and Jean Piaget. He was also ranked as the most cited living psychologist until his passing in 2021. Bandura (1973) investigated the learning of aggression, the processes that trigger violence, and the rewards and punishments of aggression. He also is known as the originator of self-efficacy, which he defined as a person's belief in their capability to accomplish a specific task. Bandura's research shows that highly perceived self-efficacy leads teachers and students to be motivated to set higher goals. Instructors may encourage self-efficacy by encouraging students to compare their performance with their own previous performance (not with that of other students), by pointing out links between effort and improvement, and by providing feedback about performance focused on facts, not evaluative judgments.

Robert Rosenthal and Lenore Jacobson

Robert Rosenthal defined the Pygmalion effect as the phenomenon whereby one person's expectation of another person's behavior serves as a self-fulfilling prophecy (Rosenthal & Jacobson, 1992). The Pygmalion effect occurs because others' expectations have an impact on both their own behavior and an individual's behavior. If someone believes one is likely to succeed, they will treat them differently to help achieve goals. The Pygmalion effect is a common feature of leader–follower dynamics, observed in relationships with managers or supervisors, military commanders, athletic coaches, or teachers. When leaders have high expectations of their followers, their followers tend to perform better.

The Pygmalion effect is a motivational phenomenon that occurs in interpersonal relationships, starting with leaders who have high expectations of their followers. These expectations are communicated verbally or nonverbally through the leader's behavior and have a positive impact on the followers' self-expectations and self-efficacy. As a result, the followers are motivated to exert more effort, leading to enhanced performance. This improved performance reinforces the leader's high expectations, creating a cycle of high expectations leading to high performance, which justifies continued high expectations and produces even higher performance. In this way, the self-fulfilling prophecy can become a self-sustaining prophecy. On the other hand, the self-fulfilling prophecy has a negative counterpart, known as the Golem effect, which can have detrimental effects. Unlike the Pygmalion effect, the Golem effect involves a decrease in leader expectations, resulting in a decrease in follower performance. In teaching, the Pygmalion effect occurs when teachers treat students differently because of their expectations. For example, students with low expectations may receive less attention or less detailed feedback. "When we expect certain behaviors of others, we are likely to act in ways that make the expected behavior more likely to occur" (Rosenthal & Babad, 1985). Box 7.2 discusses the origination of the term Pygmalion effect and Box 7.3 discusses that of the Golem effect.

Box 7.2   Pygmalion effect

The Pygmalion effect was named after the Greek sculptor Pygmalion, who fell in love with one of his own sculptures in the poem "Metamorphoses" by Ovid. In the story, Pygmalion begged the gods to grant him a wife who resembled his beloved sculpture, and the gods brought the sculpture to life. Rosenthal and Jacobson were inspired by this tale and gave their findings the same name in reference to the power of expectations in influencing behavior.

Box 7.3   Golem effect

The Golem effect shares similar foundational concepts with the Pygmalion effect, its theoretical counterpart. It was named after the clay creature from Jewish mythology, the golem, which was brought to life by Rabbi Loew of Prague. The golem's original purpose was to protect the Jewish community from Blood Libel, but it eventually became corrupt and uncontrollable, leading to its destruction. Babad, Inbar, and Rosenthal named this effect after the golem legend in 1982 to highlight the negative consequences of self-fulfilling prophecies that concern social scientists and educators.

> **Box 7.4 Types of metacognitive knowledge**
>
> Declarative knowledge, also known as "person knowledge," refers to the understanding of one's own capabilities. However, this type of metacognitive knowledge may not always be accurate, as an individual's self-assessment can be unreliable.
>
> Procedural knowledge, also known as "task knowledge," encompasses understanding the content (what needs to be known) and length (how much space is available to convey what is known) of a task. This type of knowledge is associated with an individual's perceived level of task difficulty and self-confidence.
>
> Strategy knowledge, also known as "conditional knowledge," refers to an individual's ability to use strategies for learning information and adapting them to new situations. This type of knowledge is dependent on the individual's age and/or developmental stage. For instance, a kindergartener can be taught strategies but may need to be reminded to use them, such as sounding out words when learning to read.

John Flavell

Flavell was one of the first psychologists to study the ways in which children think about their thinking processes, which he termed metacognition (Flavell, 1979). Metacognition is thinking about one's thinking process, including study skills, memory capabilities, and the ability to monitor learning. The term itself literally means "cognition about cognition" or, more colloquially, "thinking about thinking" (Flavell, 1979). Flavell found that, as children get older, they demonstrate more awareness of their thinking processes. Flavell identified two elements of metacognition: (1) knowledge, that is, understanding what you know about yourself as the cognitive processor, and (2) regulation, that is, managing or controlling how you go about learning or problem-solving. Box 7.4 lists Flavell's types of metacognitive knowledge (Flavell, 1985).

Metacognition involves the capacity of individuals to contemplate their thinking processes and their learning approach. Metacognitive processes play a vital role in planning, problem-solving, evaluation, and numerous aspects of language learning. Specifically, these processes are utilized to plan, monitor, and evaluate one's understanding and performance.

Leon Festinger

Cognitive dissonance theory, developed by Festinger in 1950 (Festinger, 1950), explains the mental conflict that arises when new information contradicts an individual's beliefs or assumptions. An inconsistency between thoughts or between thoughts and actions causes discomfort (dissonance), which motivates individuals to alter their thoughts or behaviors. The resulting unease or tension is typically relieved by engaging in one of several defensive maneuvers: rejecting, explaining away, or avoiding the new information; convincing oneself that there is no actual conflict; reconciling the differences; or adopting any other defensive measures to maintain stability or order in their worldview and self-concept.

John Stacey Adams

Adams's equity theory of motivation (Adams, 1963) posits that individuals require a perception of fairness in the rewards they receive for their contributions and that these rewards are comparable to those received by their peers in order to be motivated. If individuals perceive their rewards as unfair, they will experience distress and attempt to create a sense of equity. This process model of motivation holds that motivation is influenced by the degree of reward received in comparison to the individual's sense of contribution. The equity theory emphasizes the need for an equitable balance to be maintained between an employee's "inputs" (such as hard work, skill level, acceptance, and enthusiasm) and their "outputs" (such as salary, benefits, and intangible benefits such as recognition).

7.3 Content and Process Theories of Motivation

Content models of motivation define what motives or needs are present and focus on what people need (e.g., what motivates actions). Examples of content theories of motivation include McClelland's needs theory, Alderfer's existence, relatedness, and growth (ERG) theory, Herzberg's two factors theory, and Maslow's hierarchy of needs.

Process theories explain how and why motivations affect behaviors at the psychological and behavioral process levels, which in turn affect an individual's motivation. Examples of process theories of motivation include Locke's goal-setting theory, Skinner's reinforcement theory, Vroom's expectancy theory, and Adams's equity theory.

7.4 Summary

This chapter provides a supplement to Chapters 3 and 4 in that the theorists presented in this chapter offer a context for the previously presented creativity and motivation theories.

References

Adams, J. S. (1963). Towards an understanding of inequity. *The Journal of Abnormal and Social Psychology*, 675, 422–436.

Arts, G. H. P., Maltby, L., Arnold, D. et al. (2009). Aquatic macrophyte risk assessment for pesticides (AMRAP). In *2nd SETAC Europe Special Science Symposium on Current developments on Environmental Risk Assessment for Plant Protection Products*, (pp. 50–53). Brussels: SETAC Europe.

Bandura, A. (1973). *Aggression: A Social Learning Analysis*. Upper Saddle River, NJ: Prentice-Hall.

Festinger, L. (1950). Informal social communication. *Psychological Review*, 57(5), 271–282. https://doi.org/10.1037/h0056932.

Flavell, J. H. (1979). Metacognition and cognitive monitoring: A new area of cognitive–developmental inquiry. *American Psychologist*, 34(10), 906–911. https://doi.org/10.1037/0003-066X.34.10.906.

Flavell, J. H. (1985). *Cognitive Development* (2nd ed.). Englewood Cliffs, NJ: Prentice-Hall.

Gordon, A. D. (1987). A review of hierarchical classification. *Journal of the Royal Statistical Society: Series A (General)*, 150(2), 119–137.

Piaget, J. (1971). The theory of stages in cognitive development. In D. R. Green, M. P. Ford & G. B. Flamer (eds.). *Measurement and Piaget*. New York: McGraw-Hill.

Rogers, C. (1951). *Client-Centered Therapy: Its Current Practice, Implications and Theory*. London: Constable.

Rogers, C. (1959). A theory of therapy, personality and interpersonal relationships as developed in the client-centered framework. In S. Koch (ed.), *Psychology: A Study of a Science. Vol. 3: Formulations of the Person and the Social Context*. New York: McGraw Hill.

Rogers (1989). A client-centered/person-centered approach to therapy. In H. Kirschenbaum & V. L. Henderson (eds.), *The Carl Rogers Reader* (pp. 135–152). Boston: Houghton Mifflin.

Rosenthal, R. & Babad, E. Y. (1985). Pygmalion in the gymnasium. *Educational Leadership*, 43(1), 36–39.

Rosenthal, R. & Jacobson, L. (1992). *Pygmalion in the Classroom* (expanded ed.). New York: Irvington.

Shultz, D., & Schultz, S. (2019). *Theories of Personality*. Boston: Cengage Learning.

CHAPTER 8

Neuroscience of Creativity, Mindfulness, and Mind/Brain/Education Science

Advance Organizer. This chapter addresses the neuroscience of creativity in the context of the trends related to creativity and motivation; namely mindfulness and mind/brain/education (MBE) science. The topics covered in this chapter are the neuroscience of creativity, neuroscience methodology, mindfulness, mindfulness and creativity, mindfulness and motivation, mindfulness techniques, the benefits of mindfulness in education, and MBE science.

8.1 Introduction

Studies on the neuroscience of creativity challenge the common "neuromyth" of left-brain versus right-brain specialization that has been popular for the last several decades. Although debunked, this neuromyth tenaciously struggles to keep its hold in the public consciousness. Such neuromyths are hard to kill. Studies over the last ten years have shown that creativity involves multiple brain regions and various cognitive functions involving many areas across the brain's two hemispheres, refuting the notion of "analytical" left-brain versus "creative" right-brain specialization. Thus, creativity is not dependent upon any specific mental process or brain region. Such misunderstandings of the relationship between the brain and creativity highlight how poorly most people understand creativity and how to measure it. Sawyer (2011), a creativity researcher, points out a lack of consistency in how the term "creativity" is used in tasks designed to measure creativity and notes that these tasks involve a wide variety of cognitive processes that result in broad brain activity. This chapter seeks to understand the neuroscience of creativity related to creativity and motivation through the concepts of *mindfulness* and *mind/brain education*.

The concept of mindfulness is an emerging trend in the field of creativity and motivation that involves our own awareness of our own thoughts, feelings, bodily sensations, and surroundings. This concept has a rich history and is integrated into various techniques and practices. This chapter goes into the history of mindfulness, mindfulness techniques, mindfulness and meditation, the impact of mindfulness, how to practice mindfulness, mindfulness as a treatment for psychological disorders, and the benefits of mindfulness for educators. For example, mindfulness meditation involves intentionally focusing one's attention on the present moment without judgment. Research has shown that mindfulness can have a positive impact on creativity. Mindfulness can facilitate the creative process by enhancing attentional focus, reducing cognitive rigidity, and promoting divergent thinking. Practicing mindfulness can also assist individuals in managing stress, regulating emotions, and cultivating a more open and receptive mindset, further enhancing creativity.

Mind/brain/education (MBE) science is an interdisciplinary approach to learning that combines insights from neuroscience, psychology, and education to inform teaching methods, lesson designs, and school programs. This approach considers multiple factors that have an impact on learning, including cognitive development, social and emotional maturation, and individual differences in learning styles. By understanding how the brain learns and develops, educators can design better instructional strategies that optimize the learning process and foster creativity. For example, incorporating activities that promote active engagement, critical thinking, and problem-solving can enhance creativity in the classroom. Moreover, considering the social and emotional aspects of learning, such as creating a positive classroom environment and promoting self-regulation, can also support the development of creative-thinking skills.

The field of creativity and motivation is informed by the neuroscience of creativity and by mindfulness and MBE. These fields highlight the complex and multifaceted nature of creativity, which involves various cognitive processes and brain regions. Understanding these concepts can provide valuable insights for promoting creativity and motivation in educational settings and beyond.

8.2 Neuroscience of Creativity

The neuroscience of creativity is an interdisciplinary field that draws upon the principles of psychology, neurology, and biology to understand the brain-based mechanisms underlying creative processes. There has been a relatively new focus in the neuroscience of creativity on merging techniques that can "see" and measure brain activity as electrical recordings with newly established brain-imaging methods, and this has provided

8 Neuroscience of Creativity, Mindfulness, and MBE

valuable insights into how the brain functions during creative tasks. The following are four of the most common techniques currently used to record a person's cognition.

1. An electroencephalogram (EEG) creates brain images that measure the electrical activity of the brain, allowing researchers to study how different brain regions communicate during creative tasks.
2. Magnetoencephalography (MEG) creates brain images by measuring the magnetic fields produced by the brain's electrical activity, which can provide detailed information about the timing and location of brain activity during creativity.
3. Functional magnetic resonance imaging (fMRI) measures changes in blood flow within the brain, which can provide information about which brain regions are activated during creative tasks.
4. Positron emission tomography (PET) uses radioactive tracers infused into the bloodstream to detect areas of the brain that are involved in specific cognitive processes, including creativity.

The use and research of these techniques demonstrate that creativity involves complex interactions between various brain regions and neural networks, including those responsible for cognition, including sensory perception, attention, memory, language use, problem-solving, decision-making, reasoning, and intelligence (Colom et al., 2010).

The findings from neuroscience research suggest that creativity is not a separate or isolated mental process. Instead, it is a component of ordinary cognitive processes that occur in the brain. Therefore, creativity is grounded in ordinary mental processes (Boden, 1998; Ward, Smith & Finke, 1999; Weisberg, 1993), making creativity an integral part of neuroscience. Pfenninger and Shubik (2001, p. 217) proposed that "any theory on creativity must be consistent and integrated with contemporary understanding of brain function." The idea that creative thinking may come from everyday mental processes of creativity that can be measured has important implications for areas such as psychology, education, and the arts. It could also help us develop ways to improve creativity, treat creative difficulties, and encourage creative thinking in different areas.

8.3 Neuroscience Methodology

Chapter 1 discusses three primary methodologies that cognitive neuroscientists use to determine the relationship between the brain and cognition: the EEG, fMRI, and PET scan techniques. These techniques allow researchers to investigate how different brain regions are involved in cognitive functions. Neuroscientists agree that all cognitive function involves many regions of the brain (Dietrich, 2004; Onarheim & Friis-Olivarius, 2013).

However, there are limitations to using fMRI and PET scans due to the large size and cost of the scanners, as well as the requirement for participants to lie still and endure the loud noise of the scanner's motor. Even small bodily movements during the scans can introduce noise and potentially confound the results: Such movements can activate large brain regions and disrupt the signals associated with the cognitive processes being examined. As a result, studying individuals engaged in normal activities in their everyday lives using these methods is difficult because they may not capture all the complexity and dynamics of mental processes in real-world settings (Sawyer, 2011).

Sawyer (2011) grouped neuroscience studies relevant to creativity research into the following five categories.

1. **Insight.** Insight is a fundamental aspect of the creative process and refers to the sudden and often unexpected realization or understanding of a problem or solution. The exact nature and role of insight in creativity is widely debated by creativity researchers, with some researchers emphasizing the critical role played by insight (Cunningham et al., 2009; Ohlsson, 1992) and others arguing that insight plays no role and that creativity is essentially identical to everyday problem-solving (Patrick et al., 2015; Perkins, 1981; Weisberg, 1993, 2006). Insight is often described as a sudden "Aha!" moment, whereby a solution or understanding seems to come out of nowhere. Research has shown that insight is associated with distinct neural processes that occur at different time points during the creative process. Experiencing an "Aha!" moment may be influenced by an individual's cognitive load or cognitive capacity. Insight often involves the ability to make new connections between seemingly unrelated concepts, which requires the integration of different pieces of information in the brain.

    Cognitive overload refers to an individual's cognitive resources being overwhelmed by the demands of a task or situation or other stress, potentially hindering their ability to experience insight. While sleeping, the brain is engaged in memory consolidation whereby newly acquired information is integrated into existing knowledge structures. By consolidating memories during sleep, the brain clears neural interference from external stimuli and distractions, freeing up neural networks and pathways that may hinder the "Aha!" moment. Often, when external interference is reduced and the brain is not engaged in a rote-type act such as showering, laundry, washing dishes, ironing, etc., the insight will rise to the consciousness creating the "Aha" moment.

2. **Incubation and mind wandering.** Creative ideas involve a four-step process, according to Graham Wallas in his classic book entitled *The Art of Thought* (Wallas, 1926): preparation, *incubation*, illumination, and verification. The process provides a structured approach for generating creative ideas, but it is also important to allow for flexibility, experimentation, and open-mindedness to foster true creativity. Incubation is an important step in the creative idea process. It allows your mind to process information and ideas subconsciously, leading to new insights and connections that may not have been apparent during the active problem-solving phase.

    Sawyer (2011), who studied the cognitive processes underlying creativity, believes that *mind wandering* (i.e., allowing one's thoughts to drift while working on a task) is important to creativity, as it allows the mind to engage in divergent thinking, make new connections, and generate innovative ideas. It also facilitates incubation.

3. **Creative brains versus noncreative brains.** This comparison between creative and noncreative brains is important, as research has found that creative people show higher levels of alpha wave activity when engaged in creative tasks than medium- and low-creative groups, which have lower alpha wave activity (Martindale & Hines, 1975).

4. **Musical improvisation.** Improvisation studies (Bangert & Schlaug, 2006; Berkowitz & Ansari, 2010) indicate that there are domain-general mental processes in creativity, although no brain areas are uniquely associated with improvisation. However, musical improvisation offers a unique window into understanding the neural mechanisms underlying creative processes in the brain. It requires a combination of cognitive functions such as divergent thinking, working memory, attention, decision-making, and motor planning. Studying brain activity during improvisation can help researchers understand how these cognitive processes interact and contribute to generating novel musical ideas (see also Section 2.5, "Domain-General versus Domain-Specific Creativity," in Chapter 2).

5. **Differences with training.** Although studies have shown that experience and learning can lead to changes in neural patterns (e.g., Posner

& Raichle, 1994; Reiterer, Pereda & Bhattacharya, 2011), establishing causation between expertise in a domain and changes in brain structure or function requires careful investigation through longitudinal studies. Cross-sectional studies that compare experts and nonexperts can reveal differences in brain activity or structure between the two groups. However, they cannot definitively determine whether these differences are the result of expertise or if they existed prior to the acquisition of expertise. It is hypothesized that individuals who naturally have certain brain characteristics may be more inclined to pursue and excel in certain domains, such as music, art, or dance. In other words, individual differences in brain structure or function may predispose individuals to develop expertise in certain areas (Sawyer, 2011).

8.4 Mindfulness

In recent years, mindfulness has become increasingly popular, with many individuals and organizations embracing it to reduce stress, increase focus, and improve overall well-being. Mindfulness is practicing paying attention to the present moment purposefully and without judgment. It involves awareness of one's thoughts, feelings, bodily sensations, and the surrounding environment, while maintaining a nonreactive and nonjudgmental attitude. Mindfulness is often practiced through meditation but can also be incorporated into everyday activities such as walking, eating, and working.

The goal of mindfulness is to increase awareness and acceptance of the present moment and to cultivate a sense of calm and clarity. By paying attention to the present moment and becoming more aware of one's thoughts and emotions, mindfulness can help individuals better manage stress, reduce anxiety and depression, and improve overall well-being. Additionally, practicing mindfulness has been shown to improve cognitive function, including attention, memory, and decision-making.

8.5 Mindfulness and Creativity

Mindfulness can be a valuable tool for enhancing creativity. The following are six ways in which mindfulness and creativity often intersect.

1. **Enhanced focus.** Mindfulness practices can help improve concentration and focus, which are crucial components of the creative process. By being fully present and attentive to the task at hand, without

8 Neuroscience of Creativity, Mindfulness, and MBE

getting caught up in distractions or worries about the past or future, mindfulness can help creative individuals stay in the flow of their work, leading to enhanced productivity and creativity.

2. **Expanded awareness.** Mindfulness encourages individuals to be fully aware of their thoughts, emotions, and bodily sensations without judgment. This increased self-awareness can help creative individuals become more attuned to their own internal experiences and thought patterns, which can lead to insights and new perspectives that can fuel their creative process.

3. **Reduced judgment and fear of failure.** Mindfulness promotes a nonjudgmental attitude, allowing individuals to let go of self-criticism and fear of failure, which are common barriers to creativity. By accepting and acknowledging thoughts and emotions without judgment, mindfulness can help creative individuals to cultivate a more open, compassionate, and accepting mindset, freeing them to take risks and explore new ideas without the fear of being judged or failing.

4. **Cultivated curiosity and fresh perspectives.** Mindfulness encourages a beginner's mind, that is, an attitude of curiosity and openness to the present moment as if experiencing it for the first time. This mindset can help creative individuals to approach their work with fresh perspectives, allowing them to see familiar things in new ways and generate novel ideas.

5. **Improved emotional regulation.** Creativity often involves navigating complex emotions, and mindfulness can help individuals develop emotional regulation skills. By being aware of and accepting one's emotions without reacting impulsively, mindfulness can help creative individuals manage difficult emotions and use them as a source of inspiration and expression in their creative work.

6. **Enhanced sensory awareness.** Mindfulness involves being fully present and attuned to one's sensory experiences, namely seeing, hearing, smelling, tasting, and touching. This heightened sensory awareness can help creative individuals connect more deeply with their surroundings, drawing inspiration from their environment and incorporating sensory details into their creative work.

Mindfulness can foster a conducive mindset for creativity by enhancing focus, expanding awareness, reducing judgment and fear of failure, cultivating curiosity, improving emotional regulation, and enhancing sensory awareness. By incorporating mindfulness practices into their creative process, individuals can potentially tap into new sources of inspiration, gain fresh perspectives, and improve their overall creative output.

Mindfulness Enhances Creativity

Research suggests that mindfulness has a supportive relationship with creativity, particularly in the possibility of enhancing creativity. Henriksen, Richardson and Shack's (2020) comprehensive article captures various aspects of the relationship between mindfulness and creativity.

> Research demonstrates that mindfulness improves a person's ability to concentrate (Sedlmeier et al., 2012), decreases the fear of being judged, and enhances open-minded thinking while reducing aversive self-conscious thinking (Brown, Ryan & Creswell, 2007). These points map directly onto key characteristics of creative habits of working, thinking, and being in the world, including relaxation or flow states (improved concentration), risk-taking (requiring a lack of fear about judgment), and curiosity or open-mindedness/openness to experience (reducing self-conscious experience) (Prabhu, Sutton & Sauser, 2008). Logically, these effects suggest that mindfulness supports the skills associated with creativity, and research findings suggest that high levels of self-reported mindfulness correlate to creative practices (Colzato, Ozturk & Hommel, 2012).

Henriksen, Richardson and Shack (2020) further highlight that the skills gained in training to develop skills to improve mindfulness also help to increase creativity. As mindfulness is shown to assist in expanding open-mindedness (Carson & Langer, 2006), it thereby helps to increase one's ability to react to situations and problems differently (i.e., a "non-habitual fashion – which is at the crux of creativity" [Moore & Malinowski, 2009]). Overall, mindfulness training has also been shown to lesson anxiety and self-consciousness while improving working memory (Chiesa, Calati & Serretti, 2011). Fear and peer pressure can negatively affect creativity, particularly the risk-taking creativity factor of the Reisman Diagnostic Creativity Assessment, as discussed in Chapter 2.

8.6 Mindfulness and Motivation

Research studies suggest that mindfulness is "differentially related" to "different types" of motivations (see Chapter 3 for a list and descriptions of various types of motivation and their uses). Mindfulness therefore plays a facilitating role for highly autonomous forms of motivation, but not for externally controlled or self-controlling forms of motivation (Bradshaw

8 Neuroscience of Creativity, Mindfulness, and MBE

et al., 2020). This phenomenon is also in accord with self-determination theory, as explained in Chapter 3 (Ryan & Deci, 2017), whereby mindfulness increases mental clarity and self-awareness and promotes and facilitates the attainment of *intrinsically* motivated goals, but does *not* facilitate *extrinsically* motivated goals (e.g., money and prizes).

8.7 Mindfulness Techniques

The goal of any mindfulness technique is to achieve a state of focused relaxation by paying attention to one's emotions, thoughts, and sensations (free of judgment) so that the mind focuses on the present. Mindfulness can be enhanced by certain practices or activities, such as meditation, as described next.

Basic Mindfulness Meditation

Sit quietly and focus on breathing or one of the other areas of focus listed below. Notice that the mind will wander and, when this happens, bring awareness back in focus.

- **Body sensations**. Become aware of body sensations, such as tingling, pulsing, or no feeling, and pay attention to each body part in succession from head to toe.
- **Sensory**. Become aware of sights, sounds, smells, tastes, and touches without judgment. When the mind begins to wander, refocus your attention.
- **Emotions**. Focus on an emotion (e.g., joy, anger, or frustration).

The Mayo Clinic (2020) has shared the following mindfulness exercises on their website that might be helpful in mindfulness meditation training in addition to basic mindfulness meditation.

- **Pay attention.** It's hard to slow down and notice things in a busy world. Try to take the time to experience your environment with all of your senses – touch, sound, sight, smell, and taste. For example, when you eat a favorite food, take the time to smell, taste, and truly enjoy it.
- **Live in the moment.** Try to intentionally bring open, accepting, and discerning attention to everything you do. Find joy in simple pleasures.
- **Accept yourself.** Treat yourself the way you would treat a good friend.
- **Focus on your breathing.** When you have negative thoughts, try to sit down, take a deep breath, and close your eyes. Focus on your breath as

it moves in and out of your body. Sitting and breathing for even just a minute can help.
- **Body scan meditation.** Lie on your back with your legs extended and arms at your sides, palms facing up. Focus your attention slowly and deliberately on each part of your body, in order, from toe to head or head to toe. Be aware of any sensations, emotions, or thoughts associated with each part of your body.
- **Sitting meditation.** Sit comfortably with your back straight, feet flat on the floor, and hands in your lap. Breathing through your nose, focus on your breath moving in and out of your body. If physical sensations or thoughts interrupt your meditation, note the experience and then return your focus to your breath.
- **Walking meditation.** Find a quiet place 10 to 20 feet in length and begin to walk slowly. Focus on the experience of walking, being aware of the sensations of standing and the subtle movements that keep your balance. When you reach the end of your path, turn and continue walking, maintaining awareness of your sensations.

Source: Mayo Clinic (2020)

8.8 Benefits of Mindfulness in Education

Benefits for Teachers

Research demonstrates that when a teacher learns and implements mindfulness they benefit particularly in areas such as reduced stress and burnout, improved efficacy in their work, a more emotionally supportive classroom, and better classroom organization (Flook et al., 2010; Jennings et al., 2013; Zarate, Maggin & Passmore, 2019). In addition, they demonstrate greater compassion, connect better with students, are more at ease with teaching the curriculum, and are more satisfied with their jobs.

Benefits for Students

Studies find that students who practice mindfulness develop attention and learning skills, social and emotional skills, and resilience. They have also be found to have improved attention and focus, improved cognitive outcomes and behavior in school, improved social skills including enhanced empathy and perspective taking, and a decline in post-traumatic symptoms and depression (Baijal et al., 2011; Barnes, Bauza

& Treiber, 2003; Cheang, Gillions & Sparkes, 2019; Etherington & Costello, 2018; Jones, Greenberg & Crowley, 2015; Liehr & Diaz, 2010; Metz et al., 2013; Napoli, Krech & Holley, 2005; Raes et al., 2013; Schonert-Reichl et al., 2015; Sibinga et al., 2015). The generic influences on learning presented in Chapter 5 provide complementary tools to understand student needs and behavior.

Benefits for Schools

Young people in the United States are experiencing increasing rates of mental illness. Research demonstrates that mindfulness training in schools helps to prevent anxiety and depression. School-based mindfulness programs also promote engagement, emotion regulation, social skills, optimism, and productive behavior. Studies have demonstrated a link between positive emotional classroom climates and academic achievement (Mindful Schools, 2019). Research finds that mindfulness practice decreases stress and anxiety, increases attention, improves interpersonal relationships, and strengthens compassion. There appears to be a movement internationally to teach mindfulness in schools. Mindfulness education is a term that means the purposeful inclusion of mindfulness and mindful meditation principles, theories, and practices in education. Schools that incorporate mindfulness environments focus on the following goals: self-awareness, empathy, and techniques to calm and focus the mind.

Benefits for Corporations

Mindfulness programs help leaders and employees reflect effectively, focus sharply on the task at hand, master peak levels of stress, and recharge quickly. On an organizational level, mindfulness reduces sick days, increases trust in leadership, and boosts employee engagement.

The benefits of mindfulness and its impact on creativity are not limited to teachers, students, and school employees. The benefits of practiced mindfulness on creativity are transferable to the business and corporate world. Corporations and small businesses also experience similar benefits of mindfulness, namely improved focus, reduced stress, burnout avoidance, and improved motivation when their leadership and employees engage in mindfulness. Box 8.1 lists a sample of large corporations that have formally embraced mindfulness practices in their work settings.

> **Box 8.1 Companies that have embraced mindfulness**
>
> UnitedHealth Group, Target, Google, Sun Life Financial, Aetna, Hearst Publications, eBay, General Mills, Twitter, Apple, Nike, Deutsche Bank, Ford Motor Company, Cargill, Genentech, Facebook, Kaiser Permanente, Compusense, Green Mountain Coffee Roasters, Plantronics, Intel, Proctor & Gamble, McKinsey & Company, Astra Zeneca

8.9 Mind/Brain/Education Science

The field of MBE has implications for the study of creativity, as it can shed light on the cognitive and neural processes that underlie creative thinking and learning. MBE research can help us better understand how the mind and brain interact in the context of creativity, and how educational practices can optimize creative thinking.

The study of MBE emerged as an interdisciplinary field that focuses on the intersection of cognitive science, neuroscience, psychology, and education. Although several universities and institutions have been involved in the study of MBE, one of the prominent institutions that has been at the forefront of MBE research is Harvard University. The institution began MBE programming in the early 2000s. Other institutions that have significantly contributed to the field include Stanford University, the University of California, Berkeley, the University of Cambridge, and the Max Planck Institute for Human Development. The field is continuously evolving and continues to grow rapidly, with ongoing research and contributions from multiple institutions and scholars around the world.

The field of MBE is based on empirical research and scientific findings related to how the mind and brain develop and learn, and how these insights can be applied to educational practice. While there is no universally agreed upon set of principles for MBE, some common themes and principles that underpin the field include the following.

- **Taking an interdisciplinary approach.** MBE brings together knowledge and research from different fields, such as cognitive science, neuroscience, psychology, and education, to better understand how the mind and brain function in educational contexts.
- **Understanding brain plasticity.** The brain can change and adapt throughout life based on experiences and the environment, which can affect how we teach and learn. MBE acknowledges the importance of brain plasticity and how it can be used to improve educational outcomes.

- **Considering developmental changes.** MBE recognizes that the mind and brain develop and change over time and that educational practices should consider these changes. This includes understanding how the mind and brain change from infancy to adulthood and how these changes affect learning and education.
- **Acknowledging individual differences.** MBE understands that learners are diverse and have unique cognitive, emotional, and social characteristics. It is important to consider and address these individual differences, such as learning styles, cognitive strengths and weaknesses, and cultural backgrounds, when designing effective educational practices.
- **Using evidence-based practice.** MBE emphasizes using rigorous scientific research and empirical evidence to inform educational practices. It encourages integrating research findings into educational policies and practices and critically evaluating educational interventions and strategies.

MBE principles are not set in stone by one person or group but are based on the combined knowledge and research of experts in fields studying MBE. As new research and insights come to light, the field of MBE will continue to evolve, and the principles may change as our understanding of the mind, brain, and education grows.

Mind/Brain/Education in the Education Field

An interdisciplinary approach is a key aspect of MBE. The approach integrates findings from cognitive science and neuroscience to uncover the cognitive processes involved in creative thinking. It examines the brain networks associated with creativity – such as those involved in divergent thinking, idea generation, and mental flexibility – to identify how each is activated and coordinated during the creative process. This knowledge can inform educational practices that foster creativity, such as providing opportunities for open-ended problem-solving, encouraging exploration and experimentation, and promoting flexible thinking.

Lopata et al. (2022) note, "Given that creativity is a 21st century educational priority, it is imperative for educators to begin considering how to design creativity-supportive learning experiences with these modes at the front of their minds." They also note that Bloom's original taxonomy of educational objectives (Anderson & Krathwohl, 2001; Bloom,

1956) classified twenty-one learning goals in the cognitive dimension of the taxonomy's learning objective, which became the standard framework for lesson design in schools. Those learning goals were further delineated into six categories of processes: knowledge, comprehension, application, analysis, synthesis, and evaluation. In 2001, the six categories of the taxonomy were "rephrased" to include the cognitive component: as well as remembering, understanding, analyzing, and evaluating, and, significantly, "synthesis" was recharacterized as "creating" and elevated to the top of the hierarchy (Lopata et al., 2022). "This revision marked the formal recognition of creativity as a critical, higher order learning objective, and the arrival of creativity's position at the summit of educational priorities" (Lopata et al., 2022).

Although acceptance of creativity as a component of education has been slow and contentious, the acceptance of "creating" as a critically important objective is gaining momentum. Particularly in the context of the COVID-19 pandemic and various societal and political changes during the last several years, Lopata et al. (2022) note that, "With the arrival of the 21st century, the challenges of uncertain socioeconomic and planetary reality are becoming increasingly apparent, and more are joining the call to transform education to appreciably emphasize creativity" (p. 81). Creativity is identified as one of the critical skills, if not the top critical skill, needed by students for employability and general success following graduation (Whiting, 2020). Creativity needs to be an educational priority, and both educators and education administrators need to immediately begin designing and delivering curricula that support creativity (Lopata et al., 2022).

8.10 Summary

This chapter addressed three trends related to creativity and motivation, namely the neuroscience of creativity, mindfulness, and MBE. This information should form a basis for teachers' education curricula if pedagogy is to incorporate the latest learning and teaching research. Chapters 9 and 10 provide twenty-nine lesson plans in the form of modules that translate research into practice. In addition, the Freddie Reisman Center for Translational Research in Creativity and Motivation is available for readers of this book to use these modules, provide suggested lesson modifications, and share ideas for future related research to the FRC via http://frcenter.net.

References

Anderson, L. W. & Krathwohl, D. R. (2001). *A Taxonomy for Learning, Teaching, and Assessing: A Revision of Bloom's Taxonomy of Educational Objectives*. Harlow, UK: Longman.

Baijal, S., Jha, A. P., Kiyonaga, A., Singh, R. & Srinivasan, N. (2011). The influence of concentrative meditation training on the development of attention networks during early adolescence. *Frontiers in Psychology*, 2. https://doi.org/10.3389/fpsyg.2011.00153.

Bangert, M. & Schlaug, G. (2006). Specialization of the specialized in features of external human brain morphology. *European Journal of Neuroscience*, 24(6), 1832–1834. https://doi.org/10.1111/j.1460-9568.2006.05031.x.

Barnes, V. A., Bauza, L. B. & Treiber, F. A. (2003). Impact of stress reduction on negative school behavior in adolescents. *Health and Quality of Life Outcomes*, 1(10), 1–7.

Berkowitz, A. L. & Ansari, D. (2010). Expertise-related deactivation of the right temporoparietal junction during musical improvisation. *NeuroImage*, 49(1), 712–719. https://doi.org/10.1016/j.neuroimage.2009.08.042.

Bloom, B. S. (1956). *Taxonomy of Educational Objectives. Vol. 1: Cognitive Domain*. Midland, MI: McKay.

Boden, M. A. (1998). Creativity and artificial intelligence. *Artificial Intelligence*, 103 (1–2), 347–356. https://doi.org/10.1016/s0004-3702(98)00055-1.

Bradshaw, C. J. A., Ehrlich, P. R., Beattie, A. et al. (2020). Underestimating the challenges of avoiding a ghastly future. *Frontiers in Conservation Science*, 1(10), 1–13. https://doi.org/10.3389/fcosc.2020.615419.

Brown, K. W., Ryan, R. M. & Creswell J. D. (2007). Mindfulness: Theoretical foundations and evidence for its salutary effects. *Psychological Inquiry*, 18(4), 211–237.

Carson, S. H. & Langer, E. J. (2006). Mindfulness and self-acceptance. *Journal of Rational-Emotive & Cognitive-Behavior Therapy*, 24(1), 29–43. https://doi.org/10.1007/s10942-006-0022-5.

Cheang, R., Gillions, A. & Sparkes, E. (2019). Do mindfulness-based interventions increase empathy and compassion in children and adolescents: A systematic review. *Journal of Child and Family Studies*, 28(7), 1765–1779. https://doi.org/10.1007/s10826-019-01413-9.

Chiesa, A., Calati, R. & Serretti, A. (2011). Does mindfulness training improve cognitive abilities? A systematic review of neuropsychological findings. *Clinical Psychology Review*, 31(3), 449–464. https://doi.org/10.1016/j.cpr.2010.11.003.

Colom, R., Karama, S., Jung, R. E. & Haier, R. J. (2010). Human intelligence and brain networks. *Dialogues in Clinical Neuroscience*, 12:4, 489–501. https://doi.org/10.31887/DCNS.2010.12.4/rcolom.

Colzato, L. S., Ozturk, A. & Hommel, B. (2012). Meditate to create: The impact of focused-attention and open-monitoring training on convergent and divergent thinking. *Frontiers in Psychology*, 3. https://doi.org/10.3389/fpsyg.2012.00116.

Cunningham, J. B., MacGregor, J. N., Gibb, J. & Harr, J. (2009). Categories of insight and their correlates: An exploration of relationships among classic-type insight problems, rebus puzzles, remote associates and esoteric analogies. *The Journal of Creative Behavior*, 43(4), 262–280. https://doi.org/10.1002/j.2162-6057.2009.tb01318.x.

Dietrich, A. (2004). The cognitive neuroscience of creativity. *Psychonomic Bulletin & Review*, 11(6), 1011–1026.

Etherington, V. & Costello, S. (2018). Comparing universal and targeted delivery of a mindfulness-based program for anxiety in children. *Journal of Psychologists and Counsellors in Schools*, 29(01), 22–38. https://doi.org/10.1017/jgc.2018.22.

Flook, L., Smalley, S. L., Kitil, M. J., et al. (2010). Effects of mindful awareness practices on executive functions in elementary school children. *Journal of Applied School Psychology*, 26(1), 70–95.

Henriksen, D., Richardson, C. & Shack, K. (2020). Mindfulness and creativity: Implications for thinking and learning. *Thinking Skills and Creativity*, 37(37), 100689. https://doi.org/10.1016/j.tsc.2020.100689.

Jennings, P. A., Frank, J. L., Snowberg, K. E., Coccia, M. A. & Greenberg, M. T. (2013). Improving classroom learning environments by Cultivating Awareness and Resilience in Education (CARE): Results of a randomized controlled trial. *School Psychology Quarterly*, 28(4), 374–390. https://doi.org/10.1037/spq0000035.

Jones, D. E., Greenberg, M. & Crowley, M. (2015). Early social-emotional functioning and public health: The relationship between kindergarten social competence and future wellness. *American Journal of Public Health*, 105(11), 2283–2290. https://doi.org/10.2105/ajph.2015.302630.

Liehr, P. & Diaz, N. (2010). A pilot study examining the effect of mindfulness on depression and anxiety for minority children. *Archives of Psychiatric Nursing*, 24(1), 69–71. https://doi.org/10.1016/j.apnu.2009.10.001.

Lopata, J. A., Barr, N., Slayton, M. & Seli, P. (2022). Dual-modes of creative thought in the classroom: Implications of network neuroscience for creativity education. *Translational Issues in Psychological Science*, 8(1), 79–89. https://doi.org/10.1037/tps0000317.

Martindale, C. & Hines, D. (1975). Creativity and cortical activation during creative, intellectual and EEG feedback tasks. *Biological Psychology*, 3(2), 91–100. https://doi.org/10.1016/0301-0511(75)90011-3.

Mayo Clinic (2020). Mindfulness exercises. Mayo Clinic. www.mayoclinic.org/healthy-lifestyle/consumer-health/in-depth/mindfulness-exercises/art-20046356.

Metz, S. M., Frank, J. L., Reibel, D., Cantrell, T., Sanders, R. & Broderick, P. C. (2013). The effectiveness of the learning to BREATHE program on adolescent emotion regulation. *Research in Human Development*, 10(3), 252–272. https://doi.org/10.1080/15427609.2013.818488.

Mindful Schools (2019). Research on mindfulness in education. www.mindfulschools.org/about-mindfulness/research-on-mindfulness/.

Moore, A. & Malinowski, P. (2009). Meditation, mindfulness and cognitive flexibility. *Consciousness and Cognition*, 18(1), 176–186. https://doi.org/10.1016/j.concog.2008.12.008.

Napoli, M., Krech, P. R. & Holley, L. C. (2005). Mindfulness training for elementary school students. *Journal of Applied School Psychology*, 21(1), 99–125. https://doi.org/10.1300/j370v21n01_05.

Ohlsson, S. (1992). Information-processing explanations of insight and related phenomena. In M. T. Keane & K. J. Gilhooly (eds.), *Advances in the Psychology of Thinking* (pp. 1–144). London: Harvester Wheatsheaf.

Onarheim, B. & Friis-Olivarius, M. (2013). Applying the neuroscience of creativity to creativity training. *Frontiers in Human Neuroscience*, 7. https://doi.org/10.3389/fnhum.2013.00656.

Patrick, J., Ahmed, A., Smy, V., Seeby, H. & Sambrooks, K. (2015). A cognitive procedure for representation change in verbal insight problems. *Journal of Experimental Psychology: Learning, Memory, and Cognition*, 41(3), 746–759. https://doi.org/10.1037/xlm0000045.

Perkins, D. N. (1981). *The Mind's Best Work*. Cambridge, MA: Harvard University Press.

Pfenninger, K. H. & Shubik, V. R. (2001). Insights into the foundation of creativity: A synthesis. In K. H. Pfenninger & V. R. Shubik (eds.), *The Origins of Creativity* (pp. 213–236). Oxford: Oxford University Press.

Posner, M. I. & Raichle, M. E. (1994). *Images of Mind*. New York: Scientific American Library.

Prabhu, V., Sutton, C. & Sauser, W. (2008). Creativity and certain personality traits: Understanding the mediating effect of intrinsic motivation. *Creativity Research Journal*, 20(1), 53–66. https://doi.org/10.1080/10400410701841955.

Raes, F., Griffith, J. W., Van der Gucht, K. & Williams, J. M. G. (2013). School-based prevention and reduction of depression in adolescents: A cluster-randomized controlled trial of a mindfulness group program. *Mindfulness*, 5(5), 477–486. https://doi.org/10.1007/s12671-013-0202-1.

Reiterer, S., Pereda, E. & Bhattacharya, J. (2011). On a possible relationship between linguistic expertise and EEG gamma band phase synchrony. *Frontiers in Psychology*, 2. https://doi.org/10.3389/fpsyg.2011.00334.

Ryan, R. M. & Deci, E. L. (2017). *Self-Determination Theory: Basic Psychological Needs in Motivation, Development, and Wellness*. New York: Guilford Press.

Sawyer, K. (2011). The cognitive neuroscience of creativity: A critical review. *Creativity Research Journal*, 23(2), 137–154.

Schonert-Reichl, K. A., Oberle, E., Lawlor, M. S., et al. (2015). Enhancing cognitive and social–emotional development through a simple-to-administer mindfulness-based school program for elementary school children: A randomized controlled trial. *Developmental Psychology*, 51(1), 52–66. https://doi.org/10.1037/a0038454.

Sedlmeier, P., Eberth, J., Schwarz, M., Zimmermann, D., Haarig, F. & Jaeger, S. (2012). The psychological effects of meditation: A meta-analysis. *Psychological Bulletin*, 138(6), 1139–1171. https://doi.org/10.1037/a0028168.

Sibinga, E. M. S., Webb, L., Ghazarian, S. R. & Ellen, J. M. (2015). School-based mindfulness instruction: An RCT. *Pediatrics*, 137(1), e20152532. https://doi.org/10.1542/peds.2015-2532.

Wallas, G. (1926). *The Art Of Thought*. Poole, UK: Solis Press.

Ward, T. B., Smith, S. M. & Finke, R. A. (1999). Creative cognition. In R. J. Sternberg (ed.), *Handbook of Creativity* (pp. 189–212). Cambridge, UK: Cambridge University Press.

Weisberg, R. W. (1993). *Creativity: Beyond the Myth of Genius*. New York: W. H. Freeman.

Weisberg, R. W. (2006). Modes of expertise in creative thinking: Evidence from case studies. In K. A. Ericsson, N. Charness, P. J. Feltovich & R. R. Hoffman (eds.), *The Cambridge Handbook of Expertise and Expert Performance* (pp. 761–787). Cambridge, UK: Cambridge University Press. https://doi.org/10.1017/CBO9780511816796.042.

Whiting, K. (2020). These are the top 10 job skills of tomorrow – and how long it takes to learn them. World Economic Forum. www.weforum.org/agenda/2c20/10/top-10-work-skills-of-tomorrow-how-long-it-takes-to-learn-them/.

Zarate, K., Maggin, D. M. & Passmore, A. (2019). Meta-analysis of mindfulness training on teacher well-being. *Psychology in the Schools*, 56(10), 1700–1715. https://doi.org/10.1002/pits.22308.

CHAPTER 9

Creativity Modules

Advance Organizer. This chapter consists of modules that incorporate the foundational knowledge on creativity presented in Chapter 2, as well as instruction regarding creativity. The module design incorporates the topic name, background information, instructional activities, suggested assessment techniques, and module references. Teacher scenarios are sprinkled throughout the chapter in boxes entitled "Voice from the field." These modules also are available to teachers, corporate trainers, and parents of students of kindergarten to twelfth grade (K–12) through the Freddie Reisman Center for Translational Research in Creativity and Motivation (FRC) at Drexel University, as described in Chapter 1 and on the FRC website: www.frcenter.net/. Readers of this book are invited to send feedback, suggest module modification, and share ideas for further related research to freddie@drexel.edu.

9.1 Introduction

Creativity characteristics include imaginative thinking; the ability to come up with unusual, unique, or clever responses; an adventurous spirit or a willingness to take risks; the ability to generate a large number of ideas or solutions to problems or questions; a sense of humor; and a tendency to see humor in situations that may not appear to be humorous to others.

This chapter provides modules (analogous to lesson plans) based on the information presented in Chapters 2 and 5 on creativity. Creativity Modules 9.1 to 9.4 and 9.17 and 9.18 include a variety of discussions regarding creativity, while Creativity Modules 9.5 to 9.14 are designed around the research-based Reisman Diagnostic Creativity Assessment (RDCA) factors, namely originality, fluency, elaboration, tolerance for ambiguity, smart risk-taking, resistance to premature closure, flexibility, divergent thinking, convergent thinking, and intrinsic and extrinsic motivation.

Creativity Module 9.15 incorporates a new place value pedagogy that rejects the wrong and ineffective bundling of the tens approach, and Creativity Module 9.16 uses the counting boards for computation.

One can either pursue activities to further enhance the factors that are already considered strong for practicing and expanding upon creative strengths or focus on those factors considered weak that one might wish to strengthen. The RDCA-related modules also incorporate generic influences on learning, as described in Chapter 5. The creativity modules are for K–12 regular and special education students, as well as corporate employees, and thus offer creative pedagogies for a broad learner population. Stories and scenarios are sprinkled throughout the chapter and provide practical contributions from end-users' perspectives. Modules comprise a title, background information, activities, assessment suggestions, and relevant references.

9.2 Modules

The following modules are based on content from previous chapters, especially Chapters 2 and 5, which address creativity.

Creativity Module 9.1
What is creativity?

Background Information

Since the 1800s, there have been debates on how to define creativity, ranging from simple to complex (Plucker, Beghetto & Dow, 2004). Some researchers have proposed an element of surprise, while others think creative things should be "worthwhile" (Runco & Jaeger, 2012). The first clear definition of creativity was offered by New York University Emeritus Professor Moe Stein (Stein, 1953):

> The creative work is a novel work that is accepted as tenable or useful or satisfying by a group in some point in time. By "novel" I mean that the creative product did not exist previously in precisely the same form. The extent to which a work is novel depends on the extent to which it deviates from the traditional or the status quo. This may well depend on the nature of the problem that is attacked, the fund of knowledge or experience that exists in the field at the time, and the characteristics of the creative individual and those of the individuals with whom he (or she) is communicating.

Thus, a creative idea or product must be original, novel, unique, unusual, and relevant or useful.

The following 14 components of creativity (Jordanous, 2012), which we first introduced in Chapter 2, provide a structure for understanding creativity.

1. **Active involvement and persistence.** Being actively involved in, reacting to, and having a deliberate effect on a process. The tenacity to persist with a process throughout, even at problematic points. This is sometimes referred to as grit (Duckworth, 2016).
2. **Dealing with uncertainty.** Coping with incomplete, missing, inconsistent, uncertain, or ambiguous information. There is an element of risk and chance, without guaranteeing that problems can or will be resolved. Not relying on every step of the process to be specified in detail and avoiding routine or preexisting methods and solutions.
3. **Domain competence.** Domain-specific intelligence, knowledge, talent, skills, experience, and expertise. Knowing a domain well enough to be equipped to recognize gaps, needs, or problems that need solving, as well as to generate, validate, develop, and promote new ideas in that domain.
4. **General intellect.** General intelligence and intellectual ability. Flexible and adaptable mental capacity.
5. **Generation of results.** Working toward some end target, goal, or result. Producing something (tangible or intangible) that previously did not exist.
6. **Independence and freedom.** Working independently with autonomy over actions and decisions. Freedom to work without being bound to preexisting solutions, processes, or biases, perhaps challenging cultural or domain norms.
7. **Intention and emotional involvement.** Personal and emotional investment, immersion, self-expression, and involvement in a process. Intention and desire to perform a task; a positive process giving fulfillment and enjoyment.
8. **Originality.** Novelty and uniqueness – a new product, doing something in a new way, or seeing new links and relations between previously unassociated concepts. Results that are unpredictable, unexpected, surprising, unusual, or out of the ordinary.
9. **Progression and development.** Movement, advancement, evolution, and development during a process. While progress may or may not be linear, and an actual end goal may be only loosely specified (if at all), the entire process should represent some developmental progression in a particular domain or task.

10. **Social interaction and communication.** Communicating and promoting work to others persuasively and positively. The mutual influence, feedback, sharing, and collaboration between society and individual.
11. **Spontaneity/subconscious processing.** No need to be in control of the whole process – thoughts and activities may inform a process subconsciously without being fully accessible for conscious analysis. Being able to react quickly and spontaneously during a process when appropriate, without needing to spend time thinking about options too much.
12. **Thinking and evaluation.** Consciously evaluating several options to recognize potential value in each and identify the best option, using reasoning and good judgment and then proactively selecting a decided choice from possible options, without allowing the process to stagnate under indecision.
13. **Value.** Making a useful contribution valued by others and recognized as an influential achievement; perceived as special.
14. **Variety, divergence, and experimentation.** Generating a variety of different ideas to experiment with different options without bias and multitasking during a process (Jordanous, 2012).

Activities

Activity 1
The following are activities that elicit creative thinking:

- viewing things in new ways or from a different perspective
- generating new possibilities or unique alternatives to situations
- practicing adding details to ideas through drawings, writing, or speaking
- practicing being comfortable with the unknown
- practicing generating many ideas in a situation
- practicing generating many categories of ideas
- practicing keeping an open mind to situations
- practicing coming up with multiple possibilities when analyzing a problem by looking at every angle of the situation
- practicing making a decision when there are multiple possibilities or choices
- taking calculated risks in selected situations

Activity 2
Review Appendix 5C in Chapter 5, which provides tips for teachers in applying the generic influences on learning.

Activity 3
Self-awareness is key to many different aspects of creativity, including mindfulness. In fact, the World Health Organization lists self-awareness as one of the ten life skills that promote well-being across all cultures (Positive Action Staff, 2020). The following is a list of the other nine critical life skills:

- empathy
- critical thinking
- creative thinking
- responsible decision-making
- problem-solving
- effective communication
- interpersonal relationships
- coping with stress
- coping with emotions

Recognizing one's emotions and the emotions of others is the first step to becoming self-aware, which is complementary to creativity. Self-aware individuals hold a basic conviction in their capacity to reach their objectives. This characteristic enables them to prosper in all aspects of their lives, including recognizing and improving their artistic aptitudes. To attain self-awareness, it is necessary to possess the following four abilities.

1. **Identify your emotions.** Your students need to be able to recognize their emotions. Distinguishing between frustration and anger will aid them in managing their emotions effectively. Once they acknowledge the connection between their feelings, thoughts, and behaviors, they can deal with their emotions and respond suitably.
2. **See yourself honestly.** Teaching your students to examine themselves truthfully can enable them to receive compliments, feedback, and criticism candidly and forthrightly. As their self-awareness develops, they will learn to recognize and accept their positive and negative qualities.
3. **Recognize your strengths and weaknesses.** Developing the capacity of your students to perceive themselves, recognize their limitations, and embrace their abilities is an excellent way to enhance their self-assurance. Being aware that it is acceptable to acknowledge their mistakes or lack of understanding sets them up for progress. Similarly, acknowledging their proficiency also helps to strengthen their self-confidence.
4. **Work toward growth.** These competencies collectively lead students to develop self-efficacy. They understand that self-improvement and

progress are beneficial endeavors that motivate contented and confident individuals to attain their goals.

The following are some ideas for how to develop self-awareness.

- **Positive awareness.** Ask the students to list the qualities they appreciate about themselves. If necessary, provide suggestions such as "I am optimistic" or "I am innovative." Motivate the older students to introspect more profoundly. The students should keep this list in a prominent location where they can frequently glance at it to strengthen their confidence in their positive attributes.
- **Keep an emotion journal.** Have the students maintain an emotion journal as they learn to recognize and categorize their emotions. This may entail the younger students using emoji faces, while older students keep an electronic journal. Allocating a daily "emotional assessment" period enables the students to comprehend and examine their emotions.
- **Establish and work toward goals.** Accomplishing self-awareness targets and objectives provides students with accomplishments that will reinforce confidence in their abilities. Encourage students to establish practical objectives and note the necessary steps to achieve them. Also consider creating a collective objective for the class to strive toward throughout the academic year.
- **Use your strengths.** Assist the students in recognizing their areas of expertise. The process of identifying their strength areas helps with a more positive self-perception. Finding ways to enhance these strength areas fosters self-assurance, which helps lay the groundwork for future achievements.

Activity 3 is adapted from Positive Action Staff (2020)

Assessments

1. List your new insights regarding creativity.
2. Work through *The Teaching Self-Reflection Tool and Skills Checklist*, which contains examples that reflect effective teaching as identified by a majority of Thomas Jefferson University's occupational therapy faculty (Lorch, 2013a, 2013b; see Box 9.1 for permission statement).

Box 9.2 contains the checklist of *The Teaching Self-Reflection Tool and Skills Checklist*.

> **Box 9.1** *The Teaching Self-Reflection Tool and Skills Checklist*: permission statement
>
> This article is brought to you for free and open access by the Jefferson Digital Commons. The Jefferson Digital Commons is a service of Thomas Jefferson University's Center for Teaching and Learning (CTL). The Commons is a showcase for Jefferson books and journals, peer-reviewed scholarly publications, unique historical collections from the University archives, and teaching tools. The Jefferson Digital Commons allows researchers and interested readers anywhere in the world to learn about and keep up to date with Jefferson scholarship. This article has been accepted for inclusion in Department of Occupational Therapy Faculty Papers by an authorized administrator of the Jefferson Digital Commons. For more information, please contact: JeffersonDigitalCommons@jefferson.edu.
>
> Source: Lorch (2013b)

> **Box 9.2** *The Teaching Self-Reflection Tool and Skills Checklist*: checklist
>
> **Organization of Teaching**
> 1. Has informed students about preparation (reading or other assignments) they should have completed prior to class
> 2. Arranges materials/information before class and is well prepared for class
> 3. Begins class on time in an organized manner
> 4. There is a clear organizational plan, but instructor is flexible if adaptations to the plan are needed
> 5. Manages class time effectively (structures time so session objectives/topics are covered and activities implemented)
> 6. Adapts smoothly to back-up plan when necessary (uses board, etc., if Microsoft PowerPoint malfunctions, addresses misunderstandings, provides further application activities, if needed)
> 7. Presents the amount of material that is appropriate to allotted time and student level
>
> **Presentation of Content**
> 1. Main ideas are clear and specific
> 2. Provides a clear statement of the purpose of the lesson and/or overview/objectives/agenda of the lesson
> 3. Defines relationship of this lesson to previous lessons when relevant
> 4. Presents topics within a logical sequence
> 5. Paces lesson appropriately
> 6. Responds to problems raised during lesson
> 7. Relates assignments to objectives at some point, either first day of class or as it comes up
> 8. Distinguishes between fact and opinion

Box 9.2 (cont.)

9. Relates information to future, practical, real-world application, depending on the content
10. Shares/encourages diverse/more than one point of view (depending on the topic)
11. Shares thought-provoking information, or if basic content, makes it interesting
12. Shares up-to-date info information
13. Develops assignments and tests that are consistent with course goals

Classroom Instruction
1. Instructor is clearly seen and heard
2. Introduction captures attention
3. Demonstrates command of subject matter (knowledgeable, makes accurate statements, relates current research, identifies resources and authorities)
4. Shares key terms visually (Microsoft PowerPoint, board, etc.)
5. Uses examples and analogies to explain
6. Defines/explains difficult or unfamiliar terms (or directions or procedures, etc.)
7. Clearly explains relationships among topics/facts/theories, especially in foundational courses, etc.
8. Uses a variety of educational tools (lecture, learning activity, media, technology)
9. Uses instructional strategies that encourage student participation in the learning process (rhetorical questions, probing questions, individual or group problem-solving tasks, learning activities at the analysis, synthesis, and evaluation level)
10. Uses instructional methods that enhance learning for particular learning tasks (e.g., cooperative learning, case-based, problem-based, self-paced, etc.)
11. Uses supplemental methods/materials (such as online quizzes and modules, learning activities) that are effective and enhance learning (note: online course instruction will use a separate peer review format)
12. Introduces and directs in-class activities effectively
13. Prompts awareness of students' prior learning and experience
14. Encourages students to apply concepts to "real-world" situations
15. Relates class to course goals, students' personal goals, or societal concerns, if relevant to the topic
16. Covers an appropriate (not too little or too much) amount of material during class
17. Microsoft PowerPoint content clear, well organized, and easily read
18. Videos, websites, and other audiovisual materials have a clear and relevant purpose

Box 9.2 (cont.)

Interaction/Teaching Strategies in the Classroom
1. Promotes student participation in classes
2. Prompts or encourages students to ask questions
3. Incorporates student responses
4. Asks questions to entire class
5. Encourages students to answer each other's questions
6. Encourages students to answer difficult questions by providing cues
7. Praises student answers/uses probing questions to build on answers
8. Answers questions clearly and directly
9. Encourages critical thinking and analysis
10. Explains important ideas as simply and clearly as topic allows
11. Shows respect/sensitivity to diverse learners
12. Encourages/facilitates relevant student-led discussion
13. Guides students when they make an error
14. Constructively admits error or insufficient knowledge (i.e., suggests options to finding correct info)

Verbal/Nonverbal Communication in the Classroom
1. Speaks in language that is understandable
2. Articulates words and phrases clearly in a volume that can be easily heard
3. Has an appropriate rate of delivery
4. Makes eye contact with students
5. Projects confidence and enthusiasm
6. Speaks in expressive manner (not monotone) and uses gestures to emphasize points
7. Shows respectful facial expressions
8. Appears relaxed with class
9. Does not read continually from notes or Microsoft PowerPoint
10. Does not embarrass or belittle students in any way

Establishing Rapport with Students
1. Accessible to students outside of class (i.e., office hours, online access)
2. Admits errors with honesty/integrity
3. Responds to students by name (especially in classes of thirty students or less)
4. Encourages mutual respect, honesty, and integrity among class members
5. Responds to distractions effectively
6. Encourages constructive criticism
7. Treats students/class equitably
8. Listens effectively/closely to student comments/concerns/questions
9. Develops a warm classroom climate (students speak freely, relates to students as people, appropriate humor)
10. Responds to student misunderstanding or confusion respectfully
11. Pays attention to cues of boredom, confusion
12. Provides students opportunities to mention problems/concerns with the class, verbally or written

Adapted from Lorch (2013a)

Reflections on The Teaching Self-Reflection Tool and Skills Checklist

1. Think of your last student course evaluations and what is being assessed. Describe the heart of each of your courses and your approach to teaching. Create a list of teaching skills that are reflected as effective teaching according to faculty survey items. They typically address the following categories: (1) organization of teaching, (2) presentation of content, (3) classroom instruction interaction and teaching strategies in the classroom, (4) verbal and nonverbal communication in the classroom, and (5) establishing rapport with students. Now think back to previous student course evaluations of your courses. Can you identify themes in students' comments that might relate to one or more of these categories? What are the positive themes of student responses? What are the less positive or negative themes of student responses?

    Consider the type of content, subject area, and specific topics you most enjoy teaching or feel you teach most effectively. What about this content makes it more enjoyable or easier for you? Possible factors include interest level in the content, familiarity with the content, nature of the content, level of content (foundational versus higher level), and the specific content. The content and logistical considerations, such as class size, can influence your teaching style.

    Then identify the subject/content that you enjoy teaching the most and the content you least enjoy teaching or consider most challenging. What about this content, subject, or topic makes it more challenging for you? (Lorch, 2013a, 2013b).

2. Take time to reflect on your teaching, assess the teaching skills checklist (see Box 9.2), and ask yourself the following questions: What are the attributes that make me an efficient teacher? What is one quality of an effective teacher that I lack and want to cultivate? What sort of activities or learning opportunities can help me preserve and enhance my desirable teaching qualities? Describe the evidence, data, or feedback that you use to appraise and refine your teaching strategies (Lorch, 2013a, 2013b).

3. For learners from grade 8 to adults, administer the RDCA. The RDCA is a free online forty-item self-report creativity assessment that may be accessed via https://drexel.qualtrics.com/jfe/form/SV_exPnHxf9uPfptrv (Reisman, Keiser & Otti, 2016).

The results of the RDCA are intended "to be used diagnostically to identify one's creative strengths, rather than to predict creativity" (Tanner & Reisman, 2014, p. 25). The RDCA assesses an individual's self-perception on eleven major creativity factors that have emerged from the creativity research: originality, fluency, flexibility, elaboration, resistance to premature closure, tolerance of ambiguity, convergent thinking, divergent thinking, risk-taking, and intrinsic and extrinsic motivation. Some of the RDCA factors are similar to those tapped by the Torrance tests of creative thinking (Torrance, 1974), which in turn stems from Guilford's (1967) creativity research. The RDCA may be completed in fewer than ten minutes, is automatically scored, and provides immediate results that users may email to themselves or others. Reliability and validity information for the RDCA may be found in Reisman, Keiser, and Otti (2016).

The RDCA score interpretation (see the following section) is a diagnostic tool that provides a profile of one's RDCA that contains the RDCA factor maximum points possible, total score, and equivalent percent score for each creativity factor; classification of score meanings (very high, moderately high, average, low, very low); factor definitions; RDCA items categorized by factor; and two scoring examples. Test takers rate themselves on a six-point Likert-type scale ranging from strongly disagree to strongly agree. The test taker immediately gets a profile of relative strengths and weaknesses, ranked from very high to very low on each of the eleven factors. In addition to the eleven creativity factors tapped by the RDCA, Box 5.8 in Chapter 5 lists additional creative student characteristics.

Reisman Diagnostic Creativity Assessment Interpretation
The RDCA score interpretation table (Table 9.1) is a diagnostic tool that provides a profile of one's RDCA, the meaning of results reported as a percentage on the related creativity factors scale, and an indication of strong creativity characteristics and those that one might wish to enhance.

Example 1: A total score of 240 reflects that the user selected the highest scoring option for each item for 100 percent of the items.

Example 2: A score of 22 for the originality factor reflects that you obtained 61 percent of the possible thirty-six originality factor points comprised of the six originality RDCA items.

Table 9.1 *RDCA score interpretation table*

RDCA maximum possible score	Score and equivalent percentage	Classification	Factor definition	RDCA items related to factors
Total score (240: highest possible score)	199–240 (83–100 percent) 146–198 (61–82 percent) 120–145 (50–60 percent) 94–119 (39–49 percent) 41–93 (17–38 percent)	Very high Moderately high Average Low Very low		
Originality (36: highest possible score)	30–36 (83–100 percent) 22–29 (61–82 percent) 18–21 (50–60 percent) 14–17 (39–49 percent) 6–13 (17–38 percent)	Very high Moderately high Average Low Very low	Unique and novel	3. I regularly come up with novel uses for things. 4. I come up with new and unusual ideas. 8. I come up with unique suggestions, thought up wholly or partly independently of other people. 13. I think in unconventional ways. 20. I usually think out of the box. 29. I am very innovative.
Fluency (24: highest possible score)	20–24 (83–100 percent) 15–19 (62–82 percent) 12–14 (50–61 percent) 9–11 (34–49 percent) 4–8 (17–33 percent)	Very high Moderately high Average Low Very low	Generates many ideas	7. I can generate many relevant solutions. 28. I can rapidly produce a lot of ideas relevant to a task. 36. I generate many ideas when I draw. 40. I generate many ideas.
Flexibility (18: highest possible score)	15–18 (83–100 percent) 11–14 (61–82 percent) 9–10 (50–60 percent) 7–8 (39–49 percent) 3–6 (17–38 percent)	Very high Moderately high Average Low Very low	Generates many categories of ideas	14. I come up with different categories of approaches to solving problems. 21. I come up with different types of responses to a situation. 31. I can generate different categories of uses for a specific item.

Elaboration (24: highest possible score)	20–24 (83–100 percent) 15–19 (63–82 percent) 12–14 (50–62 percent) 9–11 (38–49 percent)	Very high Moderately high Average Low	Adds detail	9. I fill in details when drawing. 19. I tend to elaborate on my ideas when speaking. 27. I tend to keep adding to my drawings. 39. I tend to elaborate on my ideas when writing.
Tolerance of ambiguity (12: highest possible score)	11–12 (91–100 percent) 9–10 (75–90 percent) 7–8 (58–74 percent) 4–6 (33–57 percent) 2–3 (17–32 percent)	Very high Moderately high Average Low Very low	Comfortable with the unknown	24. I can tolerate the unknown. 35. I can cope with uncertainty.
Resistance to premature closure (24: highest possible score)	20–24 (83–100 percent) 15–19 (62–82 percent) 12–14 (50–61 percent) 9–11 (38–49 percent) 4–8 (17–37 percent)	Very high Moderately high Average Low Very low	Keeps an Open Mind	1. I keep an open mind. 11. When faced with a problem, I evaluate possible solutions and select the best one. 23. I gather as much information as possible before making a decision. 32. I keep listening even when I think I know what someone is saying.
Divergent thinking (18: highest possible score)	15–18 (83–100 percent) 11–14 (52–61 percent) 9–10 (50–60 percent) 7–8 (39–49 percent) 3–6 (17–38 percent)	High Moderately high Average Low Very low	Generates many solutions (related to fluency)	6. I follow many paths to come up with possible solutions. 18. I come up with multiple possibilities when analyzing a problem by looking at every angle of the situation. 37. I prefer problems where there are many or several possible right answers.
Convergent thinking (18: highest possible score)	15–18 (83–100 percent) 11–14 (52–61 percent) 9–10 (50–60 percent) 7–8 (39–49 percent) 3–6 (17–38 percent)	Very high Moderately high Average Low Very low	Comes to closure	5. I can make a decision when there are multiple possibilities or choices. 26. I can select one solution from many possibilities. 30. I do well on standardized tests that require a single correct response.

Table 9.1 (*cont.*)

RDCA maximum possible score	Score and equivalent percentage	Classification	Factor definition	RDCA items related to factors
Risk-taking (24: highest possible score)	20–24 (83–100 percent) 15–19 (62–82 percent) 12–14 (50–61 percent) 9–11 (38–49 percent) 4–8 (17–37 percent)	Very high Moderately high Average Low Very low	Adventuresome	2. I am willing to tackle challenging tasks even when success is uncertain. 10. I am afraid of the unknown. 16. I share and advocate ideas I believe in, even when those ideas are unconventional. 34. I am willing to take calculated risks.
Intrinsic motivation (24: highest possible score)	20–24 (83–100 percent) 15–19 (62–82 percent) 12–14 (50–61 percent) 9–11 (38–49 percent) 4–8 (17–37 percent)	Very high Moderately high Average Low Very Low	Inner drive	12. I do well on activities or tasks that I find personally challenging. 17. I engage in activities that are personally satisfying. 25. Curiosity, enjoyment, and interest energize me to complete a task. 38. My motivation to perform well does not depend on external recognition.
Extrinsic motivation (18: highest possible score)	15–18 (83–100 percent) 11–14 (61–82 percent) 9–10 (50–60 percent) 7–8 (39–49 percent) 3–6 (17–38 percent)	Very high Moderately high Average Low Very low	Needs reward or reinforcement	15. I will use more effort on an activity or task if there is some kind of incentive. 22. I perform tasks better knowing there will be a reward or recognition. 33. Knowing that I am going to be rewarded enhances my creativity.

Note: RDCA Items 10, 15, 22, and 33 are reversed scored (i.e., "strongly disagree" was the highest scoring option instead of "strongly agree").

References

Duckworth, A. (2016). *Grit: The Power of Passion and Perseverance.* New York: Scribner/Simon & Schuster.

Guilford, J. P. (1967). Creativity: Yesterday, today, and tomorrow. *The Journal of Creative Behavior*, 1(1), 3–14. https://doi.org/10.1002/j.2162-6057.1967.tb00002.x.

Jordanous, A. (2012). A : Computational creativity evaluation based on what it is to be creative. *Cognitive Computation*, 4, 246–279. https://doi.org/10.1007/s12559-012-9156-1.

Keig, L. (2000). Formative peer review of teaching: Attitudes of faculty at liberal arts colleges toward colleague assessment. *Journal of Personnel Evaluation in Education*, 14, 67–87.

Lorch, A. (2013a). The Teaching Self-Reflection Tool and Skills Checklist, *Department of Occupational Therapy Faculty Papers.* Paper 59. https://jdc.jefferson.edu/otfp/59.

Lorch, A. (2013b). *The Teaching Self-Reflection Tool and Skills Checklist. Jefferson Digital Commons.* Philadelphia, PA: Thomas Jefferson University. https://jdc.jefferson.edu/cgi/viewcontent.cgi?article=1060&context=otfp.

Plucker, J. A., Beghetto, R. A. & Dow, G. T. (2004). Why isn't creativity more important to educational psychologists? Potentials, pitfalls, and future directions in creativity research. *Educational Psychologist*, 39(2), 83–96.

Positive Action Staff (2020). Teaching Self-Awareness to Students: 5 effective activities. www.positiveaction.net/blog/teaching-self-awareness-to-students.

Reisman, F., Keiser, L. & Otti, O. (2016). Development, use and implications of diagnostic creativity assessment app, RDCA – Reisman Diagnostic Creativity Assessment. *Creativity Research Journal*, 28(2), 177–187. https://doi.org/10.1080/1040.

Runco, M. A. & Jaeger, G. J. (2012). The standard definition of creativity. *Creativity Research Journal*, 24(1), 92–96.

Stein, M. I. (1953). Creativity and culture. *The Journal of Psychology*, 36(2), 311–322.

Tanner, D. & Reisman, F. (2014). *Creativity as a Bridge Between Education and Industry: FOSTERING NEW INNOVATIONS.* North Charleston, NC: CreateSpace.

Torrance, E. P. (1974). *The Torrance Tests of Creative Thinking: Norms-Technical Manual.* Princeton, NJ: Personal Press.

Creativity Module 9.2

Instructors and creativity

Background Information

Creativity involves a different way of looking at problems and solving them. A learner's creative activity provides instructors with a different view of their students' strengths. Creativity also fosters opportunities for trying out new ideas and new ways of thinking and problem-solving. Instructors who frequently incorporate creativity-focused lessons are more likely to observe higher order cognitive skills (e.g., problem-solving, critical thinking, and making connections between subjects). Creativity requires two different types of knowledge: (1) knowledge and skills in a discipline referred to as *domain specific*, and (2) knowledge and skills related to the creative process referred to as *domain general*, as discussed in Chapter 2.

Activities

1. Establishing a creative learning environment is necessary for creativity to exist. Students need to feel a sense of psychological safety when being creative. Thus, ensure that all ideas are listened to and feedback is given in a respectful manner.
2. Foster students' creative thinking, which involves persistence, discipline, resilience, and curiosity. Students who are more intellectually curious are more open to new experiences. Encourage students to offer multiple paths to a solution to identify one correct answer.
3. Support the creative process by having students engage in "identifying the REAL problem" using the creative problem-solving grid shown in Table 9.2.
4. Engage students in idea generation through brainstorming, in which the individual or a group generates as many ideas as possible (see Creativity Module 9.12 for more on brainstorming).
5. Encourage students to self-reflect during the creative process, as this provides students with increased skills in metacognition (see Chapters 1 and 7) and a deeper understanding of their creative competencies. Box 9.3 is provides a perspective from the field that illustrates an instructor's appreciation of creativity.

Table 9.2 *Creative problem-solving grid: find the real problem*

	Evaluation criteria				
Student learning needs	Learner centered	Increases communication between teacher and students	Desirable	Workable	Total
1. Prerequisite knowledge missing	3	2	1	1	7
2. Students need instruction at the concrete level	1	3	3	3	10
3. Students need more time to reflect on teacher's presentation	2	1	2	2	7

Directions:

1. Rank each possible student learning need vertically within each evaluation criteria: important/desirable/effective=3, least desired=1. Three to eight options are usually a manageable list.
2. Add horizontally across the evaluation criteria, with the highest total score being your first option.
3. If you are not comfortable with the option with the highest score, then consider the next highest score. Remember, this grid is merely a heuristic (tool) for making a decision.

> **Box 9.3   Voice from the field: elementary school teacher**
>
> As an elementary school teacher, I strive to live by Teresa Amabile's words: that people are most creative when the "interest, enjoyment, satisfaction and challenge is in the work itself" (Amabile, 2017). I try to create lessons for my students that use critical thinking skills, solve real world problems, and provide an avenue to express their creativity in imaginative and thoughtful ways. Because I know my students trust my intentions, they are easily impressionable. So, if I lead by example, teach with creativity, give them opportunities for creative thought, and demonstrate that creativity **can** be taught, learned, and improved, they will be engaged and motivated to learn. If I show them that I not only value the product but the creative process that comes from their expressive artifacts, they will, in turn, learn to love the process as well. But what teacher doesn't love to have their students' highly polished final pieces to hang in the hallway? Celebrating my students' creative process and teaching them to appreciate their experiences over their final product is something that has taken me time to accept. Over the years I've learned to find value in their creative process because it encourages them to explore new ideas, deepen their learning, and share their lived experience.
>
> A few years ago, my school district was in the process of building two new elementary schools. Administrators formed a committee of stakeholders so they could have a say and share their ideas regarding the aesthetic environment of the schools. But one important group was left out: the students. My authentic problem-solving teaching method went into overdrive. The youngest learners, those who would be most directly impacted by these decisions, needed to be involved. So, I contacted the architect and he was overjoyed to come and present to my class. The students listened intently, asked thoughtful questions, and were proud to be considered part of the stakeholder team. This project was a true design-thinking project. Through empathy and ideation, prototyping and sharing, my students found joy in the creative process.

Assessments

It may be more beneficial to formatively assess the process that the students are going through than to assess the final product. Exploring how students generate ideas and whether the method of recording ideas is effective, whether the final solutions are practical, and whether they demonstrated curiosity or resilience can often be more useful than merely assessing the final product (Patston, 2021). It may, in fact, mean that the outcome of an activity should take into account a combination of the creative process as observed by the teacher and the creative process as experienced and reported by the student (Patston, 2021) and should use the creative problem-solving grid (Reisman & Severino, 2021; Torrance & Reisman, 2000). Remember, the creative problem-solving grid shown in Table 9.3 is merely a heuristic (tool) for helping a decision to be made.

Table 9.3 *Creative problem-solving grid: strategies*

Goal: creative strategies	Effective strategy	Help reach goals	Creative	Total
Persistence/grit				
Trigger original/novel ideas				
Generate many ideas				
Resist premature closure				
Tolerate ambiguity				
Divergent thinking				
Convergent thinking				
Intrinsic motivation				

Directions:
1. Rank each possible strategy vertically across each evaluation criteria (8=important desirable, 1=least desired).
2. Add across the evaluation criteria by row and enter the total in the "Total" column.
3. Consider the characteristics of identifying the strategy, with the highest total score as your first option.
4. If you're not comfortable with the choice with the highest score, then consider the next highest option.

References

Amabile, T. (2017). In pursuit of everyday creativity. *Journal of Creative Behavior*, 51(4), 335–337. https://doi.org/10.1002/jocb.200.

Patston, T. (2021). What is creativity in education? The Education Hub. https://theeducationhub.org.nz/what-is-creativity-in-education/.

Reisman, F. & Severino, L. (2021). *Using Creativity to Address Dyslexia, Dysgraphia, and Dyscalculia*. London: Routledge.

Torrance, E. P. & Reisman, F. K. (2000). *Learning to Solve Mathematics Word Problems*. Bensenville, IL: Scholastic Testing Services, Inc.

Creativity Module 9.3
Characteristics of creative teaching

Background Information

The *International Encyclopedia of Teaching and Teacher Education* (Anderson, 1995) classifies the concept of teaching into three categories:

1. teaching as success – success being signified and defined as an activity that necessarily affects learning
2. teaching as an intentional activity – that is, teaching may not logically imply learning, but there is an expectation that it will result in learning
3. teaching as normative behavior – action undertaken to bring about learning in another (Green, 1966)

Rajagopalan (2019) described characteristics of creative teaching as follows:

- Teaching is an effective interaction between teacher and students.
- Teaching is both an art and a science.
- Teaching is an art, as it calls for the exercise of talent and creativity. Teaching as a science involves a repertoire of techniques, procedures, and skills that can be systematically studied, described, and improved. A good teacher is one who adds creativity and inspiration to the basic repertoire.
- Teaching has various forms, such as formal and informal training, conditioning, or indoctrination.
- Teaching is dominated by the skill of communication.
- Teaching is a tripolar process; the three poles are educational objectives, learning experiences, and change in behavior.
- Teaching should be well planned, and the teacher should decide the objectives, methods of teaching, and evaluation techniques. Teaching is suggesting and not dictating.
- Good teaching is democratic, and the teacher respects the students and encourages them to ask questions, answer questions, and discuss things.
- Teaching provides guidance, direction, and encouragement to the students.
- Teaching is a cooperative activity and the teacher should involve students in different classroom activities, such as organization, management, discussion, recitation, and the evaluation of results.
- Teaching is kind and sympathetic, and a good teacher develops emotional stability among children.

- The teacher solves the learning problems of students.
- Teaching helps children to make adjustments in life.
- Teaching is a professional activity that helps to bring about the harmonious development of children.
- Teaching stimulates students' power of thinking and directs them toward self-learning.
- Teaching can be observed, analyzed, and evaluated.
- Teaching is a specialized task and may be taken as a set of component skills for the realization of a specified set of instructional objectives.

Activities

1. Teaching methods historically have fallen within a range of activities that include explaining, describing, demonstrating, exemplifying, guiding, etc. Use these various instructional methods to provide an environment that supports student interest and motivation.
2. Discuss the concept of teaching with colleagues.
3. Discuss characteristics of teaching with colleagues.
4. List conclusions resulting from your collaborative discussions with colleagues and reflect upon and record new insights in a journal on instruction ideas.

Assessments

Based upon the seventeen characteristics of creative teaching listed in the background information of this module and your conclusions resulting from your collaborative discussions with colleagues, create a plan of action to enhance being a creative instructor (e.g., What creative strategies will you use? What characteristics will define a creative student? What instructional changes will you make to enhance teaching creatively?).

References

Anderson, L. W. (1995). *International Encyclopedia of Teaching and Teacher Education*. Oxford, UK: Pergamon.

Green, T. (1966). The concept of teaching: A reply. *Studies in Philosophy and Education*, 4(3) 339–345.

Rajagopalan, I. (2019). Concept of teaching. *Shanlax International Journal of Education*, 7(2), 5–8.

Creativity Module 9.4
Critical thinking

Background Information

Critical thinking can be traced back 2,500 years to Socrates, followed by Plato and Aristotle who analyzed basic concepts and asked probing questions. Critical thinking enables folks to discern what is important and what is not and separate the truth from fake news. Historically, the emphasis on instruction focused on rote learning rather than critical thinking, that is, retaining information given in books or lectures and designing assessments that tap this knowledge with little regard for self-reflection and analysis from students' perspective.

Robinson (1987, p. 16) stated: "If students are to function successfully in a highly technical society, then they must be equipped with lifelong learning and thinking skills necessary to acquire and process information in an ever-changing world." Teaching students to think critically is important because, although originality helps produce ideas that are imaginative and unique, critical thinking evaluates these ideas in order to solve a problem or reach a logical conclusion. Original thinkers generate many ideas; critical thinking skills convert the ideas to a workable solution.

Definitions of critical thinking include reflective and reasonable thinking that is focused on deciding what to believe or do (Presseisen, 1986, p. 24), providing evidence to support one's conclusions or to request evidence from others before accepting their conclusions (Hudgins and Edelman 1986, p. 333) or to determine the authenticity, accuracy, and worth of information or knowledge claims (Beyer, 1985, p. 276).

Activities

1. **Questioning.** Guidelines include the following:
   - Ask clear questions in simple, clear language that students can understand.
   - Avoid ambiguous, confusing constructions and excess verbiage.
   - Ask your question before designating a respondent.
   - Ask the question, wait for the class to think about it, and then ask someone for an answer. As usual, there are exceptions to this rule. When you call on an inattentive student, it is often better to call the name first so that the question will be heard. Similarly, you should

call the name first when you address slow or shy students, so that they can prepare themselves.
- Ask questions that match your lesson objectives. When facts are wanted, ask factual and empirical questions (remember or understand the levels on Bloom's taxonomy described in Box 9.5). When you want to stimulate student thinking, ask higher level questions as per Bloom's taxonomy.
- Distribute questions about the class fairly. Avoid directing all questions to a few bright students. However, also avoid developing a mechanical system for asking questions. Students soon catch on to such systems as going by alphabetical order or row by row, and they will pay attention only when they know it is their turn.
- Ask questions suited to all ability levels in the class. Some questions should be easy and some should be difficult, so that all students will have a chance to respond to some questions correctly.
- Ask only one question at a time. Asking two or three questions at once often confuses students. Multiple questions permit no time to think and, if several questions are asked, students are not sure which question to answer first.
- Avoid asking questions too soon. It usually is much more effective to establish a knowledge base before initiating a questioning sequence.
- Pause for at least three seconds following each question to allow students time to think and to formulate their answers (Jacobsen, Eggen & Kauchak, 1993).

2. **Questioning techniques.** These techniques include clarifying, redirection, prompting, probing, and wait-time.
    - Examples of **clarifying questions** (Arizona University, 2013) include the following:
        – Is this what you said?
        – What resources were used for the project?
        – Did I hear you say . . . ?
        – Did I understand you when you said . . . ?
        – What criteria did you use to . . . ?
        – What's another way you might . . . ?
        – Did I hear you correctly when you said . . . ?
        – Did I paraphrase what you said correctly?
    - **Redirection questions** ask a question by prodding students to answer a question just asked. When a student responds to a question, the instructor can ask another student to comment

(University of Illinois, 2019). Redirecting may involve asking several students to respond to a question, in light of previous responses such as: "We have now studied the contributions of several great men and women of science. Which scientist do you think made the greatest contribution? (University of North Florida, n.d.).
- **Prompting** is a technique to move on to another student in response to a wrong answer to a question. Prompting questions use hints and clues to aid students in answering questions or to assist them in correcting an initial question with clues or hints.
- **Probing** works when a student's reply is correct but insufficient because it lacks depth; ask the student to supply additional information. Probing questions force the student to elaborate on their initial response. Examples include the following:
  – Why do you think this is the case?
  – What do you think would happen if . . . ?
  – What sort of impact do you think . . . ?
  – How did you decide . . . ?
  – How did you determine . . . ?
  – How did you conclude . . . ?
  – What is the connection between . . . and . . . ?
  – What if the opposite were true? Then what?
- **Wait time.** Students need time to think. On average, most teachers on the average wait about one second for students to answer questions. However, when teachers wait for approximately three seconds or longer for the answer to a question, the quality of students' responses improves (Rowe, 1974; University of North Florida, n.d.) in the following ways: (1) the length of student responses increases, (2) failure to respond decreases, (3) questions from students increase, (4) unsolicited responses increase, (5) the confidence of students increases, and (6) speculative thinking increases.

Box 9.4 provides a perspective from the field that addresses critical thinking.

Assessments

1. Discuss your awareness and implementation of critical thinking with one or more colleagues.
2. Write questions at different levels of thinking as per Bloom's taxonomy (expanded upon in Chapter 4; Anderson & Krathwohl, 2001). Figure 9.1 and Box 9.5 set out the levels of Bloom's taxonomy.

Box 9.4 Voice from the field: elementary grades teacher

Critical thinking involves the connections that students make with themes in literary texts and characters' point of view. In this case I chose one of my favorite texts that takes place in a school setting: *Thank You Mr. Falker*, by Patricia Polacco. By engaging with the literature in numerous ways, including defining the author's purpose, discussing how the characters changed throughout the story, and writing about a struggle they've endured, students were able to engage in critical thinking and empathize with the main character.

Another activity that enhances critical thinking is the "brainwriting" technique. This is an approach to brainstorming that eliminates group consensus without hearing from all the members first. Instead of traditional brainstorming where only one person speaks at a time, brainwriting gives everyone equal opportunity to participate in a nonthreatening way. It starts with every student having their own paper. They write the problem at the top but leave out their name. Students have two minutes to write down and/or draw as many ideas as possible. They write in "free form" without the teacher editing their writing. It should also be quiet – students are not allowed to share or talk about their ideas at this time. After the two minutes are up, students pass the papers clockwise. They read and digest the previous students' information and then add more ideas and solutions to their classmates' initial suggestions. This continues until all students have the chance to write on each other's papers. Then, the class comes together as a whole and discusses common themes. Students feel free to be their creative selves because ideas are essentially anonymous. This empowers them to make suggestions that perhaps they thought would not be received well.

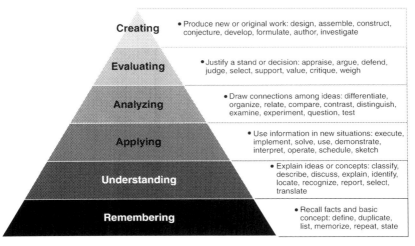

Figure 9.1 Levels and descriptions of Bloom's taxonomy, revised.
Source: Vanderbilt University Center for Teaching

> **Box 9.5 Levels of Bloom's taxonomy**
>
> **Create.** Putting elements together to form a new coherent or functional whole, or reorganizing elements into a new pattern or structure. Examples include arranging, assembling, building, collecting, combining, compiling, composing, constituting, constructing, creating, designing, developing, devising, formulating, generating, hypothesizing, integrating, inventing, making, managing, modifying, organizing, performing, planning, preparing, producing, proposing, rearranging, reconstructing, reorganizing, revising, rewriting, specifying, synthesizing, and writing.
>
> **Evaluate.** Making judgments based on criteria and standards. Examples include appraising, apprising, arguing, assessing, comparing, concluding, considering, contrasting, convincing, criticizing, critiquing, deciding, determining, discriminating, evaluating, grading, judging, justifying, measuring, ranking, rating, recommending, reviewing, scoring, selecting, standardizing, supporting, testing, and validating
>
> **Analyze.** Breaking material into its constituent parts and determining how they relate to one another and/or to an overall structure or purpose. Examples include analyzing, arranging, breaking down, categorizing, classifying, comparing, connecting, contrasting, deconstructing, detecting, diagramming, differentiating, discriminating, distinguishing, dividing, explaining, identifying, integrating, inventorying, ordering, organizing, relating, separating, and structuring.
>
> **Apply.** Using information or a skill in a new situation. Examples include applying, calculating, carrying out, classifying, completing, computing, demonstrating, dramatizing, employing, examining, executing, experimenting, generalizing, illustrating, implementing, inferring, interpreting, manipulating, modifying, operating, organizing, outlining, predicting, solving, transferring, translating, and using.
>
> **Understand.** Demonstrating comprehension through explanation. Examples include abstracting, arranging, articulating, associating, categorizing, clarifying, classifying, comparing, computing, concluding, contrasting, defending, diagramming, differentiating, discussing, distinguishing, estimating, exemplifying, explaining, extrapolating, generalizing, giving examples of, illustrating, inferring, interpreting, matching, outlining, paraphrasing, predicting, rearranging, reordering, rephrasing, representing, restating, summarizing, transforming, and translating.
>
> **Remember.** Recalling or recognizing relevant knowledge from long-term memory. Examples include citing, defining, describing, identifying, listing, outlining, quoting, recalling, reproducing, retrieving, showing, stating, tabulating, and telling.

3. Categorize assessment questions and activities according to levels of Bloom's taxonomy.
4. Categorize assessment questions and activities according to the developmental curriculum described in Chapter 4, namely arbitrary associations, lower level relationships, lower level generalizations, concepts, higher level relationships, and higher level generalizations.

References

Arizona University (2013). Handout: Clarifying and probing questions. In *Deliberation for Global Perspectives in Teaching and Learning* (p. 1). https://global.indiana.edu/documents/global-perspectives/clarifying-and-probing-questions-handout-step-2-define.pdf.

Anderson, L. W. & Krathwohl, D. R. (2001). *A Taxonomy for Learning, Teaching, and Assessing: A Revision of Bloom's Taxonomy of Educational Objectives.* New York: Longman.

Beyer, B. K., (1985). Critical thinking: What is it? *Social Education*, 49(4), 270–276.

Hudgins, B. & Edelman, S. (1986). Teaching critical thinking skills to fourth and fifth graders through teacher-led small-group discussions. *Journal of Educational Research*, 79(6), 333–342.

Jacobsen, D., Eggen, P. & Kauchak, D. (1993). *Methods for Teaching: A Skills Approach* (4th ed.). Storm Lake, IA: Merrill.

Presseisen, B. Z. (1986). Critical thinking and thinking skills: State of the art definitions and practice in public schools. Paper presented at the Annual Meeting of the American Educational Research Association (AERA), San Francisco, CA, April.

Robinson, I. S. (1987). *A Program to Incorporate High-Order Thinking Skills into Teaching and Learning for Grades K–3.* Lisbon: Nova University.

Rowe, M. B. (1974). Reflections of wait-time: Some methodological questions. *Journal of Research in Science Teaching*, 11(3), 263–279.

University of Illinois (2019). Questioning strategies. https://citl.illinois.edu/citl-101/teaching-learning/resources/teaching-strategies/questioning-strategies.

University of North Florida (n.d.) Questioning techniques. www.unf.edu/~noo632624/ece4473/q-techni.htm.

Creativity Module 9.5
Originality

Background Information

Originality involves generating unique and novel ideas. The word original comes from the Latin word *originem*, which means "beginning or birth"; original means "first." Synonyms for originality include boldness, brilliance, cleverness, daring, freshness, imagination, imaginativeness, individuality, ingeniousness, ingenuity, invention, inventiveness, innovativeness, modernity, newness, nonconformity, resourcefulness, and spirit (Thesaurus.com, n.d.).

Activities

1. **Environment.** Our senses – what we see, hear, feel, taste, smell, and touch – influence our learning. An environment that contributes to a positive and creative mindset enhances original thinking. Some people thrive in loud, crowded areas bristling with activity; others need quiet and calm to think clearly and creatively. Students need to find that place, noisy or quiet, crowded or isolated, that makes them feel comfortable. They should be encouraged to recognize their sensory preferences and seek the best learning environment. Identifying their sensory preference opens up one's comfort zone and enables original thoughts to emerge.

2. **Classroom climate.** Research shows that positive classroom climates characterized by high expectations, teacher warmth, encouragement, and pleasant physical surroundings enhance learning. Teachers and administrators should systematically evaluate the general environment of their classrooms and schools and should estimate how this environment affects their ability to promote original and critical reasoning habits among students (Orr & Klein, 1991, p. 131). Students who experiment with new ways of looking at things need to feel free to explore and express opinions and examine alternative ideas (Doyal & Gough, 1984). Fostering a climate conducive to the development of originality includes (Cotton, 1988, 1991):
   - setting ground rules well in advance
   - providing well-planned activities
   - showing respect for each student
   - providing nonthreatening activities
   - being flexible
   - accepting individual differences

- exhibiting a positive attitude
- modeling novel thinking skills
- acknowledging every student's response
- allowing students to be active participants
- creating experiences that will ensure success at least part of the time for each student
- using a wide variety of teaching modalities

3. **Brutethink.** The idea of the Brutethink (Michalko, 2007) creative-thinking technique is that, by forcing a random idea into a challenge or problem situation, you produce out-of-the-ordinary choices to solve your problem. The steps in the Brutethink process are as follows:
   (a) Bring a random word into a problem situation, such as the low self-esteem of students with math anxiety: *Fear* is the random word.
   (b) Think of words associated with the word *fear* that are related in some way. Using pictures, magazines, phone books, junk mail, cereal boxes, poetry, crossword puzzles, sounds, etc., can help come up with words.
   (c) Force connections between the random word and the problem and also between the associated words and the problem. For example, fear – alarm clock – timer – control – regulate – calm – unruffled – chill out.
   (d) List all ideas.
   This is a great group activity as well as an individual.

4. **Group originality.** Discuss and clarify a specific problem. Have the group write ideas on index cards, one idea per card. Then they pass the cards to the right. Based on what they read, they write new ideas on blank cards and pass them to the right. Then collect all cards and tape them to the wall, eliminating duplicates. Have students vote on ideas using dot stickers (five stickers per person). The key is to stay silent and generate original ideas in parallel.

5. **Write a six-word story.** Using only six words as the title, write a related story (e.g., "eat vegetables and fruit for health," "homework can be fun or not," etc.).

6. **Avoid the letter "E."** This exercise involves having a conversation without using the letter "E." (Byster & Loberg, 2014). It will help you become a faster and more productive thinker. Bored with not using "e"? Move on to other common letters such as R, S, T, or A.

7. **Eliminate "I," "me," "my," and "mine" from your vocabulary.** Write a letter without using the words I, me, mine, and my or talk for fifteen minutes a day without saying those same words.

256 Connecting Creativity and Motivation Research with End Users

8. **Look at things from a new perspective.** Consider a friend's perspective or point of view about something; this will help you develop the ability to look at things in new and different ways.
    Note: Activities 5–8 are adapted from Barringer (2016)
9. **Consider student motivation.** Chapters 3 and 6 on motivation and Assessment 3 below focus on tapping student creativity and motivation characteristics via the RDCA and Reisman Diagnostic Motivation Assessment (RDMA).

Assessments

1. Observe which students generate original solutions to a problem.
2. Observe learner responses to the activities listed in the previous section.
3. For participants in grade 9 up to adulthood, administer the RDCA assessment to obtain diagnostic information regarding creative strengths and weaknesses that may be used to design instruction or merely enhance one's awareness of their creativity (see RDCA in Chapter 5).
4. For students in grades K–8, administer the RDCA/RDMA K–8 assessment to obtain diagnostic information that will form the basis of instruction. Table 9.4 contains the RDCA/RDMA K–8 assessment with the items categorized by creativity factors.

Table 9.4 *RDCA and RDMA K–8 assessment*

Question	Category: creativity	Category: motivation
1. I come up with new uses for things.	Originality	
2. I have a great imagination.	Originality	
3. **I am afraid to take risks**.	Risk-taking	
4. I can produce a lot of ideas.	Fluency	
5. I am not afraid to be different.	Risk-taking	
6. I am persistent when finding out information on topics of interest.		Grit
7. **I try hard in school to please my teacher**.		Extrinsic motivation
8. I feel good about myself.		Bandura: self-esteem
9. I often like to work alone.		McClelland: achievement need
10. I give in to the wishes of people whose friendship and companionship I value.		McClelland: affiliation need
11. I like to win arguments.		McClelland: power need

Table 9.4 (cont.)

Question	Category: creativity	Category: motivation
12. My effort influences my learning.		Argyris: motivation management theory
13. I avoid schoolwork and dislike responsibility.		McGregor: X Y theory
14. I do better in school when I am involved in activity planning.		Ouchi: theory Z
15. I believe more effort will result in better learning.		Vroom: expectancy Theory
16. Creative teachers can improve my creativity.		Urwick: theory Z principles
17. **I am not a good student.**		Merton: self-fulfilling prophecy
18. I can win whenever I play games.		Deci and Ryan: self-determination theory
19. My teacher thinks I am smart.		Merton: self-fulfilling prophecy
20. I like to have choices.		Deci and Ryan: self-determination theory
21. I like to know what will happen next.	Tolerate ambiguity	
22. I keep an open mind.	Resistance to premature closure	
23. I like to keep adding to my drawings.	Elaboration	
24. I am good at making choices.	Convergent thinking	
25. I like to brainstorm ideas.	Divergent thinking	

Note: Items 3, 7, 17, and 21 are reverse scored.

Rather than receiving an interpretive score like in the RDCA, it is suggested to use the RDMA results diagnostically to identify creative strengths and weaknesses and design related instruction.

References

Barringer, D. (2016). 10 exercises to spark original thinking and increase creativity. www.adobe.com/express/learn/blog/10-exercises-to-spark-original-thinking-and-unleash-creativity.

Byster, M., & Loberg, K. (2014). *The Power of Forgetting: Six Essential Skills to Clear Out Brain Clutter and Become the Sharpest, Smartest You.* New York: Harmony Books.

Cotton, K. (1988) *Classroom Questioning: Close-up No. 5.* Portland, OR: Northwest Regional Educational Laboratory.

Cotton, K. (1991). Close-Up#11: Teaching thinking skills. School Improvement Research Series. Northwest Regional Educational Laboratory. https://educationnorthwest.org/sites/default/files/TeachingThinkingSkills.pdf.

Doyal, L. & Gough, I. (1984). A theory of human needs. *Critical Social Policy*, 4(10), 6–38. https://doi.org/10.1177/026101838400401002.

Michalko, M. (2007). *Thinkertoys.* Berkeley, CA: The Rocks Campus Ten Speed Press.

Orr, J. & Klein, M. F. (1991). Instruction in critical thinking as a form of character education. *Journal of Curriculum and Supervision*, 6(2).

Thesaurus.com (n.d.). Originality. www.thesaurus.com/browse/originality.

Creativity Module 9.6
Fluency

Background Information

Fluency involves generating many ideas (Cotton, 1991; Michalko, 2006; Sternberg, 1988) and is defined as the number of ideas and approaches used to accomplish a task or solve a problem.

Activities

1. Name as many colors as you can. Substitutes for "colors" include girls' names, boys' names, toys, uses of a brick, fruits, sandwiches, states, oceans, etc. (Crockett, Jukes & Churches, 2011).
2. Guideline for practicing fluency:
   (a) Write down your thoughts and ideas as they come to you.
   (b) Working in a group can be beneficial, as people often build upon each other's ideas.
3. Generate lists
   (a) Generate many different uses for common items, such as a pencil, a ruler, or a paper towel tube.
   (b) Generate synonyms for common words or phrases, such as "Good job."
   (c) Generate many different ways to arrange the desks in the classroom (draw pictures).

(d) Generate names for a classroom pet or a team or alternative titles to a book.
(e) Generate ideas for a class party.
(f) Generate questions about a given topic. This works well at the start of a social studies or science unit.
(g) Generate solutions to a reoccurring classroom problem, for example the noise level is too high during work times or students are feeling that they are not treated fairly during foursquare games at recess.
(h) Generate solutions to a regional or world issue, such as poverty or global warming.

Note: Activities 2 and 3 are adapted from Minds in Bloom (2009)

Assessments

1. Observe if there is an increase in the number of responses to other activities related to fluency after you have practiced. Box 9.6 is a perspective from the field that shares several fluency activities, as well as a suggested assessment.

Box 9.6   Voice from the field: fluency activity

While the definition of creative fluency is generating many ideas, the concept of fluency also includes communicating those ideas. Consider fluency when teaching young children to speak, read, and write, or when trying to learn a new language.

Communication is often a latent factor of fluency. I tell students that ideas that remain in the mind are only available to the thinker. In addition to forming an idea, they will also need to figure out how to explain it to others. To illustrate, I provide this type of authentic experience for students:

> Provide a prompt that allows easy generation of ideas that beg to be shared. For example, request ideas after shaking a container with something hidden inside, request ideas for an outside game to play, request ideas for how a character might solve a problem in a shared story, request ideas to solve a classroom related problem.

Other prompt ideas include naming as many colors, girls' or boys' names, toys, uses of a brick, fruits, sandwiches, states, oceans, etc. Remind students to "hold onto that thought." This is code for – don't talk out loud – just talk in your mind, and give them time to generate ideas. I encourage wonder and

Box 9.6 (cont.)

excitement – "the thing about ideas is ... once you get one ... you have to figure out how to share it." I provide some think time. Many are just about to burst with their ideas. Just before releasing them I say, "notice this feeling, we are going to talk about it later." One more pause, and then I release them to share their ideas.

Usually, the room erupts into noise as they share the ideas. I circle about helping anyone who needs it. After the sharing comes to a natural end, I gather the students to reflect on the importance of not only generating many ideas but also communicating our ideas. I specifically teach the word fluency and explain its important place in the creative process. A few favorite activities follow.

BUILD YOUR IDEA STATION ACTIVITY

During this activity, I confess to my students that truly new ideas are rare. Rather, most creative ideas are formed when two unrelated concepts are somehow connected in a new way. Often, these unrelated concepts were someone else's idea. While the parts of the idea may have come from another, the joining of ideas in a new way is creativity. The best way to generate new ideas is to gather inspiration from objects and concepts that you find interesting. Teachers can designate idea stations in an area of the classroom or ask students to create a personal idea station in a notebook or box. Encourage students to visit idea stations when they need inspiration.

Once at the idea station, students select two items. The students are encouraged to touch, manipulate, and play with the objects. As the students maneuver the objects, they consider how the objects relate to their task. For example, if a student is tasked with making up a game, the objects should be considered in relation to game playing. Use prompts such as "How does X remind me of a game?", "How is Y like a game?", and "How could X and Y be used to play a game?"

BUILD A SENTENCE ACTIVITY

My students love this group fluency activity. Give each student three index cards and tell them to open a book to any page or website. Decide on about three or four numbers between 1 and 50. In this example I will use 4, 12, and 22. Ask the students to count words until they determine the 4th, 12th, and 22nd words on the page. Once they identify the words, ask them to write each one on a notecard. It is fine if the students do not know the word; that will only help build their vocabulary. Divide the students into groups of three and set a timer for a few minutes. When told to start, the groups try to build a sentence that makes sense with as many of the words as possible. After the designated time has passed, gather the groups to share the sentences.

Box 9.6 (cont.)

STAGE TAG ACTIVITY

Select several students and provide them with a prompt to begin acting out. Designate a stage area. The acting should be improvised on this stage area. The other students remain in the audience until someone gets a new idea to join the scene. The new actor taps the actor they wish to replace. The goal is to continue the improvisation without interrupting the scene.

CUE THE STORY ACTIVITY

Select several students and provide them with a stage area. The actors should be seated or standing in a line parallel with the audience. The teacher is the story director and begins with a short prompt such as "I am really funny." The teacher cues a student to continue the story. That actor continues to improvise a story until the teacher cues another student to take over.

MOVE THAT FLUENCY ACTIVITY

Visualizing movement and athletic skills can build creative fluency and can be practiced inside or outside the classroom. Rather than having students mindlessly repeat muscle-building activities, teachers can use this opportunity to build fluency through movement. The groups are tasked with inventing a way to practice the skill together. Divide students into groups and assign each group a skill. Suggestions might include squatting, walking lunges, jumping jacks, or sit ups. Require the group to generate a verbal chant to accompany the movements. A group of middle-school students invented a squatting circle. With each deep knee squat, the students clapped hands in various patterns, sometimes clapping their own hands and other times clapping a neighbor's hands. To assist them with moving fluently, the group created a chant to help synchronize their movements.

THE GOOD, THE BAD, THE REAL? ACTIVITY

While all these fluency activities can be used with any age group, this activity works especially well with teens and adults to get the idea generation started. To begin the activity, present students with what I call a juicy prompt. To help motivate the generation of ideas, it's helpful to use prompts that are complex enough to allow multiple perspectives. Then simply ask the students to think of examples when this prompt is good. After a period, stop the group and ask for ideas of when the prompt is bad. Prompts to consider include: When is pain good/bad? When is love good/bad? When is curiosity good/bad? When is surprise good/bad?

2. **Pre-assessment to determine who may need fluency support.** Teachers of writing recognize that generating fluent ideas can be challenging for some students. Each school year, the teacher may kick off a writing workshop (Shubitz & Dorfman, 2019) with personal narratives. This approach is taken for two reasons: first, most K–12 curricula require it and, second, it helps the teacher get to know their students. This "getting to know students" includes identifying early those who struggle and excel with creative fluency.

   It is common to experience a wide variety of abilities in student use of creative fluency. When asked to brainstorm or generate ideas for a writing topic, teachers will notice some students quickly get to work, some students freeze, and others fidget or seek help from others, and a few will state that they have no ideas. This is a teacher's first assessment of student fluency. Within minutes, a creatively minded educator can become aware of who needs support developing creative fluency and who excels at this creative skill.

3. **Student ongoing self-assessment.** Authoring their own texts provides students with opportunities to analyze and reflect upon both the creative writing process and their creative-thinking process. Utilize language from the RDCA (see Chapter 5) to develop appropriate rubrics and tools to support students in self-assessment throughout the creative writing process (Figure 9.2).

The RDCA targets fluency through the following four Items:

7: I can generate many relevant solutions.
28: I can rapidly produce a lot of ideas relevant to a task.
36: I generate many ideas when I draw.
40: I generate many ideas.

Name:	😊	😐	☹️
I can generate many solutions.			
I can produce a lot of ideas.			
I generate many ideas.			
I generate many ideas when I draw.			

Figure 9.2 Fluency self-assessment.

The goal, for both teacher and student, is to utilize language from the RDCA to conceptualize, reflect upon, and refine creativity skills, in this case generating ideas or fluency in writing. Figure 9.2 provides a fluency self-assessment.

4. See suggested assessment in Figure 9.2.
5. Record the number and quality of a learner's performance in various fluency activities and, based on these data, decide who excels and who needs more experience with fluency.

References

Cotton, K. (1991). *Teaching Thinking Skills*. Washington, DC: Northwest Regional Educational Laboratory, School Improvement Program.

Crockett, L., Jukes, I. & Churches, A. (2011). *Literacy Is NOT Enough: 21st Century Fluencies for the Digital Age*. Thousand Oaks, CA: Corwin.

Lynette, R. & Noak, C. (2009). Creative thinking: Fluency. Minds in Bloom. https://minds-in-bloom.com/creative-thinking-fluency/.

Michalko, M. (2006). *Thinkertoys: A Handbook of Creative-Thinking Techniques* (2nd ed.). Berkeley: The Ten Speed Press.

Rasinski, T. V. (2004). *Assessing Reading Fluency*. Honolulu: Pacific Resources for Education and Learning.

Shubitz, S. & Dorfman, L. R. (2019). *Welcome to Writing Workshop: Engaging Today's Students with a Model that Works*. Grandview Heights, OH: Stenhouse Publishers.

Sternberg, R. (1988.) *The Nature of Creativity: Contemporary Psychological Perspectives*. Cambridge, UK: Cambridge University Press.

Creativity Module 9.7
Elaboration

Background Information

Elaboration involves adding detail to something (e.g., writing, speech, drawing).

Activities

1. **Describe a place in detail.** At times when writing, we overlook the significance of describing a place in detail, as we might consider other aspects of the story to be more important. Adding more information about the place where the story occurs can enhance the reader's experience by allowing them to imagine themselves in that particular

place. It makes the characters and events seem more authentic. To practice elaboration regarding the story place, write a paragraph describing only that place (Verner, 2011).

2. **Use specific words to paint pictures.** Look at the following examples:
   - Mary sang a song.
   - Mary belted out a song.
   - Mary squeaked out a song.
   - Mary sang a song very quietly in a large space.

   The speaker sang a song in each sentence, but the images are quite different when visualized in the mind (Verner, 2011).

3. **Show how something feels, smells, tastes, sounds, or looks.** Elaboration helps us to expand a description of something using the five senses (e.g., when describing an apple, one could elaborate by stating that "it's round and usually red, it feels smooth, it smells sweetish, it tastes juicy" (Verner, 2011).

4. **Compare two different things through simile or metaphor.** A simile is a phrase that compares two things using the words *like* or *as*.
   - He is as nervous as a cat.
   - She is like a racing car.

   Both phrases compare a person to another object. A metaphor compares two things by saying that one is the other:
   - The boy was a nervous cat hiding behind the couch.
   - The girl was a racing car moving so fast.

5. **Show someone's feelings through what they do.** Communicate feelings through actions. Instead of writing "She was exalted," write about the character's actions:

   > She was exalted. She jumped up from her seat and let out a whoop of excitement. She could hardly contain her energy as she danced around the room, her heart racing with joy. She grabbed her phone and called her friends, telling them the good news with a voice that was breathless with excitement. She couldn't sit still, and she paced back and forth, feeling like she was on top of the world. Note: These activities were adapted from Verner (2011)

Assessments

Perform pre–post assessments that reflect the elaboration activities set out previously; that is, for each activity, observe improvement as a result of practice in the specific activity.

1. Describe a place in detail. Does the amount and quality of detail improve with practice?
2. Use specific words to paint pictures. Are more action words apparent with practice?
3. Show how something feels, smells, tastes, sounds, or looks. Are five-senses words more prevalent with practice?
4. Compare two different things through simile or metaphor. Are similes or metaphors employed more with practice?
5. Show someone's feelings through what they do. Do writing activities improve regarding communicating feelings through actions?

Reference

Verner, S. (2011). How to teach writing: 7 strategies for elaboration. Busy Teacher. https://busyteacher.org/6451-7-strategies-for-elaboration.html.

Creativity Module 9.8
Tolerance of ambiguity

Background Information

Else Frenkel-Brunswik (1949) introduced ambiguity tolerance–intolerance. The construct defines "how well an individual responds when presented with an event that results in ambiguous stimuli or situations" (Budner, 1962). Budner (1962) provided three examples regarding the cause of ambiguous situations:

1. situations in which there are inadequate amounts of information available to make a decision or draw a conclusion
2. situations in which there are conflicting or inconsistent pieces of information that make it difficult to determine the appropriate course of action
3. situations in which there are multiple possible interpretations of the available information, and it is unclear which one is the most accurate or appropriate

Using Frenkel-Brunswik's theory, Bochner (1965) categorized individuals who demonstrated intolerance to ambiguity with the following attributes:

- a need for categorization
- a need for certainty

- an inability to allow good and bad traits to exist in the same person
- an acceptance of attitude statements representing a white–black view of life
- a preference for familiar over unfamiliar
- a need to reject the unusual or different
- a resistance to reversal of fluctuating stimuli
- a tendency to come to premature closure

Bochner (1965) additionally attributed secondary characteristics to those who demonstrated intolerance to ambiguity:

- authoritarian
- dogmatic
- rigid
- closed-minded
- ethnically prejudiced
- uncreative
- anxious
- extra-punitive
- aggressive

Tolerance of ambiguity or ambiguity tolerance is a term used to describe how well someone handles uncertain and complex situations. It is crucial because it can help individuals navigate through an ever-changing world. Having a strategy to handle ambiguity is important, as it helps people work effectively in areas of uncertainty. Zenasni, Besancon, and Lubart (2008) looked into the relationship between ambiguity and creativity and found that those with high ambiguity tolerance tended to be more creative. Essentially, having a high ambiguity tolerance means that a person can handle uncertainty, unpredictability, and multiple demands effectively, which can be useful in many different situations.

Ambiguity tolerance refers to how well a person or group can handle situations that are unclear, confusing, or stressful. Someone with low ambiguity tolerance may feel anxious or avoid these kinds of situations altogether. On the opposite side of the scale, however, someone with a high tolerance for ambiguity perceives ambiguous situations as desirable, challenging, and interesting (Furnham & Ribchester, 1995). They are often motivated by it. Ambiguity tolerance can be defined as the degree to which a person has the ability to be comfortable with uncertainty, change, and conflicting information, and it can be seen in how well they can function in uncertain environments. Essentially, ambiguity tolerance involves being comfortable with the unknown.

The ability to tolerate ambiguity is an important factor in fostering creativity, as it allows people to approach problems and situations with an open and flexible mindset, leading to more original and innovative thinking. Having a higher ambiguity tolerance allows a person to embrace uncertainty and ambiguity rather than be afraid of it. It allows someone to see things from multiple perspectives and make connections between seemingly unrelated ideas (Zenasni, Besancon & Lubart, 2008). Someone that is able to tolerate ambiguity generally demonstrates the common characteristics shown in Box 9.7.

Box 9.7   Tolerance of ambiguity

Source: (Skaggs, 2019)

NOT BOUND BY CATEGORIZATION

Categorization is the act of arranging items or concepts according to their shared characteristics and distinctions. Being unencumbered by this means that one can reorganize and restructure their ideas based on the context. They also stay clear of being stuck by functional fixedness, which refers to the tendency to perceive ideas or objects only through their initial grouping (see Creativity Module 9.15 on a traditional, but wrong, approach to teaching place value).

COMFORTABLE WITH NOT KNOWING

Ambiguity and uncertainty are often linked. Ambiguity refers to something that lacks a clear meaning, whereas uncertainty refers to a lack of knowledge or constancy. Making a decision becomes difficult when all of the necessary information is not available. Tolerating uncertainty requires being open to uncertainty until enough information is gathered or until one is comfortable with trusting their intuition.

LOW FEAR RESPONSE TO THE UNKNOWN, THE UNFAMILIAR, OR CHANGE

Unlike those people with a tolerance for ambiguity, those with a low tolerance often have a hard time making a decision or come across as being indecisive, particularly when confronted with new information that conflicts with their existing belief.

ACCEPTANCE OF NOVELTY

Novelty is synonymous with originality. People with tolerance of ambiguity also tolerate things that are out of the ordinary.

Activities

Engage the learner in a role play that involves needing to become comfortable in situations in which the short-term and long-term future is unknown, such as the following:

1. What questions will be on the test?
2. Will my grandmother visit us for the (e.g., upcoming) holiday?
3. Will my new teacher like me?
4. Will I become class president?
5. When you don't know what's coming do you feel afraid, anxious, surprised, or curious?
6. When you don't know what's coming do you feel overly upset, moody, happy, or sad?
7. When you don't know what's coming do you ask others if they know?

Assessments

1. Observe and take notes regarding the results of student performance in the module activities. Engage the students in a group discussion on these results with the goal of increasing their tolerance for ambiguity.
2. Administer the following selected items from the ambiguity tolerance scale (Budner, 1965). The scoring guide is located after the scale items.
   (a) A good job is one where what is to be done and how it is to be done are always clear.
   (b) What we are used to is always preferable to what is unfamiliar.
   (c) People who insist upon a yes or no answer just don't know how complicated things really are.
   (d) A person who leads an even, regular life in which few surprises or unexpected happenings arise really has a lot to be grateful for.
   (e) I like parties where I know most of the people more than ones where all or most of the people are complete strangers.
   (f) Teachers or supervisors who hand out vague assignments give people a chance to show initiative and originality.

   Note: Items are scored on a five-point Likert-type scale (ranging from 1=strongly disagree to 5=strongly agree, with the midpoint being 3=neither agree nor disagree; the higher the score, the greater the level of tolerance for ambiguity)

3. Devise your own assessment, such as discussing with learners items similar to those in activity 1.

References

Bochner, S. (1965). Defining intolerance of ambiguity. *The Psychological Record*, 15(3), 393–400. https://doi.org/10.1007/bf03393605.

Budner, S. (1962). Intolerance of ambiguity as a personality. *Journal of Personality*, 30(1), 29–50.

Frenkel-Brunswik, E. (1949). Intolerance of ambiguity as an emotional and perceptual personality variable. *Journal of Personality*, 18(1), 108–143. https://doi.org/10.1111/j.1467-6494.1949.tb01236.x.

Furnham, A. & Ribchester, T. (1995). Tolerance of ambiguity: A review of the concept, its measurement and applications. *Current Psychology: A Journal for Diverse Perspectives on Diverse Psychological Issues*, 14(3), 179–199. https://doi.org/10.1007/BF02686907.

Skaggs, P. (2019). Tolerance for ambiguity. Industrial Designers Society of America (IDSA). www.idsa.org/educationpaper/tolerance-ambiguity.

Zenasni, F., Besancon, M. & Lubart, T. (2008). Creativity and tolerance of ambiguity: An empirical study. *The Journal of Creative Behavior*, 42(1), 61–73. https://doi.org/10.1002/j.2162-6057.2008.tb01080.x.

Creativity Module 9.9

Risk-taking

Background Information

Risk-taking is important in creativity and creative thinking, as it allows individuals to venture into new and uncharted territories to explore the unknown while accepting uncertainty and possible failure, leading to novel and innovative ideas. To come up with such ideas, individuals need to take risks, experiment with new approaches, and push boundaries. The late Sir Ken Robinson (2006) expressed risk-taking as follows: "If you're not prepared to be wrong, you'll never come up with anything original." Taking risks also helps individuals to overcome the fear of failure, which is a common obstacle to creativity. When people are afraid of failing, they may be reluctant to try new things or take risks, which can limit their creativity. When people embrace risk-taking, they are more willing to take on challenges and try out new ideas, even if they may not succeed at first. This mindset can lead to greater resilience and persistence, and a more positive attitude toward failure, all of which are important for fostering creativity.

In regard to a corporate setting, Dewett (2004, 2006, 2007) found that creative behavior requires an employee to be willing to take risks in their work and that risk is an important influence on creative behavior. A willingness to take risks is a significant predictor of employee creativity and, in addition, mediates the relationship between encouragement and creativity. Shen et al. (2018) showed that low risk-taking relates to convergent thinking.

What is a risk? People should be clear about the term risk and what an actual risk is, that is, the willingness to try something without clearly knowing the final outcome. The focus here is on smart risks, that is, being venturesome, daring, and exploratory. Failed risks aren't always negative. They sometimes provide the most valuable lessons one can learn on the journey to discovering or creating something new (Karwowski et al., 2020). Box 9.8 lists the benefits of risk-taking.

Box 9.8   Benefits of risk-taking

The following list of benefits is adapted from Perper's (2014) *The Psychological Benefits of Risk Taking*:

- Unforeseen opportunities may arise.
- Risk-taking builds confidence and develop new skills.
- It develops a sense of pride and accomplishment.
- Through risk-taking, you learn things you might not otherwise.
- It provides the chance to actively pursue success.
- Risk-taking spurs creativity.
- It provides the opportunity to create change in your life.
- Risk-taking develops emotional resilience.
- Risk-takers feel more engaged and happier.

Activities

1. A strategy to become more comfortable with taking larger risks is to first try taking small risks. Try some of the following risk-taking activities:
   (a) try new foods
   (b) learn a new skill
   (c) speak in public
   (d) ask for help
   (e) travel alone
   (f) take a new route to go somewhere
   (g) share your writing or art project with someone
2. Ask students to respond to the following prompts.

(a) Define what a risk is.
(b) Provide some examples of when taking a risk has led to a positive outcome.
(c) Provide some examples of when taking a risk has led to a negative outcome.
(d) Give examples of when taking a risk has been a bad thing to do.
(e) Describe a situation in which you "had" to take a risk against your better judgment.
(f) Has anyone been forced to take a risk to help yourself or someone else?
3. Draw or write about two risks that you have taken in your life. What were the consequences? Would you do them again?

Assessments

1. Observe and discuss with colleagues the results of this module's activities.
2. Develop a list of pros and cons when assessing a risk and use these results in evaluating whether or not to take the risk.

References

Dewett, T. (2004). Employee creativity and the role of risk. *European Journal of Innovation Management*, 7(4), 257–266. https://doi.org/10.1108/14601060410565010.

Dewett, T. (2006). Exploring the role of risk in employee creativity. *The Journal of Creative Behavior*, 40(1), 27–45. https://doi.org/10.1002/j.2162-6057.2006.tb01265.x.

Dewett, T. (2007). Linking intrinsic motivation, risk taking, and employee creativity in an R&D environment. *R&D Management*, 37(3), 197–208. https://doi.org/10.1111/j.1467-9310.2007.00469.x.

Karwowski, M., Jankowska, D. M., Brzeski, A. et al. (2020). Delving into creativity and learning. *Creativity Research Journal*, 32(1), 4–16.

Perper, R. (2014). The psychological benefits of risk taking. Therapy Changes. https://therapychanges.com/blog/2014/06/psychological-benefits-risk/.

Robinson, K. (2006). Do schools kill creativity? [Video file]. www.ted.com/speakers/sir_ken_robinson.

Shen, T., Zhou, T., Long, G., Jiang, J., Wang, S. & Zhang, C. (2018). Reinforced self-attention network: A hybrid of hard and soft attention for sequence modeling. arXiv:1801.10296.

Creativity Module 9.10
Resistance to premature closure

Background Information

Resistance to premature closure involves keeping an open mind and weighing several alternatives before coming to a decision. Box 9.9 discusses an example of premature closure, referred to as functional fixedness.

Activities

1. Role play helps make abstract problems more concrete and real, allows for immediate feedback, facilitates the expression of attitudes and feelings, provides opportunities to speculate on what-if situations, and involves applying knowledge to solving problems. In role-playing, a student may assume the perspective of a participating character in a scenario designed to create a greater understanding of a topic, surrounding issues, and human interaction. To implement role play, the following steps are suggested:
   (a) Identify the goal of the activity, for example non-challenged students, in collaboration with challenged peers, engage in understanding each other's perspectives and emotions and students become aware of issues that motivating behavior and agree upon expected outcomes of the role play.
   (b) Before the role play begins, students should research the topic at hand (e.g., dyslexia, shyness, bullying, etc.), discuss their anticipated

---

Box 9.9 Example of premature closure

It appears that "experts" in a field become so committed to a standard way of doing something that they do not even consider alternative approaches. This is currently referred to as *functional fixedness*. This is an example of coming to premature closure due to blindly accepting the status quo. Torrance (1979, p. 74) stated that when "faced with any incompleteness or unsolved problem, almost everyone tends to jump to some conclusion immediately. Frequently, this jump is made prematurely – before the person has taken the time to understand the problem, considered important factors involved in the problem, and thought of alternative solutions." It is necessary to defer judgment in order to resist premature closure and remain open.

roles, and have a preliminary knowledge of the context and meaning of the situation presented (e.g., How can we as a class be more accepting of those with learning challenges so that we become a community of learners that support one another?).

(c) This preliminary preparation allows the students to express the perspectives they represent in a safe practice environment and identify changes they want to incorporate as a result of the practice run.

(d) The role-play activity should culminate in follow-up class discussions that emphasize that all of us have some sort of need (e.g., see discussion of cognitive, social, emotional, physical, and sensory, or psychomotor, generic influences in Chapter 5) and that implementing knowledge of special learning needs will enhance everyone's learning.

Role play is related to the "six thinking hats" exercise described next (DeBono, 1985). Hats may be found in costume stores or represented by other means (e.g., participants holding an index card with the color indicated or some other option to indicate the hat colors).

2. The "six thinking hats" exercise is used as a structure for role play. It is an effective thinking process that helps students use different types of thinking. The activity shows how to separate thinking into six clear functions and roles. Each thinking role is identified with a colored symbolic "thinking hat." Students can redirect their thoughts and subsequent discussion by physically or mentally wearing and switching hats. The thinking hats creative activity is a way for students to approach problems and ideas from different points of view and to contemplate an issue from a different perspective (De Bono, 1985; Kivunja, 2015). Box 9.10 provides the definitions for each hat and the role they play in the six thinking hats technique.

Box 9.10   Six thinking hats definitions

De Bono's six thinking hats exercise enables decision-making to be considered from different viewpoints. Each thinking style is represented by a different colored hat. This is a fun activity for all ages.

White Hat	Calls for Information known or needed
Blue hat	manage the thinking process
Green hat	creative thinking
Red hat	feelings and instincts
Yellow hat	brightness and optimism
Black hat	risk assessment

Source: De Bono (1985)

> **Box 9.11 Voice from the field: six thinking hats as an assessment strategy**
>
> The thinking hats strategy can be employed as a decision-making tool by teachers to involve the class in making a decision that will affect them (e.g., Should the teacher give tests on Fridays or another day of the week?).
>
> The six thinking hats strategy can help students prepare for writing a paper by brainstorming ideas from different perspectives. By using this activity, students can consider various points of view and evaluate counter-arguments to help prepare for writing a persuasive paper.

Assessments

1. Using the six thinking hats activity, participants will learn how to use a disciplined process that will:
   - help them to view a problem or situation from multiple perspectives, using different types of thinking
   - help them to avoid making snap judgments or jumping to conclusions
   - encourage creativity and innovation by exploring new ideas and possibilities
   - improve communication and collaboration by fostering open-mindedness and respect for diverse viewpoints
   - help them to make better decisions by considering a range of factors and weighing different options
   - help them to increase self-awareness and metacognition by reflecting on their own thinking and the thinking of others
2. There are endless scenarios in which it would be appropriate to use the six thinking hats strategy to encourage students to think creatively. Box 9.11, as a perspective from the field, offers other ideas for using the six thinking hats as assessment activities.
3. Engage learners in role play and record instances in which resistance to premature closure is apparent.
4. Have the learners write a short scenario in which they engage in either resisting premature closure or not, and describe the consequences.

References

De Bono, E. (1985). *Six Thinking Hats*. Boston: Little Brown and Company.

Kivunja, C. (2015). Using De Bono's six thinking hats model to teach critical thinking and problem solving skills essential for success in the 21st century economy. *Creative Education*, 6(3), 380–391. https://doi.org/10.4236/ce.2015.63037.

Torrance, E. P. (1979). *The Search for Satori and Creativity*. New York: Creative Education Foundation.

Creativity Module 9.11
Flexibility

Background Information

Flexibility is defined here as generating many *categories* of ideas. For example, categories might involve color, thickness of blocks, shape, trees, toys, articles of clothing, etc. The category color might contain objects that are red, blue, green, etc.; the category trees might contain pine, oak, walnut, etc.; and the category toys might contain truck, ball, doll, etc.; and so forth. This definition is distinguished from thinking flexibly, also called cognitive flexibility, which is the ability to shift gears and see things in more than one way. A flexible thinker would be able to think about one thing in multiple different ways. An inflexible thinker would be thinking about things in one way and not having an open mind to other thoughts or opinions. However, it is important to be aware of this distinction in definition; creativity-related flexibility relates to generating different categories of something.

Activities

1. **Good, bad, interesting** (Michalko, 2006). Creative thinking involves considering your central theme, idea, or challenge, and thinking about what's good about it, what's bad about it, and what's interesting about it. Generate as many examples of each as you can think of, but try to be fairly equal about it. Too much of one or another demonstrates bias in your thinking.

    This is not about finding the "right" answer. It is about looking at all the possible interpretations of an idea. Most people react to a new idea by either liking or disliking it.

    The good, bad, interesting exercise forces creative thinking to generate multiple perspectives on an idea. It shows that ideas can be seen as good, as bad, or as interesting, depending on the particular frame of mind you are coming from. Any idea can be looked at in a different way by reframing it. The idea changes in the mind of a person depending on how they are looking at it. This is important to remember in all interactions among people with opposing viewpoints as they generate different categories of ideas.

2. **How are they alike?** This activity enhances flexibility, generating numerous categories. Using the list "orange, apple, banana, potato, rock, water, and air," ask: How are an orange and an apple alike? They are both fruit (nominal category). They both grow on trees (intrinsic functional category, that is, what they do). They are round (perceptible category). You can eat them both (extrinsic functional category, that is, what you do to them). Next, ask: How are an orange, an apple, and a banana alike? Keep adding an object. Commonalities change as you add more objects and the commonality becomes more abstract. Box 9.12 presents the results of a related study based on the work of Jerome Bruner (1960).

3. **Absence thinking** (Michalko, 2006). This technique relies on the fact that we are very good at seeing what is there but not at all good at seeing what is not there. Absence thinking compensates for this by deliberately forcing us to notice things that are not usually apparent. For example, watch people and notice what they do not do. Make lists of things to remember that you normally forget. In other words, deliberately and carefully think about what is absent. This activity is helpful when you are stuck and unable to shift your thinking to some other approach. It is analogous to the importance of negative space to artists – especially in sculptures, as described in Box 9.13.

Box 9.12   Jerome Bruner

In a study by Denney (1975), categories changed as a function of normal and intellectually challenged youngsters matched for mental ages ranging from 5 to 11 years. The youngsters considered to be in the normal range intellectually used nominal and functional concepts as opposed to perceptible concepts when asked to pair pictures of objects. Interestingly, Reisman (personal unpublished investigation), when clinically diagnosing mathematically gifted and challenged first- through third-graders, found that adhering to Bruner's developmental theory of representing curriculum (enactive or concrete, iconic or picture, and symbols levels) led to differentiated results. The younger students could compare more objects at the enactive level (e.g., handling an apple and an orange) than at the more abstract levels (e.g., pictures or words).

> **Box 9.13 Absence thinking**
>
> Negative space in art refers to the space surrounding the main subject or object in a composition. It is the area that is not occupied by the subject or object but is just as important in defining the overall image. Negative space can be used to create a sense of balance, depth, and contrast in a piece of art.
>
> An excellent example of negative space in design is the FedEx logo. The logo features a bold, purple-and-orange typeface with the company's name, but what makes it unique is the hidden arrow created by the negative space between the "E" and the "X." This clever use of negative space not only creates a sense of intrigue and curiosity in the viewer but also subconsciously reinforces the company's brand message of being fast and efficient in delivering packages.
>
> The FedEx logo is a testament to the power of negative space in design and its ability to convey meaning and messaging in subtle and effective ways. It demonstrates that negative space is not just empty space but a crucial element in the overall composition of a piece of art or design.

Assessments

1. Observe, record, and discuss with colleagues the results of this module's activities.
2. Upon completing one of the module's activities with a group of learners, have them write a short reflection statement for the instructor who will abstract themes from the statements and share them with the group with the goal of enhancing their understanding of creativity flexibility.

References

Bruner, J. S. (1960). *The Process of Education*. Cambridge, MA: Harvard University Press.

Denney, D. R. (1975). Developmental changes in concept utilization among normal and retarded children. *Developmental Psychology*, 11(3), 359–368.

Michalko, M. (2006). *Thinkertoys: A Handbook of Creative-Thinking Techniques* (2nd ed.). Berkeley, CA: Ten Speed Press.

Creativity Module 9.12
Divergent thinking

Background Information

Divergent thinking is a creative process that generates many ideas (e.g., problems and solutions) and is related to fluency (see Creativity Module 9.6). Divergent thinking is one half of the creative-thinking process; convergent thinking is the other half, as presented in Figure 2.2 (Tanner & Reisman, 2014) in Chapter 2.

Divergent Thinking Versus Convergent Thinking

Divergent thinking involves generating a wide range of ideas or solutions for a problem, while convergent thinking involves using logical steps to determine the best solution. Unlike convergent thinking, divergent thinking does not have a single best answer and is more spontaneous and free flowing. This type of thinking is useful for open-ended problems that require creativity. Conversely, convergent thinking is effective when there is a single correct answer that can be found by analyzing available information. Convergent thinking does not rely on creativity and is often used in multiple-choice questions on school exams. Tests such as the alternative uses test and incomplete figure test have been shown to enhance divergent thinking and measure creativity.

Activities

1. **Brainstorming.** Alex Osborn (1964), known as the father of the brainstorming, said: "It is easier to tone down a wild idea than to think up a new one." Brainstorming is a method of thinking up solutions, ideas or new concepts and typically involves three steps: (1) idea capture, (2) discussion and critique, and (3) selection. Box 9.14 contains the four rules of brainstorming.

    Creativity is encouraged by not allowing ideas to be evaluated or discussed until everyone has exhausted the ideas they wish to generate. Any and all ideas are considered legitimate. It is often the most far-fetched ideas that lead to new connections and the most creative solutions. According to Osborn, other rules for brainstorming include creating an environment in which team members are not criticized for their ideas. Ideas are to be evaluated *after* the actual brainstorming

> **Box 9.14 Four rules of brainstorming**
>
> Rule 1: Focus on quantity
> Rule 2: Withhold criticism
> Rule 3: Welcome wild ideas
> Rule 4: Combine and improve ideas

component of a session. Judgments during the act of brainstorming process tend to alienate team members. The following are two modifications of brainstorming (SkyMark, 2019).

   (a) **Reverse brainstorming** (Michalko, 2006) is a different approach to brainstorming. It involves stating the problem in reverse to help solve problems by looking at them from a completely different angle and generating more creative solutions.

   (b) **Brainwriting** (Michalko, 2006) is a technique invented shortly after Osborn published his brainstorming technique. A German marketing professional named Bernd Rohrbach (1969) developed a process called 6-3-5. These numbers represent six people coming together around a common problem, then each jotting down three initial ideas on their own and then, after five minutes, rotating their notes and repeating the process. This way, people can learn from each other, and no one gets silenced in the process. This technique alleviates three of the biggest brainstorming shortcomings by (1) avoiding unbalanced conversation, (2) ensuring that everyone has the opportunity to contribute, and (3) eliminating the bias toward the first idea.

2. **Figure storming** (Michalko, 2006) is a useful creativity tool for generating fresh ideas and encouraging innovative thinking. It involves creating visual representations of a problem or idea to generate new and innovative solutions. It is similar to brainstorming, but instead of using only words, participants use drawings, diagrams, and other visual aids to represent their ideas. The process begins with a problem or idea, and participants are given time to sketch their initial ideas. These sketches are then shared and discussed in the group, with participants building on and refining each other's ideas.

3. **Starbursting** (Michalko, 2006) is a creative-thinking technique that involves generating questions related to a specific problem or topic in order to identify potential opportunities, challenges, and solutions. The process of starbursting involves creating a star-shaped diagram with the topic or problem in the center and lines radiating outward to six points, each representing a different question: Who? What? Where? When? Why? and How?

    For each of the six questions, participants brainstorm additional questions that help to explore the topic or problem more deeply. For example, for the question "What?" participants might ask "What are the possible outcomes?" or "What are the different options?" For "Why?" they might ask "Why is this important?" or "Why does this problem exist?" By generating a wide range of questions, starbursting helps to identify areas of focus and potential avenues for exploration.

    Starbursting is often used in the early stages of idea generation and problem-solving to help expand thinking beyond initial assumptions and identify potential areas for further exploration. By exploring the topic or problem from multiple angles, starbursting can help to generate new and unexpected ideas, challenge assumptions, and facilitate more informed decision-making.

4. **SCAMPER** is an activity that relies on divergent thinking, proposed by Alex Osborn's brainstorming process (Osborn, 1964). It involves looking at situations from new perspectives. Osborn's ground rules for group brainstorming comprise the following: judicial judgment is ruled out, wildness is welcomed, quantity is wanted, and combination and improvement are sought. These four guidelines provide the power that underlies divergent thinking. The acronym SCAMPER (Eberle, 1996) refers to the following skills: substitute, combine, adapt, modify/magnify/minify, put to other uses, eliminate, and reverse/rearrange. Box 9.15 sets out a perspective from the field addressing divergent thinking.

> **Box 9.15 Voice from the field: divergent thinking**
>
> To stimulate students' creativity around divergent thinking, I often provide my middle-school students with what I call simulations. Many of my students love video gaming or even board games, so this is an opportunity for them to be part of the "game." One example of my simulations relates to our classical unit of study on how technology and innovation impacted ancient warfare. After building background knowledge on ancient Greek city-states using readings, videos, and creating symbols to represent them, students enter the classroom. They are given a card with the name of a Greek city-state.
>
> This creates their simulation team for the day. Next, they discuss all the strengths and weaknesses of their given city-state and record them on a chart. For example, based on our studies, students would know that Athenians were excellent sailors because Athens was built on a harbor and created a vast trade network. To enhance their idea generation, I allow them to use pictures, symbols, or words to express their ideas. Students also would have been taught how to brainstorm in previous sessions, so they know to let the ideas flow and withhold judgment.
>
> Once the group has identified their city-states' strengths and weaknesses, I give the class a real-life historical scenario and the "game" begins. For this particular simulation, I provide an example from the Persian Wars. The Persians have attacked one of the Greek city-states and they have called upon all city-states to help. I provide them with details about the Persian strategy, weaponry, and military on a one-page fact sheet. Based on what the groups have contributed on their charts about the strengths and weaknesses of their Greek city-states, they devise a plan to support their fellow Greeks and defeat the Persians. They can draw or list their ideas directly under their city-states' strengths and weaknesses.
>
> To keep their focus on creative idea generation and finding as many unique solutions as possible, I do not assess their ideas. On occasion, some students are not used to this type of autonomy, so I circulate the classroom and reinforce their ideas with lots of positive encouragement. I often yell out to the class when a group adds another idea to their list in celebration! I try not to give examples, but, if necessary, I will lead them through one of their strengths. If Athens is really good at sailing, what could they do to help? Usually, students will say, "Send a fleet of ships!". One small spark can set off another. If a student asks me who really won or what really happened, I usually reply that who won is ancient history. The true win is what was learned both then and now and how it will help them or the next civilization be greater. They are excited the next day to share their group's ideas with their classmates and we tally up how many ideas we have generated as a class. It's a creative win!

Assessments

1. Observe and discuss with colleagues the results of the voice role play activity with the goal of modeling instruction to enhance divergent thinking.
2. After each activity attempted, ask the learners to write a reflection of what they gained from the activity, how and why they either liked or disliked a particular activity, and how they would modify it. The teacher then abstracts themes from the students' reflections and shares them with the class for discussion. The goal is for the learners to become aware of what divergent thinking is.

References

Eberle, B. (1996). *Scamper: Games for Imagination Development*. Waco, TX: Prufrock Press Inc.

Michalko, M. (2006). *Thinkertoys: A Handbook of Creative-Thinking Techniques* (2nd ed.). Berkeley, CA: Ten Speed Press.

Osborn, A. F. (1964). *How to Become More Creative*. New York: Scribners.

Rohrbach, B. (1969). *Kreativ nach Regeln – Methode 635, eine neue Technik zum Lösen von Problemen* (Creative by rules – Method 635, a new technique for solving problems). *Absatzwirtschaft*, 12, 73–75.

SkyMark (2019). Alex F. Osborn: The father of brainstorming. www.skymark.com/resources/leaders/osborne.asp.

Tanner, D. & Reisman, F. (2014). *Creativity as a Bridge between Education and Industry: Fostering New Innovations*. North Charleston, NC: CreateSpace.

Creativity Module 9.13

Convergent thinking

Background Information

Convergent thinking is the process of combining or joining different ideas together based on common elements, whereas divergent thinking involves separating topic components for the purposes of expanding and exploring the various parts. Closure may be interpreted as the resolution of tension. When we experience tension, we strive to arrive at a resolution. For example, the resolution or closure of a dangerous situation takes the form of some sort of protection. Reading an exciting murder mystery novel results in closure with the knowing "who dunnit." A long, thought-out purchase builds the tension of wanting and is resolved with the purchase, resulting in closure. Thus, the anticipation of pleasure is finalized when closure occurs.

We better remember that which is unfinished or incomplete. Russian psychologist Bluma Zeigarnik (2007) identified what became known as the Zeigarnik effect. In essence, the Zeigarnik effect describes how people remember uncompleted or interrupted tasks better than completed tasks (Mann, 2005). For example, give folks a problem at the end of the day. By the next day, they will have thought hard about it. To remember things, something should remain incomplete, with the ongoing thinking helping to keep important facts in mind. Mann (2005) further shared that Zeigarnik theorized that an incomplete task or unfinished business creates "psychic tension" within us. This tension acts as a motivator to drive us toward completing the task or finishing the business. In Gestalt terms, we are motivated to seek "closure," and creative thinkers resist premature closure. Figure 2.2 in Chapter 2 shows the central role of convergence in creative thinking. Box 9.16 provides biographical data regarding Zeigarnik.

Box 9.16   Bluma Wulfovna Zeigarnik

Bluma Zeigarnik conducted a study on memory in the 1920s, comparing memory related to incomplete and complete tasks. She found that incomplete tasks were easier to remember than successful ones, and this phenomenon is now known as the Zeigarnik effect. This was described in a diploma prepared under the supervision of Kurt Lewin. In the 1930s, she worked with Lev Vygotsky at the All-Union Institute of Experimental Medicine. During World War II, she assisted Alexander Luria in treating head injuries. She cofounded the Moscow State University Department of Psychology and the All-Russian Seminars in Psychopathology. She passed away in Moscow at the age of 87 in 1988 (Zeigarnik, 2007).

Activities

1. Practice making a choice from many options, as follows:
   (a) Given a menu of food choices, select one.
   (b) From an array of toys (colors, writing utensils, colored blocks, etc.), pick one and describe why.
   (c) Given four baby (girls, boys) names, pick your favorite.
   (d) Given a choice of pets, pick one.
2. Create a situation in which a choice must occur, for example:
   (a) Select a homework buddy from a group of five options.
   (b) Create a situation in which a learner must choose an answer to a difficult multiple-choice question and must explain reasons for the choice made.

Assessments

Assessment 1: Creative Problem-Solving Grid – Cardinality Versus Ordinality
This activity is designed to help individuals or groups identify the root or real problem and then select the best solution. First, have the students brainstorm possible problems related to an issue. For example, "Why do students have difficulty grasping the teacher's explanations of a particular concept such as cardinality (the how muchness of a set of objects) versus ordinality (the sequencing of objects according to a specific rule such as size, length, shades of a color, etc.)."

Next, decide on the criteria that will be used to evaluate each possible solution. Rank the nine possible problems within each evaluation criteria column, with "9" assigned to the most likely cause and "1" assigned to the least likely. Then, add up the totals for each possible problem across the rows. Table 9.5 provides an example of how this activity works for identifying the real problem. Remember that the same grid format can be used to determine the most desirable solution once the *real* problem is identified.

The following are directions for using Table 9.5 and other creative problem-solving grids you may create.

1. To use Table 9.5, evaluate each possible cause vertically within each evaluation criterion. Start by counting the number of factors being ranked, which will be the top ranking for each horizontal category. In the case of Table 9.5, there are nine possible causes listed in the first column. Typically, a list of five to ten options to be ranked is manageable.
2. Next rank each cause from 1 (least probable cause) to 9 (most probable cause) within each of the evaluation columns (clear teacher instructions, use of instructional activities at the concrete manipulative level, creative instruction, motivating instruction).
3. Next find the sum for each option by adding horizontally across the evaluation criteria.
4. Finally, decide upon the major cause, that is, the total score for the option that is most likely causing the ineffective instruction. If this option isn't reasonable, then go to the next highest total. Remember, this grid is only a tool and it relies upon human judgment.

Table 9.5 *Creative problem-solving grid: identifying the real problem*

Possible problem relating to instruction	Clear teacher instructions	Use of instructional activities at the concrete manipulative level	Creative instruction	Motivating instruction	Totals
Persistent in using concrete-level instructional activities					
Triggers original/novel ideas in students					
Generates many ideas					
Resists premature closure					
Tolerates ambiguity					
Emphasizes divergent thinking					
Emphasizes convergent thinking					
Encourages intrinsic motivation					
Encourages extrinsic motivation					

Assessment 2: Creative Problem-Solving Grid – Innovation Pedagogy
Table 9.6 has twenty-two elements (thus one would need to rank from 22 to 1). The exhaustive list is presented so the reader may select those that are most appropriate for their issue (i.e., do not try to rank all twenty-two items!). The directions for using this table are as follows.

1. Add across the evaluation criteria by row and enter the sum in the "Totals" column.
2. Consider the characteristics of the possible innovative pedagogy with the highest total score as your first option for designing a creative pedagogy.

Table 9.6 *Creative problem-solving grid for a possible innovative pedagogy*

Characteristics of possible innovative pedagogy	Evaluation criteria A=desirable, B=possible, C=viable, D=beneficial, E=sustainable, F=creative, G=learner centered							
	A	B	C	D	E	F	G	Total
Instructor facilitator								
Student problem-solving								
Cooperative learning								
Reflective thinking								
Metacognition								
Persistence/grit								
Deal with change								
Manage/analyze information								
Trigger original/novel ideas								
Generate many ideas								
Elaborate verbally/in writing/graphically								
Resist premature closure								
Tolerate ambiguity								
Divergent thinking								
Convergent thinking								
Intrinsic motivation								
Extrinsic motivation								
Generate many categories of ideas								
Take smart risks								
Self-initiated learning								
Self-efficacy								
Diagnostic teaching/learning								

3. If you are not comfortable with the option that obtained the highest score, then consider the next highest. Remember, this grid is merely a heuristic (tool) for making a decision.

The creative problem-solving grid in Table 9.6 exemplifies how the use of the grid may result in a new and innovative pedagogy.

References

Mann, E. L. (2005). Mathematical creativity and school mathematics: Indicators of mathematical creativity in middle school students. *Doctoral Dissertations*, 1–120. https://opencommons.uconn.edu/dissertations/AAI3205573/.

Zeigarnik, A. (2007). Bluma Zeigarnik: A memoir. International Society for Gestalt Theory and Its Applications. www.gestalttheory.net/uploads/pdf/GTH-Archive/2007Zeigarnik_Memoir.pdf.

Creativity Module 9.14
Intrinsic and extrinsic motivation

Background Information

Intrinsic motivation describes all motivational types driven by internal incentives, while extrinsic motivation describes all motivational types driven by external rewards. Table 3.2 in Chapter 3 presents subsets of motivation that highlight specific motivating factors. For example, intrinsic or internal motivation provides satisfaction during the performance of the task itself; it is satisfied by the inner joy of the task. Extrinsic motivators include recognition, status, authority, grade, and promotion. Sometimes, intrinsic and extrinsic motivation work together to achieve an optimal balance of motivating factors.

Activities

1. **Hall of fame** (Michalko, 2006). Using real or fictional people can be helpful when trying to explain intrinsic and extrinsic motivation. When we put ourselves in another person's shoes (real, fictional, historic) we can feel their inner satisfaction regarding completing a task and their need for some sort of reward.

2. **Role play** provides opportunity for students to become aware of their emotional and cognitive experiences in scenarios involving intrinsic and extrinsic motivation. Have your students engage in role play as follows:
   (a) In the first scenario, two groups of three students discuss their feelings about two different teacher–student interactions:
      (i) Teacher A always gives positive feedback.
      (ii) Teacher B always gives negative feedback.
   (b) In the second scenario, a girls' basketball team that receives supportive instruction from their male coach at halftime goes on to win, while another team that is yelled at by their male coach to the point of the star player crying goes on to lose, with the star player eventually transferring to another university.

Assessments

1. Observe and discuss with the students the results of the various role play scenarios with the goal being for them to experience both intrinsic and extrinsic situations.
2. Have students write a short reflection describing a situation in which extrinsic motivation is necessary to encourage intrinsic motivation. Discuss their ideas to recognize that both extrinsic and intrinsic motivation may sometimes be needed.

Reference

Michalko, M. (2007). *Thinkertoys*. Berkeley, CA: The Rocks Campus Ten Speed Press.

Creativity Module 9.15
Creative place value pedagogy

Background Information

It is no wonder that the traditional approach to teaching place value causes confusion to the learner because it is wrong. Place value is a pervasive difficulty in learning arithmetic, which, if not corrected early, affects students' understanding of computation well into adulthood – and is especially apparent in those students with math anxiety and dyscalculia. A creative new approach to learning place value uses place value/counting boards, which represent a physical embodiment of the rationale for moving from the units (ones) place to the tens place to the hundreds place, etc. In the beginning stages of learning, children do not think, "I have ten units; that's one group of ten and no units." Rather, initial learning takes the form of a count-on-by-one model and incorporates a horizontal move to the next position to the left *after the count of nine, not ten.* The place value/counting boards are a truer physical embodiment of our numeration system.

The place value/counting boards were created by Reisman and Severino (2021) after many years of diagnosing why students had so much difficulty learning place value. Place value charts, Dienes blocks, Cuisenaire rods, the abacus, and bead charts have been used for years. All these methods rely on the "exchange model," whereby multiples of ten are exchanged for the next higher place value. By contrast, each board has nine spaces with increasing values from 1 to 9 (see Figures 9.2 to 9.7). An empty board has a value of zero. The counting boards represent the finite set of digits in our Hindu/Arabic numeration system (0, 1, 2, 3, 4, 5, 6, 7, 8, 9). The following activities correctly address teaching place value (Torrance & Reisman, 2000).

Activities

1. In using the boards, a value of one is obtained by jumping a chip onto the board to land on space *one*. It is important to represent the board's initial value as *zero* by starting with an empty board (Figures 9.3 and 9.4).
2. By the time students are in eighth to twelfth grade, a different physical representation is needed if they still do not understand place value, which underlies the algorithms for operations on whole numbers, as well as computation with decimals. An analysis of place value reveals that two very different relationships are involved in understanding place value – a "count-on-by-one" model and an "exchange" model (bundling of tens).

   The count-on-by-one model emphasizes the fact that, when recording the counting sequence, a change in thinking from units to tens occurs after the count of nine. On the other hand, the bundling-of-tens model involves a shift in thinking after the count of ten. We count ten objects and then bundle them to represent 1 ten. In fact, we count to nine and then make our move to the tens place; we change place values after the count of nine, not ten. Therefore, the bundling-of-tens model does not accurately represent our notational system. However, we will see later in this chapter that the exchange/bundling model is

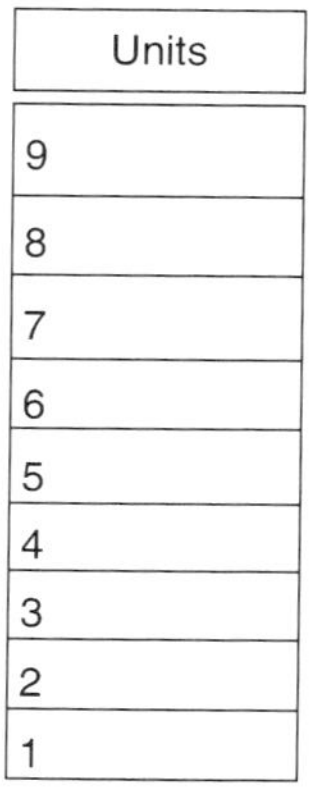

290 Connecting Creativity and Motivation Research with End Users

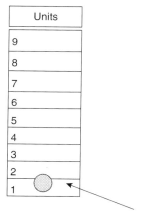

Figure 9.3 Board showing zero.

Figure 9.4 Board showing value of one.

appropriate for teaching addition and subtraction of whole numbers with renaming (carrying and borrowing).

Have students practice counting board values from zero to nine by jumping a chip onto the board to count "one," moving the chip up one space to show "two," and so on up to "nine" (Figure 9.5). Continue counting one more beyond nine and call out "ten" as the chip is moved up and off the top of the counting board (Figure 9.5). Although there is now no chip on the board, set a rule that, once the

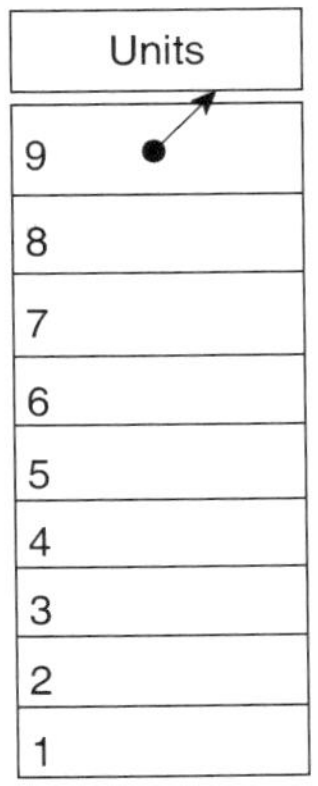

9 Creativity Modules 291

	Units
9	● ↗
8	
7	
6	
5	
4	
3	
2	
1	

Figure 9.5 Counting board showing impending count of "ten."

count starts, the counting board continues to have value, especially when the count is greater than nine and the units board appears empty. Otherwise, students might focus on the visual emptiness of the board and forget that they had been counting upward beyond nine to ten, with the chip now sitting in the space just above the board (Figure 9.5).

3. After the student has had practice using one board, provide a second counting board. Position the second board (the "tens board") to the upper left of the "units board" (Figure 9.6) to continue the upward counting sequence beyond nine.

The board to the upper left represents the "tens" place value. Each space on the "tens" board is worth ten, just as one space on the "hundreds board" is worth 100, etc. Remind students that, as the chip is moved up a space, the board value increases by its value. Thus, moving up a space on the tens board is twenty, thirty, forty, etc.

Present the following problem-solving situation: What will the count be if the chip is moved up one beyond nine? It is now just above the units board. Move the chip horizontally to the left onto the bottom space of the board to the upper left (Figure 9.7). Since only a horizontal move and no upper move occurred, there was no increase in value. Consequently, the value of the bottom space on the board in the "tens" place is ten; the boards show one "ten" and zero "units" or ten.

292 Connecting Creativity and Motivation Research with End Users

Figure 9.6 Counting board showing count of "ten."

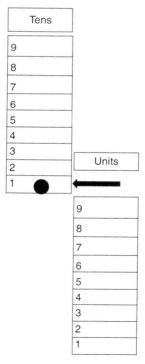

Figure 9.7 Units and tens counting boards showing that the horizontal move from units to tens remains "ten."

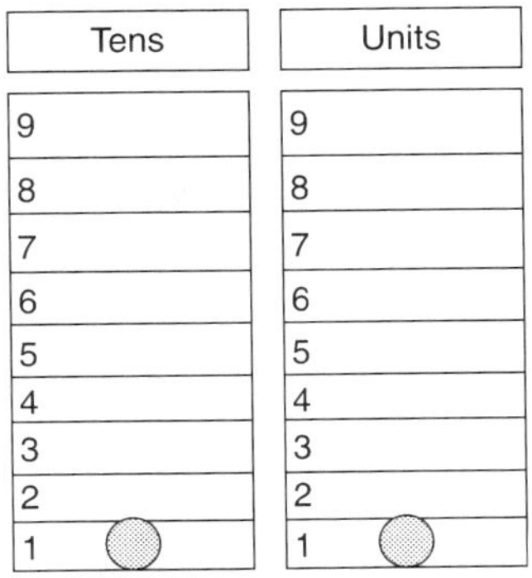

9 *Creativity Modules* 293

Tens	Units
9	9
8	8
7	7
6	6
5	5
4	4
3	3
2	2
1 ●	1 ●

Figure 9.8 Tens and units boards representing "eleven."

Offer the student a second chip and instruct them to show the number eleven. They should move a second chip onto the one-space of the units board. Be sure that students understand that eleven should be shown with a chip on the ten-space of the "tens" board and a chip on the one-space of the units board. If a student attempts to show eleven by moving the second chip to the twenty-space on the "tens" board, use the following diagnostic questions to help them understand that they are showing twenty, not eleven. Ask: If you move the chip on the tens board up a space, what will the value of the boards be? Answer: twenty. What number would you write under the "tens" board if your chip was in the second space? Answer: two. Next, instruct students to show eleven using both boards (Figure 9.8).

Repeat the process as students count to nineteen. At the count of twenty, the counting boards show a chip in the one-space on the "tens" board with a second chip sitting atop the "units" board. Make sure that students understand that, just as two digits cannot be written in one space, two chips (representing digits) cannot be in one space.

The chip with a count of ten, sitting above the units board, needs to move horizontally to the tens board, maintaining the value of twenty, which results in two chips in the bottom tens board space. This cannot be, just as we do not write two digits, one over the other, in the same number position. So how do we solve the dilemma?

There now is the opportunity to allow a two-for-one exchange, by exchanging the two chips worth ten each for one chip placed on the second space whose value is twenty.

Assessments

Place value items (answer in **bold**).

1. Circle the place value that tells the value of three in the number 3,520.
   ones
   tens
   hundreds
   thousands
2. Round 193 to the nearest hundred. Circle your answer.
   200
   190
   210
   100
3. Circle the number 3,243 rounded to the nearest hundred.
   3,000
   3,200
   3,240
   3,300
4. Circle the order from least to greatest.
   7980, 7890, 7750
   5780, 5879, 5889
   6980, 6978, 6877
   5780, 5680, 5670
5. Circle the number with the GREATEST value that can be made with the digits 4, 8, and 5 using all the digits only once.
   854
   584
   548
   845

Other Place Value Questions Using the Computational Counting Boards

6. The teacher asks students to count from one to nine on the units counting board.
7. The teacher asks students to count from one to ten on the units and tens counting boards.
8. The teacher asks students to count from one to thirteen on the units and tens counting boards and write the digit 1 under the tens board and the digit 3 under the ones board to show thirteen.

9. The teacher says numbers from one to ninety-nine for students to show on the units and tens counting boards.
10. The teacher asks students to show 111 on the counting boards. Allow creative problem-solving discussion until someone says they need a third board to show hundreds. Teacher asks students to explain why they need the third counting board.
11. The teacher asks students to show numbers 1 to 999 on the counting boards.
12. For fifth or sixth graders, extend the counting boards to the right to show decimal place values. Place the board worth tenths to the lower right of the units board and continue with hundredths, thousandths, etc. Finally, have all boards moved to the same level so that digits written below their respective board will appear as a normal number, e.g., 13.1.

References

Reisman, F., & Severino, L. (2021). *Using Creativity to Address Dyslexia, Dysgraphia, and Dyscalculia*. New York: Routledge.

Torrance, E. P. & Reisman, F. K. (2000). *Learning to use place value creatively*. Bensenville, IL: Scholastic Testing Service.

Creativity Module 9.16
Counting boards computation

Background Information

Addition and Subtraction on the Counting/Computation Boards
The place value or counting boards can be used for learning about computation. The teacher might have students make their own set of counting boards out of heavy construction paper.

Counting boards (also referred to as place value or computation boards) may be used for either teaching place value or providing a concrete activity in computation from simple addition and subtraction through operations with decimals and signed numbers.

Activities

1. An individual counting board has nine spaces with increasing values from one to nine (see Figure 9.3). An empty board has a value of zero.

296 Connecting Creativity and Motivation Research with End Users

Tens	Units
9	9
8	8
7	7
6	6
5	5 ●
4	4
3	3 ●
2 ●	2
1 ●	1

Figure 9.9 Addition without renaming: 25+13.

A value of one is obtained by "jumping" a chip onto the board, to land on space one (see Figure 9.4).

The boards can be a hands-on activity for computation, such as in addition without renaming, for example 25+13=38 (see Figure 9.9). Then have students problem solve to show only one chip on a space that involves making two-for-one exchanges on each board to show that the sum remains 38.

2. For the example 35+9 (Figure 9.10), have the student add nine and five on the units board. Several approaches allow for creative problem-solving and are especially appropriate for those with dyscalculia due to the concrete mode of engagement. Start with a chip on the nine-space of the units board, a chip on the five-space of the units board, and a chip on the three-space of the tens board.

Exchange the single chip on the five-space of the units board for five individual chips placed on the one-space. Overloading a board space is a special instance to allow for regrouping. Now there is a chip on the nine-space of the units board and five chips on the one-space of the units board. Make a two-for-one exchange of the chip on the nine-space with a chip from the five chips on the one-space of the units board, leaving a value of four on the one-space of the units board and a value of ten (9+1 exchange) for the other chip that now sits atop the units board.

Now place the tens board to the upper left of the units board. Make a horizontal move of the chip on the top of the units board to its equivalent value to the bottom space on the tens board. There now is a chip on the one-space of the tens board that is

9   *Creativity Modules*   297

Tens		Units	
9		9	●
8		8	
7		7	
6		6	
5		5	●
4		4	
3	●	3	
2		2	
1		1	

Figure 9.10 Addition with renaming: 35+9.

valued at ten and a chip on the three-space of the tens board with a value of thirty. Exchange the four chips on the units board to one chip on the four-space of the units board. Thus, the value of the boards is 3+1 chips on the tens board, valued at four tens, and four chips on the one-space of the units board, yielding a sum of four tens and four ones, or forty-four. For learners with dyscalculia who have challenges with visualizing operations on numbers, the computation boards provide a hands-on vehicle for making addition and subtraction concrete.

3. First, have students investigate addition on the boards using a count-on approach. This means starting with a number that represents an addend. Then count up the number of spaces representing the second addend. For the example 2+3, place a chip on the two-space and then count three spaces by moving the original chip up to the five-space. To show the commutative property for addition, reverse the activity to 3+2 and the chip will again end on the five-space; the sum will still be five, thus showing that the order of addends does not affect the sum.

4. To show that subtraction is the inverse operation of addition, for the example 5–3, place a chip on the five-space and count down three spaces to land on the two-space, or for 5–2, count down two spaces from the five-space to land on the three-space.

5. Allow practicing with many examples with the maximum sum of nine (Box 9.17).

298 Connecting Creativity and Motivation Research with End Users

---

Box 9.17   Counting board activities: maximum sum of nine

- Show 1+1, 2+1, 3+1, etc.; continue with sums fewer than nine.
- Illustrate two-for-one exchanges.
- Show 1+1+1+1+1+1+1+1.
- Show 2+1+1+1+1+1+1.
- Show 2+2+1+1+1+1
- Show 2+2+2+1+1.
- Show 2+2+2+2.
- Show 4+4.
- Show 8+0.

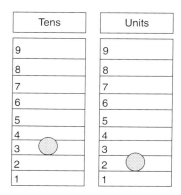

Figure 9.11 Subtracting without renaming on the computation boards.

6. Subtracting without renaming for the problem 32–12=20.
   The student shows the number thirty-two on the boards as a chip on the three—space of the tens board and a chip on the two-space of the units board. Regroup the three chips on the tens board as a chip on the twenty-space and the ten-space. This makes visible the subtrahend of ten. Remove the two chips from the unit board leaving zero units. Remove the chip on the ten-space and your boards now have a value of twenty (Figure 9.11).

7. The additive identity activity uses red (−) and black (+) checkers. The rule is when a red and black checker are on the same space, a null match occurs and the result is zero: the additive identity (Figure 9.12).

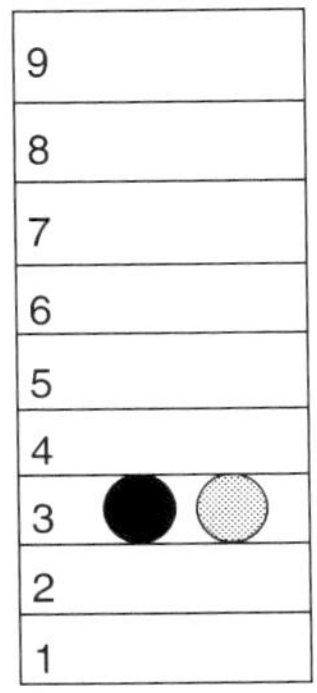

```
┌───┐
│ 9 │
├───┤
│ 8 │
├───┤
│ 7 │
├───┤
│ 6 │
├───┤
│ 5 │
├───┤
│ 4 │
├───┤
│ 3 │ ● ○
├───┤
│ 2 │
├───┤
│ 1 │
└───┘
```

Figure 9.12 Adding signed numbers on the computation boards to show the additive identity.

8. Show addition and subtraction with renaming on the counting boards.
9. Show multiplication on the counting boards.

Assessments

1. The teacher provides students with counting boards and addition and subtracting problems involving whole numbers.
2. The teacher provides students with counting boards and asks them to work in teams of two or three to show addition and subtraction with renaming on the counting boards.
3. The teacher provides students with counting boards and asks them to work in teams of two or three to show addition and subtraction computations with decimal numbers.
4. The teacher provides students with counting boards and asks them to work in teams of two or three to show multiplication computations with whole numbers.
5. The teacher provides students with counting boards and asks them to work in teams of two or three to show whole number multiplication with renaming.

Creativity Module 9.17
Neuroscience of creativity

Background Information

The idea that creativity only comes from the right side or the left side of the brain is wrong, according to the neuroscience of creativity. Creativity is a complex process that involves many different parts of the brain, both conscious and unconscious. The process includes preparation, incubation, illumination, and verification (Wallas, 1926). Depending on the stage of the creative process and the task at hand, different brain regions are involved. Effective communication between these regions is key to creative thinking (Patnaik, 2021).

Three distinct brain networks are at work during most creative thinking, namely (1) the executive control network, which activates and operates when a person needs to focus; (2) the default network, related to brainstorming and daydreaming; and (3) the salience network, which is for detecting environmental stimuli and switching between the executive and default brain networks (Patnaik, 2021); see Chapter 8 for more information on the creativity of neuroscience. Box 9.18 describes in detail these three networks.

Box 9.18   Three distinct brain networks in creative thinking

Network 1. The executive attention network is activated when we need to focus our attention on a specific task that requires problem-solving and reasoning. This network is active when concentrating on a challenging issue or problem or engaging in complex problem-solving that demands the brain's working memory.

Network 2. The default network, sometimes referred to as the imagination network, is involved in constructing mental simulations based on personal experiences. It is active during activities such as remembering the past, thinking about the future, and social cognition. An example of when this network would be active is when we are imagining what someone else is thinking.

Network 3. The salience network, located in the insular cortex, selects which stimuli we pay attention to and is important for detecting important stimuli and coordinating our neural resources in response.

Adapted from Patnaik (2021)

Activities

Research in the neuroscience of creativity is finding that highly original thinkers show very strong connectivity between three activities of the brain, namely mind wandering, visualization, and divergent thinking, and all three can be strengthened with practice.

1. Mind wandering or daydreaming involves different parts of our brains becoming activated, accessing information that may have previously been dormant or is out of memory. This activity accounts for the emergence of creativity, insights, and solutions to problems that had not been considered.

    Stop participants during a task and ask them where their attention is directed (Weinstein, 2017).
    (a) Engage in both voluntary and involuntary mind wandering.
    (b) Involuntary mind wandering happens when we actually don't intend to mind wander.
    (c) Voluntary mind wandering occurs when one drifts off deliberately.

2. Visualization is an innate process that allows us to create mental images of objects, ideas, and concepts without the use of our five senses. The ability to imagine and visualize things in our minds is closely linked to our creativity, problem-solving skills, and memory (Metivier, 2019).

    Research suggests that, when we visualize something, the same regions of the brain are activated as when we actually experience it. When you imagine engaging in an activity such as walking, the same neural pathways in the cortex are stimulated and activated as if you had walked (Metivier, 2019). This implies that visualization can have a significant impact on our cognitive and emotional responses, as well as our overall well-being. Humans have been using visualization for thousands of years, from cave paintings to modern-day art, and it remains an essential part of our cognitive abilities.

    The following are a couple of visualization exercises.
    (a) Picture a burning candle incorporating kinesthetic, auditory, visual, emotional, and olfactory senses.
    (b) Envision eating a cool, smooth, juicy apple.

3. Divergent thinking (see Creativity Module 9.12) was a term coined by psychologist J. P. Guilford (1967). It is the ability to generate many ideas or solutions from a single idea or piece of information. Divergent thinking is one of the characteristics of creativity tapped by the

RDCA. Divergent thinking tends to be spontaneous and free flowing. It occurs when individuals attempt to make new connections while keeping their minds open to new possibilities as they present themselves. The more possibilities one comes up with during the process, the stronger their divergent thinking. We can intentionally enhance our creativity by engaging in creative activities or practicing creative exercises and utilizing our executive functions to stimulate our salience network by actively seeking out more unconventional ideas and refraining from suppressing them (Patnaik, 2021). The following are techniques to stimulate divergent thinking:
   (a) Brainstorming. Generate a list of ideas about a category (e.g., toys with wheels or boys' names) to generate as many ideas as possible in a designated period.
   (b) Keeping a journal. Write one's thoughts on a topic for later analysis.
   (c) Freewriting. Analogous to the written form of brainstorming, this involves writing non-stop about a topic for a short period of time. Write whatever comes to mind without stopping to proofread or revise the writing.
4. Topics that learners can investigate further via the internet relating to the neuroscience of creativity are:
   - How is neuroscience related to creativity?
   - What does neuroscience say regarding the link between creativity and madness?
   - Do creative brains work differently?
   - According to neuroscience, at what age is the mind most creative?
   - Why are some people born creative?
   - Why do adults lose their creativity?
   - Why is creativity in decline?
   - What are the neuroscientific approaches to the scientific study of creativity?
   - What are the neural bases of creativity?
   - Is creativity inheritable?
   - Does brain damage affect creativity?
   - Do neurodegenerative conditions affect creativity?
   - Neuroimaging studies of creativity
   - What is the neuroscientific basis of creativity-enhancing methodologies?
   - How is the neuroscience of creativity applied to creativity training?
   - Are creative brains built differently?

- Is there a neurological relationship between intelligence and creativity?
- Is there brain connectivity that is associated with idea generation?

Assessments

1. Define the three brain activities described in Box 9.15.
2. Give examples of mind wandering, visualization, and divergent thinking.
3. For learners from grade 5 to adulthood, have them select a topic from this module's activities to research and create a final project; it may be a written paper, an oral presentation, or a media creation such as an infographic (see https://venngage.com/blog/how-to-make-an-info graphic-in-5-steps/).

References

Guilford, J. P. (1967). *The Nature of Human Intelligence*. Los Angeles: McGraw Hill.
Metivier, A. (2019). Magnetic memory method – Memory improvement made easy with Anthony Metivier. www.magneticmemorymethod.com/visualization-exercises.
Patnaik, T. (2021). The neuroscience of creativity – A short guide. Jeffbullas's Blog. www.jeffbullas.com/neuroscience-of-creativity/.
Wallas, G. (1926). *Art of Thought*. New York: Harcourt, Brace and Company.
Weinstein, Y. (2017). Mind-wandering, how do I measure thee with probes? Let me count the ways. *Behavior Research Methods*, 50(2), 642–661. https://doi.org/10.3758/s13428-017-0891-9.

Creativity Module 9.18
Mindfulness and creativity

Background Information

The concept of mindfulness involves awareness of our thoughts, feelings, bodily sensations, and surroundings. Mindfulness is defined as a state of "nonjudgmental, moment-to-moment awareness" (Kabat-Zinn, 1990, p. 2). Key characteristics of mindfulness include (1) being nonjudgmental, (2) being patient, (3) remaining open and curious, (4) trusting, and (5) accepting. There exists a mindfulness–creativity relationship in that mindfulness can enhance creativity as "research demonstrates that mindfulness improves a person's ability to concentrate, decreases the fear of being judged, and enhances open-minded thinking while reducing self-conscious thinking" (Brown, Ryan & Creswell, 2007; Sedlmeier et al., 2012). These are all characteristics of creativity, especially risk-taking, divergent thinking, and intrinsic motivation. Colzato, Ozturk, and Hommel (2012) point out that "these effects suggest that mindfulness supports the skills associated with creativity, and research findings suggest that high levels of self-reported mindfulness correlate to creative practices" (see Chapter 8 for more information on the creativity of mindfulness).

Activities

The goal of any mindfulness technique is to achieve a state of focused relaxation by paying attention to one's emotions, thoughts, and sensations (free of judgment) so that the mind focuses on the present. Mindfulness can be enhanced by certain practices or activities, such as the following.

1. **Sit quietly** and focus on breathing.
2. **Body sensations.** Become aware of body sensations, such as tingling, pulsing, or no feeling, and pay attention to each body part in succession from head to toe.
3. **Sensory.** Become aware of sights, sounds, smells, tastes, and touches without judgment. When the mind begins to wander, refocus your attention.
4. **Emotions.** Focus on an emotion (joy, anger, frustration).
5. **Pay attention.** Focus on the environment via touch, sound, sight, smell, and taste.

    Note: Activities 1–5 are adapted from Mayo Clinic Staff (2020)
6. **Engage in open monitoring**, which is the practice of observing and attending to any sensation or thought without focusing on any specific task or concept. This approach may increase creative thinking and, in fact, Colzato, Ozturk, and Hommel (2012) found a relationship between open-monitoring meditation and divergent thinking.
7. **Engage in focused-attention meditation**, which emphasizes attention and awareness to a particular task, item, thought, or stimuli.

It has been hypothesized that open-monitoring meditation encourages divergent thinking and that focused-attention meditation stimulates convergent thinking (Colzato, Ozturk & Hommel, 2012; Henriksen, Richardson & Shack, 2020; Kudesia, 2015).

Assessments

1. Have students keep a reflective log of their activities and invited them to share the content with teacher and peers.
2. Share these activities with teacher colleagues and compare observations of student behaviors related to the activities.
3. Instructors should keep their own reflective logs related to module activities and compare observations of learner behaviors related to the module activities.

References

Brown K. W., Ryan R. M. & Creswell J. D. (2007). Mindfulness: Theoretical foundations and evidence for its salutary effects. *Psychological Inquiry*, 18(4), 211–237.

Colzato, L. S., Ozturk, A. & Hommel, B. (2012). Meditate to create: The impact of focused-attention and open-monitoring training on convergent and divergent thinking. *Frontiers in Psychology*, 3. https://doi.org/10.3389/fpsyg.2012.00116.

Henriksen, D., Richardson, C. & Shack, K. (2020). Mindfulness and creativity: Implications for thinking and learning. *Thinking Skills and Creativity*, 37(37), 100689. https://doi.org/10.1016/j.tsc.2020.100689.

Kabat-Zinn, J. (1990). *Full Catastrophe Living: A Practical Guide to Mindfulness, Meditation, and Healing*. Gloucester: Delacorte.

Kudesia, R.S. (2015). Mindfulness and creativity in the workplace. *Mindfulness in Organizations: Foundations, Research, and Applications*, 190–212.

Mayo Clinic Staff (2020). Mindfulness exercises. Mayo Clinic. www.mayoclinic.org/healthy-lifestyle/consumer-health/in-depth/mindfulness-exercises/art-20046356.

Sedlmeier P., Eberth J., Schwarz M., Zimmermann D., Haarig F. & Jaeger S. (2012). The psychological effects of meditation: A meta-analysis. *Psychological Bulletin*, 138(6), 1139.

9.3 Summary

This chapter provides an array of modules that are meant to enhance instruction dealing with creativity. Also included are perspectives from the field that share instructor experiences related to selected modules. Fluency, flexibility, originality, and elaboration can be thought of as the cornerstones of creative thinking. Fluency is all about generating a lot of different ideas. It is a valuable skill to practice because, when you have many different ideas, you have more options and are therefore more likely to find more viable solutions to your problem. In addition, often one idea leads to another, so by generating many ideas, you are allowing that process to flow naturally. Flexibility involves selecting many categories of ideas, while elaboration refers to embellishing ideas and originality addresses the novelty and uniqueness of ideas. The remaining modules provide foundational content in creativity and also present current topics involving neuroscience, gamifications, and mindfulness.

CHAPTER 10

Motivation Modules

Advance Organizer. This chapter comprises modules that incorporate foundational knowledge and instruction regarding motivation previously presented in Chapters 3 and 6. The module design includes the topic name, background information, instructional activities, suggested assessment techniques, and module references. In addition to teachers, these modules are available to corporate trainers and parents of kindergarten to twelfth grade (K–12) students through the Freddie Reisman Center for Translational Research in Creativity and Motivation (FRC) at Drexel University, as described in Chapter 1 and on the FRC website: www.frcenter.net/. Readers of this book are invited to send feedback, suggest module modifications, and share ideas for further related research to freddie@drexel.edu.

10.1 Introduction

This chapter provides modules (analogous to lesson plans) based on the information presented in Chapters 3 and 6 on motivation. Motivation is the act of inspiring one to attain a desired goal. There are generally two broad types of motivation: intrinsic and extrinsic. Intrinsic motivation comes from within; the behavior is the reward, not the end goal. Extrinsic motivation involves some sort of reward – positive or negative – such as good grades, praise, a gift, or avoidance of punishment. Extrinsic positive motivation, or the "carrot approach," offers positive incentives such as appreciation, promotion, status, and enticements. Extrinsic negative motivation, or the "stick approach," emphasizes penalties, fines, and punishments. Box 10.1 provides examples of intrinsic and extrinsic motivation.

Motivation characteristics include the ability to concentrate intently on a topic for an extended period, behavior that requires little direction from teachers, sustained interest in particular topics or problems, tenacity for finding out information on topics of interest, persistence in working on

> **Box 10.1   Extrinsic and intrinsic motivation**
>
> EXTRINSIC MOTIVATION
> - Participating in a basketball event because you want to win the trophy
> - Studying especially hard to win a scholarship
> - Studying hard because your parents promised you that they would buy you your favorite toy if you got a good grade
> - Helping to wash dishes to get extra pocket money
> - Completing tasks at work to get a promotion
> - Taking ballet lessons because your parents expect you to do so
> - Cleaning your room to avoid punishment
> - Organizing your home because your spouse told you that both of you would be having dinner at a romantic restaurant
>
> INTRINSIC MOTIVATION
> - A sense of accomplishment because you've learned a new scale on the piano
> - A sense of fulfillment because you see progress in your work
> - Feeling that you belong when you participate in group activities
> - Washing the dishes because you like it when things are spotless
> - Feeling fulfilled when you volunteer at a shelter
> - Feeling gratified when you complete your homework because you've had the chance to practice your skills
>
> Source: Liew (2019)

tasks even when setbacks occur, a preference for situations in which one can take personal responsibility for the outcomes of efforts, follow-through when interested in a topic or problem, intense involvement in specific topics or problems, commitment to long-term projects when interested in a subject, persistence when pursuing goals, and little need for external motivation to follow through on initially exciting work.

Measuring motivation takes work, as it is difficult to define and measure. It is reminiscent of the age-old question "Which came first, the chick or the egg?" The chicken-and-egg question in this context is: Does motivation lead to successful learning or does success in learning increase motivation? Brown (1987) defines motivation as "an inner drive, impulse, emotion or desire that moves one to a particular action." Thus, a motivated learner is a learner who wants to achieve a goal and who is willing to invest time and effort in reaching that goal. Brown remarked that "all human beings have needs or drives that are more or less innate, but their intensity depends on the environment." Ausubel (1968) identified six needs and desires integral to motivation, namely the need for (1) exploration, (2) manipulation, (3) activity, (4) stimulation, (5) knowledge, and (6) ego enhancement.

Naiman et al. (1978) and Ur (1991) indicated that the most successful learners are not always those who have a natural aptitude for learning but are instead those who possess specific motivation-related characteristics, as shown in Box 10.2.

Box 10.2   Motivation-related characteristics

- **Positive task orientation.** The learner is eager to take on assignments and challenges and has confidence in their success.
- **Ego involvement.** The learner values achievement in education to preserve and enhance their own (favorable) self-image.
- **Need for achievement.** The learner has a need to achieve to overcome challenges and succeed in what they set out to do.
- **High aspirations.** The learner is ambitious, goes for demanding challenges, has high proficiency, and has top grades.
- **Goal orientation.** The learner is highly conscious of learning goals of learning or specific learning activities and focuses their efforts on attaining them.
- **Perseverance.** The learner consistently puts forth significant effort in learning and is undeterred by setbacks or seemingly slow progress.
- **Tolerance of ambiguity.** The learner is not frustrated and remains unperturbed by situations involving a temporary lack of understanding or confusion. They can endure such situations patiently with self-knowledge that understanding will eventually occur.

Additionally, a motivated classroom reflects the following five features (Horn, 2017):

1. students' sense of belongingness
2. the meaningfulness of learning
3. students' competence
4. structures for accountability
5. students' autonomy

Note: The word "employees" may be substituted for "students," as these modules apply to the corporate as well as the education field.

Introduction References

Ausubel, D. P. (1968). *Educational Psychology: A Cognitive View*. New York: Holt, Rinehart and Winston.

Brown, A. L. (1987). Metacognition, executive control, self-regulation, and other more mysterious mechanisms. In F. E. Weinert & R. H. Kluwe (eds.), *Metacognition, Motivation, and Understanding*. Mahwah, NJ: L. Erlbaum Associates.

Horn, I. (2017). *Motivated: Designing Math Classrooms Where Students Want to Join In*. Portsmouth, NH: Heinemann.

Liew, M. (2019). 14 examples of intrinsic and extrinsic motivation and how to use both. Learning Mind. www.learning-mind.com/examples-of-intrinsic-and-extrinsic-motivation/.

Naiman, N., Frohlich, M., Stern, H. & Todesco, A. (1978). *The Good Language Learner*. Research in Education Series No. 7. Toronto: The Ontario Institute for Studies in Education.

Ur, P. (1991). *A Course in Language Teaching, Practice and Theory*. Cambridge, UK: Cambridge University Press.

The following modules are based on content within previous chapters, especially Chapters 3 and 6, which address motivation.

Motivation Module 10.1
What is motivation?

Background Information

One definition of motivation is a psychological state or process that drives individuals to pursue goal-oriented behavior. The following are synonyms for behavior oriented toward attaining a particular goal: career-minded, ambitious, high-reaching, self-starting, career-focused, determined, committed, and spirited.

Many motivators drive people to pursue their goals (Ofoegbu, 2004; Ponmozhi & Balasubramanian, 2017; Sharot, 2017; Singh, 2015; Touré-Tillery & Fishbach, 2017). As individuals embody a variety of motivations, they are motivated by different triggers, demands, and requirements, as exemplified by the sources of motivation shown in Box 10.3 (Heshmat, 2019),

> **Box 10.3   Sources of motivation**
>
> - **Rely upon external incentives.** External rewards encourage focusing on short-term results at the expense of long-term results.
> - **Avoid losses.** Loss aversion produces a strong desire to stick with one's current status.
> - **Hit rock bottom.** This motivating concept involves one needing to hit rock bottom before one can change (Kirouac & Witkiewitz, 2017).
> - **Intrinsic motivation.** Behavior is driven by internal rewards (wanting to do something for its own sake) (Ryan & Deci, 2017).
> - **Positive self-image.** This includes how someone sees themselves, how others see them, and how one perceives how others see them.
> - **Self-validation.** This involves confirming one's existing self-views.
> - **Curiosity.** This motivating factor arises when one needs to obtain missing information to reduce or eliminate a deficit feeling. The opposite of curiosity is boredom or disengagement.
> - **Autonomy.** People like to feel in control.

Activities

Activity 1: Observation Log for (1) Sources of Motivation and (2) Measuring Grit Activity

First, select several individuals (students or colleagues) within your work setting and ask if they would allow you to keep an observation log on them. Record in the log the sources of motivations listed in Box 10.3 that you see. Identify and document in writing patterns of possible relationships between students and specific sources of motivation.

Activity 2: Test Your Grit Activity

"Grit" is one's passion and perseverance for long-term goals. In this activity, after you have taken the Duckworth grit scale self-assessment as set out in the following (Duckworth, 2016) and become familiar with your personal sources of motivation, administer the grit scale to selected individuals from Activity 1. Observe their grit scale results and their dominant sources of motivation, as listed in Box 10.3. Compare their scores with yours and compare the scores between the individuals you observed. How did you fare with your early observations? What did you glean?

The grit scale is useful as a self-reflection tool. There are several versions of Duckworth's scale, including the scale set out in the following, which is a generic administration guide for this activity. The scoring information is set out in Box 10.4.

> **Box 10.4 Duckworth grit scale scoring**
>
> The total possible score for the Duckworth grit scale is 50. Add up each individual score for the 10 statements to obtain your total score. Divide your total score by 10 to ascertain your grit score. The higher your grit score, the more grit you have demonstrated. The following are the different percentiles of the Duckworth grit scale.
>
> | Percentile | Grit score |
> | --- | --- |
> | 10 percent | 2.5 |
> | 20 percent | 3.0 |
> | 30 percent | 3.3 |
> | 40 percent | 3.5 |
> | 50 percent | 3.8 |
> | 60 percent | 3.9 |
> | 70 percent | 4.1 |
> | 80 percent | 4.3 |
> | 90 percent | 4.5 |
> | 95 percent | 4.7 |
> | 99 percent | 4.9 |

Duckworth Grit Scale Assessment. One method for assessing an individual's level of grit is through a grit test that measures specific characteristics. To evaluate your level of grit, you can complete the test by indicating your degree of agreement with ten statements using a scale of 1 to 5:

5 = Not at all like me
4 = Not much like me
3 = Somewhat like me
2 = Mostly like me
1 = Very much like me

The 10 statements of the Duckworth grit scale assessment are as follows:

1. New ideas and projects sometimes distract me from previous ones.
2. Setbacks discourage me. I give up easily.
3. I often set a goal but later choose to pursue a different one.
4. I am not a hard worker.
5. I have difficulty maintaining my focus on projects that take more than a few months to complete.

6. I have trouble finishing whatever I begin.
7. My interests change from year to year.
8. I don't consider myself diligent. I give up often.
9. I have been obsessed with a certain idea or project for a short time but later lost interest.
10. I don't often overcome setbacks to conquer an important challenge.

This activity is adapted from Duckworth (2019)

Activity 3: Motivational Quotes
Box 10.5 lists motivational quotes. Transfer the quotes onto multiple poster boards or sheets of paper and display them around the classroom or office. Discuss the quotes with your community with the purpose of presenting different perspectives of motivation.

Box 10.5   Motivational quotes

- "It is the supreme art of the teacher to awaken joy in creative expression and knowledge." Albert Einstein
- "Technology is just a tool. In terms of getting the kids working together and motivating them, the teacher is the most important." Bill Gates
- "Children must be taught how to think, not what to think." Margaret Mead
- "The one exclusive sign of thorough knowledge is the power of teaching." Aristotle
- "The dream begins, most of the time, with a teacher who believes in you, who tugs and pushes and leads you on to the next plateau, sometimes poking you with a sharp stick called truth." Dan Rather
- "The teacher who is indeed wise does not bid you to enter the house of his wisdom but rather leads you to the threshold of your mind." Khalil Gibran
- "No man can be a good teacher unless he has feelings of warm affection toward his pupils and a genuine desire to impart to them what he believes to be of value." Bertrand Russell
- "That is the difference between good teachers and great teachers: good teachers make the best of a pupil's means; great teachers foresee a pupil's ends." Maria Callas
- "In a completely rational society, the best of us would be teachers and the rest of us would have to settle for something else." Lee Iacocca
- "There is no system in the world or any school in the country that is better than its teachers. Teachers are the lifeblood of the success of schools." Sir Ken Robinson
- "The greatest sign of success for a teacher is to be able to say: The children are now working as if I did not exist." Maria Montessori

Assessments

1. The grit scale, as shown in Activity 2, can also serve as an assessment of motivation. Box 10.4 contains scoring and score interpretation information.
2. Abstract themes from the discussions of the sources of motivation listed in Box 10.3 and log the results for selected students for use in designing instruction.
3. After discussing themes from the motivation quotes listed in Box 10.5, ask the students to come up with their own motivation quotes. Have students revisit their quote after a couple of weeks for the purpose of seeing if they wished to modify their original quote and provide the reason for the change.

References

Duckworth, A. (2016). *Grit: The Power of Passion and Perseverance*. New York: Simon and Schuster.

Duckworth, A. (2019). Grit scale. https://angeladuckworth.com/grit-scale/.

Heshmat, S. (2019). The 10 most common sources of motivations: What motivates you to change? *Psychology Today*. www.psychologytoday.com/us/blog/science-choice/201904/the-10-most-common-sources-motivations.

Kirouac, M. & Witkiewitz, K. (2017). Identifying "Hitting Bottom" among individuals with alcohol problems: Development and evaluation of the noteworthy aspects of drinking important to recovery (NADIR). *Substance Use & Misuse*, 52(12), 1602–1615. https://doi.org/10.1080/10826084.2017.1293104.

Ofoegbu, F. (2004) Teacher motivation: A factor for classroom effectiveness and school improvement in Nigeria. *College Student Journal*, 38, 81–88.

Ponmozhi, D. & Balasubramanian, R. (2017), Work motivation of school teachers. *International Journal of Humanities and Social Science Invention*, 6(7), 20–23.

Ryan, R. M. & Deci, E. L. (2017). *Self-Determination Theory: Basic Psychological Needs in Motivation, Development, and Wellness*. New York: Guilford Press.

Sharot, T. (2017). *The Influential Mind: What the Brain Reveals about Our Power to Change Others*. London: Picador.

Singh, J. (2015) Work motivation and job satisfaction of secondary school teachers of Shekhawati region. *Journal of Psychological and Educational Research*, 5(2), 203–207.

Touré-Tillery, M. & Fishbach, A. (2017). Three sources of motivation. *Consumer Psychology Review*, 1(1), 123–134. https://doi.org/10.1002/arcp.1007.

Motivation Module 10.2
Why should teachers know about motivation?

Background Information

The motivation of teachers and students is interconnected. Teachers who are driven to teach can inspire and enhance their students' motivation to learn. The influence of teachers on their students can be either positive or negative, and motivated teachers are more likely to have a positive impact. Dar (2002) quoted Guilford and Skinner as follows:

- "Motivation is any internal factor or conditions that needs to initiate or sustain an activity." J. P. Guilford
- "Motivation in school learning involves arousing, persisting, sustaining and directing desirable behavior of the students." B. F. Skinner

Three major components of motivation are:

1. activation – the decision to initiate a behavior
2. persistence – a continued effort in working toward a goal even though obstacles may exist (this is referred to by Angela Duckworth (2016) as grit)
3. intensity – the pursuit of a goal observed through the level of intensity and the focus applied toward achieving it

The level of each motivation component can significantly influence the attainment of one's goals. For instance, high activation increases the likelihood of initiating goal pursuit. Persistence and intensity, on the other hand, dictate the extent of effort invested in working toward the goal and the ability to sustain it.

Activities

Activity 1: Role Play Components of Motivation
Engage students in role play that represents the components of motivation (activation, persistence, and intensity) listed previously under "Background Information". Role play can be a fun activity and is a key component in children's learning that develops speaking and listening skills. It also gives children the opportunity to reflect on and develop their knowledge of a topic, while enhancing creativity and imagination skills.

Activity 2: Additional Role Play Activities
Additional role play activities may include those shown in Table 10.1.

Table 10.1 *Role play activities*

Activity	Description
Do not criticize yourself	Learn from mistakes and forgive yourself
List ten things that you like about yourself	This will help improve self-perception
Do the things that interest you	This will prevent boredom
Do something that you have always wanted to do	This will prevent disengagement
Write down all your traits, good and bad	Writing them down will help in recognizing them

Assessment

Administer the Reisman Diagnostic Motivation Assessment – Student (RDMA-S). This self-assessment heuristic is relevant for middle-school-age through post-secondary students. The RDMA-S items are based on related motivation theories presented in Chapter 3 and as shown in Table 10.2 that follows the Reference section. The table includes the theory definition for each of the theories reflected in the RDMA-S. Box 10.6 describes a possible score interpretation for the RDMA-S.

References

Alderfer, C. P. (1969). An empirical test of a new theory of human needs. *Organizational Behavior and Human Performance*, 4(2), 142–175.

Amabile, T. & Kramer, S. (2011). *The Progress Principle – Using Small Wins to Ignite Joy, Engagement and Creativity at Work*. Boston: Harvard Business Review Press

Argyris C. (1997). Learning and teaching: A theory of action perspective. *Journal of Management Education*, 21(1), 9–26. https://doi.org/10.1177/105256299702100102.

Bandura, A. (1994). Self-efficacy. In R. J. Corsini (ed.), *Encyclopedia of Psychology* (2nd ed., Vol. 3, pp. 368–369). New York: Wiley.

Dar, A. (2002). Importance of teacher motivation as a tool to effectiveness in teaching learning process. *The Communications*, 27(01).

Deci, E. L. & Ryan, R. M. (1985). *Intrinsic Motivation and Self-Determination in Human Behavior*. New York: Plenum.

Herzberg, F. (1987). One more time: How do you motivate employees? *Harvard Business Review* 65(5).

Maslow, A. H. (1954). *Motivation and Personality*. New York: Harper & Row Publishers.

McClelland, D. C. (1978). Managing motivation to expand human freedom. *American Psychologist*, 33(3): 201–210. https://doi.org/10.1037/0003-066x.33.3.201.

McGregor, D. (1960). *The Human Side of Enterprise*. New York: McGraw-Hill.

Murray, H. (1973). *The Analysis of Fantasy*. Huntington, NY: Robert E. Krieger Publishing Company.

Piaget, J. (1933). The moral judgement of the child. *Philosophy*, 8(31), 373–374.

> **Box 10.6 Possible score interpretation for the RDMA-S**
>
> This box describes a possible score interpretation for the RDMA-S. The user rates their agreement on a six-option Likert-type scale (from strongly disagree to strongly agree) with the lowest possible point value being one and the highest point value being six.
>
> The following represents a hypothetical interpretation of percentile rankings based upon total score. Since the RDMAs are still undergoing analysis, these percentile rankings were arbitrarily determined by multiplying the maximum number of correct scores (306 for the RDMA-S) by the following percentiles or percentile rank score: 99, 95, 90, 80, 60, 40, 20, and 10. The highest possible score is 306 (51 items × 6 maximum points per item = 306).
>
> Someone with a score of 306 would rate higher than 99 percent of those taking this assessment. The percentile rank in this scenario would be expressed as "99%tile." The expression is created by combining the rank number (99 percent) with the word "percentile" (tile). Here is a listing of these scores and their related percentile rank:
>
> 297 = **95%tile** rank (score represents that the user scored higher than 94 percent of possible test takers)
>
> 275 = **90%tile** rank (score represents that the user scored higher than 89 percent of possible test takers)
>
> 244 = **80%tile** rank (score represents that the user scored higher than 79 percent of possible test takers)
>
> 183 = **60%tile** rank (score represents that the user scored higher than 59 percent of possible test takers)
>
> 122 = **40%tile** rank (score represents that the user scored higher than 39 percent of possible test takers)
>
> 61 = **20%tile** rank (score represents that the user scored higher than 19 percent of possible test takers)
>
> 30 = **10%tile** rank (score represents that the user scored higher than 9 percent of possible test takers)

Porter, L. & Lawler, E. (1968). *Managerial Attitudes and Performance*. Homewood, IL: Irwin-Dorsey.

Rogers, C. (1980) *A Way of Being*. Boston: Houghton Mifflin.

Ryan, R. M. & Deci, E. L. (2000). Self-determination theory and the facilitation of intrinsic motivation, social development, and well-being. *American Psychologist*, 55(1), 68–78. https://doi.org/10.1037/0003-066X.55.1.68.

Skinner, B. F. (1963). Operant behavior. *American Psychologist*, 18(8), 503.

Urwick, L. (1944). *The Elements of Administration*. New York: Harper & Brothers.

Vroom, V. H. (1968). Towards a stochastic model of managerial careers. *Administrative Science Quarterly*, 13(1), 26–46. https://doi.org/10.2307/2391260.JSTOR2391260.

Table 10.2 *RDMA-S item source interpretation grid*

Motivation theorist and theory	Theory definition	RDMA-S items related to motivation theory
Amabile: intrinsic motivation (Amabile & Kramer, 2011)	Amabile discovered the intrinsic motivation principle of creativity: People are most creative when they are motivated primarily by the interest, enjoyment, satisfaction, and challenge inherent in the work itself.	1. I do something for the pleasure of accomplishing a task with no expectation of outside reward such as a grade or money.
Piaget: intrinsic motivation with a focus on adaptation and needs-based motivation (Piaget, 1933)	Piaget believed that the best way to motivate a child was through intrinsic means (e.g., drivers that motivate an individual to do something for the pleasure of satisfying a task with no expectation of an outside (extrinsic) reward such as a grade or money). Piagetian theory relates to his concept of equilibration, whereby people engage in assimilation (i.e., transform incoming information so that it fits within their existing thinking or needs) and accommodation (i.e., people adapt their thinking and needs to incoming information). Both are components of adaptation (i.e., an individual's ability to adapt to one's environment). For example, for a toothless person who is hungry and motivated to eat, a carrot can be mashed and become chewable (assimilation). The eater either grows teeth as a baby or obtains false teeth as an adult so they can eat (accommodation) so the hunger need becomes satisfied (equilibrium).	2. I adapt my thinking and needs to incoming information. 3. I adapt to my environment.

Maslow: needs hierarchy (Maslow, 1954)	Humanistic theories of motivation build upon the idea that people have strong cognitive reasons to perform various actions. The view is famously illustrated in Maslow's hierarchy of needs, which describes multiple levels of needs and motivations. Maslow's hierarchy suggests that people are motivated to fulfill basic needs before moving on to other, more advanced, needs. For example, people are first motivated to meet basic biological needs for food and shelter, then to progress through higher levels of needs (e.g., safety, love, and esteem). Upon meeting those needs, the primary motivator shifts to meet the self-actualization need or the desire to fulfill one's individual potential.	4. My self-confidence and feeling that I can do a specified task motivate me.
Herzberg: two-factor (also known as motivation–hygiene) theory (Herzberg, 1987)	Herzberg's two-factor theory is for application in the workplace. However, the theory's ideas are transferable to other areas. Specifically, the theory argues that mutually exclusive factors determine satisfaction and dissatisfaction by employees. The factors for satisfaction are related to self-growth and self-actualization (intrinsic), and the factors for dissatisfaction (aka hygiene factors) resulting from outside forces (extrinsic) (e.g., physical workspace, organization policies, and co-worker relationships).	1. Challenging classes, recognition, and responsibility give me positive satisfaction. 2. Status, job security, salary, fringe benefits and work conditions do not give me positive satisfaction, but dissatisfaction results from their absence.
Vroom: expectancy theory (Vroom, 1968)	Expectancy motivation theory centers on people thinking about the future and formulating expectations about what they think will happen. By anticipating a positive outcome, people believe they can take action to make that future "real." The belief in a positive outcome motivates people to pursue the activities required to create the imagined future.	3. I value money, promotion, time-off, and benefits. 4. I am confident about what I am capable of doing. 5. My perception of whether I will get what I desire, as promised by my teacher(s), affects my motivation.

Table 10.2 (*cont.*)

Motivation theorist and theory	Theory definition	RDMA-S items related to motivation theory
		6. My teacher(s) ensure(s) that promises of rewards are fulfilled and that I am aware of that.
7. I act in ways that bring me pleasure and avoid pain.
McClelland: acquired needs motivation theory or three needs theory (McClelland, 1978)	McClelland's acquired needs motivation theory states that every person's motivation is a result of a mix of three primary driving emotional needs motivators: 1. achievement (getting things done) 2. affiliation (having good relationships with others) 3. power (having influence over others) These motivators are not intrinsic but develop over time through an individual's culture and life experiences.	1. I have a strong need to set and accomplish goals.
2. I take calculated risks to accomplish my goals.
3. I like to receive regular feedback on my progress and achievements.
4. I often like to work alone.
5. I want to belong to the group.
6. I want to be liked.
7. I will often go along with whatever the rest of the group wants to do.
8. I favor collaboration over competition.
9. I don't like high risk or uncertainty.
10. I want to control and influence others.
11. I like to win arguments.
12. I enjoy competition and winning.
13. I enjoy status and recognition.
Murray: theory of motivation (Murray, 1973)	Murray believed that individuals' motivations were based on a combination of basic human *needs* and the individual's *motives* coupled with the "environmental press." He defined a need as a drive that has the potential to prompt a person's behavior.	25. I need to enjoyably share with another.
26. I need to be free and independent of others.
27. I need to control or influence others.
28. I need to be seen and heard and to entertain.

Skinner: reinforcement theory (Skinner, 1963)	Environmental press is the interaction leading to adaptation between one's behavior and the situation encountered within one's surroundings toward the individual attempting to become comfortable. The reinforcement theory of motivation states that past behavior, and the resulting consequences (response) of previous behavior to a certain situation (stimulus) will dictate whether the individual chooses to repeat the same behavior in similar circumstances.	29. I need to avoid injury and take precautions. 30. I need to help, console, and nurse the weak 31. I have a need for organization and neatness. 32. I need enjoyment and fun. 33. I need to form stimulating relationships. 34. I need to be loved. 35. I need to analyze, speculate, and generalize.
Bandura: self-efficacy (Bandura, 1994)	Known as the originator of self-efficacy, Bandura defined it as a person's belief in their capability to accomplish specific tasks and challenges.	36. My motivation influences my behavior. 37. My need for achievement is positively related to my self-concept. 38. I repeat behavior that leads to positive consequences and avoid behavior that has had negative effects.
Rogers: unconditional love or unconditional positive regard (Rogers, 1980)	Humanistic theories of motivation are based on the idea that people have strong cognitive reasons to perform various actions (see the Maslow entry earlier in the table.) Specifically, Rogers hypothesized that humans have a basic need and tendency to work toward self-actualization.	39. My perceived self-efficacy (belief that I can do something) leads me to set higher goals. 40. My motivation becomes directed toward the satisfaction of others' expectations.

Table 10.2 (*cont.*)

Motivation theorist and theory	Theory definition	RDMA-S items related to motivation theory
Argyris: management practices theory of motivation (Argyris, 1997)	This theory is founded on the principle that management practices affect employees' behavior. Similar to Vroom (see earlier in the table), employees are motivated to expend more effort when the management practices create an environment in which there are recognized links between employees' efforts, their level of success in their performance, and the result or compensation of their efforts.	41. I am motivated to exert a high level of effort when I believe there are relationships between the effort I put forth, the performance I achieve, and the outcomes/rewards I receive. 42. My effort will improve my performance. 43. My performance will lead to rewards. 44. Rewards will satisfy my individual goals. 45. In contrast to a person refusing to learn, I am a person relishing the opportunity to learn.
McGregor: participation theory or theory X and theory Y (McGregor, 1960)	McGregor's participation theory comprises two theories that potentially inhabit each person, theory X (negative connotation) and theory Y (positive connotation), with supervisors using strategies of each theory as needed in managing their workforce on the theories X and Y continuum. Theory X presumes that people are extrinsically motivated and in need of firm supervision, as they are generally self-centered, dislike responsibility, and – left to their own devices – would work as little as possible with no regard for the needs of the organization or others. Supervisors, therefore, need to motivate workers using external rewards and punishments. Theory Y presumes that people are intrinsically motivated, requiring more general oversight than theory X. The employee is more connected to the organizational goals and other employees, enjoys their work, and takes responsibility for their behavior.	
Urwick: theory Z (Urwick, 1944)	Theory Z was a response to McGregor's theory X and theory Y. Rather than a continuum, theory Z contends that managers should ensure that their employees are confident and positive and that they know the organization's goal and how each of their specific roles contributes to them (Note:	46. A supportive teaching style helps cultivate my creativity.

Porter and Lawler: expectancy theory model (Porter & Lawler, 1968)	the "Z" in theory Z is for labeling purposes only. It has no specific meaning.) The theory requires that the "manager" develops trust between them and the employees and that the employees will be "involved" and invested in the company, working as part of a team.
Porter and Lawler's expectancy theory model contends that an individual's perception of the value of the reward in the context of the perceived effort required will affect motivation. The employee, upon being successful with the task, experiences both intrinsic reward (self-satisfaction) for having done a good job and extrinsic reward (monetary or another form of external recognition).
Alderfer: existence, relatedness, and growth (ERG) theory of motivation (Alderfer, 1969)	Alderfer's ERG motivation theory condenses Maslow's five human needs into a three-factor model: existence, relatedness, and growth. He believed that multiple levels of need simultaneously influenced a person's motivation and that the levels fluctuated and changed over time.
Alderfer's theory differs from Maslow's theory in that ERG is not hierarchical. In ERG, a lower level need does not necessarily have to be gratified for a higher level to become relevant (e.g., a person may satisfy a higher level need, whether or not a lower level need was met).
Existence needs include physiological needs (e.g., food, water, air, clothing, and safety), which relate to Maslow's first two levels: physiological and safety.
Relatedness needs involve relationships with family, friends, co-workers, and employers and correspond to Maslow's third and fourth levels: belonging and esteem.
Growth needs overlap with Maslow's fourth need (esteem) and comprise the fifth level of self-actualization, which includes creativity and productivity.

4.7 I have a need to perceive that I am good at something.

4.8 I have choices and control over my decisions.

Table 10.2 (*cont.*)

Motivation theorist and theory	Theory definition	RDMA-S items related to motivation theory
Deci and Ryan: self-determination theory (Deci & Ryan, 1985; Ryan & Deci, 2000)	Deci and Ryan's self-determination theory (SDT) is important in that it changed the previous dominant belief, namely that reinforcing people's behavior through extrinsic rewards was the best way to get humans to perform tasks. SDT identifies three basic psychological needs that everybody has, regardless of environment (school, work, or personal pursuits), to allow them to thrive using high-quality motivation: autonomy, competence, and relatedness.	49. I am connected to others through positive relationships. 50. I do not believe that the best way to get someone to perform tasks is to reinforce their behavior with rewards. 51. I believe that a basic psychological need is autonomy.

Motivation Module 10.3
Instructor motivation characteristics

Background Information

Goal-oriented behavior is a key ingredient of motivation and is an integral component of characteristics that represent instructor motivation. The following list is an example of the characteristics of motivated instructors:

- They are purposeful and intentional.
- They have a ready answer to questions (e.g., What do you believe is the next step for you, professionally speaking? and What goals do you have for your role here?)
- They tend to be competitive and are willing to work hard for the "win."
- They constantly review their goals to remind themselves of what they want to accomplish and what they need to do to achieve the goal.
- They demonstrate goal-oriented skills that indicate they can effectively manage their workload, complete tasks, and meet deadlines in the workplace.
- They set targets and objectives and meet appropriate deadlines. Goals that are too long term or offer no method of measuring progress may influence behavior negatively, encouraging people to put off their work until a later date.

Gorham & Millette (1997) found differences among teachers in perceptions of their ability to influence motivation, with those who were more optimistic about motivation in their classrooms perceiving a more significant influence on both the motivation and the demotivation of students. Aji, Martono, and Fakhruddin (2019) reported that several factors – including teacher commitment, professional competence, and motivation – influenced teachers' performance. The higher a teacher's commitment, professional competence, and motivation, the better their performance.

Kocabas (2009) found that teachers are motivated mainly by the following factors: a sense of safety in school, pupil achievement, the levels of attraction to the teaching profession, levels of self-reliance, their perception of their status in society, the sense of self-fulfillment, a positive atmosphere in school, positive relationships among teachers, an appreciation of their achievements and values, effective administration and management, and a sense of security on matters such as health and security, sickness, and retirement arrangements. On the other hand, teachers identified a competitive climate among teachers as negatively affecting teachers' motivation levels.

Activities

Shernoff (2013) suggests that the following activities be used by teachers related to motivation and flow (Csikszentmihalyi, 1990) in the classroom:

- **Challenge but not overwhelm.** An activity should present a challenge slightly above the student's current skill level without overwhelming them. Students may feel anxious and give up if the challenge is too difficult. Conversely, if a challenge is too easy, they may become disinterested. Striking the right balance is essential. To do so, it may be necessary to scaffold the lesson by breaking it down into manageable pieces and allowing the students to find the optimal level of challenge.
- **Create assignments that are relevant to students' lives.** Motivate students to explore how the topic might relate to their own experiences. Exploring a topic that resonates personally is helpful if there is an expectation or hope that the students will enter a flow state.
- **Provide autonomy and multiple options to demonstrate understanding or mastery.** Research shows that students will engage more with a challenge or task when they can choose their activities and work with autonomy.
- **Provide structure but allow the students to assist in setting clear goals and provide students with ongoing formative feedback.** Students develop a sense of ownership regarding a challenge when they help define the assignment goal and understand how their efforts are assisting in reaching it.
- **Cultivate positive relationships with students.** Teachers can assist in fostering positive relationships with their students by valuing their input.
- **Allow for time and limit distractions.** Build time into assignments to give students time to incubate ideas and engage in flow.
- **Be hands-on and real-world!** Create experiences that are hands-on and engage the students and their intrinsic motivation. Engage students in identifying the "real problem" and problem-solving solutions.
- **Model enthusiasm for the topic and their work.** Be the Idea Agent and the cheerleader for your students in their project-based work. Encourage, praise, and acknowledge attempts and collaboration. Set

the stage, provide the resources they need – and then get out of the way and let them at it!

Assessments

Assessment 1: Likert-type Scale Related to Instructor Motivation Characteristics
Use the following Likert-type scale for each statement related to instructor motivation characteristics in Box 10.7 to record your confidence level for each statement: not at all, slightly, somewhat, quite, and extremely. Use the results as a self-reflection to identify strengths and areas to be investigated.

Assessment 2: Complete the Reisman Diagnostic Motivation Assessment – Teachers
Table 10.3 sets out the trailblazer motivation researchers presented in Chapter 3 upon whose work the Reisman Diagnostic Motivation Assessment – Teachers (RDMA-T) items are based; the table also presents the theory definitions. The score interpretation is given in Box 10.8. Score each item on the following Likert-type scale: 1, very untrue of me; 2, untrue of me; 3, somewhat untrue of me; 4, neutral; 5, somewhat true of me; 6, true of me; and 7, very true of me.

Box 10.8 describes a possible score interpretation for the RDMA-T. The user rates their agreement on a six-option Likert-type scale (from strongly

---

Box 10.7 Instructor motivation characteristics self-assessment

1. How confident are you that you can engage students who typically are not motivated?
2. How confident are you that you can help your school's gifted students to learn at their full potential?
3. Thinking about your students' creativity, how confident are you that you can enhance their creative strengths?
4. If your students have a problem while working toward an important goal, how well do you motivate them to keep working?
5. How often are your students motivated to stay focused on the same goal for several weeks at a time?
6. When working on a project that matters a lot to you, how focused can you stay when there are lot of distractions?

Box 10.7 (cont.)

7. If your students fail to reach an important goal, how likely are they to be motivated to try again?
8. At your school, how valuable are the available professional development opportunities dealing with creativity?
9. How helpful are your colleagues' ideas for improving your motivation as a teacher?
10. How often do your professional development opportunities help you explore new ideas regarding motivation?
11. On most days, how motivated are the students about being at school?
12. To what extent are teachers in your school trusted to teach in the way they think is best?
13. How positive are the attitudes of your colleagues regarding creativity?
14. How supportive are students in their interactions with each other?
15. How confident are you that you can help your students with learning disabilities to learn?
16. When one of your teaching strategies fails to work for a group of students, how easily can you think of another approach to try?
17. How confident are you that you could have a productive conversation with a parent?
18. How effective do you think you are at managing particularly disruptive students?
19. How confident are you that you can enrich your creative students' learning?
20. How clearly can you explain the most complicated content to your students?
21. How confident are you that you can meet the learning needs of your most advanced students?

Adapted from Wisconsin Department of Public Instruction (2015)

disagree to strongly agree) with the lowest possible point value being one and the highest point value being six.

The following represents a hypothetical interpretation of percentile rankings based upon total score. Since the RDMAs are still undergoing analysis, these percentile rankings were arbitrarily determined by multiplying the maximum number of correct scores (336 for the RDMA-T) by the following percentiles or percentile rank score: 99, 95, 90, 80, 60, 40, 20, and 10. The highest possible score is 336 (56 items × 6 maximum points per item = 336).

Table 10.3 *RDMA-T item source interpretation grid*

Motivation theorist and theory	RDMA-T items related to motivation theory
Amabile: intrinsic motivation	1. I do something for the pleasure of accomplishing a task with no expectation of outside reward such as a grade or money.
Piaget: intrinsic motivation with a focus on adaptation and needs-based motivation	2. I adapt my thinking and needs to incoming information. 3. I adapt to my environment.
Maslow: needs hierarchy	4. My self-confidence and feeling that I can do a specified task motivate me.
Herzberg: two-factor (also known as motivation–hygiene) theory	5. Challenging classes, recognition, and responsibility give me positive satisfaction. 6. Status, job security, salary, fringe benefits, and work conditions do not give me positive satisfaction, but dissatisfaction results from their absence.
Vroom: expectancy theory	7. I value money, promotion, time-off, and benefits. 8. I am confident about what I am capable of doing. 9. My perception of whether I will get what I desire, as promised by my teacher(s), affects my motivation. 10. My teacher(s) ensure(s) that promises of rewards are fulfilled and that I am aware of that. 11. I act in ways that bring me pleasure and avoid pain.
McClelland: acquired needs motivation theory or three needs theory	12. I have a strong need to set and accomplish goals. 13. I take calculated risks to accomplish my goals. 14. I like to receive regular feedback on my progress and achievements. 15. I often like to work alone. 16. I want to belong to the group. 17. I want to be liked. 18. I will often go along with whatever the rest of the group wants to do. 19. I favor collaboration over competition. 20. I don't like high risk or uncertainty.

Table 10.3 (*cont.*)

Motivation theorist and theory	RDMA-T items related to motivation theory
	21. I want to control and influence others.
	22. I like to win arguments.
	23. I enjoy competition and winning.
	24. I enjoy status and recognition.
Murray: theory of motivation	25. I need to enjoyably share with another.
	26. I need to be free and independent of others.
	27. I need to control or influence others.
	28. I need to be seen and heard and to entertain.
	29. I need to avoid injury and take precautions.
	30. I need to help, console, and nurse the weak
	31. I have a need for organization and neatness.
	32. I need enjoyment and fun.
	33. I need to form stimulating relationships.
	34. I need to be loved.
	35. I need to analyze, speculate, and generalize.
	36. My motivation influences my behavior.
	37. My need for achievement is positively related to my self-concept.
Skinner: reinforcement theory	38. I repeat behavior that leads to positive consequences and avoid behavior that has had negative effects.
Bandura: self-efficacy	39. My perceived self-efficacy (belief that I can do something) leads me to set higher goals.
Rogers: unconditional love or unconditional positive regard	40. My motivation becomes directed toward the satisfaction of others' expectations.
Argyris: management practices theory of motivation	41. I am motivated to exert a high level of effort when I believe there are relationships between the effort I put forth, the performance I achieve, and the outcomes/rewards I receive.
	42. My effort will improve my performance.
	43. My performance will lead to rewards.

McGregor: participation theory or theory X and theory Y

Urwick: theory Z

Ouchi: the focus is on the well-being of the employee

Porter and Lawler: expectancy theory model

Alderfer: ERG theory of motivation

Deci and Ryan: self-determination theory

Hackman and Oldham: job characteristics theory – characteristics (i.e., skill variety, task identity, task, significance, autonomy, and feedback) affect work.

44. Rewards will satisfy my individual goals.
45. In contrast to a person refusing to learn, I am a person relishing the opportunity to learn.
46. A supportive teaching style helps cultivate my creativity.
47. I believe a person may satisfy a particular need whether or not a previous need has been satisfied.
48. I have a need to perceive that I am good at something.
49. I have choices and control over my decisions.
50. I am connected to others through positive relationships.
51. I do not believe that the best way to get students to perform tasks is to reinforce their behavior with rewards.
52. I believe that a basic psychological need is autonomy.
53. I prefer a job that involves just one skill.
54. When I receive clear, actionable information about my teaching performance, I have better understanding of what specific actions I need to take (if any) to improve.
55. I prefer a job that involves just one skill.
56. When I receive clear, actionable information about my teaching performance, I have better understanding of what specific actions I need to take (if any) to improve.

Note: Assessment items 20 and 53 are to be reverse scored.

> **Box 10.8 Possible score interpretation for the RDMA-T**
>
> Someone with a score of 336 would rate higher than 99 percent of those taking this assessment. The percentile rank in this scenario would be expressed as "99%tile." This expression is created by combining the rank number (99 percent) with the word "percentile" (tile). The following is a list of these scores and their related percentile rank:
>
> 319 = **95%tile** rank (score represents that the user scored higher than 94 percent of possible test takers)
>
> 302 = **90%tile** rank (score represents that the user scored higher than 89 percent of possible test takers)
>
> 268 = **80%tile** rank (score represents that the user scored higher than 79 percent of possible test takers)
>
> 201 = **60%tile** rank (score represents that the user scored higher than 59 percent of possible test takers)
>
> 134 = **40%tile** rank (score represents that the user scored higher than 39 percent of possible test takers)
>
> 67 = **20%tile** rank (score represents that the user scored higher than 19 percent of possible test takers)
>
> 33 = **10%tile** rank (score represents that the user scored higher than 9 percent of possible test takers)

References

Aji, A. P., Martono, S. & Fakhruddin, F. (2019). The effect of teacher motivation in mediating commitment and professional competence on teachers' performance of vocational school in Blora Regency. *Educational Management*, 8(2), 150–156.

Csikszentmihalyi, M. (1990). *Flow: The Psychology of Optimal Experience* (1st ed.). New York: Harper Collins.

Gorham, G. & Millette, D. (1997). A comparative analysis of teacher and student perceptions of sources of motivation and demotivation in college classes, *Communication Education*, 46(4), 245.

Kocabas, I. (2009). The effects of sources of motivation on teachers' motivation levels. *Education* 129(4), 724–733.

Shernoff, D. J. (2013). *Optimal Learning Environments to Promote Student Engagement*. New York: Springer.

Wisconsin Department of Public Instruction (2015). Social-emotional learning: User guide. https://dpi.wi.gov/sites/default/files/imce/sspw/pdf/seluserguide.pdf.

Motivation Module 10.4
Self-determination theory

Background Information

The self-determination theory (SDT) is a motivational theory that was developed by the psychologists Richard Ryan and Edward Deci (Deci & Ryan, 2008, 2012); it is discussed in Chapter 3. The SDT posits that every individual has three basic psychological needs that help us feel motivated: autonomy, competency, and relatedness. These are defined as (Deci & Ryan, 2000, 2008, 2012; Ntoumanis et al., 2020):

1. **Autonomy.** Individuals desire to perceive themselves as having control over their fate and possessing some degree of power in shaping their existence. Above all, people seek to feel in command of their actions.
2. **Competence.** This need pertains to our accomplishments, expertise, and abilities. Individuals desire to enhance their proficiency and acquire expertise in tasks that are significance to them.
3. **Relatedness (also called connection).** Individuals require a sense of inclusion and interconnectedness with others.

Taking charge of one's life involves setting goals, evaluating options, making choices, and then working to achieve those goals. Each person's behavior is, in part, determined by intrinsic and extrinsic motivation, and both drive us to meet these three basic needs. Self-determination involves many attitudes and abilities including self-awareness, assertiveness, creativity, pride, problem-solving, and self-advocacy skills.

The SDT challenged the widely held notion that rewarding behavior is the most effective way to motivate people to perform tasks. To better understand motivation, Ryan and Deci introduced the self-determination continuum, a framework that categorizes motivational styles into six levels, ranging from least motivational to most motivational. The ultimate goal is to achieve self-determination, which is at its highest point at the intrinsic regulation or intrinsic motivation stage (O'Hara, 2017). Self-determination is the sense that each person is in control of their own life and choices, is motivated, and can meet their potential.

Activities

1. **Choice-making.** Express your preference between two or more options and exert control over your actions to implement your choice.

2. **Decision-making.** Similar to making choices, decision-making requires effective judgments about what choices or solutions are right at any given moment. Identify possible alternatives for an action, consider the potential consequences of each action, assess the probability of each result occurring, select the best alternative, and, finally, implement the alternative decision.
3. **Problem-solving.** Identify a problem, generate possible solutions, consider the potential pros and cons of each solution, and, finally, decide upon a solution.
4. **Goal-setting.** For goal-setting activities to work, they need two key things: (1) to be small, achievable, and measurable over time and (2) to have specific and clear outcomes. Write three goals that reflect these two criteria.
5. **Self-regulation.** Self-regulation involves setting goals, developing a plan to achieve goals, implementing and following the action plan, evaluating the outcomes of the action plan, and adjusting accordingly. Write a scenario that incorporates the self-regulation component

Assessments

1. Record observations of students displaying autonomous behavior and this list becomes the template for identifying the meaning of autonomous behavior.
2. Discuss with a colleague the steps you now take to encourage relatedness that become the structure for instruction.
3. List new pedagogy you now use to cultivate competence in student behavior.

References

Deci, E. L. & Ryan, R. M. (2000). The "what" and "why" of goal pursuits: Human needs and the self-determination of behavior. *Psychological Inquiry*, 11, 227–268.

Deci, E. L. & Ryan, R. M. (2008). Self-determination theory: A macrotheory of human motivation, development, and health. *Canadian Psychology / Psychologie canadienne*, 49(3), 182–185. https://doi.org/10.1037/a0012801.

Deci, E. L. & Ryan, R. M. (2012). *Self-determination theory*. In P. A. M. Van Lange, A. W. Kruglanski & E. T. Higgins (eds.), *Handbook of Theories of Social Psychology* (pp. 416–436). Thousand Oaks, CA: Sage Publications Ltd. https://doi.org/10.4135/9781446249215.n21.

Ntoumanis, N., Ng, J. Y. Y., Prestwich, A. et al. (2020). A meta-analysis of self-determination theory-informed intervention studies in the health domain:

effects on motivation, health behavior, physical, and psychological health. *Health Psychology Review*, 15(2), 1–31. https://doi.org/10.1080/17437199.2020.1718529.

O'Hara, D. (2017). The intrinsic motivation of Richard Ryan and Edward Deci. *American Psychological Association*. www.apa.org/members/content/intrinsic-motivation.

Ryan, R. M. & Deci, E. L. (2000). Self-determination theory and the facilitation of intrinsic motivation, social development, and well-being. *American Psychologist*, 55(1), 68–78.

Motivation Module 10.5

Self-directed learning

Background Information

Self-directed learning involves one taking the initiative and responsibility for one's personal learning. It involves the processes of:

- diagnosing learning strengths and weaknesses
- identifying and selecting learning goals
- reaching out to teachers and/or mentors for help
- choosing and implementing pedagogical approaches
- assessing attainment of preselected goals

Westphal (in conversation) described the unschooling/self-directed environment as *independent meaningful learning*. This depiction captures several related concepts that this book encapsulates, namely (1) the autonomy portion of Ryan and Deci's theory described in Motivation Module 10.4 entitled self-determination theory, (2) the meaningfulness that underlies the MeaningSphere (www.meaningsphere.com/our-mission) philosophy and the Mosaic perspective (we are born to learn – https://weareborntolearn.org/) that emphasizes intrinsic learning approaches that honor the whole child and create a pathway to thrive, and (3) attention to the learner's needs.

Malcolm Knowles (1975) focused on individuals taking the initiative, with or without the help of others. His definition of self-directed learning includes the following five steps (Brandt, 2020; Knowles, 1975):

1. diagnosing one's learning needs
2. formulating appropriate learning goals
3. identifying both human and material resources for learning
4. choosing and implementing appropriate learning strategies
5. evaluating learning outcomes

Self-directed learning involves the following (Brandt, 2020; Dweck, 2007; Eisenberg, Spinrad & Eggum, 2010):

- **Self-regulation** is planning, directing, and controlling one's emotions, thoughts, and behaviors during a learning task.
- **Motivation** is the desire to participate in an activity anticipating the intrinsic pleasure resulting from the activity or a feeling of responsibility to perform a task. A growth mindset plays a significant role in influencing motivation, as it involves the belief that intelligence, personality, and capabilities can evolve and adapt over time through experience.
- **Personal responsibility** (also called initiative or ownership) is taking full responsibility for one's actions.
- **Autonomy** is recognizing available choices, taking charge of one's learning, and controlling choices through ongoing reflection and evaluation.

Instructional models for self-directed learning generally support various practices throughout the following stages:

- **Planning.** Educators assist students in assuming responsibility for their learning by prompting them to reflect on and assess their learning requirements (i.e., gaps in knowledge and skills), establish realistic but challenging learning goals, and plan individual steps and the resources necessary to accomplish a task.
- **Monitoring and adjusting.** Teachers provide targeted, detailed, and timely feedback, and students incorporate this feedback into their learning activities.
- **Reflecting and evaluating.** Learners showcase their work while educators foster discussion and reflection to encourage learners to consider which resources were most helpful, which strategies were most effective, where they encountered difficulties, and what alternative methods could have been used.

Note: The self-directed learning list and the instructional models for self-directed students were adapted from Brandt (2020)

Self-Directed Learning versus Self-Determined Learning
Self-directed learning and self-determined learning may appear similar, but they are fundamentally different. Although both terms describe learning initiated and controlled by the learner rather than external factors, such as a teacher or a curriculum, their differences are explained in Box 10.9.

> **Box 10.9 Difference between self-directed learning and self-determined learning**
>
> Self-directed learning is "a process in which individuals take the initiative, with or without the help of others, to diagnose their learning needs, formulate learning goals, identify resources for learning, select and implement learning strategies, and evaluate learning outcomes" (Knowles, 1975, p. 18).
>
> Self-determined learning is "an active, constructive process whereby learners set goals for their learning and then attempt to monitor, regulate, and control their cognition, motivation, and behavior, guided and constrained by their goals and the contextual features in the environment" (Pintrich, 2000, p. 453).

Thus, self-directed learning refers to a learning process whereby the learner takes responsibility for their own learning by identifying their learning needs, setting their own goals, and choosing the resources and strategies they will use to achieve those goals. Self-directed learners may still follow a predetermined curriculum or learning plan, but they have more autonomy and control over how they learn. Self-directed learning emphasizes acquiring knowledge within a set context and typically follows a linear path.

Self-determined learning, on the other hand, emphasizes the role of personal agency and choice in the learning process. In self-determined learning, the learner not only sets their own goals and chooses their own resources, but also has the power to make decisions about the direction and scope of their learning. This may involve choosing topics of interest, determining the pace of learning, and deciding when and how to demonstrate their learning. Self-determined learning prioritizes the learning process itself and is entirely directed by the learner. It involves questioning assumptions and beliefs and is designed to be metacognitive (Deol, n.d.).

Boxes 10.10 and 10.11 explain the concept of "double-loop learning," a key difference between self-directed and self-determined learning. Box 10.10 explains double-loop learning and Box 10.11 provides an analogy to assist in understanding the differences between single-loop learning and double-loop learning.

Performance and motivation increase when students believe that they are engaging in self-governed behaviors. The following objectives form the structure for the activities: (1) support autonomy, (2) encourage relatedness, and (3) cultivate competence (Mahavongtrakul et al., 2021).

The FRC has an opportunity – an obligation – to provide a framework to support the acquisition of critical content knowledge within an unschooling/

> **Box 10.10 Double-loop learning**
>
> The "double-loop" element is a significant difference between self-directed and self-determined learning. Double-loop learning is a concept that was introduced by Chris Argyris (1977) and Donald Schön (Argyris & Schön, 1974), which refers to a deeper level of reflection and inquiry that goes beyond simply adapting to feedback or changing behaviors in response to external factors. In double-loop learning, the learner questions their underlying assumptions and values and critically examines the goals and strategies they set for themselves.
>
> While self-directed learning may involve adapting strategies to achieve predetermined goals, self-determined learning involves questioning and revising those goals based on a deeper understanding of oneself and one's values. Double-loop learning involves scrutinizing variables, questioning original concepts and learning processes, and reflecting upon these activities (Argyris, 1991).

> **Box 10.11 Difference between single-loop learning and double-loop learning**
>
> Single-loop learning and double loop learning are two different approaches to learning and problem-solving. Single-loop learning involves using a set of predetermined goals or decision-making rules to try to solve a problem. If the desired outcome is not achieved, adjustments are made to the strategies used to achieve the goal. This approach assumes that the goals and decision-making rules are correct and that any issues can be resolved through a more effective application of those rules.
>
> Double-loop learning involves questioning and potentially revising the goals or decision-making rules themselves based on the outcomes of the initial attempts to solve a problem. This approach recognizes that the goals and rules may be part of the problem and that deeper reflection and inquiry are necessary to address underlying issues and achieve more effective solutions. The process is called "double loop" because it involves two distinct phases. The first loop uses the existing goals or decision-making rules to try to solve a problem, while the second loop involves modifying those goals or rules based on the outcomes of the first phase.
>
> The importance of double-loop learning lies in recognizing that how a problem is defined and solved can sometimes be a source of the problem itself. By questioning and potentially revising the goals or decision-making rules that are being used, double-loop learning enables learners to not only solve immediate problems but address underlying issues that may be contributing to those problems (Argyris, 1991).

Box 10.11 (cont.)

Argyris describes the distinction between single-loop and double-loop learning using the following analogy (Argyris, 1977):

> A thermostat that automatically turns on the heat whenever the temperature in a room drops below 69°F is a good example of single loop learning. A thermostat that could ask, "why am I set to 69°F?" and then explore whether or not some other temperature might more economically achieve the goal of heating the room would be engaged in double loop learning.

self-directed learning environment. This became apparent in the documentary film *Unschooled* (Gold, 2020), which told the story of Natural Creativity in Germantown, a neighborhood in Philadelphia, where parents' main concern centered on whether their children would receive the content knowledge necessary for adulthood. Box 10.12 tells the story of a high schooler who dropped out of his ninth grade and, with the guidance of his mother, opted into a self-directed learning school.

Box 10.12 Story of a high schooler who opted into a self-directed learning school

A solution to meld learner interest with traditional school content became apparent in the story of the boy whose interest in photography not only kept him in school but also resulted in a show of his photos under the mentoring of a professional photographer, some of which were sold.

Mathematics content is embedded in photography, as is other school content (e.g., literacy, biology, history), and is embedded within other careers. To implement this groundbreaking new component of the FRC, we will need to develop a cadre of relevant practitioners (scientists, lawyers, doctors, writers, filmmakers, chefs, photographers, etc.) who can help teachers meld school content with related disciplines as well as learners' main interest.

This was the missing component of the story of the Natural Creativity in Germantown photography student who received instruction and mentoring from a professional photographer, but no emphasis on the math that is so richly a part of photography; thus, the missing link was the math teacher. A consideration of the need for a new learning collaboration between teachers and career professionals who together can address discipline content needs and applications of the content must be a next step.

The following activities are related to Deci and Ryan's (1991) three basic needs of the intrinsic motivation process (autonomy, competency, and relatedness).

Activities

Activity 1: Math Examples
The following are some examples of how mathematics can be embedded within a learner's interest and thus be a motivator to learn both the subject and the career competencies.

What Type of Math Is Used in Photography? Photography involves numbers and math. The number on the apertures (e.g., 2.8, 4, 5.6) are all fractions. These numbers are known as f-numbers: the ratio of focal length to effective aperture diameter.

How Do Photographers Use Algebra? Photographers use algebra to calculate everything from shooting the photo to developing the print. Photography involves math through many camera parts and how to use them, such as shutter speed, aperture openings, the inverse square law, the "rule of thirds," and more.

Focal Length In photography, focal length refers to the length of the lens and is used to calculate the distance between you and your subject. Focal length is measured in millimeters.

Photographers Use Chemicals to Develop Film and Photographs Math is needed to determine the amount of each chemical used and how much water is to be added to each step of the developing process.

Shutter Speed Each change of shutter speed indicates a halving or doubling of the time that the shutter remains open, in full stops (f/stops). If a photo is underexposed by a certain number of f/stops, you'll need to know how to calculate the proper aperture or shutter speed to make a perfect exposure. (The f/stop on a camera refers to its aperture setting. Aperture is one of the two exposure controls on a camera, the other being shutter speed. Aperture controls the diameter of the lens' diaphragm that lets light into the camera.)

10 Motivation Modules

Activity 2: Self-Directed Learning versus Lecture-Style Learning
Describe the difference between self-directed learning and lecture-style learning. Self-directed learning is an offshoot of self-determination theory, which explains how external events, such as rewards or praise, sometimes produce positive effects on motivation, but at other times can be quite detrimental (Deci & Ryan, 2008; Ryan & Deci, 2008). The hidden cost of certain types of rewards is that they undermine intrinsic motivation by decreasing the sense of autonomy and competence.

Activity 3: Support Autonomy in the Classroom
Providing students with opportunities to help make decisions fosters student autonomy and empowerment.

- Give students choices.
- Establish deadlines for assignments but allow for early submissions.
- Collaborate with students to set their own learning goals.
- Take a poll among the students to make class decisions concerning learning.
- Get learners to take risks.
- Give learners options.
- Use learner-generated content.
- Give students opportunities to self-assess progress.
- Develop strategies for independent learning

Activity 4: Encourage Relatedness in the Classroom
To feel motivated, a student must feel a sense of belonging and feel connected to their teacher and their peers.

- Learn the students' names and use them often.
- Speak to each student individually at least once a week.
- Facilitate group projects and active learning assignments.
- Give individualized and personal feedback.
- Accept feedback from your students.
- Use an online discussion board to continue communication outside class.
- Provide opportunities for learners to work collaboratively.

Activity 5: Cultivate Competence in the Classroom
When a student feels able and effective in their learning environment, they will experience higher levels of motivation.

- Avoid micromanaging and allow students to make their own mistakes.
- Equip students with learning strategies early on such, as note-taking techniques or reading strategies.
- Give specific advice on how to succeed in the class.
- Present content in multiple formats so different types of learners can feel comfortable with learning.
- Encourage students to participate in and contribute to their own learning.
- Divide students into groups and ask different groups to work together to complete a task.
- Praise and encourage students when appropriate.

Activity 6: Self-Directed Learning in Language Instruction
The development of self-directed learning in language learning and teaching and acquiring the necessary skills of self-directed learning, along with school-based teaching/learning strategies and processes, can significantly motivate students to plan and make decisions for their learning activities and evaluate their own progress, which finally leads to effective learning (Moradi, Harvey & Helldin, 2018).

Activity 7: How to Teach Reading in a Self-Directed Learning Environment
Provide a glossary of content-related terms in the reading selection. Use visual or audio support to help the student understand written materials in the text. Give step-by-step directions and read written instructions out loud. Simplify directions using key words for the most important ideas. Highlight key words and ideas on worksheets for the student to read first.

Research demonstrates that students who possess strong self-directed learning skills exhibit considerably better reading outcomes, measured by the number of books completed and days spent reading, than those with weaker self-directed learning abilities. Additionally, the students with strong self-directed learning skills demonstrated a greater tendency to engage in planning behaviors, which were significantly linked to better reading outcomes, than students with weaker self-directed learning skills (Li et al., 2021).

Activity 8: Self-Directed Learning – A Four-Step Process
Self-directed learning essentially means that students direct all of the main aspects of their study, such as the objectives, methods, materials, and evaluation. That way, students can tailor their studies to their own needs

(Li et al., 2021). The following are four steps to implement self-directed learning:

1. Students need various skills and attitudes to learning for successful independent study. Signs of readiness for self-directed learning include being autonomous, organized, self-disciplined, able to communicate effectively, able to accept constructive feedback, and able to engage in self-evaluation and self-reflection.
2. Students need to set learning goals.
3. Students need to understand themselves as learners.
4. Students need to engage in self-reflection and self-evaluation of their learning goals and progress in a unit of study.

Assessments

1. Record observations of students displaying autonomous behavior and this list becomes the template for identifying the meaning of autonomous behavior.
2. Discuss with a colleague the steps you can take now take to encourage relatedness that becomes the structure for instruction.
3. List new pedagogy you now use to cultivate competence in student behavior.
4. Assess student interest, which forms the basis to recruit a professional (perhaps a parent) to honor the student interest and collaboratively address content and application goals.
5. Develop an assessment checklist like that in Table 10.4, which the teacher and student can complete together and discuss.
6. Write a short reflection essay critiquing Knowles's statement in Box 10.13 and receive feedback on your reflection essay from colleagues with the purpose of initiating a self-directed learning environment in your worksite.

References

Argyris, C. & Schön, D. A. (1974). *Theory in Practice: Increasing Professional Effectiveness*. Hoboken, NJ: Jossey-Bass.

Argyris, C. (1977). Double loop learning in organizations. *Harvard Business Review*. https://hbr.org/1977/09/double-loop-learning-in-organizations.

Argyris, C. (1991). Teaching smart people how to learn. *Harvard Business Review*. https://hbr.org/1991/05/teaching-smart-people-how-to-learn.

Table 10.4 *Self-directed learning assessment grid*

Competency/goal	Importance (1, very; 2, fairly; 3, not very; 4, unimportant)	Rating (1, excellent; 2, good; 3, adequate; 4, poor)
1. Diagnosing my learning needs		
2. Stating my learning goals		
3. Identifying resources for learning		
4. Identifying a learning coach/mentor		
5. Choosing and implementing appropriate learning strategies		
6. Evaluating learning outcomes		
7. Organizing my time and resources		
8. Cooperating/working with others		
9. Demonstrating self-motivation		
10. Being resourceful		
11. Being independent		
12. Having the ability to find information		
13. Interpreting data (e.g., charts, tables, graphs)		
14. Having an awareness of task demands		
15. Demonstrating self-knowledge of learning preferences		
16. Having the ability to develop strategies for meeting learning sequentially		
17. Having the ability to carry out a plan systematically		
18. Having the ability to formulate relevant questions		
19. Having the ability to engage in self-evaluation		
20. Having the ability to analyze and organize information		
21. Having the ability to select and use the most effective means of acquiring information		
22. Having the ability to select the most relevant and reliable information sources		
23. Having the ability to communicate clearly through writing		
24. Having the ability to communicate clearly through speaking		
25. Having the ability to accept constructive feedback from others		
26. Having the ability to collect evidence of accomplishments and have it evaluated		
27. Having the ability to elaborate in writing		
28. Having the ability to elaborate in speaking		
29. Having the ability to generate unique/original ideas		
30. Having the ability to tolerate ambiguity		

Table 10.4 (*cont.*)

Competency/goal	Importance (1, very; 2, fairly; 3, not very; 4, unimportant)	**Rating** (1, excellent; 2, good; 3, adequate; 4, poor)
31. Having the ability to resist premature closure		
32. Having the ability to generate many ideas		
33. Having the ability to generate any categories of ideas		
34. Having the ability to engage in divergent thinking (e.g., brainstorming)		
35. Having the ability to engage in convergent thinking (e.g., coming to closure, making a decision)		
36. Preferring to get a reward for hard work (e.g., extrinsic motivation)		
37. Working hard for task-related enjoyment (e.g., intrinsic motivation)		

Box 10.13 Knowles's statement

Knowles (1975) stated "Self-directed learning describes a process in which individuals take the initiative, with or without the help of others, in diagnosing their learning needs, formulating learning goals, identifying human and material resources for learning, choosing and implementing appropriate learning strategies, and evaluating learning outcomes."

This quote is in contrast to direct learning, whereby a learner receives educational instruction directly from the teacher, typically in a classroom setting.

Brandt, C. (2020). 21st century skills self-directed learning. Center for Assessment. www.nciea.org/blog/instructing-assessing-21st-century-skills-a-focus-on-self-directed-learning/.

Deci, E. & Ryan, R. (1991). A motivational approach to self: Integration in personality. In R. Dienstbier (ed.), *Perspectives on Motivation* (Vol. 38, pp. 237–288). Lincoln, NE: University of Nebraska Press.

Deci, E. L. & Ryan, R. M. (2008). Self-determination theory: A macrotheory of human motivation, development, and health. *Canadian Psychology / Psychologie canadienne*, 49(3), 182–185. https://doi.org/10.1037/a0012801.

Deol, K. (n.d.). Self-directed learning vs. self-determined learning. Karen Deol: My Journey through Education. https://tinyurl.com/hznz2xn6.

Dweck, C. S. (2007). *Mindset: The New Psychology of Success*. New York: Ballantine Books.

Eisenberg, N., Spinrad, T. L. & Eggum, N. D. (2010). Emotion-related self-regulation and its relation to children's maladjustment. *Annual Review of Clinical Psychology*, 6(1), 495–525. https://doi.org/10.1146/annurev.clinpsy.121208.131208.

Gold, B. (2020). Unschooled [Film]. Wavelength Productions.

Knowles, M. (1975). *Self-Directed Learning: A Guide for Learners and Teachers*. New York: Association Press.

Li, H., Majumdar, R., Chen, M.-R. A. & Ogata, H. (2021). Goal-oriented active learning (GOAL) system to promote reading engagement, self-directed learning behavior, and motivation in extensive reading. *Computers & Education*, 171, 104239. https://doi.org/10.1016/j.compedu.2021.104239.

Mahavongtrakul, M., Hooper, A., Mann, D. & Sato, B. (2021). Beyond instructional development: An exploration of using formal pedagogy training to benefit perceived quality of life and sense of community in graduate students. *To Improve the Academy: A Journal of Educational Deve*, 40(2). https://doi.org/ https://doi.org/10.3998/tia.406.

Moradi, H., Harvey, P. D. & Helldin, L. (2018). Correlates of risk factors for reduced life expectancy in schizophrenia: Is it possible to develop a predictor profile? *Schizophrenia Research*, 201, 388–392. https://doi.org/10.1016/j.schres.2018.05.035.

Pintrich, P. (2000). The role of goal orientation in self-regulated learning. In M. Boekaerts, P. Pintrich & M. Zeidner (eds.), *Handbook of Self-Regulations* (pp. 451–502). Cambridge, MA: Academic Press.

Ryan, R. M. & Deci, E. L. (2008). Self-determination theory and the role of basic psychological needs in personality and the organization of behavior. In O. P. John, R. W. Robins & L. A. Pervin (eds.), *Handbook of Personality: Theory and Research* (pp. 654–678). New York: The Guildford Press.

Motivation Module 10.6
Intrinsic motivation

Background Information

Intrinsic motivation is the feeling associated with the drive to do something for its own sake and is a key characteristic of creativity. The four types of intrinsic motivation are creative motivation, competence motivation, learning/exploring motivation, and attitude motivation (Brown, 2020).

Creative Motivation
People are likely to display the highest level of creativity when motivated by their deep involvement and passion for the work (i.e., finding interest, enjoyment, satisfaction, and challenge in it; Amabile, 1996). The higher the creator's intrinsic motivation, the more creative and original they will be. Conversely, the more focused they are on extrinsic motivation (e.g., rewards or punishments for doing well or badly), the less creative they will be (Amabile, 1979; Deci & Ryan, 2008; Torr, 2008).

Competence Motivation
Competence motivation theory explains individuals' motivation to participate, persist, and work hard in any particular achievement context (Psychology, 2019). Thus, individuals are attracted to participation in activities in which they feel competent or capable.

Learning/Exploring Motivation
Learning/exploring motivation causes people to look for new things and see new perspectives and is related to self-directed learning, whereby students take an active rather than a passive role in managing their time and assessing their own progress. This encourages intrinsic motivation, as there is no outside pressure to perform or meet deadlines.

Attitude Motivation
Attitude motivation is a type of intrinsic motivation that relates to social status and behavior; it addresses making people around them feel good, which brings joy, and folks are motivated to do more.

Activities

Using Competence Motivation in Education and the Workplace
Learners' competence motivation increases when instructors emphasize meaning and individual development within the classroom. The same concept applies and is transferable to employees in the workplace. The following are a few ways to use competence motivation:

1. Assign tasks that are personally interesting to the learner.
2. Provide the right kind of feedback.
3. Assign tasks that are moderately and appropriately challenging.
4. Encourage mastery, skill development, and the learning process.
5. Encourage challenging but achievable goals.
6. Give praise when earned.

Activity 1: Assign Tasks that Are Personally Interesting to the Learner Whether the learner is a K–16 student or an industry employee, they will be more interested in mastering an area if they are personally interested in the topic or task. This will create a kind of peak involvement, whereby they are not thinking about objectives, rewards, or anything else extrinsic. In addition, by being wholly involved in learning, the learners are more likely to achieve competency in the subject.

Activity 2: Provide the Right Kind of Feedback Teachers or team leaders can help leaners feel in control of their learning and achievements by providing feedback that encourages them to recognize their power over what and how they learn. Feedback focuses on how far the learner has come since first trying the task and emphasizes the process they are using to learn.

Activity 3: Assign Tasks that Are Moderately and Appropriately Challenging Encourage learners to try tasks that are appropriately challenging for their skill levels. To do this successfully, encourage them to focus on mastery goals that are just out of reach. Also focus on the constructive value of failure and mistakes, providing comfort in knowing that occasional errors are okay.

Activity 4: Encourage Mastery, Skill Development, and the Learning Process Unlike performance goals, which focus on a specific outcome, mastery goals are about mastering a task and being better each day than the day before. One never quite reaches them because there is always room for improvement. By focusing on mastery, skill development, and the learning process, learners will be less likely to give up in difficult circumstances and more likely to persevere when experiencing setbacks.

Activity 5: Encourage Challenging but Achievable Goals According to the competence motivation theory, success or mastery of a task can lead to an overall increase in the perception of one's competence. However, if the person continually fails at a task or does not receive teacher support, it can have the opposite effect. That is why it is essential to encourage challenging but achievable goals. If the goals are too easily achieved, the learner can become bored or even embarrassed by the simplicity of the tasks they are given.

Ways to Cultivate Intrinsic Motivation in Learners

1. **Rethink rewards.** Rewards incentivize learners for simple, mechanistic tasks performed well. However, rewards lead to poor performance for tasks that require thinking outside the box.
2. **A higher purpose.** Learners who feel that they are working to contribute to the greater good or something greater than their personal needs find the work exhilarating.
3. **Don't use fear of punishment as a motivator.** Fear is not an effective motivator and should not be used as a substitute for intrinsic motivation.
4. **Expect self-direction, not compliance.** Motivating learners to follow the rules by threatening or goading won't help in the long run. Help them become more self-directed so that they end up complying as a result of their own decisions.
5. **Visualize and conquer.** Have learners visualize a moment in their lives when they felt very proud of themselves for an accomplishment.
6. **Make every learner feel capable.** Some learners may feel incapable of completing a task before trying it. Say, "You're capable," which speaks to the task at hand and the learner's sense of self-worth.
7. **Cooperation and competition.** Intrinsic motivation can increase when learners gain satisfaction from helping their peers. Motivation is also increased in cases in which they can compare their own performance favorably to that of others.
8. **Help learners trust themselves to succeed.** Learners who trust themselves to succeed at a task are more likely to challenge themselves in other situations. Be sure to recognize learner achievement in terms of personal worth and not just success on a particular assignment; this will encourage the learner to carry that confidence into other learning situations.

Adapted from Briggs (2016)

Assessments

1. Learner describes creative motivation, competence motivation, learning/exploring motivation, and attitude motivation orally or in writing.
2. Learner gives at least one example of creative motivation, competence motivation, learning/exploring motivation, and attitude motivation either orally or in writing.
3. Learner displays self-directed behavior when engaged in rule compliance.
4. Learner displays self-directed behavior when engaged in task completion.
5. The teacher keeps a log of selected students engaged in assessments 1 to 4 to provide them with relevant feedback.

References

Amabile, T. M. (1979). Effects of external evaluation on artistic creativity. *Journal of Personality and Social Psychology*, 37, 221–233.

Amabile, T. M. (1996). Motivation for creativity in organizations. *Harvard Business School Background Note*, 396–240. www.hbs.edu/faculty/Pages/item.aspx?num=13674.

Briggs, S. (2016). 25 ways to cultivate intrinsic motivation. InformED. www.opencolleges.edu.au/informed/features/intrinsic-motivation/.

Brown, E. (2020). 4 types of intrinsic motivation. Learnfromblogs. https://learnfromblogs.com/4-types-of-intrinsic-motivation.

Deci, E. L. & Ryan, R. M. (2008). Self-determination theory: A macrotheory of human motivation, development, and health. *Canadian Psychology / Psychologie canadienne*, 49(3), 182–185. https://doi.org/10.1037/a0012801.

Psychology (2019). *Competence motivation theory*. IResearchNet. https://psychology.iresearchnet.com/sports-psychology/sport-motivation/competence-motivation-theory/.

Torr, G. (2008). *Managing Creative People: Lessons in Leadership for the Ideas Economy.* New York: John Wiley.

Motivation Module 10.7

Extrinsic motivation

Background Information

Extrinsic motivation is reward-driven behavior. It is a type of operant conditioning, that is, a method of changing behavior by using rewards or punishments to increase or decrease the likelihood of certain actions being repeated. Extrinsic motivation uses rewards (e.g., money, gifts, or special favors) to motivate others for doing or performing the desired action. Although extrinsic motivation often involves tangible rewards, it also occurs through abstract rewards, such as praise, promotion, or fame (Financial Issues Solver, n.d.; Meadows-Fernandez, 2018).

In the context of businesses, extrinsic rewards refer to rewards given to employees that are typically monetary or concrete, such as salary increases, bonuses, and perks. These rewards are extrinsic because they are not inherent to the work and are determined by someone other than the employee. There are four categories of extrinsic motivation: external regulation, introjection regulation, regulation through identification, and integrated regulation (Bravo Wellness, 2019; Vallerand, 1997).

- **External regulation** means you do something to satisfy an external demand or receive external incentives. An example would be a student who studies hard to get good grades to receive material rewards from their parents. Although the behavior is intentional, it is controlled by an external source and, therefore, this action is externally regulated.
- **Introjection regulation** involves accepting the cause of doing something. An example would be a student who spends lots of time practicing piano for a recital to avoid embarrassing themselves in front of others. This type of regulation is performed due to internal pressure to reduce guilt or anxiety, enhance ego or pride, or maintain self-esteem or the feeling of self-worth.
- **Regulation through identification** is a less controlling form of extrinsic motivation. Identification means the person consciously values a goal and believes the activity is personally important.
- **Integrated regulation** occurs when one has fully accepted the reason for an action (i.e., a person has examined the cause and found it compatible with their own values and needs). The action then becomes self-initiated and is autonomous and not controlled by external motivators (Ryan & Deci, 2000). Despite being extrinsic, integrated motivation shares many qualities with intrinsic motivation. Some researchers even refer to integrated regulation as intrinsic because the person has completely internalized the extrinsic cause into their values.

Illustrations of Extrinsic Motivation
Money Money is widely used as a motivator in the workplace, enabling employees to buy goods and services to fulfill their wants and needs. Furthermore, it gives employees a gauge to evaluate how much the organization values their contributions.

Name and Recognition Acknowledging employees' efforts and achievements in the workplace can be a powerful motivator, giving them a sense of achievement and making them feel appreciated. Such recognition can lead to increased engagement, higher productivity, and greater loyalty to the company, resulting in improved retention rates.

Awards Awards include bonuses, commissions, or prizes to foster interest and complete a particular task.

Public Praise and Appreciation Praise and appreciation in public settings (e.g., group meetings, board of directors meetings, all-school meetings) by the worker's supervisor is ego boosting to the receiver of the praise. It tends to make the induvial or group "feel" valued and special, while encouraging them to continue the good work with hopes of receiving public recognition again.

Activities

Activity 1

Extrinsic motivation can be used to motivate someone to do different things. Extrinsic motivation is involved if a known reward is tied to the task or outcome. The following are examples of extrinsic rewards. Write a story in which one of the following situations is involved:

- competing in sports for trophies
- completing work for money
- customer loyalty discounts
- buy one, get one free sale
- frequent flyer rewards

Activity 2

Write about characters in a story, historical figures, or current events that focus on the extrinsic motivation of the characters using the following sample prompts. Fill in the blank space with an extrinsic motivator.

Prompts for Reading Comprehension   What outside forces are driving the character?

- Why does _____ not motivate the character?
- How does _____ impact what the character loves?
- In what way does _____ impact what the character thinks they need?
- In what way does _____ impact what the character despises?

Prompts for Historical Figures   What outside forces pushed this person toward that act?

- Why did _____ not push this person to act?
- How did _____ impact what this person loves more than anything else?
- How did _____ impact what the person believes they needed?
- How did _____ motivate the character's enemy?

Prompts for Current Events What forces are pulling the group toward that idea?

- Why does _____ not motivate the group to act?
- How does _____ impact what the group wants?
- In the view of the group, how does _____ impact others?
- Why does the group consider _____ wrong?

Assessments

Mark each of the following examples with an "E" to show that it is an extrinsic motivation characteristic or an "I" to show that it is an intrinsic motivation characteristic:

____ Going to work to get paid
____ Studying to get a good grade
____ Working because you enjoy the job
____ Studying because you find the subject interesting
____ Working hard to get a raise or recognition from your boss
____ Tackling a new project because you love a challenge
____ Tidying your house to avoid feeling embarrassed when company comes over
____ Tidying your house because a clean home keeps you calm

Answers
Extrinsic motivation examples:

- Going to work to get paid
- Studying to get a good grade
- Working hard to get a raise or recognition from your boss
- Tidying your house to avoid feeling embarrassed when company comes over
- Intrinsic motivation examples:
- Working because you enjoy the job
- Studying because you find the subject interesting
- Tackling a new project because you love a challenge
- Tidying your house because a clean home keeps you calm

Adapted from Cherry (2021)

References

Bravo Wellness (2019). Intrinsic vs. extrinsic rewards to improve employee engagement. www.bravowell.com/resources/intrinsic-vs.-extrinsic-rewards-to-improve-employee-engagement.

Cherry, K. (2021). 6 key ideas behind theories of motivation. Verywell Mind. www.verywellmind.com/theories-of-motivation-2795720v.

Financial Issues Solver (n.d.). What are extrinsic motivators? https://financial-issues-solver.com/.

Meadows-Fernandez, A. R. (2018). Extrinsic motivation: What is it and how does it work? Healthline. www.healthline.com/health/extrinsic-motivation.

Ryan, R. M. & Deci, E. L. (2000). Self-determination theory and the facilitation of intrinsic motivation, social development, and well-being. *American Psychologist*, 55(1), 68–78. https://doi.org/10.1037//0003-066x.55.1.68.

Vallerand, R. J. (1997). Toward a hierarchical model of intrinsic and extrinsic motivation. *Advances in Experimental Social Psychology*, 29, 271–360. https://doi.org/10.1016/S0065-2601(08)60019-2.

Motivation Module 10.8
Gamification

Background Information

Gamification in education is transforming a classroom into a gaming environment. Creating a gaming metaphor requires choosing a theme (e.g., medieval times, fantasy, space battles, military, spy/secret agent) and referring to everything in the classroom with gaming terms (student = player, assignment = quest, grade = quest points).

Studies on gamification show that using gamification in the classroom increases student engagement. It is also a strategy for increasing motivation, involving creativity and student choice. It gives students immediate feedback (through peer comments, progress charts, badges, teacher response, etc.) and allows them to easily track their progress toward academic goals. Box 10.14 presents a further description of gamification related to learning.

Activities

There are many ways to establish gamification in classrooms. These range from minor tweaks to significant changes in the existing instructional

> **Box 10.14 Gamification related to learning**
>
> The gamification of education is an instructional technique that incorporates game-like elements and video game design to motivate students and enhance their learning experience in different educational settings.
>
> The objective is to increase fun and involvement by capturing learners' attention and inspiring them to pursue learning. Gamification is identifying the components that make games enjoyable and motivating players to continue playing, then incorporating those elements into a non-game setting to influence behavior. Gamification involves introducing game-like features into a context not typically associated with games (Ryan & Deci, 2000; Toda et al., 2019).
>
> Gamification in educational settings has added benefits in terms of encouraging students to exhibit desired behaviors, such as attending classes, actively engaging in meaningful learning activities, and showing initiative (Borges et al., 2014; Borys & Laskowski, 2013).

design used in the classroom. The following are a couple of common methods for gamifying a classroom.

1. **"Repackaging grades"** refers to exchanging a letter or a number grade on assignments with experience points. In most games, players earn points for each challenge met. At pre-described intervals, characters "level up" or increase to the next level of the game. In gamification of the classroom, leveling up is synonymous with the student's grade improving by a letter grade. For example, Johnny receives 150 points for his homework assignment, so levels up to "master level" (which is recorded on official school records as an A). An alternative approach is to award badges to students as they level up or accomplish challenging tasks.

2. **Positive reinforcement** can boost student confidence. Some ways of rewarding students in a gamified learning environment include coins, whereby students receive "coins" upon the successful completion of an activity (e.g., students receive ten coins for the completion of a learning activity). The coins can be accumulated and redeemed for a class store gift or badge to recognize their efforts (see Chapter 11 for a description of badges).

Assessments

Gamification is a good idea only when it supplements classroom teaching and empowers students to get more out of their education. If bringing games and competition into the curriculum doesn't complement the normal instructional strategies, then it might be better to avoid these ideas. Successful gamification will tap into the user's intrinsic motivation, such as becoming successful as a student, while offering extrinsic motivation, such as rewards, points, or badges. The emphasis on extrinsic motivation should be balanced with intrinsic motivation that emphasizes learning for personal enjoyment.

References

Borges, S., Durelli, V., Reis, H. & Isotani, S. (2014). A systematic mapping on gamification applied to education (pp. 216–222). ACM Symposium on Applied Computing. Gyeongju, Republic of Korea.

Borys, M. & Laskowski, M. (2013). Implementing game elements into didactic process: A case study. In V. Dermol, N. T. Sirca & G. Dakovic (eds.), *Active Citizenship by Knowledge Management & Innovation: Programme of the Management, Knowledge and Learning International Conference* (pp. 819–824). Celije, Slovenia: ToKnowPress.

Ryan, R. M. & Deci, E. L. (2000). Self-determination theory and the facilitation of intrinsic motivation, social development, and well-being. *American Psychologist*, 55(1), 68–78. https://doi.org/10.1037//0003-066x.55.1.68.

Toda, A. M., Klock, A. C. T., Oliveira, W. et al. (2019). Analysing gamification elements in educational environments using an existing Gamification taxonomy. *Smart Learning Environments*, 6(1). https://doi.org/10.1186/s40561-019-0106-1.

Motivation Module 10.9
Mindfulness and motivation

Background Information

Mindfulness is a practice that originated from ancient eastern and Buddhist philosophy and dates back around 2,500 years (Mindfulness Supervision, 2022). The term "mindfulness" comes from a Sanskrit word that literally translates to "that which is remembered" (Parth, Harris & Forthun, 2019; Williams Leumann & Cappeller, 2004). In essence, mindfulness is thinking about and reminding ourselves to pay attention to the present moment experience (Black, 2011; Parth, Harris & Forthun, 2019; Shapiro & Carlson, 2009). Over the years, mindfulness has been studied and practiced to a point that it now has an inherent quality of consciousness that can be measured empirically and scientifically (Black, 2011; Kohls, Sauer & Walach, 2009; Walach et al., 2007; see Chapter 8 for a discussion of mindfulness).

There are three key features of mindfulness (Parth, Harris & Forthun, 2019):

1. **Purpose:** mindfulness requires actively and deliberately focusing your attention rather than allowing it to drift.
2. **Presence:** mindfulness requires complete involvement and attentiveness to the current moment.
3. **Acceptance:** mindfulness involves impartially observing and acknowledging experiences without categorizing them as positive, negative, pleasurable, or uncomfortable. Instead, they are accepted as they are and observed until they naturally dissipate.

Box 10.15 summarizes mindfulness's psychological, physiological, and spiritual benefits (Davis & Hayes, 2011; Parth, Harris & Forthun, 2019).

The goal of engaging in mindfulness is to achieve a state of focused relaxation by paying attention to one's emotions, thoughts, and sensations so that the mind focuses on the present while being free of judgments.

Motivation is a process that drives people to act (see Chapters 3 and 6 on motivation), while motives describe why a person does the things they do. The motivational forces that direct and maintain our goal-directed actions include biological, emotional, social, and cognitive forces (Cherry, 2022). Motives are rarely directly observable; therefore, we must often infer why people do the things they do based on their observable behaviors (Nevid, 2013).

Box 10.15   Mindfulness: psychological, physiological, and spiritual benefits

PSYCHOLOGICAL BENEFITS

The psychological benefits of mindfulness include increased self-awareness of one's mind, which significantly reduces stress, anxiety, and negative emotions. With this increased awareness comes greater control over self-reflective thinking and more working memory, leading to fewer distracting thoughts and an increased capacity for intentional, responsive behaviors. Furthermore, mindfulness practice has been found to increase empathy, compassion, and conscientiousness of others' emotions.

> **Box 10.15** (cont.)
>
> ### PHYSIOLOGICAL BENEFITS
> The physiological benefits of mindfulness practice include improved immune system functioning, increased brain density, and neural integration in the areas responsible for positive emotions, self-regulation, and long-term planning. It also lowers blood pressure and increases resistance to stress-related illnesses (e.g., heart disease).
>
> ### SPIRITUAL BENEFITS
> The spiritual benefits of mindfulness include increased self-insight and self-acceptance, which leads to increased acceptance of others. This practice also increases compassion and empathy and enhances one's sense of morality, intuition, and courage, leading to greater self-discipline.

Activities

Activity 1: Ways to Motivate Yourself
- Intention involves awareness of why we are doing something.
- Keeping a routine ensures that at least one of your goals will be addressed.
- Recognize the power of now by focusing on just getting through today's goal.
- Being present involves focusing on what you're doing at a given moment.
- Building trust through practice includes thinking of a goal as a series of repeated steps that build with repetition.
- Keep in mind that there is an antidote for every obstacle; thus, understand the specific obstacle and come up with a plan to address it.
- Don't be too hard on yourself when you mess up; rather, recommit to continuing toward satisfying the goal.
- Recognize that intentions can change by staying open to awareness of the change.

Adapted from Headspace (2021)

Activity 2: Positive Phrases to Employ to Be Super Positive
- I admire you.
- You can do it.
- I value you.
- You can count on me.
- I believe in you.

- You are kind.
- I trust you.
- You are smart.

Adapted from Economy (n.d.)

Activity 3: Possible Answers to the Question "What Motivates You?"
- Learning new things
- Acquiring new skills
- Meeting deadlines, goals, and targets
- Coaching others
- Improving processes/finding ways to solving problems
- Leading a team or being a part of a team
- Completing a difficult project
- Overcoming challenges
- Coming up with creative ideas

Adapted from Targetjobs (n.d.)

Activity 4: Mindfulness
Practicing mindfulness in the classroom can help students calm themselves, focus, and engage in learning and positive social interactions. The following are suggested mindfulness techniques for elementary school, middle school, and high school or college classrooms.

Elementary School Classrooms
1. Use breath control by suggesting that students breathe in slowly for three counts, then exhale for three counts. Alternatively, they can imagine a peaceful scene, such as a beach or a forest, and visualize themselves inhaling the fresh air and exhaling any tension or worries.
2. Sensory activities can be a great way to help students relax and focus. For example, you might encourage them to try some gentle stretching exercises, suggest they use a stress ball or fidget toy to occupy their hands, or have them hold a warm cup of tea or hot cocoa to enjoy the comforting aroma and taste.
3. Getting students moving can also be a powerful way to help them calm down and focus. For instance, you might suggest they take a short walk around the classroom or campus, practice some yoga poses, or do some simple exercises such as jumping jacks or lunges. Another idea is to have them engage in a guided mindfulness activity that involves paying attention to their body and surroundings, such as a body scan or a mindful walking exercise.

Middle School Classrooms

1. To help students transition calmly, you could suggest they focus on their breath while listening to the sound of a chime. Alternatively, you might guide them through a progressive muscle relaxation exercise in which they tense and relax each muscle group in their body while sitting in their chairs.
2. As a way to encourage self-reflection and promote growth, you might ask students to write about a positive experience they had that day, such as a moment of kindness they witnessed or an accomplishment they achieved. Alternatively, you could provide a writing prompt that invites them to think about a challenge they faced and how they overcame it, or a lesson they learned from a mistake they made.

High School or College Classrooms

1. For students who are feeling anxious or overwhelmed, a helpful mindfulness technique is to imagine a peaceful scene, such as a beach or a forest, and picture themselves in that environment. They can focus on the sights, sounds, and smells of this scene, and use their breath to anchor themselves in the present moment. Another mindfulness exercise is to practice gratitude by reflecting on something they are thankful for each day, such as a good friend or a supportive family member. By cultivating an attitude of gratitude, students can shift their focus away from stress and anxiety and toward positive emotions and experiences.
2. Keep a log reflecting on the actions in Box 10.16 that may be used while engaged in mindfulness.

Adapted from School of Education Online (2021)

Box 10.16   Mindfulness actions

I am able to observe my thoughts and feelings without getting lost in them.
I am aware of my body and physical sensations throughout the day.
I can easily find words to describe my feelings.
I can easily describe different sensations that I am feeling.
I notice when my mind is wandering and return it to the present.
I am aware of the thoughts and emotions influencing my actions and behaviors.
I can accept unpleasant experiences without judging them.

Box 10.16 (cont.)

I can be aware of my thoughts and emotions without judging them to be good or bad.
I can notice my thoughts and emotions without having to react to them.
I can pause before reacting in difficult or stressful situations.

Source: Baer et al. (2006)

Assessments

1. Record the observed positive effects of mindfulness, including:
   - improved attention and learning skills
   - better social and emotional skills
   - increased empathy and classroom participation
   - reduced negative effects of stress on students' ability to stay engaged
   - increased focus, attention, self-control, classroom participation, and compassion
   - improved academic performance, ability to resolve conflict, and overall well-being
2. Share the results of assessment 1 with colleagues for the purpose of incorporating mindfulness activities into instruction.

References

Baer, R. A., Smith, G. T., Hopkins, J., Krietemeyer, J. & Toney, L. (2006). Using self-report assessment methods to explore facets of mindfulness. *Assessment*, 13(1), 27–45. https://doi.org/10.1177/1073191105283504.

Black, D. S. (2011). A brief definition of mindfulness. Mindfulness Research Guide.

Cherry, K. (2022). Motivation: Psychological factors that guide behavior. Verywell Mind. www.verywellmind.com/what-is-motivation-2795378.

Davis, D. M. & Hayes, J. A. (2011). What are the benefits of mindfulness? A practice review of psychotherapy-related research. *Psychotherapy*, 48(2), 198–208. https://doi.org/10.1037/a0022062.

Economy, P. (n.d.). 9 powerful phrases super positive people say. Inc. www.inc.com/peter-economy/9-powerful-phrases-super-positive-people-always-say.html.

Headspace (2021). How to get motivated. www.headspace.com/mindfulness/how-to-get-motivated.

Kohls, N., Sauer, S. & Walach, H. (2009). Facets of mindfulness – Results of an online study investigating the Freiburg mindfulness inventory. *Personality and Individual Differences*, 46, 224–230. https://doi.org/10.1016/j.paid.2008.10.009.

Mindfulness Supervision (2022). What is mindfulness meditation in Buddhism? https://mindfulness-supervision.org.uk/what-is-mindfulness-meditation-in-buddhism/.

Nevid, J. (2013). *Psychology: Concepts and Application*. Belmont, CA: Wadsworth.

Parth, N., Harris, V. & Forthun, L. (2019). Mindfulness: An introduction. Askifas. https://edis.ifas.ufl.edu/publication/FY1381.

School of Education Online (2021). How to incorporate mindfulness in the classroom. https://soeonline.american.edu/blog/mindfulness-in-the-classroom/.

Shapiro, S. L. & Carlson, L. E. (2009). *The Art and Science of Mindfulness: Integrating Mindfulness into Psychology and the Helping Professions*. Washington, DC: American Psychological Association.

Targetjobs (n.d.). "What motivates you?" Tricky graduate interview question. https://targetjobs.co.uk/careers-advice/interviews-and-assessment-centres/what-motivates-you-tricky-graduate-interview-question.

Walach, H., Nord, E., Zier, C., Dietz-Waschowski, B., Kersig, S. & Schupbach, H. (2007). Mindfulness-based stress reduction as a method for personnel development: A pilot evaluation. *International Journal of Stress Management*, 14(2), 188–198. https://doi.org/10.1037/1072-5245.14.2.188.

Williams, M., Leumann, E. & Cappeller, C. (2004). *Etymo – Logically and Philologically Arranged with Special Reference To Cognate Indo-European Languages*. New Delhi: Bharatiya Granth Niketan.

Motivation Module 10.10
Neuroscience of motivation

Background Information

The neuroscience of motivation studies how the environment and daily events activate specific brain structures and how these are associated with the motivational states that energize, direct, and sustain behavior (Carver & Scheier, 1998). Our evolving understanding of the human brain provides new clues as to what makes specific individuals more motivated than others – whether it be an employee working harder at their job than their colleagues or students engaging more in learning than their peers.

The chemical dopamine primarily deals with motivation. Dopamine generates positive and negative motivation depending on where in the brain it is acting. High dopamine levels concentrated in one area of the brain drive individuals to work hard for a reward; high levels in another drive them to reject that effort. This discrepancy is because dopamine is a reward neurotransmitter and conveys what neuroscientists label "motivational salience." Dopamine transmits signals in response to rewards. It also signals responses to salient, non-rewarding stimuli such as stress or aversion. Dopamine motivates us either toward or away from something (Berridge, 2004, 2018). Dopamine neurons connect distinct brain networks and have distinct roles in motivational control (e.g., supporting brain networks for seeking evaluation and value learning). In contrast, other neurons support orienting, cognition, and general motivation (Bromberg-Martin, Matsumoto & Hikosaka, 2010).

The cortical brain contains conscious and deliberate motivations, including goals, plans, strategies, values, and beliefs about the self. Some cortical brain structures involve motivation and emotional states (Reeve, 2018). The subcortical brain involves memory, emotion, pleasure, and hormone production. Structures in the cortical and subcortical brain are linked by a network of neural pathways that communicate with each other. As part of the nervous system, these brain structures use neurotransmitters to interact, while the endocrine system relies on hormones such as cortisol, oxytocin, and testosterone, which are important for motivation (Reeve, 2018). Neuroplasticity is the capacity of neural networks in the brain to alter their connections and behavior in reaction to new information, sensory stimulation, development, damage, or dysfunction (Ceruto, 2019). Measuring motivation includes many approaches, such as observable responses, cognitive responses such as the speed of recall or quality of perception, analyzing self-reports of one's experience, and behavioral measures such as task performance and brain activation (see Chapter 8 for more on neuroscience and mindfulness).

Activities

1. Set achievable goals by breaking large goals down into a series of smaller, more achievable, goals.
2. Engage in framing. Folk do not like being told to do something they don't want to, but when one is enthusiastic about achieving a goal for intrinsic reasons, work becomes enjoyable. Thus, rather than dwell on what one *has* to do, reframe the task as a goal that one *wants* to achieve.
3. Discuss the following subcortical brain structures and how they are involved in motivation and emotional states (Reeve, 2018) with teachers and peers for the purpose of becoming familiar with this information.

Subcortical brain structures	Function
Reticular formation	Regulates arousal, alertness, and the neural process of awakening the brain's motivational and emotional concerns

(*cont.*)

Subcortical brain structures	Function
Amygdala	Detects, learns about, and responds to the stimulus properties of environmental objects, including both threat-eliciting and reward-eliciting associations
Basal ganglia (caudate nucleus, putamen, substantial nigra, and globus pallidus)	Contribute to the motivational invigoration and inhibition of movement and action
Ventral striatum (nucleus accumbens) and ventral tegmental	The brain's reward center
Ventral tegmental area	Manufactures and releases dopamine that is received by the nucleus accumbens to produce pleasure and liking
Hypothalamus	Responsive to natural rewards in the regulation of eating, drinking, and mating, and it also regulates both the endocrine and autonomic nervous systems

Adapted from Souders (2019).

4. Discuss the following cortical brain structures and how they are involved in motivation and emotion (Reeve, 2018) with teachers and peers for the purpose of becoming familiar with this information.

Cortical brain structures	Function
Insula	Monitors bodily states to produce both positive and negative gut-felt feelings; also processes feelings associated with risk, uncertainty, intrinsic motivation, empathy, and personal agency
Prefrontal cortex	Involved in making plans, setting goals, and formulating intentions
Right hemispheric activity	Associated with negative affect and "no-go" avoidance motivation
Left hemispheric activity	Associated with positive affect and "go" approach motivation
Orbitofrontal cortex	Stores and processes reward-related values of environmental objects and events to formulate preferences and make choices between options
Ventromedial prefrontal cortex	Evaluates the unlearned emotional value of basic sensory rewards and internal bodily states and is responsible for emotional control
Dorsolateral prefrontal cortex	Evaluates the learned emotional value of environmental events and possible courses of action, and is responsible for control over urges and risks during the pursuit of long-term goals

(*cont.*)

Cortical brain structures	Function
Anterior cingulate cortex	Monitors motivational conflicts and resolves those conflicts by recruiting other cortical brain structures to exert cognitive control over basic urges and emotions

Adapted from Souders (2019).

5. Explore these neuromyths (Macdonald et al., 2017):
   - We use only 10 percent of the brain. (You've probably heard this statement on several occasions, but the reality is that it has no scientific basis.)
   - Each hemisphere has a function.
   - Learning occurs in the first three years of life.
   - Some subjects are more important than others.
   - Learning is more effective in the preferred modality.

Assessments

1. Explain outcome-focused motivation directed at completing a goal (Brehm & Self, 1989; Locke & Latham, 1990; Powers, 1973).
2. Explain process-focused motivation used during goal pursuit (Higgins et al., 2003; Touré-Tillery & Fishbach, 2015).
3. Explain goal pursuit involving intrinsic motivation (Deci & Ryan, 1985).
4. Give an example of each of the following processes: (1) generating motivation, (2) maintaining motivation, and (3) regulating motivation.
5. Solve a matching test item for cortical brain structures and their function.
6. Solve a matching test item for subcortical brain structures and their function.

References

Berridge, K. C. (2004). Motivation concepts in behavioral neuroscience. *Physiology & Behavior*, 81(2), 179–209. https://doi.org/10.1016/j.physbeh.2004.02.004.

Berridge, K. C. (2018). Evolving concepts of emotion and motivation. *Frontiers in Psychology*, 9. https://doi.org/10.3389/fpsyg.2018.01647.

Brehm, J. W. & Self, E. A. (1989). The intensity of motivation. *Annual Review of Psychology*, 40, 109–131. https://doi.org/10.1146/annurev.ps.40.020189.000545.

Bromberg-Martin, E. S., Matsumoto, M. & Hikosaka, O. (2010). Dopamine in motivational control: rewarding, aversive, and alerting. *Neuron*, 68(5), 815–834. https://doi.org/10.1016/j.neuron.2010.11.022.

Carver, C. S. & Scheier, M. F. (1998). *On the Self-Regulation of Behavior*. Cambridge, UK: Cambridge University Press. https://doi.org/10.1017/CBO9781139174794.

Ceruto, D. S. (2019). The neuroscience of motivation: How our brains drive hard work and achievement. Forbes. https://tinyurl.com/3cnex3vm.

Deci, E. L. & Ryan, R. M. (1985). *Intrinsic Motivation and Self-Determination in Human Behavior*. New York: Plenum. https://doi.org/10.1007/978-1-4899-2271-7.

Higgins, E., Idson, L., Freitas, A., Spiegel, S. & Molden, D. (2003). Transfer of value from fit. *Journal of Personality and Social Psychology*, 84(6), 1140–1153.

Locke, E. A. & Latham, G. P. (1990). *A Theory of Goal Setting & Task Performance*. Upper Saddle River, NJ: Prentice-Hall, Inc.

Macdonald, K., Germine, L., Anderson, A., Christodoulou, J. & McGrath, L. (2017). Dispelling the myth: Training in education or neuroscience decreases but does not eliminate beliefs in neuromyths. *Frontiers in Psychology*, 8, 1314. https://doi.org/10.3389/fpsyg.2017.01314.

Powers, W. T. (1973). *Behavior: The Control of Perception*. Piscataway, NJ: Aldine.

Reeve, J. (2018). *Understanding Motivation and Emotion* (7th ed.). Hoboken, NJ: Wiley.

Simpson, E. H. & Balsam, P. D. (2016). The behavioral neuroscience of motivation: An overview of concepts, measures, and translational applications. *Current Topics in Behavioral Neuroscience*, 27, 1–12. https://doi.org/10.1007/7854_2015_402.

Souders, B. (2019). How to measure motivation by understanding the science behind it. PositivePsychology. https://positivepsychology.com/motivation-science-research-assessments/.

Touré-Tillery, M. & Fishbach, A. (2015). It was(n't) me: Exercising restraint when choices appear self-diagnostic. *Journal of Personality and Social Psychology*, 109(6), 1117–1131. https://doi.org/10.1037/a0039536.

Motivation Module 10.11
Diagnostic teaching

Background Information

Diagnostic teaching (Reisman, 1982) involves creative problem-solving that comprises a process of discovering student learning strengths and weakness, analyzing curriculum concepts to be taught, detecting gaps or misconceptions between the student knowledge base and the curriculum to be taught, and devising ways to mesh student learning needs with curriculum needs, thus triggering student self-efficacy that motivates wanting to succeed. Tools to identify student learning needs that involve generic influences on learning (Tanner & Reisman, 2014) are discussed in the appendices of Chapter 5, and tools to identify curriculum needs are presented in Chapter 4 in the section on developmental curriculum (Reisman & Severino, 2021).

Activities

1. Match the following literacy concepts with their curriculum level.

Literacy Concept	Key	Curriculum level
1. Manipulating phonemes	d	a. Concept
2. Summarizing	f	b. Lower level generalization
3. Word meaning	a	c. Arbitrary association
5. Alliteration	b	d. Higher level generalization
6. Hearing syllables	e	e. Lower level relationship
7. Sound/symbol relationships	c	f. Higher level relationship

2. Match the following mathematics concepts with their curriculum level.

Mathematics concept	Key	Curriculum level
1. Write digits	e	a. Lower level generalization
2. One-to-one correspondence	c	b. Higher level relationship
3. Equivalent sets	a	c. Lower level relationship
4. Shape	f	d. Higher level generalization
5. Number operations (+, −, ×, ÷)	b	e. Arbitrary association
6. Place value	d	f. Concept

3. Diagnose the gap that explains why the following student, Donald, is having trouble learning addition with renaming as exemplified in 15+7.
   Donald can bundle ten pencils to make one bundle of ten, but he cannot move to the written level, that is, the symbolic level. Thus, he can focus on the units column and state there are twelve units but he is lost at the symbols level. His answer is 112.

Answer: The physical bundling of concrete objects does NOT represent our number system where the count of nine, not ten, triggers the move to the tens place.

Suggested pedagogy: Use the place value boards presented in Chapter 9, Figures 9.3 to 9.12.

4. Diagnose why Keisha, a fourth grader, gets upset when she usually misses the point of a story and other situations.

Answer: It sounds like she has trouble noticing the salient aspects of situations (e.g., what she is reading or supposed to notice).

Suggested pedagogy: Print reading passages and provide cues such as a larger font, underlining, or coloring key words. Provide situations in which she can practice noticing the salient aspects of situations. For more on generic influences on learning, see Appendices 5A, 5B, and 5C.

5. Encourage intrinsic motivation by engaging students in activities in which no external reward, such as a grade or badge, is involved. Thus, base assessment upon student effort in relation to learning outcome. For example, focus on self-directed learning as described in Motivation Module 10.6.

Assessments

1. Keep a journal in which you describe diagnostic interactions with students and the outcome.
2. Perform a task analysis on the following topics (see Chapter 4 for basic facts task analysis):
   - subtraction without renaming
   - subtraction with renaming
   - addition of fractions with like denominators
   - time to the minute
   - find perimeter of a rectangle
   - name the number of syllables in a given word
   - tell the main idea of a reading passage
3. Reflect upon how you use diagnostic teaching to motivate learners (Reisman, Keiser & Bach, 2023).
4. Select two students at different academic achievement levels (e.g., high and low performers) and create two case studies that include (1) demographic information (family data, social and emotional observations, generic influences on learning, classroom interactions), (2)

academic achievements, (3) an instructional plan as you go forward, and (4) the log results of your instructional plan.

References

Reisman, F. K. (1982). A Guide to the **Diagnostic Teaching** of Arithmetic (3rd ed.). Columbus, OH: Charles E. Merrill.

Reisman, F. & Severino, L. (2021). *Using Creativity to Address Dyslexia, Dysgraphia, and Dyscalculia: Assessment and Techniques*. Oxford, UK: Routledge, Taylor & Francis Group.

Reisman, F., Keiser, L. & Bach, C. (2023). Reisman Diagnostic Motivation Assessment (RDMA). Online free App. Downloaded via Qualtrics.

Tanner, D. & Reisman, F. (2014). *Creativity as a Bridge between Education and Industry: Fostering New Innovations*. North Charleston, NC: CreateSpace.

10.3 Summary

This chapter provides an array of modules that are meant to enhance instruction that incorporates motivation. They are designed to translate the foundational knowledge presented in Chapter 3 on motivation so that it can be used by teachers, parents, and corporate trainers. Relevant references are placed within their related module.

CHAPTER 11

Dissemination and Communication Techniques for Translational Research

Advance Organizer. This chapter describes several pathways to non-degree options that are based on satisfying specified competencies. In addition, microcredentialing options are described that may be accumulated toward an academic degree.

11.1 Introduction

This chapter will discuss various dissemination and communication passport techniques for sharing the work of the Freddie Reisman Center for Translational Research in Creativity and Motivation (FRC). These are just examples, not an exhaustive list. The techniques are examples of the transmission of information in fields of study, much like in advertisement, public announcements, and speeches. Another way to think of dissemination and communication is "scattering of seeds". The seeds represent the information being communicated or disseminated. The following overview of the Education Passport will provide context for the techniques that follow.

11.2 Education Passport

The Education Passport is an electronic subscription-based comprehensive record of learning built on the validated achievement of competencies. Collections of achieved competencies are organized into badges, and multiple badges can lead to higher level badges or stackable microcredentials. The Education Passport supports learners in the ongoing and iterative creation of their own individual career, life, and learning pathways from kindergarten to twelfth grade (K–12) schools, through college, and into their post-graduate experiences. The Education Passport helps learners to:

- manage the validated achievement of competencies that represent their skills, knowledge, and experiences from both formal and informal

11 *Dissemination and Communication Techniques* 371

learning contexts, aligning them in relevant and meaningful ways to their career, academic, and life aspirations
- reflect on their interests, passions, and knowledge, as well as build a strong reflective sense of themselves as learners, their strengths, and their challenges in order to develop a path to achieving their educational, career, and life goals

The Education Passport supports organizations, schools, and businesses in achieving onboarding, quality retention, professional development, and training goals by helping them to:

- identify workforce development needs and align them to specific competencies and related certifications
- determine appropriate learning resources and delivery modalities to support the achievement of competencies
- support the successful implementation of the Education Passport program by providing client-side training and consulting

The Education Passport reimagines and broadens how schools and universities support individuals and organizations in meeting learning goals. The Education Passport develops systematic, data-driven, and market-oriented approaches to identifying and organizing critical competencies aligned with current workforce opportunities. It also collaborates with industry partners, researchers, and field experts to develop new competencies to support projected industry trends and future employer needs. Working with businesses, individuals, and experts, the Education Passport determines the most effective way of delivering training, documenting, and validating competency achievement and coaching learners to become the drivers of their own education across broader populations than are currently served through standard degree programs. A dyadic consumer model, comprising individual learners and organizations, is used to frame the following two goals:

1. significantly change how students and professionals manage their own learning and meaningfully improve their ability to envision, plan, and achieve their academic, career, and life aspirations
2. significantly change how organizations, schools, and businesses manage professional development and learning and improve their ability to envision, plan, and achieve their strategic goals

11.3 Dissemination and Communication Techniques

Badges

Badges are digital symbols of completion or accomplishment of a credential, knowledge, or skill. It is an online record of completion much like a paper diploma. Usually, badges are not for credit but still symbolize completion of a credential, knowledge, or skill.

Microcredentials

Microcredentials are focused credentials designed to provide competencies. Several badges can be taken together to create a microcredential. A stackable microcredential can provide a pathway to a certificate or full degree.

Spotlights

A spotlight is a two-page synopsis of research around a theme using language common to teachers, parents, and the public. There are many exciting dissemination and communication techniques that educators can use to make research accessible to a broader audience. Spotlights communicate specific information on what will work in the classroom and beyond. We know that one size doesn't fit all, and spotlights are just one example of communicating knowledge so that it is understandable to teachers, parents, and the public. The hope is that spotlights will serve as accessible information that provides new ideas to educators and parents who are leading the way in opening doors for students.

Parent Guides

A parent guide is a one-page activity for students to do at home that builds on a lesson done at school during the day. They are meant to be informative while also extending the lesson of the day into the home in a fun and meaningful way for the entire family to enjoy. Parent guides are also meant to be resources for parents to understand what their children should learn and be able to do, and provide helpful suggestions for supporting students' learning at home. Parent guides are written in easy-to-understand language with key questions (what, why, who, how, and when) for parents to ask their children during the activity.

11 *Dissemination and Communication Techniques*   373

Research Briefs

A research brief is a short (two- to three-page) summary of a discussion paper or research intended to help decision-makers make informed decisions. They provide a concise summary of research knowledge on a certain topic. Research briefs are not very in-depth but provide an overview or summary of the research. The intent is to provide decision-makers with a concentrated summary of the relevant findings of the research.

TED Talks

TED Talks are short informative video presentations given by dynamic expert speakers in the areas of education, creativity, and motivation, among other intersections of content areas. The talks examine new ideas and are relevant to a broad audience.

Digest of Research

A digest of research is a summary of an interview with a researcher on the main points and issues covered, with implications of their work for the general public. The digest is meant to allow researchers to quickly grasp the core ideas of the research in the author's own voice. Each digest of research focuses on a single topic, with the focus being on what the research means for students and teachers.

Social Media

Social media refers to web-based applications that focus on the dissemination and communication of content and on sharing content and collaboration. Social media is used by people to stay in touch and interact with various communities. The Drexel FRC will use the following types of social media to disseminate and communicate its research: Instagram, Twitter, Facebook, YouTube, LinkedIn, and blogs.

11.4 Summary

The focus of this chapter is on dissemination and communication techniques that are used by the FRC to further the center's mission of translating research in the areas of creativity and motivation for the benefit of students, teachers, corporate trainers, and the general public. The dissemination and communication of research is an important part of the research process; it allows the benefits of the results to be passed on to other researchers, to professional practitioners, and to the wider community. In addition to providing ways of accessing to the research-based instructional modules in Chapters 9 and 10 of this book, this chapter provides targeted ways of distributing information to the public about evidence-based theories and practices. Effective dissemination and communication are important for ensuring that the research has the most impact in practice and that it is reaching the intended audience. Other forms of dissemination and communication that the FRC will utilize include publishing empirical and research articles, presenting at national and international conferences, developing policy briefs, creating community and school programs, and presenting various program results to local community groups and local and national stakeholders. As the FRC grows over the years, its dissemination and communication techniques will broaden to reach a global audience.

CHAPTER 12

From Individual Compliance to Creative Collaboration: A Business Perspective

Advance Organizer. This final chapter looks ahead to the role of creativity and motivation, collaboration, and the locus of control within business and education contexts.

12.1 Introduction

From a business perspective, people are expensive, temperamental, and unpredictable. Human relationships are time-consuming, delicate, and complicated. Whether paving a new road or launching the James Webb Telescope, skillful solutions to complex challenges require diverse collections of expert individuals to make decisions together in real time. They must do so across different realms of functional expertise and across different cultures, genders, generations, and identities. For younger employees raised in the ubiquitous information era unleashed by the internet, an increasingly high set of expectations for work that is personally and socially rewarding is added to the mix.

12.2 Looking Ahead: Transition

It is no longer 1970, when people were grateful for jobs and work was simply defined in terms of tasks to enable the production of goods and services, guided by directors and overseen by line managers and supervisors who possessed all of the information and made all of the decisions. Today, the process of continuous creative destruction and reinvention is faster than ever, fueled by a constantly accelerating stream of information and an exponentially expanding ability to connect vast numbers of people at ever-plummeting costs. Fifty years ago, there were three television networks in the USA. Today, every smartphone is its own broadcast studio and there are over five million podcasts available for public consumption.

We now have software that translates languages in real time and software that guides us on the commitments we've made in our regular stream of communications with our family, friends, and colleagues, providing helpful prompts that we didn't even request. We are hyper-connected and hyper-collaborative, with the pandemic accelerating our collective reliance on virtual collaboration in a hybrid quest for economic advancement and individual relevance. Added to this is the evolving crush of information, connection, experience, and choice resulting in the metaverse – a sensory immersive virtual experience operating in parallel to the physical, which promises to eclipse the Zoom revolution by orders of magnitude.

The speed and complexity of change in this socioeconomic environment cannot be successfully navigated by individuals being trained in a system that remains essentially the same as it was fifty years ago. The individualized compulsory education model was invented when the primary purpose was to convey basic information and develop elemental skills while exposing learners to a variety of possible applications and helping them to evaluate paths of aptitude and interest at the lowest possible cost.

This systemic approach was essential if the masses were to be grounded in sound basic skills and effectively introduced to the world of opportunities and advanced paths of learning that a well-rounded citizen and economic contributor would require. When designed, knowledge was conveyed only through heavy books and through teachers who had traveled to gain additional knowledge. The system is a product of the employment need at the time, when the industrial revolution and the dawn of computing required a large proportion of the population to move from farm and menial manufacturing work into knowledge work of some kind.

When we fast forward through the explosion of the information age to today's wide-ranging information economy, we see an acceleration in the speed of changing information and the corresponding complexity of choice. This avalanche of data creates both more insight and more ambiguity, requiring participants to be skilled in the ability to quickly make complex choices, assess the effects of those choices, and revise those choices to meet evolving demands.

12.3 Moribund Business and Education Systems

However, our current education system has not evolved to meet this essential change in the nature of work. In our system, the student has little if any choice of what they will learn, when they will learn, with whom they will learn, how they will learn, or who they will learn from until perhaps their junior year of college. Operating within a system literally designed to prevent students from making decisions that matter to them – a system focused entirely on "theoretical" or "abstract" issues having no bearing on their own experience, and doing so individually without help – students are expected to enter a workforce that requires them to make complex decisions quickly with those who may be different from them in many ways.

To thrive in this dynamic environment and to create real value for employers that cannot be realized by machines or the rudimentary artificial intelligence now emerging, employees must know how to understand the needs of others, be empathetic to their feelings, and discern the role of values and purpose in making choices that have a real impact on others. These kinds of talents used to be the sole province of "leadership" or "management," but, with the pace of development and accessibility of information today, organizations can no longer employ legions of "doers" executing the instructions of the "leaders" who do all the thinking and collaborating and who exclusively possess relatively scarce static information.

12.4 Caring and Creative Collaboration: Functioning in a Complex Society

This difference between technology-enabled, localized, empowered, and collaborative decision-making, on the one hand, and legacy hierarchical command-based decision-making is no more vividly on display than what is currently happening on the battlefield in Ukraine (as of the fall of 2023). Informal Ukrainian combat units, free to innovate and improvise, are dramatically outperforming their Russian adversaries. Not only are the Ukrainians empowered by their lack of rigid hierarchy, but they are empowered by their cause of freedom from external domination. This contrasts drastically with the context of their attackers, who are executing the commands of a hierarchy founded precisely on the premise of external domination. This freedom to genuinely care about the purpose and create innovative ways to serve that purpose speaks to the essence of the Ukrainian advantage.

General Stanley McChrystal (2015), in his book *Team of Teams*, captures the essence of the difference between controlled compulsory compliance and caring creative collaboration and sets out the implications of transforming systems from the former to the latter. Describing the unique conditions faced in post-invasion Iraq, he wrote (McChrystal, 2015):

> The Task Force hadn't chosen to change; we were driven by necessity. Although lavishly resourced and exquisitely trained, we found ourselves losing to an enemy that, by traditional calculus, we should have dominated. Over time we came to realize that more than our foe, we were actually struggling to cope with an environment that was fundamentally different from anything we'd planned or trained for the speed and interdependence of events had produced new dynamics that threatened to overwhelm the time-honored processes and culture we'd built.

While not the "life or death" confrontations of the battlefield, competition in the business world has similar motivational and creative dynamics. Business missions to serve markets by delivering products and services that are essential to feeding, clothing, housing, connecting, and caring for our society take on a tremendous significance to all involved. In fact, the role of business in the Ukrainians' fight to preserve their democratic freedoms is significant. Who else but business provides the communications, logistics, transportation, finance, weaponry, and technology that the Ukrainians are employing to wage this existential battle? The same can be said of every emergency room in the world. Like education itself, without business, our entire ability to function in a complex society would grind to a halt.

Until the information era, our approach to education prepared and enhanced the ability of young employees to meet the expectations of the workplace. Expectations for performance at school were followed by the same expectations at work. Those who demonstrated an ability to scholastically meet or exceed those expectations were generally able to meet or exceed expectations vocationally, and the middle class grew, standards of living improved generally, and technology accelerated its advance.

This was the lesson that McChrystal's (2015) elite task force learned the hard way on the streets of Baghdad. The nature of the battlefield had changed, and central command and control would prove to be too slow and clumsy to keep up with the local guerillas. The Russians appear to be learning this same lesson in Ukraine. When the conditions have fundamentally changed, the way of engaging those conditions must change or even the most historically successful programs will fail.

The ubiquitous information era puts vast amounts of data, knowledge, resources, and connections at the fingertips of any worker with a keyboard. Those who must wait for their "central command" to issue directions before utilizing this tremendous resource are operating at a severe disadvantage to those who are free to act with autonomy to serve a common purpose and rapidly innovate based on guidance and real-world experience.

Like McChrystal's (2015) forces in Iraq, businesses have no choice but to evolve and enable their members to leverage this capability with autonomy, purpose, and creativity. Small, nimble groups that can quickly and iteratively learn what methods work best are becoming increasingly free to "care and create" on behalf of their customers. Those organizations that can't adapt are being creatively destroyed by legions of innovators starting up micro-businesses that are disrupting hierarchical chains of command within larger enterprises (e.g., GitHub: https://github.com/).

What about education? How are we preparing our students for this new reality? Are we presenting them with opportunities to "care and create" with others different from themselves? Are we preparing them for the workplace as it has already become, encouraging them to bring innovative ideas forward to serve purposes that are truly meaningful to them? Where do they have the opportunity to develop their choice-making ability, and where do they learn to do so with others different from themselves?

In addition to the limited autonomy and intrinsic meaning implicit in the compulsory educational experience, the legacy educational system ensures that any collaboration that occurs in school will happen only among students of the same age and from the same local community. This often implies a limited experience of collaboration and interdependence with only those from the same age groups, socioeconomic status, and cultural backgrounds.

12.5 Call to Action

If education is to serve the needs of society, preparing students who are ready to thrive and enter the workforce, we must eschew the rote and routine "paint by numbers" execution of pre-designed instructions and the expectation of information retention in favor of the proven practices described by my academic colleagues in this book. This animating call to action is not so that businesses and shareholders can make more money and is certainly not to enable military conquest. The primary purpose of this call to action is so that everyone in our society has an improved experience of contributing meaningfully to their own growth and development, the health and well-being of their families, and the effectiveness of society to meet its own needs, ultimately elevating the contribution of work to the improved wellness of humanity as a whole.

12.6 Summary

Only when we engage young people in experiences that embrace their inherent ability to tap their inner motivations and respond creatively and collaboratively with those different from themselves will they accelerate the development of information (and meaning) era skills that will help them thrive in the workplace. In so doing, we can create the world we all want.

References

McChrystal, S. A. (2015). *Team of Teams: The Power of Small Groups in a Fragmented World*. Edmonton, AB, Canada: Portfolio.

Index

Adams, John Stacey, 201, 207
alternative uses test, 114
applied research, 4
   definition, 5
   education methods, 5
Aptitudes Research Project, 114
assessments
   checklists, 110, 175
   creativity, 80
   diagnostic, 83, 178
   formative, 82
   interview, 177
   interviews, 82
   motivation, 80
   motivation assessments
      checklists, 167
      diagnostic, 167
      interviews, 167
      questionnaires, 167
      rating scales, 167
      self-reports, 167
      surveys, 167
   non-standard, 82
   observation, 83
   products, 110, 120
   questionnaires, 171
   rating scales, 110, 119, 171
   reliability, 81
   self-assessments, 109
   self-reports, 110, 167
   standard, 82, 109, 110
   summative, 82
   surveys, 175
   validity, 81

Bandura, Albert, 201, 204
basic research, 4
   definition, 4
   tools, 4
Bloom's taxonomy, 86
Brabeck, Mary, 2

business systems
   moribund, 377

cognitive dissonance theory, 207
consensual assessment technique, 121
creative and caring collaboration
   call to action, 379
   General McChrystal, Stanley, 377
   questions we should be asking ourselves, 379
creative problem-solving
   creative problem-solving grid, 86
   diagnostic teaching, 84
creative product semantic scale, 121
creative thinking process, 27
creativity
   4P framework, 23
   characteristics, 227
   common myths, 27
   components, 229
   creative collaboration, business perspective, 375
   creativity versus innovation, 23
   definition (creativity), 228
   by field
      architects, 18
      artists, 18
      corporate/business/industry, 19
      education, 21
      engineering, 18
      military, 19
      psychologists, 22
      scientists, 19
   collective components
      Jordanous, Anna, 16
   creative work
      Stein, Moe, 16
   domain-general versus domain-specific, 26
   Four-C model, 22
   future of, 48
   killers and quick fixes, 30
   motivation, connection, 165

creativity (cont.)
  neuroscience, 210
  realationship with intelligence, 26
creativity modules
  characteristics of creative teaching (Module 9.3), 246
  convergent thinking (Module 9.13), 282
  counting boards computation (Modules 9.16), 295
  creative place value pedagogy (Module 9.15), 288
  critical thinking (Module 9.4), 248
  divergent thinking (Module 9.12), 278
  enhancing elaboration (Module 9.7), 263
  enhancing flexibility (Module 9.11), 275
  enhancing fluency (Module 9.6), 258
  intrinsic and extrinsic motivation (Module 9.14), 287
  mindfulness and creativity (Module 19.18), 303
  neuroscience of creativity (Module 9.17), 300
  originality (9.5), 254
  resistance to premature closure (Module 9.10), 272
  risk-taking and creativity (Module 9.9), 269
  tolerance of ambiguity (Module 9.8), 265
  what is creativity? (Module 9.1), 228
  why should instructors know about creativity? (Module 9.2), 242
creativity trailblazers, 31
  Amabile, Teresa, 31
  Beghetto, Ronald, 31
  Betts, Kristen, 31
  Bruner, Jerome, 32
  Cramond, Bonnie, 33
  Cropley, Arthur, 33
  Cropley, David H., 33
  Csikszentmihalyi, Mihaly, 34
  De Bono, Edward, 34
  Gardner, Howard, 35
  Glăveanu, Vlad, 35
  Gowan, John Curtis, 35
  Guilford, John Paul (J. P.), 36
  Isaksen, Scott, 36
  Kaufman, Alan, 37
  Kaufman, James C., 37
  Kaufman, Nadine, 37
  Kim, Kyung-hee (Kay), 37
  Kogan, Nathan, 38
  Krippner, Stanley, 38
  Lubart, Todd, 39
  Martindale, Colin, 39
  Mumford, Michael, 39
  Neethling, Kobus, 40
  Noller, Ruth, 40
  Osborn, Alex Faickney, 40
  Parnes, Sidney, 41
  Piaget, Jean, 41, 201
  Plucker, Jonathan, 41
  Pritzker, Steven, 41
  Puccio, Gerard J., 42
  Richards, Ruth, 42
  Robinson, Ken, 43
  Runco, Mark, 43
  Sawyer, Robert Keith, 44
  Simonton, Dean Keith, 44
  Sisk, Dorothy, 44
  Stein, Morris (Moe), 45
  Sternberg, Robert, 45
  Torrance, Ellis Paul, 46
  Treffinger, Donald John, 46
  Vygotsky, Lev, 47
  Wallach, Michael A., 47
  Wallas, Graham, 47
curriculum new categorization
  developmental curriculum levels, 89

Education Passport, 370
  dissemination/communication techniques
    badges, 372
    digest of research, 373
    microcredentials, 372
    parent guides, 372
    research briefs, 373
    social media, 373
    spotlights, 372
    TED Talks, 373
education system
  little choice, 376

Festinger, Leon, 201, 207
Flavell, John H., 201, 206
Four-C model, 22
Freddie Reisman Center for Translational Research in Creativity and Motivation (FRC), xv, xvii, 2, 370
  purpose, 10
  services provided, 12

General McChrystal, Stanley, 377
generic influences on learning, 118
Guilford, Joy Paul (J. P.), 109
  address, American Psychological Association (APA), 15

Hammrich, Penny, xvii

inverted-U theory, 8

Jacobson, Lenore, 201, 204

Index 383

Kaufman Domains of Creativity Scale (K-DOCS), 119
Keiser, Larry, xvii
   RKW (Reisman, Keiser & Westphal) Student – Enhancing Self-Motivation Diagnostic, 185

Likert, Rensis, 6, 110
Likert-type scales, 6, 110

Maslow, Abraham, 203
Maslow's hierarchy of needs, 63, 160
MeaningSphere, xvii
Mind, Brain, and Education (MBE), 220
   common themes and principles, 221
   education, 221
mindfulness, 214, *See* neuroscience of creativity
   benefits
      corporations, 219
      education, 218
      employees, 219
      schools, 219
      students, 218
      teachers, 218
   creativity, enhances, 214, 216
   mindfulness technique, 217
   motivation, 216
Mosaic, xvii
motivation
   assessment explanation, 166
   Autonomy-supportive Intervention Program, 186
   Basic Psychological Need Satisfaction in General Checklist, 175
   checklists, 175
   corporate employee, enhancing motivation, 164
   corporate employer, enhancing education, 167
   creative collaboration, business perspective, 375
   creativity, connection, 165
   definition, 60, 160, 310
   diagnostic assessment, 178
   Employee Motivation Survey, 175
   extrinsic, 308
      subset, 61
   interviews, 177
   intrinsic, 308
      subset, 61
   key elements, 61
   mindfulness, 216
   Motivation Assessment Scale, 174
   neuroscience of, 76
   process of, 61

Reisman Diagnostic Motivation Assessment (RDMA), 180
RKW Student – Enhancing Self-Motivation Diagnostic, 185
Rosenberg Self-Esteem Scale (RSES), 173
school leadership, enhancing teacher motivation, 163
self-determined education, 75
self-esteem, 165
self-motivation questionnaire, 171
Situational Motivation Scale, 169
Student Motivation Survey, 176
student motivation, enhancing, 161, 167
Student Opinion Scale, 174
surveys, 175
teacher motivation, enhancing, 163
types of, 61
motivation modules
   defining motivation (Module 10.1), 310
   developing intrinsic motivation (Module 10.6, 347
   diagnostic teaching (Module 10.11), 366
   extrinsic motivation (Module10.7), 350
   gamification and education (Module 10.8), 354
   instructor motivation descriptors (Module 10.3), 325
   mindfulness and motivation (Module 10.9), 356
   neuroscience of motivation (Module 10.10, 362
   self-determination theory (Module 10.4), 333
   self-directed learning (Module 10.5), 335
   teachers' knowledge regarding motivation (Module 10.2), 315
motivation trailblazers, 62, 70
   Aargyris, Chris, 68
   Alderfer, Clayton P., 67
   Amabile, Teresa, 71
   Deci, Edward L., 74
   Herzberg, Frederick, 65
   Kramer, Steven, 72
   Latham, Gary, 73
   Lawler, Edward, 73
   Locke, Edwin, 73
   Maslow, Abraham, 63, 201
   Mayo, George Elton, 72
   McClelland, David, 68
   McGregor, Douglas, 69
   Merton, Robert K., 72
   Murray, Henry, 67
   Ouchi, William, 69
   Porter, Lyman, 73
   Ryan, Richard, 74
   Urwick, Lyndall F., 71

Index

neuroscience of creativity, 210
  methodologies, 211

Piaget, Jean, 201
Pygmalion effect, 205

RDCA, 6, 180, 227, 237
Reisman Diagnostic Creativity Assessment (RDCA), xvii, 6, 117
  creativity factors, 227
  interpretation, 237
Reisman Diagnostic Motivation Assessment (RDMA), xvii, 160
  corporate use, 180
  student use, 180
  teacher use, 180
Reisman, Fredricka, xvii
  RKW (Reisman, Keiser & Westphal) Student – Enhancing Self-Motivation Diagnostic, 185
Remote Associates Test, 114
RKW Student – Enhancing Self-Motivation Diagnostic, 185
Rogers, Carl, 201, 202
Rosenthal, Robert, 201, 204
Runco ideational behavior scale, 120

self-assessments, 115
  advantages, 117
  disadvantages, 117
  Gough personality scale, 116
  Reisman Diagnostic Creativity Assessment (RDCA), 117
self-efficacy, 204
Skinner, Burrhus Frederic (B. F.), 201, 204
standardized assessments
  achievement, 110
  aptitude, 110
  diagnostic, 110, 178
Stein, Morris "Moe," 15

Torrance tests of creative thinking, 113
translational education research, xv, 1, 2
  cycle, 3
  lab to learner model, 7, 10

voice from the field, 244, 251, 259, 281

Westphal, Jeff, xvii
  RKW (Reisman, Keiser & Westphal) Student – Enhancing Self-Motivation Diagnostic, 185